'Progress is cumulative in science and engineering, but cyclical in finance.'

James Grant in *Money of the Mind*, 1994

The Rise and Fall of

The City of
Money

A FINANCIAL HISTORY OF
Edinburgh

RAY PERMAN

BIRLINN

For the Library of Mistakes and Russell Napier, its founder

First published in 2019 by
Birlinn Limited
West Newington House
10 Newington Road
Edinburgh
EH9 1QS

www.birlinn.co.uk

ISBN 978 178027 623 6

British Library Cataloguing in Publication Data
A catalogue record for this book is available from the British Library.

Typeset by Hewer Text UK Ltd, Edinburgh
Printed and bound by Gutenberg Press, Malta

Contents

Part 3: Modernisation and internationalisation

Part 4: Triumph and disaster

List of Plates

Note issued by the Union Bank of Scotland, which merged with Bank
 of Scotland in 1955
An advertisement showing the head office of the Commercial Bank of
 Scotland, in George Street, Edinburgh
Banknote issued by the National Commercial Bank
Carlyle Gifford
Bruce Pattullo
Tom Risk
George Mathewson
George Younger
Charles Winter
Peter Burt
James Crosby
Lord Stevenson
Fred Goodwin
Lord Stevenson, Andy Hornby, Fred Goodwin and Sir Tom McKillop
 face the House of Commons Treasury Committee, 2009

Preface

THIS STORY IS bookended by two financial catastrophes – the Darien disaster at the beginning of the eighteenth century and the credit crunch in the twenty-first. There were numerous financial crashes in between, but none had the potential to bankrupt the nation as those two did. Can we learn anything from them? Why study the history of finance when the financial regulator tells us that the past is not necessarily a guide to the future? What similarities could there be between William Paterson's unsuccessful attempt to drive Bank of Scotland out of business and the failure of Royal Bank of Scotland more than three centuries later? Banking was so much simpler in 1695 than it was in 2008 that the two events cannot be compared.

And yet, the economic cycle of boom and bust has been repeated many times (and could not be abolished by political will, no matter how sophisticated the economic policy). Long periods of easily available cheap money followed by a sudden tightening of credit has been the background to several catastrophic events: the collapse of the Bank of Ayr in 1772, the financial ruin of Sir Walter Scott in 1825, the failure of the City of Glasgow Bank in 1878, the downfall of Bank of Scotland and Royal Bank of Scotland in 2008. And, although history never repeats itself exactly, there are some things that do not change.

In this book I have tried to tell the story of Scottish finance and particularly how Edinburgh came to be the only city in the UK to have resisted the pull of London and maintained an independent financial sector up until the twenty-first century. Partly that is an accident of history – the founding of Bank of Scotland before 1707 gave it rights and privileges independent of the Bank of England. These were not removed by the Act of Union, and Scotland retained sufficient autonomy and political strength to be able to keep its banks free of the restrictions which stunted the growth of rivals to the Old Lady of Threadneedle Street south of the border. The settlement also left Scotland with distinctive civic institutions, particularly a separate legal system, but also the Church, schools and universities. Lawyers played a big part in the development of finance in Scotland, but so did kirk ministers and professors of mathematics. They were joined in time by a set of independent professional institutes – banking, law, accountancy and actuarial mathematics.

This is not just a story of institutions, but also of people. Some were visionary, some energetic; some were incompetent and some comic. I have tried to sketch some of their biographies and to give links in the bibliography to where to find fuller pictures. Overwhelmingly they were men. Very few women were allowed to play full parts in this story, even though their money and their willingness to take risks were important from the very beginning.

★ ★ ★

The inspiration for this book came from Russell Napier, a finance professional with a passionate interest in economic history and a belief that there is much modern practitioners can gain from the lessons of the past. He has given that idea tangible form in two ways: the Practical History of Financial Markets is a short course for finance professionals, which is taught in Edinburgh, London and abroad;[1] The Library of Mistakes is a collection of several thousand books of financial history, first established in Edinburgh, but now being replicated in other parts of the world.[2] The library is open to anyone, is free to join, and organises regular talks and a book club. Some years ago Russell invited me to help him lead an annual financial walking tour of Edinburgh for students at the University of Edinburgh Business School. The compact historic city centre is a case study in the way that economic and financial events help shape the environment in which we live and, although fire and redevelopment have removed some of the buildings and sites which were the setting for episodes described here, enough survive to help bring the history to life. I hope this book will complement the tour and enable readers to plot their own journeys around the city.

Others have also helped me with this book and deserve my thanks. Dr Charles Munn is not only a distinguished author and financial historian, but also a former chief executive of the Chartered Institute of Bankers in Scotland, the world's oldest banking institute. His suggestions and ideas have been invaluable. I am grateful too to Dr Douglas Watt, Dr Claire Anderson and Trevor Davies for reading and commenting on parts of the manuscript. Professor Fran Wasoff helped me organise my research. Dr Paul Kosmetatos guided me to valuable sources of information. My wife, Fay Young, is an author and editor in her own right, and I'm grateful for her patience, perceptiveness and encouragement.

There are several excellent books about the financial history of Edinburgh, but none covering the whole of the period I wished to survey or the complete range of financial activities – banking, insurance, investment management, stockbroking and professional services – which make up a financial centre. Sidney Checkland's *Scottish Banking, A History 1695–1973*, published in 1975, remains the definitive history of banking in Scotland. Richard Saville's *Bank of Scotland, A History 1695–1995*, published in 1996, tells the story of Britain's first commercial bank with great authority. I have drawn on both these books, but where possible I have also gone back to the original sources, working in the archives of Bank of Scotland, Royal Bank and others (listed at the end of this book).

I could not have done this without the expertise, helpfulness and enthusiasm of Siân Yates, Rosemary Moodie and Hania Smerecka at Bank of Scotland, and Sophie Volker, Sally Cholewa and Lyn Crawford at Royal Bank. I also appreciate the help that Ashleigh Thompson and Vikki Kerr at the City of Edinburgh archives gave me, for the assistance of Karyn Williamson at Standard Aberdeen and the staff of the National Records of Scotland and the University of Edinburgh Special Collections. I am grateful to the trustees of the Stafford Trust for permission to quote from the diary and letters of William Ramsay held in the National Records of Scotland as part of the papers of the Steel Maitland Family. Staff at the University of Edinburgh Library, the National Library of Scotland, the Edinburgh City Library and the Library of Mistakes have also given me invaluable assistance.

For the last 30–40 years of this story, the archives are still closed. For that period I have relied on my own experience, records and memory, and on interviews with some of the participants, as well as on the official reports by the Financial Services Authority, the Financial Conduct Authority and the Parliamentary Commission on Banking Standards. I have used several informative and useful books about that period, particularly for Royal Bank *Making it Happen* by Iain Martin and *Shredded* by Ian Fraser, for HBOS/Bank of Scotland, my own book *HUBRIS: How HBOS wrecked the best bank in Britain* and for the government perspective, *Back from the Brink* by Alistair Darling.

A note on monetary values: at the beginning of this story Scotland still had its own currency, the pound Scots, which traded at 12 to 1 against the English pound sterling (£). But many Scots merchants and companies used sterling. The £ was divided in 20 shillings and each silver shilling into 12 pence, which were copper. Five-shilling coins were called crowns, and a half-crown coin was worth two shillings and six pence. There were silver six- and three-pence coins, the latter replaced with a nickel-brass coin in 1947. Half-pence ('ha'pennies') and quarter-pence ('farthings' or 'fourth-ings') were also in common use. These fractions continued in use until 1971, when the system was decimalised.

I have not attempted to translate historical amounts into contemporary equivalents. Depending on whether you use purchasing power, a GDP deflator, inflation or some other measure, you get very different answers. Some indication of magnitude can be had from the calculator on the website of the National Archives.[3] Suffice it to say that the losses suffered by the investors in the Darien scheme were enough to nearly bankrupt the country in 1700, that Sir Walter Scott's net worth was much less than his debts in 1825 (although the Duke of Buccleuch could have paid them off with ease, had he been allowed to) and that losses of the City of Glasgow Bank in 1878 were enough to impoverish that city for years. However, they all pale into insignificance beside the losses of RBS and HBOS in our own time. Is this historical progress?

Ray Perman
Edinburgh, August 2019

Part 1

The ascent of paper money

1

Famine and finance

THE STORY OF finance in Edinburgh starts in the depths of human misery. In the summer of 1695 the harvest in Scotland failed. It was the first of four disastrous seasons, which became known as the 'ill years'. Across Europe dramatic weather conditions caused a 'mini ice age'. The Thames froze in London and a winter festival was held on the ice. The diarist John Evelyn wrote of weeks of bitter cold and deep snow delaying the spring. In northeast Scotland coastal villages were inundated by a freak sandstorm. When spring and summer did arrive they were cold and brought periods of heavy rain interspersed with droughts. Crop failure brought famine. In the countryside people were literally dropping dead from starvation or the diseases which habitually accompanied it – smallpox, typhus, typhoid and dysentery. Their bodies lay by the roadside unburied. The physician Sir Robert Sibbald described the condition of the people in a pamphlet published in 1699:

> The Bad seasons these several Years past hath made so much Scarcity and so great a Dearth, that for Want, some Die in the Way-side, some drop down on the Streets, the poor sucking Babs are Starving for Want of Milk, which the empty breasts of their Mothers cannot furnish them: Every one may see Death in the Face of the Poor that abound everywhere; the Thinness of their Visage, their Ghostly Looks, their Feebleness, their Agues and their Fluxes threaten them with sudden Death, if Care be not taken of them . . . and in this their Necessity they take what they can get; Spoiled Victual; yea, some eat these Beasts which have died from some Disease, which may occasion a Plague among them.[1]

Rural areas suffered most, but the famine inevitably hit the towns and cities. There were food riots in many burghs, including Edinburgh, where in 1699 the magistrates were forced to take action to suppress unrest. In Leith people were said to be dying in the streets.[2] Meal was to be had, but at vastly inflated prices, and fear of unemployment meant the terror of starvation, forcing some to take direct action. A group of women wool workers, led by Sarah Grier, tried to stop the export of wool from Leith lest it deprive them of their jobs. Refugees flooded into Edinburgh in the hope of finding food. A makeshift camp set up in Greyfriars churchyard housed 300, but groups of vagrant beggars roamed the streets. Those who could scrape together the money and still had the strength to leave Scotland did so: there was an upsurge in emigration, mostly to Ulster, which was less affected. With the increased death toll and lower birth rate, the population fell by 5–15 per cent by 1700.[3]

The harvest failure brought rocketing grain prices, but the first reaction of the Scottish government was to redouble efforts to combat smuggling of food from Ireland. It was only in December of 1695 that import restrictions were relaxed and not until the following year that duties on grain were abolished. The visionary entrepreneur William Paterson, of whom we shall hear much more, wrote: 'In the summer of 1695 they were busie [sic] giving rewards for having their corn carried abroad, and a few months after, as impatiently employed in buying it back again.'[4] Neither government ministers nor the Scottish parliament, which largely represented the landed interest, saw alleviation of the suffering of the poor as their responsibility. They left that to the Church and the burghs.

It was nearing the end of the century before they realised that the famine had not only a human cost, it also hit the economy hard. With little or no crop to sell or to barter, tenant farmers could not afford their rent, which was often paid in grain. Some were evicted, others went into arrears, reducing the income of landowners. Merchants were also affected as markets were curtailed or closed. Government revenues from excise duties or taxes fell by nearly 30 per cent.[5] This was a blow to the state, but also to those who profited personally from collecting it. Lord Belhaven and David Boyle of Kelburn (the future Lord Glasgow), both directors of the newly created Bank of Scotland, were tacksmen of the inland excise, effectively franchised tax collectors. When they warned the privy council in 1696 that revenues would be hit by 'so many people falling down dead', they were also bemoaning the loss of their own income.[6]

There was no shortage of explanations for the crisis. A resurgence in witch hunting saw 50 people indicted in Renfrewshire, 6 of whom were strangled and burned.[7] In pulpits throughout the land kirk ministers attributed the crisis to the wrath of God and called on the nation to cleanse itself of its sins. Opponents of the king, William III, blamed him, stretching the four poor harvests to a Biblical 'seven lean years'. But famine in Scotland was not new. With agriculture lagging behind the modern methods used in England and on the Continent, yields were low at the best of times. When the weather turned bad, the nation could not feed itself.

Scotland in the seventeenth century had been weakened by frequent political and religious wars. The accession in 1688 of William and his wife Mary, who reigned as 'co-regents', promised a period of stability, but sparked a Jacobite rising in 1689, which had brought fresh bloody division, disruption and uncertainty. When William was proclaimed king of Scotland at the Mercat Cross in Edinburgh High Street, a few hundred yards away supporters of his father-in-law, the deposed James VII & II, were still holding Edinburgh Castle against a siege. The Jacobites were not finally defeated until the Battle of Dunkeld four months later. Prominent supporters of the new king knew that if the Stuart dynasty were to be restored they would at least suffer exile and confiscation of their assets – and possibly death. 'For these families the victory of the Revolution was a matter of survival; they were used to fighting, and most possessed armouries and travelled even in Edinburgh with armed retainers, guns, swords and hunting dogs.'[8] Three further armed rebellions and numerous false alarms were to keep Scotland in a state of tension for the next half-century.

William also plunged England and Scotland into a Continental war. As a result, several important export markets, particularly France, were now closed to Scots' exports such as black cattle, salt, herring and coal. French privateers raided so many Scottish and English ships that traders preferred to use neutral Scandinavian vessels, hitting shipping revenues and employment. Britain lost 4,000 ships in nine years of the war. Manpower, already depleted by the famine, was further worsened by conscription into the Royal Navy, although this was preferable to the press gangs active south of the border.[9] There was some compensation in increased trade with the Baltic countries, but Scotland's main export market was England. The two countries were still nominally independent, had their own parliaments and made their own laws, though they had shared a monarch since 1603 and economic and social links were well established. Nevertheless, the attitude of Scotland's nearest neighbour was hardly friendly. Import duties on Scottish manufactured goods like linen were raised and the highly protectionist English Navigation Acts, aimed principally at the Dutch, had the side effect of virtually extinguishing Scotland's trade with North America. Although no one measured these things in the 1690s, it is likely that the country entered a deep recession that lasted at least until the first decade of the next century.[10]

More important than the effect on output was the impact the famine and the economic slump had on liquidity. Money in Scotland at this time was silver and copper coins. No new gold coins had been minted since 1638,[11] although some rich landowners and merchants kept part of their fortunes in bullion and sometimes paid for large purchases with it. Foreign gold and silver coins also circulated. The value of a coin was its weight in silver or gold, but soft precious metals lent themselves easily to 'clipping' – shaving off slivers of metal to be used to make new coins. Trust in the currency was low, leading the government to have to undertake periodic 'recoinages' – recalling coins to be reminted at their full weight.

There was no paper money, although merchants could exchange bills (essentially IOUs) with trusted trading partners, which facilitated trade with London or foreign ports, but at a price – steep discounts were applied to Scots' bills. The disadvantage of having a coinage based on metals which Scotland produced in only limited quantities[12] meant that it was dependent on trade to increase the money supply. In the 1690s trade was heavily one way – exports were crippled by the war and money was going abroad to pay for grain imports or to finance King William's campaigns. The shortage of cash severely hampered economic recovery, even after harvests returned to normal and the war ended in 1697.

England also suffered from a shortage of coin, but when William had arrived from the Dutch provinces he had introduced a number of monetary innovations from his native country which were mainly aimed at financing the national debt and his war, but also boosted the money supply. These included allowing the establishment of the Bank of England in 1694 with permission to circulate a paper currency, the introduction of exchequer bills two years later and in 1704 the Promissory Notes Act, which made debts transferable and negotiable.[13] Enacted by the English parliament, these measures increased liquidity and facilitated economic expansion, but they did not apply north of the border, where Scotland had its own laws and parliament. The country was economically behind its British and closest European neighbours and further impoverished by the disasters of the last decade of the seventeenth century. It was also poorer. Scottish wage rates were typically half those of England and stagnant or falling.[14]

Astonishingly, in the middle of this depression, while hundreds were starving to death, the nation pledged nearly half its wealth to finance two audacious speculative ventures – Bank of Scotland, only the second incorporated bank in Britain and the first to rely wholly on commercial business, and the even more ambitious Company of Scotland Trading to Africa and the Indies, later known as the Darien Company. Together these enterprises raised pledges of £500,000.[15] More surprisingly they scooped up a large proportion of the nation's ready cash, either paid immediately or collected in later calls. The scale of the draw on the depleted liquidity was enormous. It is difficult to be precise about the amount of money circulating in Scotland at the time, but Douglas Watt has estimated that the Company of Scotland alone sucked up between 17 per cent and 51 per cent of the available supply.[16]

It is tempting to think that in an unequal, in some respects still feudal, society like Scotland, the money came from a handful of super-rich individuals and it is true that important aristocrats and large landowners did subscribe to the two fundraising exercises – some to both. But the burden was much more widely spread. Bank of Scotland came first, aiming to raise £1,200,000 Scots (£100,000 sterling) and opening its subscription book – an impressive heavy ledger, bound in red leather – on All Hallows Day, 1 November 1695. It was placed in the Cross-Keys coffee house and tavern in Covenant Close, leading off from the south side of the High Street in Edinburgh, and remained open every Tuesday and Friday until the end of the year. Subscribers, called 'Adventurers' by the bank's promoters, had to come in person or send an authorised representative, pay 10 per cent of their subscription in cash and agree to provide further cash as and when the bank decided it was needed. The maximum subscription was set at £20,000 Scots. It was intended that two-thirds of the capital should come from Scotland and one-third from England, so a second subscription book was opened in London.

There was a steady arrival of subscribers rather than a queue, but by the end of the year the bank had its money. The tavern owner, Patrick Steill,[17] led them by subscribing £3,000 Scots (£250 sterling). Of the 172 Adventurers who signed up, 136 were in Scotland, the rest in London. The Scottish subscribers did include the nobility (24), and featured some of the leading families and government ministers. Anne, third Duchess of Hamilton, a formidable and shrewd 64-year-old widow, subscribed £8,000 Scots and persuaded other members of her family to invest, including her son Lord Basil Hamilton. She was the first of seven women to subscribe for shares.

Altogether the nobility provided £190,000 Scots, about 16 per cent of the total. There were also 39 lairds, substantial landowners, mostly from the lowland counties and an important and growing economic and political force. They subscribed £200,000 Scots. Lawyers and judges became shareholders and there was representation from other professions, including surgeons, doctors, vintners, goldsmiths and a few army officers. Some employees of the noble families subscribed in their own right. David Crawford, secretary to the Duchess of Hamilton, and Alexander Ramsey, servitor to the Marquis of Tweeddale, each signed for £6,000 Scots. The nobility and landowners were well represented, but this was a venture conceived and largely backed and executed by the growing commercial class. But by far the largest group of Adventurers, providing £300,000 Scots, was made up of merchants. There were at least 70, mostly from Edinburgh, but including men from London, Glasgow, Dundee, Kirkcaldy and further afield.[18]

By the time the Company of Scotland started its fundraising in the following year the enthusiasm among monied Scots to invest had grown considerably. William Paterson, the principle promoter of the scheme, had considerable expertise in raising money. During his years in London he had sold shares in several new ventures – the Hampstead Water Company, the Orphans Fund and, most importantly, the Bank of England. He was a polished and experienced salesman and he knew the importance of preparing the ground before the subscription book was opened to the public. He also went first to the Duchess of Hamilton, correctly calculating that her support would be vital in giving the project credibility. She was well connected politically and in the kirk, and acknowledged as a sensible and effective manager of her own estates. However, she was not easily won over and it took all Paterson's powers of persuasion, reinforced by her son Lord Basil who was also a promoter of the project, to bring her round. Even then she initially subscribed only £1,000 sterling, raising it later to the maximum of £3,000.[19]

Paterson also realised the power of advertising. He had a handbill drawn up and distributed, and was behind the publication of a pamphlet heaping praise on himself and the scheme as an 'absolute Necessity to our Nation to keep us from being destroyed'. The subscription book was opened on 26 February 1696 at 'the house of Mrs Purdie in the North side of the High-street over against the cross'. It was less than 100 yards from where the bank's book had lain two months earlier. Mrs Purdie seems to have run a coffee house, but did not subscribe, at least not in her own name. Interestingly, the first three to sign the book were women – the Duchess of Hamilton, Margaret, eighth Countess of Rothes, and Lady Margaret Hope of Hopetoun. All three had also invested money in the bank. Women appear to have been much more attracted to the Company of Scotland than to the bank – in all 90 subscribed a total of £21,000. Not all were titled and most contributed £100 sterling each. In the story of finance in Edinburgh women hardly get a look in, but in the background, to these early ventures at least, they were significant providers of capital, investing in their own right.

If the bank had attracted a trickle, the Company of Scotland subscription attracted a more substantial flow: 'They came in shoals from all corners of the kingdom to Edinburgh, rich, poor, blind and lame, to lodge their subscriptions in the Company's house and to have a glimpse of the man Paterson.'

Watt discounts this description by William Herries, on the grounds that he was prone to exaggeration and was in London at the time and so could not have witnessed the scene for himself. However, the subscription book was open only for four hours a day and on the first day 69 Scots signed – 17 per hour. With bystanders waiting to see the 'Quality' arrive in their carriages or sedan chairs, Watt estimates a crowd of a few hundred thronged the High Street, which was 'impressive and unprecedented in Scottish joint-stock investment'.[20] No previous Scottish company had attracted this much popular interest or support. The excitement produced £50,400 sterling on the first day and the pace continued for the next two months. A second book was opened in Glasgow and also did brisk business. By April the promoters felt confident enough to increase their target from £300,000 to £400,000 sterling and by August 1 that sum was achieved.

As with the bank, the nobility and lairds were well represented, but large shareholders, contributing £1,000–£3,000 provided only 2.7 per cent of the total raised. Seventy per cent came from people or organisations subscribing £200 or less – half of it from contributions of £100 or less. Altogether 1,320 people or organisations became shareholders.

Significantly, £27,150 was put up by what Watt calls 'institutional investors', although they were not the savings and pension funds we know
today. Edinburgh and Glasgow councils subscribed the maximum
£3,000 each and burghs mostly around Edinburgh, but others as far
afield as Paisley, St Andrews, Brechin and Ayr came in with lesser
amounts.

Professional institutes, like the Faculty of Advocates and the
Incorporation of Surgeons, were represented, as were trades houses,
artisans' organisations such as the skinners, tailors, baxters (bakers),
cordiners (who made shoes and other leather goods), coopers, hammermen (metalworkers) and the Incorporation of Marie's Chapel, which
represented wrights and masons. There was a charity, Cowane's Hospital,
an almshouse in Stirling, and a commercial corporation, the Easter
Sugary of Glasgow. It would be wrong to say that all Scotland was represented, because the vast majority of the population did not have any
surplus funds, let alone £100 to invest. But it was an impressive demon-
stration of the breadth of appeal that the venture inspired amongst those
who did have surplus wealth in a period of 'Dearth and Want', to quote
Sibbald.

Why did they invest? Some were possibly driven by patriotism, the
chance to help Scotland out of its economic backwardness and to emulate
the modern institutions of England, notably the Bank of England and the
East India Company. Paterson played on this desire to see the nation
modernise and progress. But there may also have been a more basic
motive. A series of launches of joint stock companies in England had
provided investors with numerous opportunities and some had repaid
handsomely those who took the risk. Between 1682 and 1692 the East
India Company, which had a monopoly on trade between England and
India and Asia, paid out dividends equal to four times its nominal capital.
A shareholder who bought in 1660 and sold in 1688 would have made a
total return of 1,200 per cent. The return of a salvage ship laden with
silver from the wreck of a Spanish galleon paid its backers a 10,000 per
cent return and set off a flurry of similar companies, some boasting of
new diving machines. Then there was the Convex Lights Company,
manufacturing street lamps, and the Royal Lustring Company, which
raised £62,000 to manufacture fine French cloth. The White Paper
Company's shares increased by three times over four years, the Linen
Company from £10 to £45 in three years.[21] There were others: 'Water
companies, most of them quite sound; treasure seeking companies,

highly speculative; paper, linen, lead, copper, plate glass, bottle glass and mining companies, The Society for Improving Native Manufacture so as to keep out the Wet, and the Company for Sucking-Worm (fire hose) Engines.'[22]

Scotland had seen little of this opportunity and none of the excitement.

To Watt, the rush to buy into the Company of Scotland bears all the hallmarks of a classic financial mania. The urge to subscribe spread far outside the narrow merchant class who had invested in previous joint-stock companies and might be expected to more accurately assess the risks. The Company had more shareholders than either the Bank of England or the East India Company, which were larger undertakings. Given that the institutional investments were on behalf of large groups or even towns, a significant proportion of the whole population – or at least its middle and upper classes – was involved in the speculation. Sir John Dalrymple, although writing 80 years later, was unequivocal:

> The frenzy of the Scots nation to sign the Solemn League and Covenant* never exceeded the rapidity with which they ran to subscribe to the Darien Company. The nobility, the gentry, the merchants, the people, the Royal burghs without the exception of one, and most of the other public bodies subscribed. Young women threw their little fortunes into the stock, widows sold their jointures to get the command of money for the same purpose. Almost in an instant £400,000 were subscribed in Scotland although it is now known that there was not at that time above £800,000 cash in the kingdom.[23]

Was there also something in the national psyche that played a part? Watt calls in evidence Sir Walter Scott. Writing over 100 years later, he contrasted the behaviour of the Scot when acting alone to that when acting in a group: 'In his own personal affairs the Scotsman is remarked as cautious, frugal and prudent in an extreme degree ... But when a number of the natives of Scotland associate for any speculative project, it would seem that their natural caution becomes thawed and dissolved

---

* The 1643 agreement between the Scots and the English parliamentarians pledging religious freedom against the demands of King Charles I.

by the union of their joint hopes, and that their imaginations are liable in a peculiar degree to be heated and influenced by any splendid prospect held out to them.'[24]

It would not be the last time that investors were carried away by the prospect of easy riches.

2

Britain's first commercial bank

EDINBURGH AT THE end of the seventeenth century was very different from the city we see today. With a population of around 30,000 in just 5,500 households, it was the biggest settlement in Scotland and more than twice the size of Glasgow, the next largest. But it was less than a tenth the size of London (although the population of Scotland at around one million was a fifth that of England) and not among the 30 largest cities in Europe.[1] Important Continental centres with which Scotland had established links were far larger: Leiden nearly twice the size, Amsterdam four times and Paris thirteen times as big. Its geographic area was also much smaller than it is today, still mostly confined within its ancient defensive walls. Most of the population lived in narrow alleys running north or south from a single street (now the Royal Mile) which ascended 220 feet (67 metres) from the Palace of Holyrood House to the castle, sitting on the pinnacle of its rock at the west end of the city. A good idea of the city can be had from the remarkable three-dimensional plan drawn by James Gordon of Rothiemay in 1647 (see illustrations). It had changed little by the end of the century.

At the lower, eastern end of the street, the Canongate, the houses were larger and less congested, with gardens behind. But at the top, the High Street and the approach to the castle, the 'closes' or 'wynds' were narrow, steep, dark and dirty alleyways, with buildings perhaps as high as ten or twelve storeys crowding in on either side. Each tenement could contain numerous families – the more affluent at the bottom with easier access to the streets, fresh water and escape in case of fire, which was a frequent occurrence; the poorest at the top. The social classes were thus not separated by district as they are now, but by vertical distance: they met on the stairs and mingled in the streets. Sanitation was a constant problem, with household waste – including human waste – thrown into the closes, sometimes from a great height. The minutes of the town council contain several 'acts anent the muck':[2] most were ineffectual. The 'dung' was a hazard for those arriving home late after an evening in one of the taverns, but the council made a regular income from having the waste collected in the early hours of the morning and sold to farmers.

Daniel Defoe, visiting the city in 1725, described the main street as 'perhaps, the largest, longest, and finest street for buildings and number of inhabitants, not in Britain only, but in the world'.[3] However, the topography of the city had its drawbacks:

> By this means the city suffers infinite disadvantages, and lies under such scandalous inconveniences as are, by its enemies, made a subject of scorn and reproach; as if the people were not as willing to live sweet and clean as other nations, but delighted in stench and nastiness; whereas, were any other people to live under the same unhappiness, I mean as well of a rocky and mountainous situation, thronged buildings, from seven to ten or twelve story high, a scarcity of water, and that little they have difficult to be had, and to the uppermost lodgings, far to fetch; we should find a London or a Bristol as dirty as Edinburgh, and, perhaps, less able to make their dwelling tolerable, at least in so narrow a compass; for, tho' many cities have more people in them, yet, I believe, this may be said with truth, that in no city in the world so many people live in so little room as at Edinburgh.

There was room to expand to the south. On the other side of the ravine, which had the Cowgate and the Grassmarket at the bottom, the land levelled out to open fields. But to the north expansion was blocked by a fetid swamp, the Nor' Loch. It was fed by a flowing burn, but was also the recipient of much of the city's detritus, washed down with every rainfall.

Physically the city may now be different from three hundred years ago, but in one way it has not changed. Edinburgh was then and is now a city of inequality. Just as today it is home to some of the richest individuals in the UK, so in the 1690s it sheltered both the richest and the poorest in Scottish society.[4] Despite its small size and its cramped and insanitary conditions, Edinburgh was a wealthy community relative to the rest of Scotland. The city was the pre-eminent royal burgh, but it no longer had any royalty. Monarchs had deserted Holyrood Palace in 1603 when James VI became James I of England and moved to London, taking many courtiers with him. He promised to return frequently, but neither he nor his son or grandsons had been regular visitors. King William, who took the throne in the 'Glorious Revolution' of 1688, had not made the trip north at all.

It may have lacked a royal court, but the city still had many of the attributes of a capital. The Scottish parliament still met in a hall behind St Giles' Cathedral in the High Street and the high courts were located nearby. Lawyers, ministers of the Protestant Church of Scotland and academics were all strongly represented among the population. Physicians had long been considered professionals, but during the 1690s surgeons lifted their social status from craftsmen to join their fellow medics. Although the Enlightenment was still half a century in the future, Edinburgh was already an intellectual city. The university, founded 170 years after the first of the three ancient Scottish universities of St Andrews, Glasgow and Aberdeen, was growing faster than any of them. It was particularly strong in law and medicine, but had an increasing reputation in the sciences, promoting revolutionary and controversial new ideas such as those in Newton's *Principia*.[5] The Faculty of Advocates opened its library in 1689 (later to become the foundation of the present National Library of Scotland) and the surgeons theirs a decade later.

The Scottish parliament, much derided for its part in the Union with England in the next century, was conscious that Scotland was poorer and less developed than its neighbours and in the 1690s introduced measures designed to improve the economy. These included acts for 'Encouraging of Forraigne Trade' (1693) and the granting of joint stock charters to manufacturing companies, giving them limited liability in case of failure. The 'Act for the Settling of Schools' in 1696 required the establishment of a school in every parish and was the basis of a dramatic expansion of literacy in the century to come. The establishment of the Presbyterian Church cemented the role of the Protestant Church of Scotland in national life. It would become a leading force in the transformation of the country. But the shortage of cash and credit hampered the expansion of the economy and particularly the development of Edinburgh.

Before there were banks there were lenders – rich merchants or landowners would lend at interest, as would other bodies with surplus funds. Charitable institutions such as Trinity Hospital in Edinburgh and King James's Hospital in Leith advanced money. Goldsmiths lent money as a sideline to their jewellery and bullion businesses. 'Jingling Geordie', the city's most celebrated goldsmith had died in 1624, but the George Heriot Hospital, which he endowed, continued his lending business for centuries after his passing. One of the most remarkable lenders was Mary Erskine, or Mrs Hair, the surname of her dead second husband. From her office in a tenement opposite St Giles' in the High Street, she lent money on personal and heritable security, and also financed trade. From her profits she founded two schools for the education of the daughters of merchants and members of the incorporated trades. In 1944 they were renamed after her as Mary Erskine School.

The maximum legal rate of interest that could be charged in Scotland was 6 per cent, but in practice many borrowers were forced to pay more – much more for those with poor creditworthiness. Trade bills could be accepted as payment, but would usually be discounted, and if presented in London might be marked down by as much as 10–15 per cent.

The money market in Scotland was small and primitive compared to London, even before the creation of the Bank of England in 1694. By the end of the seventeenth century the London money market was already rivalling Amsterdam as Europe's leading financial centre, but the activities of the Bank of England brought a dramatic step up in size and depth. The Act of the English parliament that enabled its establishment granted the promoters (who included William Paterson) valuable concessions. Their main business was to lend the government £1.2 million in perpetuity, for which they would receive interest of 8 per cent, guaranteed from tax revenues, and a £4,000 a year management fee. In addition they were permitted to take deposits, issue notes and pay shareholders dividends from profits – the first £100,000 of which would be tax-free. They had limited liability and an effective monopoly over formal banking for at least eleven years.

In contrast to the Bank of Scotland fundraising (which came the following year), the Bank of England secured pledges for ten times as much capital in 12 days – with King William and Queen Mary among the first subscribers.[6] Only a quarter had to be paid in cash, the Bank accepting notes for the remainder. It was able to lend the whole sum to the government before the deadline set by the Act, but crucially this was in notes (promises to pay), not in coin. The government in turn used the notes to settle its own debts and make purchases. 'The Bank was thus from the start an engine to create credit, albeit an engine inevitably somewhat resented by London's goldsmith-bankers, who nevertheless often still found it convenient to have an account there,' wrote David

Kynaston, the Bank's latest biographer.[7] The Bank's non-government business – lending and deposit-taking – expanded quickly such that it was soon moving to larger premises and hiring more staff.

The success of the Bank of England was keenly watched by six London-based Scottish merchants, led by Thomas Deans. The beneficial effect it had on the money supply was attractive, but so too were the profits it was already making. In 1695 the Bank received the first of its guaranteed £50,000 half-yearly interest payment and £6,876 15s 4d for advancing the money ahead of the deadline. It was also getting its management fee and interest on its commercial loans. Its share price rose steadily. Deans quickly had a draft bill prepared, based on the charter of the Bank of England, which he took to Edinburgh to lobby the privy council and the Scottish parliament.

The proposed Bank of Scotland was not an exact replica of the Bank of England because it was not going to be allowed to lend to government, but Deans and his friends thought the commercial possibilities were sufficiently attractive and in time their bank might become agent to the Scottish government, earning extra revenue. Some of the six had previously collaborated on other ventures, including a company supplying baize cloth for army uniforms, but they had no experience in banking. One Scot who did was William Paterson, who was already falling out with his fellow directors at the Bank of England over an alleged conflict of interest. He clearly saw the benefits of creating a bank and had practical experience in fundraising and establishing enterprises, but he had bigger things on his mind. He was quietly working on his proposal for a trading house to rival the East India Company. Not a man to think small, Paterson had ambitions far larger than a parochial Scottish bank. He was thinking on a global scale.

The Scottish merchants turned instead to an Englishman, John Holland. The two men knew each other because Holland had been on the board of the Hampstead Water Company with Paterson, but they were very different in upbringing and temperament. Where Paterson was visionary, impulsive and had a reputation for being devious, Holland appears to have been the opposite, diligent, meticulous and straightforward. A contemporary described him as 'the best deserving man in a nation both of common sense, honesty and good breeding he has been a long time truly the balance that adjusted the East India Company and made them to go right'.[8] He had been born in London, the son of a sea captain who had served in both the English and the Dutch navies and was a sometime friend of Samuel Pepys. As a young man he had spent time in the Netherlands learning bookkeeping and accounting, before returning to London as assistant to the Dutchman Francis Beyer, auditor general of the East India Company. He also made his fortune by investing in some of the company's voyages.[9] Beyer supported the plan for a Bank of Scotland and was one of the original subscribers. It is likely that he recommended John Holland, although he was already well known to Scots merchants, having been a partner with another of them, James Foulis, in a textiles venture. It was Holland who provided Deans with the blueprint for the new Scottish bank.

In June 1695 Paterson got his Act enabling him to establish the Company of Scotland and to begin finding backers. Three weeks later Deans was also successful and an 'Act for Erecting a Bank in Scotland' was passed. Paterson was furious – Deans had been one of his original supporters in London, but had withdrawn after fierce opposition from the East India Company. Although his stated ambition for the Company of Scotland was to engage in trade, he also secretly intended it to be a bank and he had urged his supporters to lobby against the potential new rival. They had failed. Paterson cursed that the bank Act had been 'surreptitiously gained and which may be of great prejudice, but is never like to be of any matter of good neither to us, nor those that have it'.[10] How the promoters of the bank curried favour with the politicians we do not know, but considering what was done to secure passage of the Company of Scotland Act (see next chapter), Paterson had scant reason to complain.

Nevertheless, Bank of Scotland was born and the Scottish parliament granted it some special and valuable privileges. It was to be a 'joint stock company', that is, incorporated with limited liability, meaning that its shareholders could not be held responsible for its debts beyond the amount they had subscribed. For its first 21 years its dividends were to be tax-free, and it was to enjoy a monopoly over banking in Scotland for the same period. Further, as an inducement to contribute to its capital, any non-Scottish subscriber was to be granted Scottish citizenship. John Holland was elected its first governor and temporarily moved to Edinburgh to launch the bank, which opened for business in March 1696. The legislation specifically forbade the bank lending to the Crown. It was thus Britain's first wholly commercial bank and Scotland's first formal financial company. The story of finance in Edinburgh had begun.

Since there were no precedents, the directors and proprietors of the bank had to make up their own rules. Meeting in the Cross-Keys they drew up standing orders and conditions for lending. From the start their Presbyterian rectitude asserted itself. Although Holland was governor and manager, he was not to be allowed to decide loan applications on his own. A committee was set up consisting of men of 'Credit and Substance' who would decide each application by ballot – the first ever credit committee. There were to be similar committees in branches when they were opened. A cashier would look after the money, but there was also to be an 'overseer' to watch over him, effectively an internal auditor. The directors intended to keep a very close eye on the day-to-day running of the company and their sanction was needed to increase salaries or to sack staff, a restriction that remained in force for 200 years.[11]

Holland invented some very prudent guidelines. The bank would make money by lending, but its advances were to be made on a very cautious basis. Loans were for a maximum of one year and could be recalled by the bank at 30 days' notice. They all had to be backed by collateral, in the form of land, a personal security or pledges of 'non-perishable commodities'. In the case of personal security, the bank not only demanded the ability to seize the borrower's 'moveables' in the event of a default, but also insisted on having two 'cautioners' to act as guarantors. The bank lent at 6 per cent, but there was a 2 per cent discount for those who repaid early. It would also take deposits and, crucially, would issue its own banknotes – promises to pay the bearer on demand the face value of the note in coin. Behind its caution over lending and the pains it took to ensure political support in Scotland and London was an absolute need to establish trust in its paper. It would lend notes, not coin. Unless they were regarded by the bank's depositors and by those with whom its lenders did business as 'as good as coin' the bank would not succeed and the economy would not benefit. This trust was to be severely tested.

The bank started lending in April 1696 and at the end of that month approved its first loan to a woman: Dame Henrietta Murray borrowed £500 on her own personal bond and £1,000 on the security of her son's estate.[12]

The first issue of banknotes was to be £125,000 sterling, but it would be backed by only £6,666 13s 4d held in coin at the Edinburgh office – gearing of 19 to 1.[13] Lesser amounts were distributed to branches established in Glasgow, Dundee, Aberdeen and Montrose. Thus the bank would earn interest on money that did not physically exist as coin – it could create more than £100,000 of new money by issuing notes. It was running the risk that holders of its notes would demand that they be redeemed in cash and force it into default, and if that happened trust would be lost and its business damaged, possibly terminally. Others had been more circumspect; neither the Bank of Amsterdam, nor the well-regarded Hamburg bank issued banknotes promising to pay the bearer in coin, and attempts by other banks in Genoa, Sweden and Norway to do so had ended in failure. The Bank of England had done so, and was much better capitalised, but even it had temporarily to suspend cash payments in May 1696.

Bank of Scotland started life in rented rooms in Myln Square, but later bought an office above a coffee shop in Parliament Close, off the High Street. To manage its business and keep on top of its liabilities, the bank needed a modern and efficient accounting system. Holland had expertise and experience of his own, but the directors also appointed George Watson as accountant.[14] Like Holland, he had trained in bookkeeping in Amsterdam, the leading financial centre of the time, spoke Dutch and had a thorough knowledge of international trade. He established a double entry accounts system. In June, Holland returned to London with the thanks of the directors for getting the bank up and running. He had been paying his own expenses while living in Edinburgh and drawing no salary, his remuneration being set at 10 per cent of the bank's profit after the Adventurers had taken a 12 per cent dividend, which could only be paid from net earnings, not from capital. Since the bank was in no position to pay a dividend in 1696, he received nothing.[15] He had been called out of retirement to help with the launch and now hoped to go back to a quiet life. At a general meeting of the subscribers, the court of directors reported that Holland 'has fully performed his undertaking to the company of setting the bank upon such a clear establishment as that it cannot probably miscarry'.[16]

Or as we might say today: what could possibly go wrong?

3

The first bank war

WILLIAM PATERSON HAD spent years developing and promoting his idea for a trading company to challenge the monopolies of the East India Company and a second English trading firm, the Royal African Company – supplier of slaves to English colonies in the West Indies and North America. He had tried to raise support and finance in Amsterdam and Berlin and to tap the rich seam of animosity among independent London merchants against the arrogance and exclusivity of the two companies. There had been challenges to the East India, but it had ruthlessly used its monopoly to make money and its money to enforce its monopoly, through patronage, bribery and coercion.[1]

Although born the son of a Dumfriesshire farmer, Paterson had spent most of his life outside Scotland, first living with an aunt in Bristol, then after her death working in the West Indies in various clerical jobs. On returning to Britain his ingenuity, resourcefulness, determination and powers of persuasion enabled him to rise in wealth and status in the London business world. His promotion of the successful Hampstead Water Company had been recognised with a gift of £2,000 in 'maiden' shares, but he was resentful that his efforts on behalf of the Bank of England were not similarly rewarded. He was elected a director, but had to pay for his shares like everyone else and was refused recompense for the time and effort he had put into developing the proposal, lobbying and, at the second attempt, winning parliamentary approval for it. This may have been the reason that he attempted to launch the Orphans' Bank on the back of a typically Patersonian scheme for helping the Corporation of London escape from the mess it had got into by raiding the charitable orphans' funds entrusted to it.[2] Paterson's prospectus for his new bank included a 5 per cent profit share for himself.

When the news reached his fellow directors at the Bank of England it gave them the pretext for asking him to resign, but they may have had

other reasons. He was not one of the 'great and good' – the titled gentlemen and rich merchants who made up the rest of the Bank board – and
he was not an easy man to like. His entry in the *Dictionary of National
Biography* describes him as gaining 'a reputation for double-dealing and
insincerity, as well earned as that for imagination and persuasiveness'.[3]
One contemporary was blunter, describing him as 'one who converses in
darkness and loves not to bring his deeds into the light'.[4] Others were
more kind in their assessment: 'He trusted people he should not have
trusted and lacked any sense of humour.'[5] He was a serious man who
never told a joke or a funny story and, against the spirit of the age, he was
a teetotaller.

Paterson had initially ruled out Scotland as the place to launch his new
idea because of its seeming poverty and backwardness, but he been
persuaded to visit Edinburgh in 1692 by another London Scot, Andrew
Fletcher of Saltoun. There he was introduced to the Marquis of
Tweeddale, the King's Commissioner in Scotland, whom he tried to
interest in the idea of a Scots trading company, although with little immediate impact.[6] On a second trip a year later he had rallied support among
merchants and left them with a draft Act of Parliament in case an opportunity arose to lobby for it. By 1695 political events had moved in his
favour. The king urgently needed the Scottish parliament to renew its
war subsidies and Tweeddale needed a diversion to head off a growing
row over his failure to launch an inquiry into the Glencoe massacre of
1692. Paterson, back in London, received the news that Tweeddale had
opened a new session of the Scottish parliament with a speech indicating
that the parliament would pass an Act permitting the formation of a
trading company.

His supporters among the merchants of Edinburgh now went into
action to press for an enabling Act. Methods of winning influence have
not changed over three centuries: wining and dining played a big part in
the campaign. The merchants contributed to a lobbying fund. Robert
Blackwood seems to have taken the lead and an account of how the
money was spent was kept by James Balfour. He was the owner of a
soap-works, a glass-works, and an alum factory and, with other Edinburgh
merchants, had acquired the monopoly of the manufacture of gunpowder for Scotland. Two centuries later his descendant Barbara Balfour-
Melville found some of the receipts Balfour kept in a wooden chest (the
spelling is original):

£2119. 12s. 8d. Scots for 'procuring the Act of Parliament for the African tread.' This expenditure included treating at various coffee-houses, and we have little old yellowed accounts, in crabbed hand-writing, telling how much was expended, for instance, in dinner to the 'Provost of Glasgow, and other men of Glasgow.' The 'London men' were also fed, but which party enjoyed the following dinner we do not know; it was on the 22nd June 1695 that it was served. 'For Lambs head, & brist of mutton broth, for hering, for a gigot & loin of mutton, for 3 dwcks, for 3 chickens with gooseberrys, for fillot, for oyle, for fruit & cheese, for wyne, for bread & ale, for tobacco & pypes, for paper, for the Cook, for wyn find the bill, £33. 5s. 0d.'

Then there was money 'spent at the Ship' – to moneys 'paid to the Duck [sic] of Hamilton's servants/cash for drink money to ye president of ye parliaments servants', '12s. given the Comitioner's servants in drink money.' £570. 17s. 4d.was 'pyed for pasing our patent through'.[7]

Within two months the Act had been passed and Paterson had the legal cover he needed to raise money for his new venture. It had always been Paterson's intention that, although the company was to be legally Scottish, at least half the equity would be raised in London and the London-based Scots merchants, with more experience of trade and finance, would direct it. The Act was sufficiently wide to give the new company the ability to trade anywhere in the world and, astonishingly, gave a government guarantee against losses.

It was quickly seen as a challenge to the East India Company, which had been weakened by recent raids on its ships by French pirates and was implicated in bribery scandals, making it unpopular. Paterson called his Edinburgh backers to a meeting of directors in London and to their consternation, opened a London head office, published a prospectus (which detailed his incentives: 2 per cent of the shares and 3 per cent of the profits for 21 years) and began collecting subscriptions. He rapidly secured pledges for £300,000, but this success turned sour. The East India Company may have been down but it was not out, and began a concerted campaign against Paterson and his 'Scotch East India Company'. It started with a threat to any of the East India's own share-holders who might have promised to subscribe to the new rival (some had) and proceeded to the English parliament where the Company of

Scotland was denounced as a threat not only to the East India Company, but to English trade and taxes.

Directors of the new company were summoned to appear before the House of Lords and later the Commons, which, in January 1696, found them guilty of the crime of swearing the oath of loyalty to the company required by the Scottish Act, while in England – technically treason. They were threatened with being thrown into the Tower of London. This looked like a theoretical rather than an actual sanction; no one went to prison, but most of the Scots decided not to wait around to find out and quickly returned home.[8] Paterson took his time, closing his house in London and selling his effects before journeying north with his wife and child. But the East India Company's campaign had done its work: Paterson's London support, including the pledges of funding, melted away.

★ ★ ★

Paterson's life was a series of sharp reverses of fortune and it was about to take another 180-degree turn, this time for the better. He left London defeated, but arrived in Scotland a hero. News of his exploits in London and his brave stand against the might of the English establishment had preceded him. His fame was celebrated on the streets in popular ballads[9] and his reputation was burnished in the coffee houses of Edinburgh by his close collaborator James Smith (or Smyth – he had many aliases), who had travelled in advance. Paterson had secured influential allies, including the lord provost of Edinburgh, Sir Robert Chiesly, with whom he had been in regular correspondence. Paterson, Smith and a newly recruited accountant, Daniel Lodge, who had worked with Paterson at the Bank of England, were made burgesses of Edinburgh and 'gildbrethren' of the Merchant Company. Although virtually unknown in the city, they had become instantly admitted to the commercial community. All three were also co-opted onto the court of directors of the Company of Scotland.

Such was his fame that Paterson's mere presence in Scotland boosted the fundraising and, as we saw in Chapter 1, it proved much more fruitful than he had expected. Since a quarter of the subscriptions had to be paid immediately in cash, within a few months of his arrival he was in control of nearly £100,000 sterling – fifteen times the cash available to John Holland at Bank of Scotland. The Company purchased two houses in Myln Square, a few yards from the bank's rented office, and bought a large chest and two smaller strong boxes to safeguard its capital. Meticulous accounts of receipts and expenses were kept and the chief cashier was required to balance the cash every evening before leaving the office.[10]

Governance of the Company was theoretically in the hands of the board of 25 directors, two-thirds of whom were nobles or lairds with estates outside Edinburgh to manage and little experience of business or finance. The main source of expertise was Paterson and his two associates, Smith and Lodge. Attendance at meetings was a problem and Paterson complained that it was sometimes difficult to get a quorum,[11] but the dysfunctional board allowed him considerable scope to use the Company and its money to pursue his own ambitions. At the end of July he won acceptance for his plan to found a trading colony in the province of Darien on the isthmus of Panama, which he envisaged becoming the key to facilitating trade between the Atlantic and the Pacific – between Europe and the Indies. Yet despite his vision of a global trading empire, he decided on a more parochial, and perhaps personal, immediate use for the money – to drive his rival out of business.

Why Paterson viewed John Holland with such animosity is not clear; they had, after all, recently worked together as fellow directors of the Hampstead Water Company and Holland had acquiesced in Paterson receiving his 'maiden shares' as recognition for his part in starting the enterprise. The most likely explanation is that the relationship turned sour during the previous year. Paterson, as the principal projector and architect of the Bank of England may have resented the fact that Holland had copied his design in the proposals for Bank of Scotland – especially as Paterson had received nothing for his work for the Bank and would not even be recognised as the inspiration for the Scottish venture. Holland, with his detailed knowledge of the power and ruthlessness of the East India Company, had also carefully kept the fledgling Bank of Scotland out of the row over the launch of the Company of Scotland in London. With several directors and many subscribers in common he did not want to risk being tarred with the same brush as Paterson and have his London capital put under threat. How he could have helped is not clear, but the fact that several of the London Scots who initially backed Paterson, including Thomas Deans, deserted the Company for Bank of Scotland must have rankled.

In a small city like Edinburgh, with a tiny financial elite, it was difficult to keep secrets. The bank and the Company not only had many subscribers in common, but ten directors served on both boards too. Paterson knew that the bank was vulnerable. By the end of July 1696, it had issued notes totalling £25,846 from head office and had outstanding notes for a further £3,500 in its branches. Since these 'promised to pay the bearer on demand', the bank already had liabilities four times the amount of coin in its coffers and as it continued lending this exposure would increase.[12] Paterson, using the ambiguous wording in the Company of Scotland's Act of Parliament to justify ignoring the legal monopoly granted to the bank, began issuing his own notes, lending to his own subscribers and directors, many of whom were also the people who might borrow from Bank of Scotland. By October he had lent £20,025 to the Company's own shareholders – nearly as much as the bank and a fifth of the paid-up capital of the Company.[13]

He also started to undermine the bank by spreading rumours about its solvency and accusing John Holland of being secretly in the pay of his old employer, the by now infamous East India Company, which it was claimed wanted to destroy the Company of Scotland. More seriously, Paterson began buying up Bank of Scotland notes and, in June 1696, he appeared personally in the office of the bank and demanded that the notes be redeemed in cash. He also got others to do the same, including Lord Provost Chiesly, who was a major shareholder in the Company. News that such prestigious people were not prepared to trust Bank of Scotland notes spread quickly and had the effect of panicking the bank's smaller creditors to seek repayment too.[14] Paterson's intention was to spark a run on the bank and destroy its credibility.

Having directors in common meant that it was also clear to the bank board what lay behind Paterson's moves and they took emergency action to stave off disaster. Lending was halted, cash recalled from the branches (which were later closed), James Foulis, the London director, was instructed to delay payment on London bills and a general meeting of Adventurers was called.[15] The board wrote to Holland in London: 'A great deal of noise has been made here . . . about the business of our bank and we understand there are formed designs to break us.'[16]

Holland hit back at the rumours by publishing his own account of his activities and motives and his dealings with Paterson,[17] which he had printed in Edinburgh and distributed from the bank's head office. He instructed the directors to call up another 20 per cent of the unpaid subscription.[18] This raised £13,332, tripling the backing for the bank's outstanding notes. The bank also borrowed 26,000 silver merks (about

£1,430 sterling).[19] The total was enough to meet demands for payment and to restore confidence and for a while it looked as though the crisis had been averted. Paterson proposed a meeting 'for removing any mistakes that are or shall be twixt the companies',[20] and a high-powered delegation of bank directors met a committee from the court of the Company on two occasions, but to no avail. There continued to be demands for the redemption of the bank's notes and by October it was running out of cash again, forced to borrow and to cut its costs by sacking staff to stay in business.

Paterson, however, had overplayed his hand. He did not have the full support of either the political establishment or his own directors. In the small world of Scottish business and landowning many wealthy and influential individuals had vested interests in both the bank and the company. They could not afford to see one of their investments go bust so quickly. It also dawned on ministers that the collapse of the bank would have a disastrous effect on the already stretched public finances. Taxes were hard enough to collect, but would be made worse if some of the largest taxpayers and/or tax collectors were bankrupted.

The bank had managed to survive so far. To drive it under Paterson needed to continue his campaign, but he was running through the Company of Scotland's resources. Most of the lending he had done had been in cash rather than by issuing paper, and he had been buying up Bank of Scotland notes. The Company too had opened branches around the country and had expanded its staff. Cash was running short: its own notes were being returned, with the holders demanding coin, and it needed to set aside large sums for procuring and outfitting ships and equipping an expedition. All this was using up cash at an alarming rate – the available surplus fell from £48,000 to £30,000 between August and October and was to drop much further.[21]

The board decided to get back to its core purpose. James Smith returned to London to recruit sea captains and ships' surgeons, and source possible trade goods, while Paterson was sent to Amsterdam and Hamburg, accompanied by two directors, to raise additional finance. He was entrusted with £20,000 – the bulk of the Company's remaining cash – and he passed two-thirds of it to Smith to finance his activities in London. As soon as Paterson left, the board decided to stop issuing new notes and lending to its own shareholders.[22] But getting its money back was not easy: it took three years to recover the full amount. The Company had been lending at 4 per cent, but after bad debts were taken into account the return on capital was a derisory 0.6 per cent.[23]

The bank's difficulties were over for the time being, but the Company's problems were just beginning and Paterson's fortunes were about to take another dramatic turn. His attempts to enlist the merchants of Holland and northern Germany to his cause was undermined by Smith, who ran up huge losses in London, some of which he could not account for.

The Company had no choice but to go abroad for ships and equipment. There were no shipyards in Scotland capable of producing the ocean-going vessels it needed and it could not go to English yards, so they had to be procured in Hamburg and Rotterdam. Sails, ropes, most of the ironwork, cannon, small arms, ammunition and even gunpowder had to be imported. For this it needed cash or credit, but its standing was about to take a serious knock. Smith had been given the cash, but notes drawn on him by the Company's agents in Amsterdam, who were procuring vessels and equipment, were refused payment. An investigation by the directors uncovered the chaotic state of his accounts.

A collapse in the value of sterling and a severe shortage of coin had produced a difficult financial situation in London and Smith persuaded his fellow directors that things were not as bad as they seemed and would improve once the financial crisis was over. He was allowed to join Paterson and the others in Hamburg, but when further suspicions arose he fled to Amsterdam, where the Company's agents arrested and imprisoned him. Historians disagree on whether Smith was a crook or merely unlucky,[24] but the outcome was that the Company suffered substantial losses, very little of which was recovered. To compound the problem Paterson had made the wrong call on the way exchange rates would move, adding to the deficit. An independent inquiry cleared Paterson of any wrongdoing, but he was removed from the board and when the first expedition to Darien finally did depart in 1698 he was only a last minute addition to the passenger list.

The tables were now turned. Whereas a few months previously the political and wealthy elite could not afford to let Bank of Scotland be bankrupted by Paterson, now they could not face letting the Company of Scotland fail. If it did, more than the prestige of the nation would be lost – a large part of their personal fortunes and the liquid wealth of the country were tied up in it too.

A power struggle developed within the board of the bank between on one side those who wanted to lend to the Company and on the other those who feared that to do so was to put the bank at risk again. The Company was doing all it could to cut its commitments and conserve its cash, but there was no guarantee that it would survive, even if it borrowed from the bank. The danger then would be that both institutions would go down together. The bank was still weak. Understandably, it had made a loss in its first year of trading, but the figures in the accounts ignored the fact that some of its borrowers were significantly in arrears with their interest payments. Had this been recognised, as was the practice in some London banking operations, the deficit would have almost doubled.[25] There must have been doubts, too, about its ability to call up more capital or borrow further: its shareholders were themselves financially stressed. John Holland, writing from London, took the side of the moderates and urged caution. This was in keeping with his prudent nature, but given the bruising experience of his tussle with Paterson he cannot have been keen to help rescue the Company.

The dispute was resolved in the spring of 1697 when the cautious faction was victorious in the board elections. Lord Belhaven and Lord Ruthven, who had held places on the boards of both the bank and the Company and favoured lending to it, were defeated, as were their supporters. John Holland stood down as governor, although he was elected a London director, along with his mentor Francis Beyer. His place as governor was taken by the Earl of Leven, a staunch supporter of the king and a man who 'epitomised the Presbyterian ideal of the cautious approach to lending and discounting'.[26] He had been a soldier and a politician and was keeper of Edinburgh Castle. He held the governorship of the bank for over 30 years until his death in 1728.

The Company of Scotland mounted its expeditions to Darien, without the help of a loan from the bank, but the colony was a disaster. Disease, incompetence, hostility from Spain (the dominant colonial power in the region) and indifference from the English settlements in the West Indies combined to defeat Paterson's ambitions. Many settlers, including Paterson's wife and child, died and Scotland lost a substantial proportion of its national wealth.

4

The Equivalent and the
beginning of paper money

THE NEW CENTURY was to be transformative for Edinburgh and for Bank of Scotland, but it started with a disaster for both. On Saturday night 3 February 1700 fire broke out in the Meal Market, a small court of buildings behind Parliament Close, mostly occupied by lawyers. With tall buildings tightly packed together, the blaze quickly spread up the hill to the close itself and the High Street. Duncan Forbes, later the judge Lord Culloden, wrote to his brother: 'There are burnt, by the easiest computation, between three and four hundred families. All the pride of Edinburgh is sunk. From the Cowgate to the High Street, all is burnt and hardly one stone is left upon another. The Commissioner, the President of Parliament, the President of the Court of Session, the Bank, most of the Lords, lawyers and clerks were all burnt, besides many poor and great families. It is said just now by Sir John Cochran that there is more rent burnt in this fire than the whole city of Glasgow will amount to.'[1]

There was relatively little loss of life, but with no fire brigade the blaze had to be left to burn itself out and the damage to buildings was considerable. Walls still standing were so dangerous that they had to be pulled down. William Paterson, back in Edinburgh after being evacuated from the colony at Darien in a fever, witnessed the fire and attributed it to 'the secret hand of God'.[2] This was a widespread theory. Since the fire had consumed the houses and offices of the rich, it was believed that it was the Almighty's judgement on them for ignoring the plight of the poor and the starving. Sermons were preached on the subject in the city kirks, but if it was divine retribution, it spared the Company of Scotland's offices on the other side of the High Street, while destroying the tenement in Parliament Close to which Bank of Scotland had moved in 1696. The Earl of Leven brought troops from the castle who rescued books and papers from the burning building and the board heard that 'the whole notes, cash, papers and books belonging to the office, being revised and inspected since the bringing thereof from the company's lodging . . . is safe and again put in order'.[3] But the bank lost the building, which had been purchased for £1,111. It was not insured.[4]

The bank also had other problems. Holland's prudent lending rules had proved impossible to enforce. In the depressed economic conditions, some borrowers simply did not have the cash to repay on time. Many of its outstanding loans were overdue and the bank had to go to law to defeat a challenge to the additional 2 per cent interest charge for late payers. Lending in London had not gone as well as was hoped. Scots merchants would accept Bank of Scotland notes, but when the Bank of England recovered from the financial crisis of 1696 and began lending again London merchants preferred its paper. James Foulis, who managed the London operations, returned ten books of unissued £10 notes, ten of £5 and the plates, presses and stamps used to make them.[5]

Worse, losses were being sustained on the cross-border exchange business, which the bank had imagined would be a second source of profit. It had set itself the ambitious target of stabilising the exchange rate between Edinburgh and London and between Edinburgh and Amsterdam, where many Scots merchants did business. Using the subscription money it had raised in London, Foulis bought and sold bills of exchange, looking to make a margin on both sides of the trade. The market was very volatile,[6] but initially business went well and the bank booked reasonable profits. However, this attracted competitors into the market who slashed margins to a level that did not justify the bank's risk. In November 1700 it pulled out of Amsterdam and scaled back its London business. But Foulis, in addition to trading for the bank, had run up big losses dealing on his own account, which he financed by borrowing from his employer. In 1701 he was bankrupted.[7] His bank shares and those belonging to his son had to be sold to pay part of the debt and his debts called in, but the bank only received 10s on the £.[8]

It was a salutary lesson: the directors decided that 'this was the most dangerous of all banking trades'[9] hardly suited to a cautious Presbyterian business. There was some good news. The bank developed a small business in discounting bills of exchange (advancing money at interest against expected receivables), but the economy was still too weak to enable it to expand its lending to the level which would produce big enough profits to provide an adequate return on the Adventurers' investment. It managed to pay a first small dividend in 1699, but could not afford one the following year.

In 1704 the bank took a decision that was eventually beneficial, but in the short term led to another run and a liquidity crisis. It decided to supplement the £100, £50, £10 and £5 bills it issued with £1 notes. (The note actually had the words '£12 Scots' printed on the face, but by this time the bank was doing most of its business in sterling). This would enable it to lend in smaller sums, get its paper into many more hands and quickly expand its business and its reach into the economy. The Nine Years' War with France had ended in 1697 and King William had died in 1702, but peace did not last long. Under his sister-in-law Queen Anne, England and Scotland were dragged into another Continental conflict. Coin was again in very short supply, so the take-up of the new £1 note was encouraging.

The directors cannot have foreseen what was going to come next. Rumours that the Scots pound was going to be devalued against sterling had swept the country periodically, but never before had the reverse happened. A story began to go round the coffee houses and taverns that the government would counter the shortage of hard cash by revaluing the coinage upwards: the holders of coins would see an increase in their wealth without having to do anything. An official denial did nothing to stop the tale being believed and demands for the bank's notes to be redeemed in coin accelerated. The bank was slow to respond and calling in overdue loans had little effect: by the end of the year it was out of cash and had to suspend payments. The rumour was groundless, but confidence in the bank was shaken and the government felt it had to act. The privy council ordered an investigation into the bank's solvency and produced a balance sheet that, it was claimed, showed that the bank could honour all £50,847 of its outstanding notes and have a surplus. Letters of reassurance were sent out, but it was four months before redemptions could be resumed and the bank had to curtail some parts of its business for two years.[10]

★ ★ ★

The Union between Scotland and England came in 1707. Historians still argue about its causes and effects, but in this story it had two very positive influences. The financial settlement that accompanied the political agreement recapitalised the Scottish economy at a time when it was desperately in need of investment; and the way in which the sum was paid gave an enormous boost to the acceptance of paper money and so to the development of Edinburgh as a financial centre.

The Act gave many economic benefits to Scotland – unfettered access to the English market, the ability to trade freely and openly with the English colonies and protection for Scottish ships from privateers and foreign powers. There was also to be a common currency – sterling, which had been in increasing use by Scots merchants anxious to avoid the uncertain exchange value of the Scots pound.

Article 15 of the Act of Union provided for a capital sum of £398,085 10s to be paid by England to Scotland.[11] This was said to be the 'Equivalent' of the cost to Scotland of meeting its share of interest payments of the (English) national debt of the new Great Britain. How this very precise sum was determined the Act does not explain,[12] but Forrester claims the calculation was done by William Paterson.[13] Whether this was true or not the figure was very close to the total pledged to the Company of Scotland and the way in which the money was to be spent favoured the subscribers. The Company had done little since its putative colony had been finally abandoned in 1700. It had never managed to collect the full sum subscribed, but it had lost at least £170,000 in hard cash. Now the Act formally dissolved the Company and promised that its shareholders would be compensated. Company of Scotland shares had been changing hands rapidly in the years leading up to the Union at a quarter or less of their face value (Defoe claimed some had been sold at 10 per cent of par).[14] Now the holders were to be paid 60 per cent of the original cost, representing a considerable profit for those who had bought in the market.

Other distributions were also to be made. Army officers, noblemen and lairds who had raised troops for the war, and public servants owed money by the Scottish government were to be paid their arrears. Any loss arising from a recoinage to merge the Scottish and English currencies was to be made good. The expenses of the Scottish commissioners (who were to implement the Act) were to be met and a seven-year fund was to be set up to promote the textile, fisheries and other industries. There were high expectations from such a limited pot of gold.

It was July before a train of waggons, each pulled by six-horses, set off from London accompanied by three Bank of England officials and an escort of Scots cavalry, and August before they reached Edinburgh. Why the journey took so long and needed so many carts is a mystery. The *Edinburgh Courant* reported the arrival on 6 August deadpan: 'Yest'day the Equivalent Money in thirteen waggons was carried to our Castle, under guard of 150 Dragoons of the Lord Polwarth and the Lord Carmichel's Regiments.'[15] The reception was not as rapturous as the Bank of England staff may have hoped: 'A good share of ye mob are very angry,' reported James Houblon, 'and threw stones at ye bank officers and coachmen.'[16] It was not difficult to stir up anti-English feeling in the city and the Bank people may have got off lightly. When the waggons were unloaded the Scottish commissioners found to their dismay that little over a quarter of the payment was in gold (£100,085); the rest was in exchequer bills, redeemable only in London. Fearing more rioting they demanded more cash and a further £50,000 was despatched, this time in one of the Queen's coaches guarded by mounted grenadiers. It arrived in Berwick in record time and was conveyed to Edinburgh.[17]

The Bank of England was sitting on a lot of exchequer bills, accepted in exchange for its latest lending to the government. They were freely traded and routinely accepted in London, and in persuading the Treasury and Scottish ministers that the Equivalent could be largely paid this way the Bank was probably hoping to extend its business into Scotland.[18] But in Edinburgh they were seen as another example of English duplicity and a threat to the business of Bank of Scotland. In fact the Edinburgh bank did well from the episode and over the next few years saw big increases in its lending and the beginning of a deposit business as recipients of the Equivalent looked for safe custody of their money. As the bank began to make steady profits and to pay regular dividends its share price rose.[19]

Others did not do so well. Predictably those with political connections were first to get compensation for their losses from the Darien debacle, led by the Duchess of Hamilton, whose man of business, David Crawford, managed to jump the queue and get his own money too.[20] Altogether shareholders in the Company of Scotland took 60 per cent of the available funds, representing their loss, plus interest. This left insufficient for the other purposes and when the shortfall from reminting Scottish coins into English ones and paying the expenses of the commissioners were deducted, the losers were government creditors, officials who were hoping for their back pay and the aristocrats and landowners who had raised, equipped and paid troops. The government, without the cash to pay them, issued debentures – securities supposedly paying interest, although the holders had a long wait before seeing any.

The distribution of the financial settlement may have been marked by mismanagement and corruption, but it had a significant effect on the economic activity of Scotland. The recoinage – melting down Scottish and foreign silver and gold coins and reminting them as full-weight sterling – showed that the total circulation had been only £411,000, heavily depleted by the losses of Darien and the need to import food over the famine years. The cash element of the Equivalent increased this by over a third. Scotland and England now had a common currency and a common coinage. In theory the Pound Scots, the Scots penny, the 'bodle', the 'plack', the 'bawbee' and the 'merk' ceased to exist, although some of the names remained in common usage for years.

But more important in the long run was the paper issued. Slowly the exchequer bills were replaced by Bank of Scotland notes, its expanded lending helping Scots merchants to take advantage of the new markets they had gained through the Union and landowners to improve their estates and increase their income. Economic improvement was not fast and not even, but gradually Scotland recovered from the famine years. Even the debentures, after trading well below their face value in the years after 1707, became the seeds for the next stage in the development of the Edinburgh finance industry. One of the holders was William Paterson, who was voted £18,242-worth by a special Act of Parliament.

5

Royal Bank and the second bank war

THE DEATH OF Queen Anne in 1714 and the succession by her distant kinsman, the Hanoverian George I, prompted another Jacobite rising the following year in support of James Stuart, the 'Old Pretender', son of the deposed James VII & II. The Earl of Mar led an army which quickly took Inverness, Dundee and Perth. A separate attempt to capture Edinburgh Castle was foiled. Bank of Scotland had £30,000 of government money in its vaults, which was sent to the castle for safekeeping, and in the febrile atmosphere there was a prolonged run on the bank, which forced it to suspend redemption of its notes for cash.

In November the Jacobite army was stopped by a government force at Sheriffmuir in Stirlingshire and a parallel uprising in England was defeated at Preston. The danger was over by early 1716, but it was eight months before the bank was able to resume convertibility of it notes for cash on demand and its reputation suffered. There were rumours that it had Jacobite sympathies: two of its directors, Lord Basil Hamilton and the Earl of Panmure, had fought for the rebels and after the conflict was over the bank's treasurer, David Drummond, collected funds for the defence of Jacobite prisoners. Much more telling for the bank was the fact that its political influence was waning as the Earl of Leven, its governor, and his Tory supporters steadily lost power to the Whigs.[1] Its 21-year legal monopoly on banking in Scotland came to an end and the bank made no attempt to have it renewed.

A Whig administration, led by Sir Robert Walpole, took power in 1721 after the South Sea Bubble scandal – when shares in the South Sea Company were ramped up to dizzy heights and then crashed causing many bankruptcies – had implicated ministers in the previous government. Its rising star in Scotland was John Campbell, the Duke of Argyll. He had succeeded the Earl of Leven as commander-in-chief north of the border and so had led the government army at Sheriffmuir, earning him

considerable prestige. Significantly, he was a buyer of Equivalent debentures, as was his brother the Earl of Ilay, also a powerful politician, and
other members of the extended Campbell clan. The debenture holders
had not had much luck in securing their interest payments, but in 1719
parliament voted them £10,000 a year from Scottish customs duties.
Acting on a suggestion from William Paterson, they formed themselves
into a society and tried to claim rights to borrow, issue notes and deal in
mortgages, but were vigorously opposed by the Bank of England. Bank
of Scotland, still licking its wounds, made no objection.

Over the next three years the debenture society made three attempts
to get Bank of Scotland to agree to a merger and, after being rebuffed,
bought up £8,400 of the bank's notes and presented them for payment
trying to force a default. They also tried to get government officials to
remove their deposits,[2] but the bank stood its ground.

In 1724 the Equivalent Society was incorporated and three years later
the Duke of Argyll secured the right to transact financial business for it.
In September 1727 the society obtained a charter to establish a new
bank – Royal Bank of Scotland. Now the limits of the Union of 20 years
before became apparent: the Bank of England kept its dominant position
in England, but failed in an attempt to enforce its privileges north of the
border. This would be very significant in the century to come. England
had one dominant bank, but Scotland now had the beginning of a multi-
bank system.

Royal Bank (known as the 'New Bank', while Bank of Scotland became
the 'Old Bank') was from the start a creation of the Campbells and their
associates. It appointed the Earl of Ilay as its first governor and elected a
board of directors packed with Argyll supporters in influential positions,
including the president of the court of session as the deputy governor,
several other judges, the solicitor general, two commissioners of excise
and George Drummond, the lord provost of Edinburgh.[3] It rented premises in Ship Close, off the High Street, hired staff and began to issue its
own notes. The board ordained that 'the words Royal Bank and the sume
[sic] of the notes be of a larger character or letter that they might appear
conspicuous at first sight'.[4] It dithered over whether to commission an
engraving of the king's head because of the cost and resolved to ask Lord
Ilay, who apparently insisted since the royal portrait adorned the first
notes.

At the end of September 1727 the board heard that a total of £106,747
14s 9$\frac{1}{6}$d had been subscribed as the capital of the bank.[5] In theory this

made it stronger than Bank of Scotland, but it was not cash. Subscribers were given their shares in exchange for their debentures, but these could not be turned into ready money: the government had no intention of redeeming the debentures and they had been changing hands in the market for a lot less than face value. William Paterson was offered £3,000 for his £18,000 debenture holding.[6] They paid interest at 4.5 per cent, but the Royal was obliged to pass this on to its new shareholders to compensate for the income they had lost. Accordingly it paid its first half-yearly 2 per cent dividend at the end of December, despite having done very little lending business by then and had certainly not made a profit.[7]

Unlike Lord Leven, who chaired most Bank of Scotland board meetings, Ilay was an absentee governor. He lived mainly in London and controlled Royal Bank and other Scottish institutions through his placemen, Patrick Campbell (Lord Monzie), George Drummond and Andrew Fletcher (Lord Milton), who maintained a network of informers and spies, including paying servants of Bank of Scotland directors for information.[8] 'The dirty work was done by friends who he had helped to pick as directors and managers,' comments Ilay's biographer.[9] Ilay was a consummate politician; having fought beside his brother at Sheriffmuir to defeat the Jacobites (and been wounded twice) he hedged his bets by keeping up a correspondence with the Old Pretender's court in exile.[10] He was a judge at the court of session and an active and successful investor in partnership with his brother's protégé, the gambler and banker John Law, dealing in stocks in both London and Paris. He was a money-lender and, together with his London banker, the goldsmith George Middleton, invested heavily in Royal Bank of Scotland stock.

By 1728 Bank of Scotland had been in business for over 30 years and, apart from years when there was war, famine or a run on the bank (there was another in 1708 on a false rumour of a French invasion),[11] it was now a solidly profitable company. The improving Scottish economy and its monopoly position for most of that time enabled it to pay regular dividends of 15–20 per cent, occasionally as high as 30 per cent. Its original Adventurers had got their money back and were now getting handsome regular returns. It is unsurprising that Royal Bank looked at this performance and wanted part of the action. But Ilay, who had been a shareholder in the Old Bank since 1724, desired more, either to take it over, or to drive it out of business. 'We must either agree with the bank, or destroy it,' commented Milton.[12]

To fight a bank war, the Royal needed cash. It raised £22,000 from its shareholders and used Ilay's influence to get more, becoming banker in Scotland to the Treasury. The government had voted £20,000 for the improvement of manufacturing and fisheries in Scotland to be disbursed through a board of trustees, who were mostly Ilay's nominees. Bank of Scotland offered to borrow half this sum and to lend it to individual manufacturing and fishing enterprises,[13] but Royal Bank made a counter bid to take the whole amount and was successful.[14] The earl's connections with the Bank of England also enabled the New Bank to borrow up to £30,000 to bolster its fighting fund.[15]

The seasoned directors of the Old Bank must have had a sense of *déjà vu* when the attack came. The Royal bought up large quantities of Bank of Scotland notes and presented them for payment without warning. Bank of Scotland dragged its feet by delaying payment and sometimes redeemed the notes entirely in silver sixpences.[16] This provoked a cry of outrage among the directors of the Royal: 'So often as the servants of this bank do make demands at the Old Bank for payment of their notes, they are very ill-used and trifled with in the take of the money and very often other ways uncivilly treated.'[17]

Since the two banks were only a few hundred yards apart on opposite sides of the High Street and the protagonists must have known each other well, the conflict was very personal. The Old Bank mustered its defences by calling in its overdue debts and borrowing £8,000. The Royal pressed its assault, sending one of its staff accompanied by a notary and a witness to demand repayment of £5,000 of Bank of Scotland notes, with instructions to 'protest against the Bank for non-payment and that an instrument be extended thereupon and registered and to the end [that] Horning may be obtained on such protest'.[18] 'Horning' was a legal procedure taken against debtors who could not pay: the Royal intended to take the matter to law.

In March the New Bank launched a two-pronged legal action: on its own behalf its cashier, Allan Whitefoord, went to the court of session to press for payment of £9,374 of notes, and Andrew Cochrane, a Glasgow merchant and friend of Lord Ilay, began his case for repayment of £900. The Old Bank, which was down to £585 in cash,[19] could not pay, suspended repayment of its notes, but offered interest to the holders until such time as redemption could be resumed.[20] Royal Bank, casting itself as the protector of 'poor people' and the nation's finances made a public offer to cash 3–4 Bank of Scotland twenty-shilling (£1) notes for 'relief of such merchants who are to pay in money to the Revenues and to prevent the Revenues from suffering'.[21]

The following month George Drummond suggested to a Bank of Scotland director he had 'accidentally' met that they should begin merger talks and this was followed by a formal meeting of directors from each side. The Bank, perhaps perceiving the weakness of Royal Bank's capital position, suggested that before they proceeded any further a full valuation of each side's capital and trading accounts should be determined. Had this happened, Royal would have been shown as worth a lot less than the Old Bank. There were doubts about the real value of its stock and it was trading at a loss. It had been forced to borrow at the legal maximum (now 5 per cent) from the Bank of England and the manufacturers' trustees, but it was prevented by law from charging more on its lending.

Royal Bank was forced to reveal its hand: it wasn't interested in a merger, it was proposing a takeover – a straight swap of Bank of Scotland stock for new Royal Bank shares. When the court of session, heavily influenced by Ilay's political enemies, found against the Royal Bank and Cochrane, the Old Bank was emboldened to drag the talks out without making a commitment. In frustration, Royal Bank appealed to the House of Lords, where Ilay managed to get the verdict overturned.[22] But by this time the Old Bank had recovered. It began by redeeming twenty-shilling (£1) notes, then steadily other higher denominations. It even sent its company secretary (with a notary and a witness) to Royal Bank to offer to redeem any £50 notes it held – the offer was refused.

The Royal's attack had failed. The Old Bank rejected an amalgamation of any sort and by the spring of the following year had paid off all its borrowings and redeemed any outstanding notes. It had survived the latest, and best-financed assault on its independence, but the successful defence was not without damage: it had to pay legal costs and that year's dividend was a miserable 1.5 per cent.[23]

Having failed in its attack, Royal Bank turned its attention to its banking business. Its contacts in the Argyll/Whig dominated town councils of Edinburgh, where George Drummond was lord provost, and Glasgow, where Andrew Cochrane had been elected provost, brought it both deposits and lending, and it became banker to the army in Scotland. Its connections in London, through Lord Ilay, the Equivalent Company and the Bank of England, enabled it to make headway in the exchange and remittance trade between Scotland and London – a market that Bank of Scotland had neglected since its problems at the start of the century. It also had more success than its rival closer to home, among the merchants of Glasgow. The freedom the Union had given them to trade with the American colonies would be interrupted by Britain's continuing wars, but Glasgow merchants were beginning to expand the tobacco trade. For this they needed funds and banking facilities, which the Royal provided.

It was also responsible for an innovation which was to become ubiquitous in banking. At the height of its battle with the Old Bank, a merchant, William Hog, asked the Royal if he could overdraw his cash account. This was novel: until then borrowers took a fixed amount of money for a fixed period, paying interest on the full amount. The 'overdraft' (the name appears in the Royal Bank board minutes for the first time on 31 May 1728, but this type of account was usually called a 'cash credit') gave customers in good standing the ability to borrow variable amounts and to pay interest only for as long as they needed the cash. The bank drew up rules and demanded two guarantors, but allowed Hog to overdraw up to £1,000. The overdraft was born and it gave the bank a product that appealed to traders, whose cashflow was predictable but variable. It enabled the Royal to make progress in the merchant towns of Scotland where the Old Bank was still weak. Eventually Bank of Scotland was compelled to follow suit.

A decade later, the Royal was doing well, but it had a problem. Its charter did not give it permanence and should the government ever decide to redeem the Equivalent debentures its future might be in doubt. It needed a new charter and Lord Milton, using the influence and contacts of the Earl of Ilay, took on the task of securing it. The negotiations took six years of political arm-wrestling, but in 1738 the bank got its legal immortality and the ability to increase its capital by up to £40,000. It continued to thrive and when Allan Whitefoord retired as cashier in 1745 he was able to sell his £1,000 of shares with a 43 per cent profit.[24]

His successor was his deputy, John Campbell, who effectively became the bank's chief executive, but this was not his only job. The bank's 'servants' were full-time employees, its 'officers' had outside occupations. John Campbell, although he lived in the bank house, was the 'doer' (legal adviser) to the Earl of Breadalbane and his diary shows that he juggled both positions constantly.[25] He had been required to deposit a bond for £10,000 to guarantee 'the faithful discharge of his trust'.[26] The cashier's bond (the treasurer's bond in the Old Bank) was the security for deposits. In the event that a depositor could not get his money from the bank when he demanded it, it was the bank officer, rather than the bank as a legal entity, who stood behind it.

The widespread use of banknotes inevitably led to forgery becoming a problem. The notes were printed, but so simply that a good scribe, of which there were many, could make a handwritten copy which would fool a recipient not familiar with handling paper currency. Bank of Scotland discovered its first forged notes in 1701: Thomas Macghie had altered a £5 note to £50; he was detected, but vanished abroad before he could be prosecuted. The bank ordered new copper engraving plates with each note in different styles 'to put out of the power of man to renew Macghie's villany'.[27] It was a forlorn hope. In 1710 Robert Fleming, a teacher, a 'poor man', was condemned to death for passing twenty-shilling notes which he had copied himself by hand. Queen Anne granted several stays of execution and after her death he was reprieved. But forgery continued to be a problem and the notes had to be redesigned in 1723 and in 1726.[28]

After 1730 both banks were increasingly concerned to prevent counterfeiting and detect it where it did occur, paying informants a reward for information leading to successful prosecutions. The penalties for the criminal – banishment or execution – and the costs for the bank were severe. In 1749 Bank of Scotland brought winter closing time forward from 5 p.m. to 4 p.m. because of the risk that tellers would not be able to detect forgery by candlelight. Royal Bank followed suit shortly afterwards.[29] By 1751 the two banks were sufficiently comfortable with their rivalry to undertake a joint prosecution of a University of St Andrews professor and an Edinburgh lawyer and his wife, who were suspected of forging notes of both banks.[30]

The first paper notes were seen as holding their value better than coin because they could not be debased and clipping them did not affect their worth. It was vital to the banks' survival that credibility of their notes be maintained so they were prepared to spend tens or even hundreds of times the value of the loss to make an example of forgers. It was also important for the economy, and the courts could be harsh in taking the side of the banks. Capital punishment for forgery remained in Scotland until 1820. During the eighteenth century, 26 men were executed, with a further 18 men and 2 women sentenced to death, but subsequently pardoned. The courts were especially hard on those who were educated, owned property or were in a position of trust.[31]

6

Hard drinking ministers found the pensions industry

ALEXANDER WEBSTER'S HELLFIRE and damnation sermons filled his church to overflowing every Sunday. Like his father, whom he succeeded as minister of the Tolbooth Kirk at the top of the High Street, he was a charismatic preacher on the evangelical wing of the Church of Scotland – a fundamentalist Christian who believed in the primacy of the Bible as the revelation of the word of God. He had been instrumental in bringing the English revivalist George Whitefield to Scotland and preached along-side him in Leith and at a remarkable open-air gathering in Cambuslang in 1741 when, it was claimed, 15 preachers addressed a crowd of up to 30,000.[1] However, Webster was able to reconcile his religious fervour with a strong liking and a prodigious capacity for alcohol. 'He combined the clearest of heads with the most unctuous of spirits, was the life of supper parties in Edinburgh . . . could join over a magnum of claret on Monday with gentlemen of not too correct lives whom he had profes-sionally consigned to perdition on Sunday. He could pass with alacrity and sincerity from devote prayers by a bedside to a roystering reunion in Fortune's tavern and return home with his Bible under his arm and five bottles under his girdle.'[2]

Webster had married Mary Erskine[3], who had a fortune of £4,000 a year, which enabled him to 'keep better company than most clergy'. His contemporary in the church, Alexander Carlyle, described him as 'a clever fellow, an excellent and a ready speaker, fertile in expedient and prompt in execution, yet he had by no means a leading or a decisive mind'.[4] Carlyle may have intended this faint praise to be damning – they were not friends – but Webster's powers of persuasion and determination to get things done were to prove essential in arriving at a viable way of providing for dependents of the clergy. The 'leading decisive mind' could be provided by others.

The Church of Scotland had a problem. After the Reformation it permitted its clergy to marry, but when a married minister died his widow and children often had no income and were reduced to penury or relying on charity. John Knox had no doubt where the responsibility should rest: 'provision for the wyffis of ministers after their deceise to be remittet to the discretioun of the Kirk'.[5] Parishes made their own arrangements, or none at all. The obligation was formalised in an act of the Scottish parliament in 1672, which said that the widow and any children were to share a lump sum of half the annual stipend of the dead minister. But there would be no continuing support, and once the six-months' wages were spent many widows lived in poverty, getting any relief they could from the local provision for the poor.

The Scottish Episcopal Church faced the same issue and in 1688 the Bishop of Edinburgh and the Dean of Glasgow raised 7,615 merks (about £5,000 Scots or £425 sterling) to create the Centisma Fund. The money was to be invested and the interest used to support the 'relics and orphans' of the ministers of the 31 dioceses of Edinburgh. Dependants of professors of divinity and ministers of other denominations were later added to the beneficiaries, but the fund was small and its performance and administration were patchy.[6] The General Assembly, the Church of Scotland's annual governing conference, had several attempts to solve the problem in the 1720s and 30s, first exhorting individual presbyteries to set up arrangements, then trying to establish a scheme for the whole Church. There was opposition to a fund that would earn interest as being too close to mammon. There was also uncertainty about how much should be contributed by the ministers. One tenth of the annual stipend was suggested, but it was an arbitrary figure, perhaps inspired by the traditional 'tithe'. The scheme was also voluntary and, despite several extensions of the deadline, the take-up was small. In the 1740s a group of Edinburgh ministers decided to work out the shape and rules of an effective arrangement and propose it to a General Assembly. The lead was taken by Webster and a fellow minister, who was a very different individual.

There was a theological division in the Church of Scotland between the evangelicals and the moderates – who distrusted dogmatism and embraced rational argument. A century later the schism was to contribute to the Disruption, when the evangelicals broke away to form the Free Church of Scotland, but in the eighteenth century relations between the protagonists on both sides was still cordial. Webster's collaborator in trying to find a practical solution to the problem of ministers' dependants was Robert Wallace, minister at Greyfriars Church and a leading moderate. He believed in the power of reason to solve problems and clearly did have a 'leading mind'. At the University of Edinburgh he had studied mathematics as well as theology and had become so proficient that when the professor was ill Wallace had taught his classes. After being ordained he showed himself to be an independent spirit. He fell out of favour with the ruling Whig party until after the fall of Walpole in 1742, when Ilay lost his power of patronage in Scotland.

Wallace was not averse to a drink, but he had neither the income nor the constitution for Webster's consumption. He was a founder member of the Rankenian Club, named after Ranken's tavern in Hunter Square, to the south of the High Street, where it met to read out papers on diverse subjects and have them discussed and criticised. Members included the philosopher and historian David Hume, Principal William Wishart of Edinburgh University, John Stevenson, professor of logic at Edinburgh, George Turnbull, professor of moral philosophy at Marischal College, Aberdeen, and Colin Maclaurin, professor of mathematics at Edinburgh.

Maclaurin shared an interest in both mathematics and theology with Wallace, and he had personal experience of the challenge the two clerics were trying to meet. He was born the son of a minister in rural Argyll, but his father died when he was six weeks old. His mother moved Colin and his brother to Dumbarton so that the boys could attend school, but she died when Colin was nine and thereafter he was brought up by his uncle Daniel, also a minister. At the age of 11 he entered Glasgow University to study mathematics and three years later presented his MA thesis defending Newton's ideas on gravitation and planetary motion against the accepted theories of Descartes.[7] After graduation he stayed at Glasgow for a further year to study theology and thought about entering the Church, but at the age of 19 he won a ten-day contest against leading mathematicians to be appointed to a chair at Marischal College in the University of Aberdeen.

His move to Edinburgh some years later was supported by Newton, who had become a friend and mentor and who offered to pay part of his salary as an inducement to the university to employ him. It was at Edinburgh that he did his most important and lasting work, advocating and expanding Newton's theories on the calculus and developing the Maclaurin series, for which he is still known. He was also a popular teacher. Carlyle described him 'as the clearest and most agreeable lecturer on that abstract science that ever I heard. He made mathematics a fashionable study.'[8]

Although some of the correspondence between Wallace and Maclaurin survives, we do not know who suggested collecting mortality statistics to calculate how many kirk ministers were likely to die in each year and therefore how much would be needed to support their families. Insurance and life assurance companies already existed. A few had funds into which they put contributions and from which they paid claims, but most operated on a 'pay as you go' basis – hoping to meet each year's claims from that year's contributions, which were not calculated on any rational basis. Many London firms went bust in the South Sea Bubble crash of 1720. It is surprising that these companies were so ignorant, since the problem was not new and a paper on what we would now call actuarial mathematics had been published in 1693 by the astronomer and mathematician Edmund Halley in the *Philosophical Transactions of the Royal Society of London.*[9] Using mortality data collected by Caspar Neumann, a theologian living in Breslau (now Wrocław in Poland) and sent to the Royal Society by the German mathematician Gottfried Leibnitz, he calculated the probability of deaths in any one year and therefore worked out the price of annuities on lives.[10]

Valuing annuities – a guaranteed income for life in exchange for a lump sum – was important because many European states and cities – including England – sold them as a means of raising money. Much later they were to become the basic tool of the life assurance and pensions industry. To induce people to buy them, governments offered attractive returns – as high as twice the prevailing interest rate. This was paid irrespective of the age of the purchaser, so if too many young people with long life expectancies bought annuities, the city risked bankruptcy.

Johan de Witt, prime minister of Holland, and Johannes Hudde, mayor of Amsterdam, had already thought about the problem of computing the price of life annuities. Hudde had a record of the people who had bought Amsterdam's annuities, including the age at which the annuities had been purchased and the age at which they had died. Witt was a mathematician as well as a politician and in 1671 he published a pioneering work on valuing life annuities.[11] Fearing an invasion, they wanted to raise money to strengthen the army, but it was too late. De Witt had previously neglected the armed forces and in 1672 Holland was easily overrun by a triple alliance led by France. De Witt was lynched by the crowd in The Hague.[12] His work on annuities seems to have been forgotten. Twenty

years later Halley's work was ignored. The English government continued to sell annuities at prices which ensured that it was losing money.

We don't know whether Maclaurin knew of De Witt's work, but he was
a member of the Royal Society, so may have known about Halley's paper.
Wallace, with his interest in mathematics, may have already heard of it.
They discussed the need to gather mortality statistics with Webster, who
took on the job of contacting every presbytery in Scotland to ask how
many ministers had died during the previous 20 years, how many had
left widows, how many widows were still alive and how many had not
married again. He received answers from all but a handful and from
these Wallace constructed a table and computed that an average of 27
ministers were likely to die in any one year and that 18 of these would
leave widows. Since 1722 there had been 304 widows, and 280 of these
were still living and unmarried. He considered that 300 widows at any
one time would be a reasonable maximum figure to allow for, but, since
they would be entitled to half-a-year stipend by law and to any arrears
owing, when calculating how much money was needed the maximum
number could safely be reduced to 261.

The two ministers proposed that the contributions would be paid into
a fund, which would earn interest. Wallace calculated the level of contribution needed so that the fund would always be able to meet its obligations, without ministers being asked to pay too high a proportion of their
income. To be sure he asked his fellow Rankenian to check his calculations. Maclaurin appears to have been a very gentle man, sensitive to the
feelings of others. He began by praising the calculations, which were 'so
good that minute observations against the absolute perfection of the
scheme seem to be improper'. However, he was 'apprehensive that the
capital will not rise so fast as is proposed'. In fact Maclaurin had spotted
a material error in the calculation of the number of widows that would
have led to the fund running out of money, and sent Wallace a detailed
explanation of how he thought the arithmetic had gone wrong. Maclaurin
compared Wallace's forecast of the number of widows to the number
predicted by the 'doctrine of chances' (probability), which showed
increasingly higher numbers over time. Wallace accepted the changes
and reworked his calculations.[13]

Wallace and Webster proposed the scheme to the General Assembly,
but there was still resistance to a fund and it took them two years of argument and compromise to bring their colleagues round. The final scheme,
adopted when Wallace was Moderator (chair) of the Assembly in 1743,

offered ministers four different rates of contribution with different bene-fits accordingly. Widows would get an annuity for life, but children would receive a one-off payment of ten times the annual contribution their father had made. To get over the objections to investment, the surplus from the fund was to be offered as loans of £30 each, at 4 per cent inter-est, to university principals, professors and ministers, in a set order of seniority.

Another minister, George Wishart of the Tron Kirk, was despatched to London to press for an Act of Parliament, his task being made more difficult by constant suggestions from Edinburgh: 'When they were in London several peevish and unwise orders were sent to them and they learned by experience how difficult is was to be directed and advised by a committee at Edinburgh,' commented Maclaurin.[14] 'Mr Wallace earnestly desires me to go over the computations for the scheme and if possible I would oblige him. There are some wrong-headed people talk absurdly on the subject, which he imagines a paper from me would silence.' Maclaurin's backing gave Wallace's argument the authority it needed and the legislation was granted in 1744.

Webster was the driving force in getting the scheme implemented. Trustees and collectors were appointed (each having to put up a personal bond for £7,000 to ensure their honesty) and a report was given to the General Assembly each year. There were a few teething problems – in 1747 there was not sufficient demand from borrowers to produce the forecast interest income and in the following years there were more widows than had been anticipated, but Wallace reworked his calculations and a modified scheme was approved by a new Act of Parliament in 1749. Interestingly it allowed the Church to take legal action against ministers who did not pay their contributions or against borrowers who were late with their interest payments.

The Scottish Ministers' Widows' Fund was the first in the world to be established on actuarial principles and was soon copied. In 1761 The Corporation for the Relief of the Poor and Distressed Presbyterian Ministers and Poor and Distressed Widows was established in Philadelphia for the American Church 'in imitation of the laudable example of the Church of Scotland'. A year later the Equitable Life company of London (Society for Equitable Assurances on Lives and Survivorships) was organised on actuarial lines based on the ideas of the English mathematicians James Dodson (1710–57), who developed a scientific basis for calculating fair annual premiums using mortality tables for the town of Northampton. He was aware of Halley's work on mortality, but whether he also knew of the Scottish Ministers' Widows' scheme is unknown.[15] Equitable Life is widely credited as being the first life assurance company to use actuarial principles, but it came more than a decade after the Church of Scotland fund. Surprisingly, Scotland failed to capitalise on this lead. Although a number of life assurance companies operating on similar principles were started in London – and some opened offices in Edinburgh – it was into the nineteenth century before another Scottish life and pensions company was founded.

Wallace appears to have taken no further interest in the scheme once it was running smoothly, but Webster remained involved. In 1768 he advised the United Incorporation of St Mary's Chapel in Edinburgh on a similar scheme for the dependants of artisans and in 1771 he fiercely rebutted criticism of the fund in a book by Richard Price, an adviser to Equitable Life. Webster wrote a 5,000-word letter to Price, who was also a non-conformist minister and a mathematician, and succeeded in winning him round. Price corrected the mistakes in future editions of the book and warmly endorsed the kirk scheme.

Wallace, described by a later diarist as 'eminent as a divine, a statistician and an economist', went on to write a 'Dissertation on the Numbers of Mankind in Ancient and Modern Times' (1753), in which he took issue with the population ideas of David Hume. He also wrote an essay on the 'Art of Dancing' – however, he was 'too discreet, probably, to practice'.[16] He died in 1771.

Webster, too, became interested in population and in 1755 the government commissioned him to undertake the first census of Scotland, which he approached in much the same way as he had collected mortality statistics for ministers. He wrote to every parish in Scotland and asked not only for the number of inhabitants, but their gender, ages, how many were men of fighting age, and the number of Protestants and Catholics. The methodology would not be credible in a modern census, but the figure he calculated for the population of Scotland, approximately 1.2 million,[17] seems plausible given that the first modern census of 1801 estimated the population at 1.6 million. Webster was by marriage an uncle of James Boswell and in 1773 dined with Boswell and Dr Johnson. Boswell reported: 'At supper we had Dr Alexander Webster, who, though not learned, had such a knowledge of mankind, such a fund of information and entertainment, so clear a head and such accommodating manners, that Dr Johnson found him a very agreeable companion.'

Despite his intemperate drinking, which increased after he was left £6,000 by a grateful parishioner, he lived to age 76, dying in 1784.

The scheme which the two ministers established is still in existence, now called the Widows' Fund, with 1,500 beneficiaries – pensioners, widows and orphans. It was closed to new entrants in 2014 and is being slowly run down, but it is quite possible it will see its 300th anniversary. The fund now has assets of £35 million and, although the investment policy has been relaxed since the days when it was only allowed to make loans to ministers, it is conservatively invested in government gilts. Unusually for an occupational pension scheme these days, it has been in surplus, enabling the trustees to declare several discretionary increases in benefits.

7

Jacobites defeated by bankers

WHEN CHARLES EDWARD Stuart (Bonnie Prince Charlie), son of the Old Pretender, landed on the northwest coast of Scotland in July 1745 he brought with him 1,000 guns, 1,800 broadswords and 4,000 *Louis d'ors* – French gold pieces – which he immediately sent to Edinburgh to have changed.[1] Foreign gold coins still circulated in Scotland, but Britain was (again) at war with France and so much enemy currency would have aroused suspicion. We don't know who changed his gold coins, but the prince had many supporters in the capital. Bank of Scotland was still imagined to have Jacobite sympathies, but – unsurprisingly – there is no reference to any such transaction in the bank's minute book. Handling a large quantity of French coin would have been extremely dangerous and it is unlikely the Old Bank would have taken the risk, even if asked. It is more likely that one of the city's goldsmiths melted the coins down into bullion to be later exchanged for guineas. This is possibly the first recorded instance of money laundering in Scotland.

The rebellion of 1745 was to be the last gasp of the Jacobites. The prince had come to lead another attempt to claim the thrones of Scotland and England for his father and was to learn that in modern warfare marshalling financial resources was as important as procuring arms and men. He had been advised that at least 30,000 gold coins would be needed,[2] but he could not raise enough. Attempts to elicit loans or gifts from sympathisers before his landing had produced very little[3] and unlike the Hanoverian government, which had the financial might of the Bank of England behind it, he had no formal means of obtaining credit.

To win support of the population the prince paid the men who rallied to his standard and bought rather than commandeered the food and other supplies he needed as he marched south. This was a popular but expensive policy, and by the beginning of September he was 'down to his last guinea'.[4] Along the way several rich supporters had given him small gifts of money or payment in kind (often meals for himself and his staff), but on his arrival in Perth he demanded the sum of £500, which the magistrates agreed to pay in return for a promise that no more would be required. Clearly if the prince was to succeed in conquering Scotland and marching on London he would need much more money and Edinburgh, Scotland's richest city, was the only place he would get it.

The capital was apprehensive about the approach of the rebels. Sir John Cope, commander of the government forces, was still in the Highlands where he had tried unsuccessfully to intercept the Jacobites and two regiments of dragoons, stationed in the city, had retreated to Leith, leaving it undefended except for a small garrison in the castle. Wealthy landowners, including several directors of the two banks, left for the safety of their country estates, but some residents were prepared to fight. A citizen regiment with a contingent from the university was hastily assembled and armed with a variety of old weapons. It was commanded by former lord provost and Royal Bank director George Drummond, who had fought at Sheriffmuir in 1715 and was an ardent anti-Jacobite. Professor Colin Maclaurin left his family at his country house in Dalkeith and travelled into Edinburgh to join the defenders. The classes he taught at Edinburgh spanned an extraordinarily wide range: as well as mathematics he covered experimental philosophy, surveying, fortification, geography, theory of gunnery, astronomy and optics. He was put to work shoring up the old city walls. It did not go well.

> I was amongst the first volunteers & signed for a dozen of the town's regiment. The care of the walls was recommended to me in which I laboured night and day under infinite discouragements from superior powers. When I was promised hundreds of workmen I could hardly get as many dozens; this was daily complained of; redress was promised; but till the last two days no redress was made and then it was late. However, the town was in a condition to have stood out two or three days against men unprovided with artillery, unskilful & then ill-armed; and there was an expectation of relief . . .[5]

The town guard and volunteers had marched west to the village of Corstorphine to meet the Jacobites head on, but after a brief stay Drummond had thought better of it and marched his troops back again. A meeting was called to discuss what to do. Maclaurin recorded the decision: 'On the fatal Monday I was loading the cannon at the West Port [the west gate to the city] & pressing the finishing of some works when in a pack'd meeting (400 volunteers, mostly substantial burghers) it carried to capitulate.'

When he arrived a few days later the prince, leading an army of 1,200, entered Edinburgh unopposed.

Of the two banks the Royal, having so publicly tied its colours to the government mast, had most reason to be apprehensive. Ilay, now Duke of Argyll following the death of his brother in 1743, was no longer governor and had sold most of his Royal Bank shares, but his influence on the board remained, notably in the presence of Andrew Fletcher, Lord Milton, who was deputy governor and lord justice clerk, a senior judge. His informers in the West Highlands had been warning of a possible invasion for several years, but the duke, now out of favour with the government, had struggled to get London to take the threat seriously. Royal Bank was vulnerable, it was banker to the army and its vaults in Ship Close held £20,000 of public funds in the account of the Receiver General, £14,000 of it in gold, the rest in silver coin. There were also its own notes, bonds, Bank of Scotland notes, gold and silver coin, plus silver plate being kept for various noblemen. These were assets an army planning a military campaign in England would badly need.

John Campbell, newly promoted to be chief cashier, had faced his first crisis within weeks. The directors heard that 'false and malicious reports that the bank had stopped redemption of its notes were being industriously propagated' and offered a reward of £50 for the unmasking of the person spreading the story. Whether this was a political attempt by Jacobite supporters to undermine the bank by trying to provoke a run is not clear, but a few days later the directors were further unsettled when they received the news that the rebel army had left Perth and was on its way to Edinburgh. They were unsure how they should react, so resolved to meet twice daily to be able to respond quickly to events. An inventory of all notes, gold and silver held in the vaults was ordered and they were put into boxes for easy transportation, but for the time being they were left where they were. Rather than taking a decision themselves, the Royal Bank directors looked to Bank of Scotland for a lead.[6]

The directors of the Old Bank seem to have been fairly relaxed. Their first discussion of the impending threat came on 6 September, nearly a week after the Royal Bank directors had noted it. Hearing that the Jacobites had taken Perth, they sent to the castle to ask that a strong-room be made ready and a week later, when the prince's army had crossed the River Forth at Stirling, they moved all notes, coin and books to the house of Major Robertson inside the castle walls. In contrast to their rivals at the New Bank, they appear to have closed the bank completely and did not meet again until 13 November.[7]

John Campbell heard about the Old Bank's move to the castle the following morning. He advised his directors to follow suit, 'as it is not proper to let the same remain in the office as it is not a place of strength to hold out against an attack or any insult'. It was not an easy task. The directors assembled to oversee the loading onto carts of an iron chest containing the Receiver General's £14,000 in gold, six boxes each containing £1,000 in silver, one box containing £47,000 in Royal Bank notes, two boxes of silverware belonging to Lord Rosse [sic], another box of £13,700 Royal Bank notes, one chest containing £300 in half-guineas, eight bags each with £100 in silver, one parcel of £3,300 in Old Bank notes, another parcel with £1,860 in Royal Bank notes, books of 'unfinished' banknotes, two chests of bills, securities and cashier's papers, eight boxes from the secretary's office, eighteen boxes from the account-ant's office, and two 'great chests' and three boxes of Lord Glenorchy's plate. All the chests and boxes were locked and the keys distributed among the directors. John Campbell volunteered to see everything safely stowed in the castle and said that he and his wife would 'ly' with them in the vault. His diary makes no mention of ever spending the night there.[8]

Three days later the Jacobites had occupied Edinburgh and the prince took up residence in Holyrood Palace, with his army camped in the neighbouring King's Park. Within days they received news that Cope's force, which had left the north by sea, had landed at Dunbar and was marching on Edinburgh and they went out to meet it at Prestonpans, to the east of the city. Most of the British army was in Europe fighting the French, and Cope's troops had no battle experience. They broke before the furious charge of the prince's Highlanders and suffered heavy casu-alties. The bloody defeat changed the mood in Edinburgh and London – no longer could the rebel threat be taken lightly.

On his way to Edinburgh the prince had sent a letter to Glasgow demanding £15,000 and other goods (the magistrates, led by Andrew Cochrane, eventually paid £5,000) and he now imposed a tax on the capital of half-a-crown in the £ (one-eighth) of all rents, which Royal Bank had to pay in common with all householders and businesses. He also requisitioned taxes and other revenues which would have gone to the government and asked for 1,000 tents, 2,000 'targets' (shields), 6,000 pairs of shoes and 6,000 canteens. The news of his victory at Prestonpans had doubled the size of his army to 3,000, but clearly he expected to have more sympathisers join him on his eventual march to London. Horses and corn were also expropriated and raiding parties were sent out into the towns and villages to extort further 'contributions'.[9]

Both the New and Old Banks were effectively now closed, which disrupted the normal commerce of the city. The prince issued a proclamation asserting that the banks 'shall be intirely [sic] sure under our protection and free from all contribution to be exacted by us in any time coming so that the proprietors may return with safety to their former business of banking'. But the directors were not convinced and both banks remained shut. The prince also promised to use banknotes for making payments, which would have been acceptable in Scotland, but not once his army crossed the border. It was not long before his representatives were demanding coin.

Although they occupied the city, the rebels had no field guns and so were unable to take the castle. They contented themselves with controlling who entered and left the fortress by setting up a guard post in the 'Weigh House' within range of the main gate and firing occasional musket shots at the castle guard, who fired back. The few directors of Royal Bank who had remained in the city decided that they ought to cancel or destroy the notes held in the castle, but how to get in was a problem. John Campbell had sometimes negotiated access to do some minor pieces of bank business, but others had been rough handled by the Highlanders and sent away.[10]

The demands on Royal Bank soon became much more direct. On the evening of 1 October 1745, John Murray of Broughton, the prince's secretary, arrived at the bank office with a notary and a witness to demand that £857 he had in Royal Bank notes be redeemed in coin. Failure to comply within 48 hours, he threatened, would result in the estates and assets of each of the directors being confiscated.[11] Campbell played for time by saying that he needed a safe pass to be able to get the money from the castle and at the next board meeting asked how he should respond. It was decided to pay 'to prevent further trouble and mischief', but it was the first of frequent increasing demands.[12]

Bearing a passport issued by Murray, a delegation of directors got past the Highland guard and walked to the castle, led by Campbell waving a white flag. They burnt or tore-up as many banknotes as they could, but with no idea who might be the eventual victor they had to tread a fine line between the two sides in the conflict. Accordingly, they gave General Guest, the garrison commander, £2,000 'for the public service', but took away £6,000 in gold to meet the requirements of the rebels. Most of it was to be needed as Murray's representatives made a series of demands, 'on pain of military execution'.[13] The trip to the castle was not without danger. John Campbell wrote in his diary:

> During our continuance in the Castle which was from about 9 till near three o'clock, there was cross firing from thence upon the Gardner's house at Livingston's yeards, [sic] occupied by R. Taylor, the shoemaker, at the head of a party of volunteers for the prince, to stop the communication thereabouts with the Castle. [O]ne Watson, a soldier, was so courageous as to go down over the Castle wall upon a rope, fire upon the Gardner's house, kill some of the volunteers there, carried off a firelock or two from them, sett the house in fire, return'd with these firelocks by his rope into the Castle, where he was received with loud huzzas for his valour.
>
> On his return the garrison was preparing for a sally, but as the men were a drawing up we got liberty from General Guest to go out again, and Captain Robert Mirry [sic] escorted us to the gate, where I again rais'd my white flagg, and with my friends return'd to town in safety, landed at my house from whence we adjourn'd to dine at Mrs. Clerks, vintner. No sooner were we sett down in Mrs. Clerks than we were inform'd that upon the sally from the Castle, Taylor and some of his men were taken and carried thither prisoners, leaving others dead on the spott, their house being sett on fire, the rest of the party having made their escape.[14]

Meanwhile in London the news of Cope's defeat caused a run on the Bank of England blamed, according to the *Gentlemen's Magazine*, on 'Papists and Jacobites with design to hurt credit as much as was within their power and to get gold to send to the rebels'.[15] Whether this was true, or it was merely a general panic, the run forced the Bank to curtail redemption of bills and later to call in more subscriptions from its shareholders. In a show of solidarity, merchants meeting in Garraway's coffee house issued a statement of faith in the Bank – a public relations stunt possibly instigated by the Bank of England itself.

At the beginning of November the Jacobite army left Edinburgh and marched into England. The experience of the last few months had shaken the Royal Bank directors and they waited nearly two weeks before retrieving the cash, notes and books from the castle and reopening for business. At the end of 1745 the prince turned back at Derby and retreated to Scotland, causing a brief renewed panic and a move to again take the Royal Bank's reserves to the castle. It was only when it was learned that the Jacobite army had crossed the Forth on the way north that the bank felt it could relax. Bank of Scotland, which had burned £80,000 of its own notes to prevent them falling into the prince's hands, withdrew only a small amount of cash from the castle. It took the precaution of preparing duplicate books so that it could continue to conduct some business, but it did not fully reopen the bank until the beginning of April 1746.

The Hanoverian government recalled the army led by the Duke of Cumberland from France and in January 1746 borrowed £1 million from the Bank of England. This was military and financial firepower Bonnie Prince Charlie would be unable to match. To supply him with money, a ship was despatched from France with about £13,000 in coin, but it was intercepted and chased by the Royal Navy, finally being trapped and bombarded in the shallow waters of the Kyle of Tongue, on the north coast of Scotland. With the help of local sympathisers, the Jacobites unloaded the gold and silver from the stricken vessel and attempted to take it overland to Inverness, 100 miles away, but they were chased by the Hanoverian militia and captured.[16]

The prince, now desperate for money, decided to produce his own banknotes to pay his men and buy the provisions he needed. He ordered Robert Strange, an artist and engraver who had volunteered for the Jacobite army, to prepare plates and print the notes. Inverness had no printing industry, so Strange had to persuade local craftsmen to build a press and a local coppersmith to prepare a plate, which Strange tried to etch. A crude plate with small denomination notes (one penny to six pence) was made, but before printing could be started news was received of the approach of Cumberland's army. The Jacobites left Inverness to meet them.[17]

By the time the two armies faced each other at Culloden the prince's soldiers had not been paid for months, food was short, they were ill-equipped and exhausted. The Hanoverian army, by contrast, was battle-hardened, well supplied and well fed – they had even been given a day off and a tot of brandy the day before the battle in celebration of Cumberland's 25th birthday (even though his birthday was not for another 11 days). They had also spent time in Aberdeen training in special tactics to counter the Highland charge.

After a crushing defeat, the prince escaped to France, never to return, and the Highland clans that had supported him were ruthlessly suppressed. The Jacobite threat, which had hung over Scotland for half a century, was lifted.

★ ★ ★

After the departure of the Jacobites from Edinburgh, the main demands on Royal Bank had been from the government army, which needed coin to pay its troops and refused to take Royal Bank notes, despite the protests of the directors. George Middleton, the Duke of Argyll's London banker, had to send gold and silver by warship, drawing on the Royal Bank's account with the Bank of England. Bank of Scotland, too, supported the army, lending £10,000 to General Husk, who had arrived in Edinburgh with the first division of Hanoverian troops in January 1746. The Old Bank directors, perhaps to emphasise their loyalty, promised him further credit if needed.[18] Among the beneficiaries of the army's spending was Lawrence Dundas, the son of a minor landowner, who had used a gift from his godfather to set himself up as a wine merchant in Edinburgh. He secured the contract to provision the army with bread and fodder and he did it so well that when the opposing sides met, Cumberland's men were well supplied and the horses of his cavalry, and those pulling his artillery and baggage trains, were in good condition. His efficiency led to a second contract with the army in Flanders and later supplying the troops who were building roads in the Highlands and Fort George, near Inverness.

Royal Bank's reserves were depleted and they felt themselves at risk of the same sort of treatment they had meted out to Bank of Scotland 17 years earlier. They declared: 'If the Gentlemen of the Old Bank shall make any extraordinary demand of cash for notes of this bank in their hands, that the Cashier shall not pay the same but tell them that the bank are to keep the same for the service of the army.'[19]

But no attack came. Like the Bank of England, they also asked for a public declaration of faith in Royal Bank from merchants and others 'sensible how necessary it is at all times for the welfare of this country that public credit be maintained and guard against sundry and malicious reports tending to lessen the credit of the bank'. Overdrafts were suspended for six months and 4 per cent interest was offered for deposits. The rebellion did, however, have a silver lining for the bank. In 1748 the government abolished the judicial powers of the nobility and their feudal claims over the labour and property of their tenants. They were paid compensation of £152,000, which was channelled via the Bank of England to the Royal. As with previous rebellions, the estates of landowners who had sided with the prince were confiscated and sold, the money again being channelled through Royal Bank.[20]

Bank of Scotland directors voted Major Robertson, whose house in Edinburgh Castle they had used as a temporary bank vault, 30 guineas for his trouble.[21] The following year the 'soldiers and servants' of the castle petitioned the Royal Bank board for some financial recognition for their part in safeguarding that bank's assets. The directors voted them 5 guineas, less the £1 7s 6d 'already paid'.[22]

In the spring of 1745 Royal Bank had purchased some ruined houses 'on the east side of Fishmarket Close', with the intention of demolishing them and building a new head office. William Adam, the most famous architect of the age, was commissioned to design it, but the work was delayed several times by the conflict and Adam died before it could proceed. His son John was asked to survey the site with a view to demolishing the remaining walls and laying the foundations, but his report cannot have been favourable because the bank then tried to sell the land, without success. The directors concluded that the site was 'by no means the most eligible place to build the bank's office upon, yet as it cannot be disposed of when exposed to publick sale . . . thereby the bank is fixed down to that spot'. They accepted a tender for the precise price of £2,823 6s 3$^{4}/_{12}$d and work began on a five-storey building – but it proved to be a nightmare.[23]

A neighbouring tenement had to be purchased to provide adequate access, they had to buy off a shopkeeper who said his premises were being undermined by the foundation work and others who complained that their light was being restricted. The bank had to make a deal with a cobbler who erected a pop-up shop next to the entrance, while promising he would limit 'disturbance of fish-wives, oyster-wives, boys and others'.[24] The building work and negotiations with the council over permissions and with neighbouring proprietors over access consumed hours of the directors' time over the next few years. The building was eventually finished in 1753 at a cost 40 per cent higher than originally planned. It had an innovation – a channel in the stairwell to take water to each of the building's five floors in case of fire, but the bank had to petition the council for a supply of water.[25]

George Drummond had left the city when it was occupied by the rebels and joined Cope's army in time to witness its destruction at Prestonpans. In 1746 he returned to Edinburgh and was elected lord provost for the second time. A sad ending to the rising was the death of Colin Maclaurin. Rather than swear an oath of allegiance to the prince, he had fled to Newcastle, and then to York. When he heard that the Jacobite army had left Edinburgh he began a return journey in bad weather, but on the way fell from his horse and caught a bad cold, from which he never recovered. He dictated chapters for his biography of Newton from his sick bed, but died in June 1746, aged only 48.

8

Drummond's vision for a city on a hill

EDINBURGH WAS GROWING in population, prosperity and influence. About 50,000 people now lived in the city,[1] still mostly on top of one another in the towering tenements that lined the closes on either side of the Lawnmarket, High Street, Netherbow and Canongate – today's Royal Mile. Many of the closes and houses destroyed by the fire of 1701 had been rebuilt – although there were still gap sites and ruins – and there were new developments to the south, on the flat land across the Cowgate ravine. Argyle's Square, Brown's Square and Adam's Square were small private developments, financed speculatively by their builders, with houses around a garden. They were modest by later standards, but spacious, light and airy compared to the Old Town. They were also homes 'after the fashion of London, every house being designed for one family'[2] – the rich did not share a building with the less well off. They were being separated by district rather than by a staircase.

Since 1741 the city had also boasted a large modern hospital. The first infirmary – a tiny affair with four beds – had been established by the Royal College of Physicians in 1725, financed by charitable donations. In 1736 a Royal Charter was obtained allowing the infirmary to be incorporated and a new fundraising drive, given a boost by the energy and contacts of George Drummond, raised enough to commission the architect William Adam to build a hospital with 228 beds. The historian Hugo Arnot, writing in 1788, praised 'the large staircase in the centre of the building so spacious as to admit of sedan chairs being carried up it', the separate wards for 'female patients undergoing salivation, and cells for mad people', and the hot and cold baths for the use of patients and 'citizens at large'.[3] It also had two teaching wards and a surgical theatre where students could watch operations. It was to become important to the health of the city and establish Edinburgh as a leading centre for medical teaching and research. Drummond helped secure a position for the surgeon Alexander Munro at the university, the first salaried medical professorship in the UK.

One of the early students at the medical school was James Hutton, now better known as the father of geology and for his revolutionary theory of 'deep time'. But he was other things too: an improving farmer and an entrepreneur. In 1756 with James Davie he started a business in Edinburgh manufacturing sal ammoniac, a compound used extensively in several industrial processes, but also as a fertiliser and food additive. The raw material was soot, of which 'Auld Reekie' – the city's nickname from the myriad chimneys belching coal smoke from its hearths – had plenty. The business was profitable and financed many of Hutton's later scientific and investment activities.

After decades of slow growth or stagnation, the Scottish economy was at last taking off. Agricultural prices were increasing, encouraging land-owners to improve their estates and increase their rents. The linen indus-try had been given a boost by the launch of the British Linen Company in 1746, the creation of Lord Milton. It began by making loans to textile businesses (including Milton's own), largely for working capital, and assisted them in sales and marketing. Edinburgh had some manufactur-ing – textiles, brewing, tanning, metalworking, printing – but it was increasingly a city of service industries and the knowledge economy. It was a city of law and public administration, banking and increasingly religious and intellectual thought, literature and learning.

The philosopher David Hume, famous (or in some circles infamous) following the publication of his books and essays on human understand-ing, behaviour, morals and religion, had returned to Edinburgh after years in France and England. He had been rejected for the chair of moral philosophy at Edinburgh University because of his atheism (and was to be rejected for the chair of logic at the University of Glasgow for the same reason), but was made keeper of the Advocates' Library in 1752 and began a productive and successful period of writing and publication. Hume's treatment by the university, the council (which had a veto over professorial appointments) and the Edinburgh clergy was doubtless painful, but he recovered quickly, unlike the student Thomas Aitkenhead half a century earlier who was hanged. Blasphemy was still nominally a crime punishable by death, but since Aitkenhead no one had been executed. Edinburgh was becoming a more tolerant city and even some kirk ministers rallied to Hume's defence. Robert Wallace preached a sermon in support of Hume: *Ignorance and superstition, a source of violence and cruelty.*[4]

The city was gaining a reputation as a centre of learning and ideas. Adam Smith, although yet to publish his major books on moral philosophy and economics (or to meet and befriend Hume), gave a series of public lectures at Edinburgh University from 1748–51 on rhetoric, the history of philosophy and jurisprudence. The foundation of the Select Society and similar clubs in 1754 brought together the intellectuals and the newly wealthy gentry and nobility, 'who wished to acquire polish from consorting with the literati as much as the literati desired status from the patronage of the social elite', says the historian T.C. Smout. The attraction of the clubs had an economic as well as a social effect, in bringing visitors into the town to spend as well as to attend.[5]

However, Edinburgh was still a city of contrasts. Hugo Arnot reported that 'the Canongate was the foulest quarter of the city with respect to abandoned women and brothels'. While at the top end of the Royal Mile Alexander Webster was still packing the Tolbooth Kirk every Sunday and collecting record amounts from his congregation for the relief of the poor.[6] George Drummond took regular comfort from Webster's evangelical sermons. As neither a landowner nor a merchant, he lived on what he could earn as a public servant in central or local government and for that he was dependent on the political patronage of Lord Ilay (after 1743, Duke of Argyll) and his lieutenant in Edinburgh, Lord Milton. Drummond was their placeman on the city council, the boards of Royal Bank, British Linen Company and the Society for the Improvement of Manufacturing and Fisheries. He owed £10,000 to the duke, who manipulated him by alternately threatening to cut his salary as commissioner of Customs, sack him or promote him. As a widower with ten children to support, he needed a regular income and his diary shows constant anxiety about his debts. For several years he retreated to religion and alcohol, but remarriage to a rich widow (and after her death to another) gave him a more stable financial base.[7]

Drummond was not his own man, except in his passion and vision for the development of Edinburgh. His political masters were prepared to go along with his schemes, but not to take a lead. For 40 years he was the driving force on the city council. He was lord provost six times and when not in office was the *éminence grise* behind whoever held the post.[8] His dream, which he told a friend had driven him since he first led the council in 1725, was to drain the Nor' Loch and extend the city onto its northern bank where there was space to design and construct a modern metropolis. But several disasters nearer at hand provided an opportunity that Drummond could not miss. The first was a fire in 1750 that ravaged Mary King's Close, an abandoned seventeenth-century alley opposite St Giles' Cathedral in the High Street, running down towards the loch. The following year the side wall of a nearby six-storey tenement collapsed and an inspection showed that adjacent buildings were in an equally unstable condition and had to be pulled down. This provided a gap site which the lord provost intended to fill with buildings that would enhance the grace, elegance and commercial appeal of the city, but first he had to win public support and raise the money.

In 1752 a pamphlet, *Proposals for carrying out certain public works in the city of Edinburgh*, was published. Its author was the lawyer and writer Sir Gilbert Elliott, but its inspiration was George Drummond. Running to 7,500 words, it compared Edinburgh, as capital of Scotland, unfavourably with London and other capitals – its advantages were 'overbalanced by other disadvantages almost without number ... The meanness of Edinburgh has been too long an obstruction to our improvement and a reproach to Scotland. The increase of our people, the extension of our commerce and the honour of the nation, are all concerned in the success of this project.'

The narrative outlined some immediate projects, including an Exchange for the merchants who currently did their business in the open air around the market cross, a new library for the Faculty of Advocates, robing rooms for judges and offices for their clerks, a new home for the registers and records of Scotland, but also looked ahead. There would be a new 'Act of Parliament for extending the "royalty" of the city [the area over which it could impose local taxes] to enlarge and beautify the town, by opening new streets to the north and south, removing the markets and shambles, and turning the North-Loch into a canal with walks and terraces on each side'. And it made a pitch for a government contribution to the cost: 'The expense of these public works should be defrayed by a national contribution.'[9]

These ideas were not new, but in the past little had come of them. Drummond had the drive to realise them and since he was already 64 was impatient to make a start. In the same month that the *Proposals* appeared, he informed the city council that he had asked the architect John Adam, son of William, to draw up plans. He lobbied for an enabling Act of Parliament and appointed commissioners to begin to negotiate for the purchase of land for the Exchange and for a new north–south road to cross the High Street. But he needed money and the city did not have it. Hugo Arnot bemoaned the fact that over the previous six decades, while the city had grown, its revenues had declined. In 1690, including shore duties from the port of Leith, Edinburgh had gross revenue of more than £6,500, but by 1749, despite increased rents on houses and land and a 15-fold rise in shore duties, revenue had actually fallen slightly. He was lost for an explanation, unless to blame the general incompetence of public administrators – a charge of which he absolved 'that publick spirited and excellent magistrate George Drummond Esq'.[10]

In 1723 the council, which already had debts of £78,000, had been allowed to borrow a further £25,000, to be financed by a two-pence (Scots) a pint duty on ale in an enlarged area of the city. This money was supposed to pay for new public buildings, increased stipends for kirk ministers and salaries for professors (both of which were paid by the council), bringing fresh water into the city and other purposes. Not only was it inadequate for all the uses assigned to it, but the yield from the tax steadily declined as drinkers switched from beer to whisky or tea. From nearly £8,000 in 1724, the tax take had more than halved by 1764 (and was to decline much further). To reduce the debt and make up some of the revenue shortfall, the city had been forced to sell land and buildings.

Drummond's first thought was to fall back on the philanthropic fundraising which had served him well in the building of the infirmary. 'There can be little doubt, but the better sort of inhabitants would cheerfully contribute to ornament the area,' he told the council.[11] His inclusion in the scheme of rooms for the advocates' library, judges, merchants and a meeting room for the Convention of Royal Burghs was partly to help this effort. He also wrote to Henry Pelham, first commissioner of the Treasury, asking him to intercede with the king on Edinburgh's behalf. It paid off; the Crown pledged nearly £2,000, the royal burghs £1,500, three dukes, including his patron Argyll, gave £200 each and there were promises from the surgeons, tailors, merchants, advocates, goldsmiths, masons, wrights and painters. Some subscriptions came from London and the town of Elgin put up £10. A total of £6,000 was promised by the end of 1752 (although eight years later some of the pledges had not been backed up with cash) but it was not enough to get the work started. Drummond went to the banks.[12]

The council had previously borrowed £5,000 from Bank of Scotland for famine relief.[13] The bank had waived the interest charge and the entire council had attended a meeting of the directors to thank them.

Now Drummond, who was temporarily out of office, and William Alexander, the lord provost, appealed to the bank again for £5,000 interest-free to 'improve and ornament' the city. The directors would not go that far, but as a gesture of goodwill extended the period of the loan and made the extra year free of interest.[14] When the pair went to Royal Bank the directors first deferred a decision to a meeting of proprietors, but later agreed and matched the Old Bank's terms. However, there were strings attached: the council had to pledge £4,700 in a bond secured on the ale duty to the Old Bank and £3,400 of Royal Bank stock it owned to the New Bank. In addition each member of the council had to guarantee the rest personally.[15]

The estimated cost of the Exchange was £18,000. There was no possibility of the council funding such an ambitious scheme from its own resources and Drummond had to promise that the project would be self-financing. The city would be the contractor, but it would appoint developers (called 'undertakers') to carry out the work. He assured his colleagues: 'It is not meant nor intended that the Town shall run any risque [sic], or that the ordinary revenue should ever be burdened with, or defray any part of the expense of carrying on this or any other of the publick works.'[16] The finances would be kept separate from the town's revenues in cash accounts at the two banks.

The commissioners accepted John Adam's design for elegant neoclassical buildings on three sides of a courtyard or piazza, with the open side fronting the High Street.* Because the site sloped precipitously on the north, there were four storeys at the front of the central building, but ten at the back. There was to be a covered loggia facing the piazza where, it was hoped, merchants would conduct their business sheltered from the weather. On this slender hope – a previous covered area had been built adjacent to the market cross, but the merchants had never used it – the development was given the grand name of 'The Exchange'. However, most of the buildings were to be offices, shops and private houses. Undertakers were appointed – an architect, a mason and two wrights – and work began with Drummond laying the foundation stone in 1753.

The financial plan was always shaky and trying to piece together the income and expenditure from mentions in the council's minutes gives the impression that Drummond was flying by the seat of his pants. He did not have enough to complete the work and pay off the banks, but he

---

* The building is now the City of Edinburgh Council Chambers.

hoped that selling or leasing the buildings before completion would bring in enough to keep the work going and, despite not being able to make the stage payments promised to the undertakers as the building progressed, managed to transfer the financial risk from the council to them.

Inevitably, costs overran. Buying out the owners of the land cost more than £11,000, another £4,100 had to be advanced to the undertakers to get the work started and when interest and fees were added there was hardly anything left of the subscription pledges and the two bank loans. An early win was persuading the lords of the customs to lease the main part of the central building. Drummond hoped to either sell it to them or tie them to a 99-year lease, but he settled for a 57-year lease with an annual rent of £360.[17] The following year Adam Fairholme, a private banker, bought a large house in the west wing and other smaller flats and shops were sold. As the council had no money, the commissioners allowed the undertakers to keep the proceeds of the sale. Nevertheless, they were forced to borrow. Construction was completed around 1760. There were various sales of homes or shops and the remaining properties – mostly small rooms off Mary King's and Allen's Closes, which now ran underground beneath the new buildings – were sold by 'roup' (auction). However, the financial wrangling between the council and the undertakers continued for another six years. Drummond had managed to put onto the unhappy builders the responsibility for selling the properties and achieving the council's valuation of their worth, which they disputed:

> The undertakers cannot help mentioning the particular hardship they are under in this affair. The building which they understood was to serve as an Exchange – and the Public [council] in the contract with them declared it to be so – accordinglie [sic] on the faith of this they undertook the work upon the plan given them and executed it fairly and honestly. Upon the idea of an Exchange the subjects were valued at prices which would be drawn for shops etc. within an Exchange. But they find it turns out that there is no Exchange, so that this is only a private square, consequently the subjects decreased in their value.[18]

Drummond had not persuaded the merchants to move under the shelter of the new loggia – they persisted in conducting their business in the open air, whatever the weather. Even when the Mercat Cross was demolished they continued to meet at the spot where it had been. The council was unmoved by the undertakers' plea and insisted they still owed £2,006 – a sum they said would ruin them and their families. Two years later the undertakers gave in, acknowledging that they owed the debt, but asking for time to pay in three annual instalments. One of the four men – Patrick Jamieson, the mason – paid £400 towards his share and his son stood surety for the rest. The council accepted the offer from the others, but insisted that 'cautioners' guarantee the debt and added interest until it was finally paid.[19]

Drummond got his fine new buildings 'ornamenting' the High Street without further burdening the council's debt. After paying back the banks he even made a small profit, which was devoted to his next project. It was even more ambitious – draining the Nor' Loch and building a bridge to connect the High Street with the land owned by the council on the north side, where he planned to build the New Town of Edinburgh. Money was again a problem. Baillie John Brown, one of the commissioners who would oversee the project, suggested a solution: no contribution from the city's funds would be possible, but there would be no difficulty in selling the city's land at £400 an acre with a reasonable 'feu'* on top.[20]

In 1766 the council announced a competition to design the development and from six entries, one by James Craig, a young architect and planner, was chosen. It was a classical rectangular layout, with three broad streets connecting two large squares. After suggestions from John Adam and the other judges of the competition, a modified plan was adopted and published so that prospective property developers and owners could see what the town would look like and what they would be buying. The council also began naming the streets neighbouring the north end of the proposed bridge – Princes Street, Queen Street and St Andrew Square. Craig had the plan printed and copies were sold in bookshops and from his home at the foot of the West Bow. The marketing worked. Between 1767, when the final plan was approved, and 1769 the council received nearly £8,000 in sale proceeds and began to earn annual feu rents.[21] Sales of lots continued for at least the next decade. This was an early example of a practice now commonplace in hot property areas – buying 'off plan', but it also indicated the demand among the

---

* Under Scotland's land tenure system the 'feudal superior', in this case the city council, could sell land and impose an annual 'feu' or rent and specify some planning restrictions on any building.

more prosperous citizens for larger and more elegant homes. For the third time Drummond started a new campaign for subscriptions, which eventually raised £2,500.

Finance was not the only problem: the bridge would be a considerable engineering challenge. It would have to be 1,134 feet (345 metres) long – longer by a quarter than London Bridge – built over a swamp and would have to cope with the difference in height of the land on each side. To create access from the High Street houses had to be acquired and demolished. Sir James Clerk of Penicuik, who like his father and grandfather was an amateur architect, had submitted some sketch designs to the council and estimated the cost at £12,000. Working with John Baxter, a mason and contractor, he suggested that the bridge should be based on the design of a Roman aqueduct and offered to get advice from London and from Baxter's son who was studying in Rome.

> That this work will turn out to be one of the most ponderous and weighty, if not one of the most beautiful of any in Europe, the advice of the most able architects ought to be obtained, who I am persuaded will cheerfully give it without expecting anything for it and to boot will think themselves honoured by having it asked of them. As we architects, like lawyers and physicians are fond in difficult cases such as this is to have the assistance of our bretheren, and as I intend it only for my own intertainment [sic], to have the affair consulted by the most able in their professions.[22]

The commissioners, however, were in too much of a hurry to take advice from London or Rome. 'If it is not to be carried into execution this summer, so shall [we] dispair [sic] of ever seeing it go forward at all.'[23]

Work was begun on draining the Nor' Loch and an advertisement in the Edinburgh newspapers invited tenders for designing and constructing the bridge. From seven submissions, the bridge committee considered two, from David Henderson and William Mylne. Both men gave a range of costs, depending on options chosen. Henderson's was deemed to be the better design and entitled him to a 30-guinea gold medal, but when he was asked to provide security for the construction he could only offer £3,000. The tender therefore went to Mylne at a price of £10,140.

George Drummond laid the foundation stone with great ceremony and the work began. An Act of Parliament was obtained, extending the city's royalty to the new streets, the Physic Garden, which supplied the medical school with herbs, had to be moved from beneath the intended path of the bridge, and the council began work on the New Town. Sewers were to be constructed, rather than inhabitants throw their waste into the streets, as they had done for centuries in the Old Town. The council also agreed to a proposal from the 'feuers' who had bought plots around St Andrew Square that the garden in the centre be 'beautified' to speed up the sale of the remaining lots. Drummond died in 1766, knowing that the realisation of his vision had been started, but without seeing the bridge or even a single house completed. He was 78.

Disaster struck the bridge on 3 August 1769, three months before the scheduled completion date. The side walls, where it met the road from the Old Town, collapsed, spilling hundreds of tons of rubble. The emergency meeting of the bridge commissioners the following morning did not record the fact that five men were killed in the accident; the council's only concern was who would pay for the additional work.[24] They appointed an expert committee, which decided that Mylne had underestimated the incline needed for the bridge to meet the roadway coming down from the High Street. To make up the difference he piled rubble onto the bridge, which could not take the extra weight.

A dispute started over who was to carry out the remedial work and how it was to be paid for. The council insisted it was Mylne's responsibility to complete the bridge within the contract price. He, sickened by the incident, wanted to hand the project back to the council and asked them to pay him the difference in the money he had received and the costs he had incurred. The feuers, who had paid for their lots and started to build their houses, banded themselves into a lobby group and put pressure on the council to get the work done so that they could get access to their property. The dispute went to law, but eventually the city paid the extra £2,000 needed to complete and strengthen the bridge. Mylne, still protesting that he was owned money, fell into debt and left Edinburgh in 1773. He spent some time in a log cabin in the backlands of Georgia, where he grew corn and melons and kept chickens, but eventually he recovered and returned to Edinburgh in 1775.[25]

With the bridge completed in 1772, development of the New Town proceeded rapidly with the city financing the new roads, sewers and water supply from the sale of lots, feu duties and local taxes. The legal extension of the royalty enabled it to levy rates on the new houses and businesses. But in his determination to expand Edinburgh to the north, Drummond had missed a trick. In 1761 the council had been offered land to the south, across the Cowgate ravine. The asking price was £1,200, but the council declined to buy. It was purchased instead by the builder and property developer James Brown, who had earlier built Brown's Square. Belatedly, the council tried to buy him out for £2,000, but he demanded £20,000 and when his price was refused he 'feued' the land for a square of terraced houses around a large garden. He called it George's Square, after his brother rather than the young King George III, who had newly ascended to the throne. Brown had three marketing advantages: the square offered large houses in open airy surroundings, it was outside the city's royalty and so was free from local taxes and it was not dependent on the completion of North Bridge, which was at that time still mired in legal dispute.[26] Plots around the square went quickly to the 'great and good' of the city, Brown recovered his purchase price and was said by a later writer to be collecting a 100 per cent annual return from the feu duties.[27]

9

Glasgow rivalry and the unfortunate Mr Trotter

EDINBURGH WAS NOT the only growing Scottish city. Glasgow, although still smaller than the capital, was expanding in power and influence largely because of the tobacco trade with British colonies in America and the West Indies, where it established a dominant position over its rivals, London, Liverpool, Whitehaven and Bristol.[1] The 'Virginia Dons', as the richest of the merchants were known, made their mark, spreading the city's development westwards with large new houses, public buildings and streets – Virginia Street, Jamaica Street, and those named after individual traders: Glassford Street, Ingram Street and Buchanan Street. Tobacco was imported from the slave plantations of America and the Caribbean and most of it re-exported to Europe. It was a trade dependent on strong personal relationships and was hungry for capital.[2] Before 1707 Scotland had been excluded from the slave trade by the monopoly of the Royal African Company and the Navigation Acts, but the Union gave Scottish merchants access to the English colonies, which they exploited to great effect, trading tobacco, sugar and later cotton.

After unsuccessful attempts to establish branches in Glasgow, the two Edinburgh banks had largely ignored it. They did lend to merchants in the city and to other towns in the west of Scotland, but they let the business come to them, rather than doing anything to encourage it, and they did not finance trade. Their objection to the tobacco business was not on moral grounds. As far back as 1695 George Watson, Bank of Scotland's first accountant and James Foulis, the London manager, had part-financed a slave ship – although the deal with a London company was done on a personal basis rather than through the bank and was illegal, so had to be kept secret.[3] Much later Sir Lawrence Dundas, Royal Bank governor, and directors Charles Selkrig and Sir John Gladstone (father of the prime minister), had all owned slave estates (and received compensation when slavery was abolished in Britain).[4] The banks' objection was on commercial, rather than moral, grounds: although the potential profits could be substantial, sending wooden sailing ships across the Atlantic was still a risky business and it could be many months, or even years, before the loans were repaid.

The 'cash credit' – a current account with an agreed overdraft limit – was the foundation of Edinburgh banking business. Bank of Scotland still would not discount bills of exchange and when it or Royal Bank made larger advances they had to be backed by heritable property, or guaranteed by known and reputable 'cautioners' who would stand security for the loan. Some of the tobacco traders had grown wealthy enough to acquire estates, but others needed short-term borrowing to finance considerable sums in port and excise duties as well as sometimes supplying trade credit to dealers and maintaining warehouses in the colonies. Their working capital was provided either by retained profits or by an established network of individuals: the historian Tom Devine has listed Scottish landowners, trustees, tradesmen, physicians, military officers, spinsters, widows and university professors, among others.[5] An examination of the lists of creditors of some of the leading firms by Devine shows the absence of either the Old Bank or the Royal. As in Edinburgh, some merchants developed sidelines in banking, discounting bills, lending, insuring ships and accepting 'sugarhouse' notes – bills issued by some of the sugar businesses in the city.[6]

Rather than the banks financing the tobacco trade, the profits from tobacco financed new banks. In July 1749 five Glasgow merchants – John Graham, Andrew Buchanan, Allan Dreghorn and Robert and Colin Dunlop (later joined by Alexander Houston) – applied to Bank of Scotland for a cash account with a credit limit of £10,000. The bank directors initially viewed this as a desirable transaction; the men were 'persons of considerable estate and undoubted credit, not only able, but [they] have promised to befriend the company, promoting the circulation of banknotes in Glasgow'.[7] The Old Bank had good relationships with a number of private banking companies in Edinburgh – mostly small partnerships which discounted merchants' trade bills and did a limited amount of lending, but were not considered as serious rivals and did not issue their own banknotes. The Glasgow venture – which became known as the Ship Bank because it used a picture of a vessel in full sail on its notes – was initially viewed the same way and would be of considerable value if it spread the use of Bank of Scotland notes in the west.

The Royal Bank directors were less sanguine about the emergence of potential rivals. Their directors received intelligence from Glasgow that a company 'for erecting a bank' had employed an engraver to produce note-printing plates and was buying paper. They were also concerned about a group of Aberdeen merchants who appeared to be starting a bank. They considered trying to obtain a legal ruling preventing private companies, not authorised by Act of Parliament (as Bank of Scotland and Royal Bank were), from conducting banking business. They wrote to the directors of the Old Bank suggesting a joint approach, but the reply was not encouraging: the Old Bank did not consider it to be 'an affair of such consequence' as to justify the expense of a legal opinion.[8]

So in the following year when another group of Glasgow merchants – Andrew Cochrane, John Murdoch and Robert Christie on behalf of 31 partners – applied for an account, the Royal Bank directors agreed not only to provide them with £6,000 credit, but to train their accountant. They knew that the new operation – to be known as the Arms Bank because it used the Glasgow coat of arms on its notes – would issue its own notes and agreed to accept them, provided it promoted Royal Bank notes in Glasgow. It also offered an element of protection, saying it would provide cash in the event of a run on the new bank, but it also wanted the Arms Bank to withdraw cash from Bank of Scotland, whenever possible.[9]

A year later the mood had changed. The two new Glasgow banks had withdrawn their agents in Edinburgh, who were responsible for the mutual note exchange, and the Royal Bank directors took this badly. They feared competition for customers and they worried that the new entrants would destroy the balance between having enough notes in circulation to facilitate economic expansion, and allowing debt to grow to dangerous levels. The note exchange was the mechanism by which the two Edinburgh public banks monitored and maintained this balance: 'The number of private banks set up in different corners of the country, without the sanction of public authority or depositing a fund or stock of cash, appear to be taking an unreasonable credit and may be attended with great inconveniences to the country and greatly affect paper credit in general.'[10]

Lord Milton had been elected deputy governor of Royal Bank and, acting as agent for the Duke of Argyll, had bought shares in Bank of Scotland – the institution the duke (then as Lord Ilay) had tried to drive out of business 25 years previously. Now he brokered an agreement of 'mutual friendship and harmony' between the two Edinburgh banks. The Old Bank declared: 'Taking into consideration the circumstances of the country with regard to the great circulation of private credit occasioned by private persons erecting themselves into banking companies without any public authority ... measures must be speedily taken for preventing the Dangerous Consequences that might arise, not only in this company in particular, but to the credit of the nation.'[11]

A joint committee of the two banks was set up and a secret pact agreed and detailed in the minute books of both. It was dressed up as a measure taken for the good of the country and there was some reason for their concern. As always, gold and silver coin was scarce and the two banks had to buy more in London periodically, transporting it north under armed guard or, for very large quantities, in a chartered warship. This added to the cost of capital. They feared that an uncontrolled expansion of the note issue by new banks would make this situation worse.

But the state of the nation's finances was not their only concern: what they established was an anti-competitive cartel.[12] Gone was the rivalry between the two institutions. Now they pledged in writing to come to each other's aid in the event of a run on either one and to provide up to £10,000 in 'specie' (cash) if needed. They would accept each other's banknotes and set up regular note exchanges – effectively establishing a clearing house. To end the competition from Glasgow and Aberdeen they would close the accounts of those banks, withdraw credit from them and any merchants in Glasgow or Paisley doing business with them, and make private bankers and merchants in Edinburgh sign a pledge not to do business with the Glasgow or Aberdeen banks. Significantly, the British Linen Company, controlled by Lord Milton, was exempted from any sanctions.[13]

Strong action followed swiftly. Bank of Scotland withdrew credit from 18 Glasgow merchants and 2 in Paisley, cut the Ship Bank's overdraft limit (and later closed the account). Royal Bank stopped 22 Glasgow accounts and recalled its loan to the Arms Bank.[14] They also used their political influence to ensure that Glasgow notes would not be accepted in payment of Customs or Excise dues. But not everything went the Edinburgh banks' way. They went to law asking for a prohibition on private banks, but were turned down by the court of session, and, although most merchants agreed to sign the pledge demanded, some prominent private bankers and traders refused. These included powerful men like William Alexander, who had a thriving tobacco import–export business and was a former lord provost of Edinburgh, and Adam Fairholme, a private banker who became the city's treasurer. The banks first watered down their demand, saying that it would be sufficient to have the pledge read to customers, but even this was resisted by some businessmen who preferred to have their accounts closed than cut off their links with Glasgow.

The tiny Aberdeen bank had its account at Bank of Scotland closed and was presented with £1,400 of its own notes for immediate redemption in cash. It folded under the pressure and its partners voluntarily ceased business in 1753.[15] The Glasgow banks approached Lord Milton with a compromise, offering to limit the scale of their activities and their geographic area, but the Edinburgh banks demanded total capitulation. After several meetings and long negotiations Milton had to concede that no common ground was possible.[16] The Ship and the Arms Banks intended to continue and they would not confine themselves to the tobacco trade, but would lend on the security of land too – the core business of the established Edinburgh banks. They were not authorised by law, but were partnerships backed by some of the best-known and wealthiest men in Glasgow and they did not have limited liability. This was seen as a sign of their strength and reliability.

The Edinburgh banks had failed with threats, so they tried more direct means. In 1757 directors of Bank of Scotland were approached by Archibald Trotter with a proposition that was to lead them into frustration and farce. Trotter had been a banker. In 1744 he had joined John Coutts, his cousin by marriage, in a partnership which started as a corn dealership but soon specialised in discounting bills of exchange (trade finance), particularly for imports and exports through the smaller Scottish ports of Perth, Dundee, Montrose and Aberdeen. In 1750 Coutts, by now a successful banker, who had served as lord provost of Edinburgh, died while on a Grand Tour in Italy. Trotter continued in partnership with Coutts's sons, but it did not go well. Sir William Forbes, who later joined the firm, remembered:

> After a few years the young gentlemen and he not agreeing together, Mr Trotter resigned his share in the company. He, I have understood, differed widely in his character from Provost Coutts, not possessing that liberality of thinking and acting in business for which the latter was so greatly distinguished. The young gentlemen seem to have considered him more in the light of a governor than a

partner and, as neither his person nor manners were at all calculated to command their respect, his young friends were constantly teasing him with little boyish, roguish tricks. One that I remember hearing of when I entered the office, consisted in their putting a live mouse under the cover of his inkstand and watching with glee for the start he was to give when on his lifting the lid the animal jumped out, to the no small amusement as might be expected, of the whole counting house.[17]

Now, after trying and failing to establish himself as an accountant, the humourless Trotter proposed to the Edinburgh public banks that he set himself up in Glasgow, posing as an honest dealer in bills of exchange. His real purpose was to promote Bank of Scotland and Royal Bank by using their notes to buy up notes of the Glasgow banks. He was then to present these notes to the Ship and Arms Banks and demand payment in cash, hoping to drive them into default. His proposal was referred to the joint committee of the two Edinburgh banks, which gave him a five-year contract, paid him £150 a year each and advanced him £5,000 at 4 per cent as working capital for his nefarious activities.[18] He was to be paid a bonus if he could get the Glasgow banks to cease their note issue.[19]

The two Glasgow banks saw through Trotter immediately. The Ship Bank, whom Trotter later described as gentlemen of property who treated him civilly, met his demands for cash, which they raised from their merchant customers and by buying gold and silver in Edinburgh at a premium. The founding partners had deep pockets and meant to outlast him. The Arms Bank, whom Trotter distained as 'traders', decided to have fun at his expense. They limited the hours when they were prepared to redeem notes and paid him only in sixpences. There were 40 sixpences to the £ and Trotter was presenting £100 or more a time, giving ample scope for error and delay. The bank teller would laboriously count out the tiny silver coins, occasionally losing count and having to begin again, or dropping one on the ground, providing another excuse for restarting the process anew, or finding one which might have been tampered with and having to go off to get a second opinion as to whether it was valid or not. If they ran out of time, the process had to be restarted the following day.

Trotter reported regularly in letters to George Innes, the Royal Bank cashier. He began optimistically: 'The directors will judge well in continuing to send further supply as soon as possible as these new sums will last but a few days as the New [Arms] Bank here is again run short of both the Edinburgh notes and gold at last . . . and will pay me nothing but sixpences.'[20]

But frustration soon set in:

> I observe what you say about bad specie [counterfeit coin], but that is not in my power to help. You cannot imagine the trouble I have in collecting as I do as much for you as I could for myself. The directors will surely think it reasonable to take it as I get it . . .[21]
>
> The New [Arms] Bank is so intolerably troublesome that I believe people in time will be glad to take it knowingly short. I have already been obliged to desire my clerk not to stand with them for a sixpence or a shilling* upon £100 for otherwise he would be able to get nothing. This whole day has been spent for £110 as they will pay nothing after their pretended bank hours, which is two hours in the day, less than those in Edinburgh or I believe any place in the world, which is a gross imposition upon the public as they can certainly have not title to any such privileges more than any shopkeeper in town. But without the shelter of this refuge, the demands on them would press them sore . . .[22]

In an attempt to speed up his campaign Trotter took a legal action against the partners in the Arms Bank, seeking immediate redemption of the £3,447 bank's notes that he held, plus interest and £600 in damages. He also asked the court to rule that the bank had no right to limit its hours of business and should be ready to cash his notes at any time from 7 a.m. to 10 p.m. The case dragged on for three years. Two of the judges, who were also directors of Royal Bank, had to recuse themselves, and two of the others, including the lord president, took the opportunity to express their dislike of paper credit and banks in general. In the end it was settled out of court by the Arms Bank partners paying Trotter £600, which was roughly equal to his legal fees.[23]

The Ship and the Arms Banks remained in business, to be joined in 1761 by a third Glasgow bank, the Thistle, again backed by wealthy merchants. Trotter turned his attention to the new rival, whose partners complained to the board of Bank of Scotland in a letter 'wrote in most haughty minacing [sic] strain'.[24] It deserved, the directors decided, 'a

---

* One shilling = two sixpences.

reply in very few words'. A second letter, demanding explanation of the bank's response, written 'in most imperious threatening stile [sic]' got no reply at all.[25] Two years later the board was informed by William Alexander, a private banker and merchant, of a rumour that the Thistle was planning to turn the tables on the Edinburgh banks by making 'considerable demands' on one or both of them. The scare was sufficiently credible for the Old Bank directors to meet in emergency session at 8 p.m. In concert with Royal Bank, they invoked an 'option clause', allowing them to defer payment of notes for six months.[26] There is no evidence that the feared run came, but the following month, perhaps tongue in cheek, the partners in the Thistle Bank offered to lend Bank of Scotland £5,000 in gold, to be repaid when convenient. They were thanked for their civility, but the offer was declined.[27]

Eventually, the directors of both Edinburgh banks decided that little was being achieved, withdrew Trotter's credit and closed his account. He wrote to Innes beginning with reasoned counter arguments in his customary clear handwriting. He claimed to have exchanged notes worth more than a hundred thousand pounds a year and to have caused the Glasgow banks extra cost and stopped them exporting 'specie' [cash]. 'And all for the cost of my trifling salary, which God knows is dear bought of . . . I shall only add that I have the vanity to think that had it not been for my establishment here, which these companies here are so anxious to have an end to so as they may be at liberty to act without check, observation or control, that their notes by this time would have had a much more extensive circulation.'[28]

But as the letter went on to a total of eight pages, the quality of the argument and the handwriting deteriorated into a rant, with many passages underlined. The Royal and Old Bank directors were unmoved. He continued to live in Glasgow for a few more years, but was finally sacked.[29]

The Third Scottish Bank War, as it became known, had important after effects. The option clause had been first adopted by Bank of Scotland when it was under assault by Royal Bank, and subsequently used by Royal Bank and British Linen when it began issuing notes.[30] It was a modification of the 'promise to pay', by delaying redemption in cash for six months, with interest accruing to the bearer of the note in that period. The device helped the banks to regulate the demands for gold and silver coin, which had again become scarce during the Seven Years' War (1756–63). The Glasgow banks had also claimed the right to invoke the option, but there is no evidence they actually delayed payment on their notes. However, the existence of the clause undermined confidence in paper currency and in many parts of Scotland there were meetings protesting against the option.[31]

The affair had also demonstrated the inability of the Edinburgh banking duopoly to suppress competition and new banks began to spring up around Scotland – in Dundee, Perth, and a revival of banking in Aberdeen, Dumfries and Ayr. These banks began to issue their own notes and the shortage of coin also persuaded other business to do likewise. Notes were appearing for as little as five shillings* and Bank of Scotland itself introduced a ten-shilling note.[32] The two Edinburgh banks – again acting in concert – decided on a political strategy by promoting a new Act of Parliament 'to remedy the growing evil of so many banking companies'.[33]

Four delegates – two from each bank – were given a list of 12 demands and, well supplied with expenses, were sent to Westminster to lobby ministers and MPs. They were to press for a legal ban on any bank not authorised by law. Bank of Scotland and Royal Bank had special Acts of Parliament, but British Linen, which was becoming an irritating rival, was a difficult case, having been established by law, albeit not as a bank. It was still under the protection of Lord Milton, Royal Bank deputy governor, so the delegates were told not to mention it. To have their duopoly restored, the two banks offered to give up the option clause, restrict their note circulation by not issuing any under £10 in value and make a donation to the fund for promoting fishing and manufacturing.[34]

Not everyone saw the growth in banks the same way. Among the Scottish MPs there was practically no one who was not a shareholder in, or connected to, one or other of the banks and there was strong opposition from Glasgow and those with 'Enlightenment views' who believed banking should be free of vested interest or government sanction. Archibald Ingram, tobacco baron, lord provost of Glasgow and partner in the Arms Bank, wrote a detailed rebuttal of the Edinburgh banks' claims and sent it to the lord privy seal, who was dealing with the matter on behalf of the privy council.[35] Adam Smith was in London and had a meeting with the minister. His views, later expanded in *The Wealth of Nations*, had already been explained in his lectures at Glasgow University. He was against any government granted monopoly in banking and saw

* There were 20 shillings to the £.

the spread of banks as diversifying risk. He was also in favour of an expansion of the note issue, although he was against the option clause and believed notes should always be convertible into gold or silver. He was not completely in favour of a free market, advocating the retention of the 'usury law', which set a maximum interest rate.

David Hume took a very different view, believing that banknotes inhibited economic growth. In his *Essay on the Balance of Trade* in 1752 he argued: 'I scarcely know any method of sinking money below its level, but those of institutions of banks, funds and paper credit which we are in this kingdom so much infatuated. These render paper equivalent to money, circulate it throughout the whole state, make it supply the place of gold and silver, raise proportionately the price of labour and commodities and by that means either banish a great part of those precious metals or prevent their further increase.'[36]

The Act, when it reached the statute book, was much more a reflection of Smith's views than those of Hume. It was also a blow to the Edinburgh banks; it did not stop or even limit the spread of private banks, but it did outlaw the option clause and banned the circulation of notes valued at less than £1. Far from cementing their duopoly, the privy council declared 'that the trade of banking is a matter not of Publick favour, but of Right to every subject in common' and that public opinion would not accept an exclusive privilege for Bank of Scotland and Royal Bank. The stage was set for the next and very much larger challenge to the Edinburgh financial establishment.

10

Collapse of the Ayr bank

TOWARDS THE END of the Seven Years' War and the Treaty of Paris, which ended it in 1763, enormous fortunes could be made by young men with credit and daring by speculating on the rise and fall of government securities or shares in prominent businesses like the East India Company. Among the Scots attracted to London to try their luck in Exchange Alley* were Adam Fairholme and Alexander Fordyce.

Of the two, Fairholme had the better pedigree. He had joined his uncle in a corn dealing business, which branched out into banking and later, with his brother Thomas, he ran a successful private bank in Edinburgh. One of his rivals described the Fairholme bank as 'long eminent, and in the enjoyment of unsullied credit'[1] and the few pages from the accounts book which survive show a conservative business lending modest sums against bonds to landowners, merchants, lawyers and army officers.[2] Adam Fairholme was a respected member of the community – he had served as treasurer of Edinburgh city council, bought the first and the largest house in Provost Drummond's new Exchange building in the High Street and, together with his brother, was a director of Bank of Scotland.

Fordyce had a lowlier start in life. Although son of a provost of Aberdeen, he had begun his career as an apprentice stocking manufacturer, but quickly tired of the trade. Moving to London in search of excitement he began as an 'outdoor clerk', obtaining acceptances and payments on bills of exchange, but by 1759 had become junior partner in a bank and later managing partner in his own concern, Neale, James, Fordyce & Down.[3]

Fairholme's move to London proved his undoing. Speculating in 1761

---

* Exchange Alley actually burnt down in 1748, but the name persisted until the opening of the stock exchange in Sweetings Alley in 1773.

that government funds would rise in price if a peace treaty was agreed, he bought a large position on credit and made a paper fortune of £70,000. Had he stopped there and realised his winnings all might have been well for his bank, but he did not. Rival banker Sir William Forbes remembered: 'By his continuing his operations, they lost their imaginary profits; and being tempted like losing gamesters to enter still more deeply into the Alley, the whole affair ended most unhappily. Adam Fairholme remained in London, carrying on this scheme of stock-jobbing, probably with various success, till he was able to go on no longer, and in the month of March 1764, he declared himself bankrupt and left the kingdom. The necessary effect of this was the bankruptcy of their house at Edinburgh, which stopped payment the same month.'[4]

Among the depositors who lost their money in the failure of A. & T. Fairholme were the architects and developers Robert and John Adam. Fairholme could not face his creditors and tried to flee to France, with tragic consequences. On the ship he saw a Bow Street Runner and, believing he was about to be arrested and dragged back in shame, jumped overboard and was drowned. In fact the policeman was after a different fugitive.[5]

Fordyce was more fortunate. Apart from his activity in his bank, he traded heavily on his own account, successfully anticipating the peace treaty and movements in East India Company stock. He used his profits to improve his social standing, buying an estate in Scotland and a large house at Roehampton, Surrey, where he entertained in great magnificence. He aspired to be an MP and spent nearly £14,000 at Colchester in 1768 in an unsuccessful effort to be elected. In 1770 he married Lady Margaret Lindsay, second daughter of the Earl of Balcarres, and was twice elected rector of Marischal College, Aberdeen.[6]

Speculative dealing and financial engineering was not confined to Exchange Alley. The war had widened the discount on Scottish bills in London. A smart dealer with a little capital could employ agents (they were known as 'English Riders' but may not all have been English) and exploit the differential, buying bills at a discount in London and presenting them in Edinburgh for payment in full in gold and silver for an immediate profit.[7] That cash could then be used in London to buy more bills and the process could begin again. Each time the trades would get larger.

The demands of the war and the necessity to import food during years of poor harvests meant that coin was in short supply in Scotland in any case, but the activities of the 'Specie Exporters' made it worse. The directors of Bank of Scotland and Royal Bank worried about the drain on their reserves and they spent considerable sums bringing cash to Scotland from London.[8] Bank of Scotland commissioned private bankers Andrew St Clair and William Alexander to obtain gold and silver, while Royal Bank spent £22,000 between 1764 and 1769 bringing gold and silver from London – equal to five years' profits on £80,000 of lending.[9]

To shore up their balance sheets, the two banks jointly tried unsuccessfully to raise a loan of £200,000 from the Bank of England, or to borrow in Holland,[10] and when that failed they invoked the option clause on their notes, suspending redemption for six months.[11] They called in debts and severely cut back their lending, limiting credit on cash accounts to £2,000 – later reduced to £1,000. They also made an agreement that neither bank would grant a new credit without first informing the other. With the two biggest lenders in the country virtually closing down new lending, the effect on trade and investment was dramatic. Merchants and developers, impatient for credit and being refused by the banks, turned to bill discounting, sometimes circulating 'fictitious bills' between London and Edinburgh for months or even years at a time to avoid having to repay the loan in cash. The cost in interest and commissions added each time a bill shuttled back and forth was high.

Adam Smith drew a distinction between ordinary trade bills, which could be used to obtain credit in advance of an expected receipt of money in the near future, and 'fictitious bills', where no payment was expected and were invented purely for the purposes of getting a loan. He estimated the cost of getting credit this way at 8 per cent a year or more at a time when most mercantile projects would only expect to earn profits of 6–10 per cent: 'Many vast and extensive projects, however, were undertaken, and for several years carried on without any other fund to support them besides what was raised at this enormous expense. The projectors, no doubt, had in their golden dreams the most distinct vision of this great profit. Upon their awaking, however, either at the end of their projects, or when they were no longer able to carry them on, they very seldom, I believe, had the good fortune to find it.'[12]

Some people were making big money in this frenzied environment, but it was not the two public banks. With a few exceptions, private bankers in Edinburgh were discounting bills far beyond the level justified by their capital or the needs of the economy and funding themselves by borrowing from London finance houses. In 1769 Bank of Scotland was dragged into this market. In a shareholders' coup the cautious Earl of Elgin was removed from the court of directors and the new board began a policy friendly to the more aggressive private bankers. The Old Bank had been very timidly discounting bills for several years, but now the pace was stepped up with the board declaring 'it being the intention of the directors to encourage hereafter the discounting of bills'.[13]

This played into the hands of the private bankers, who could arrange the bill, lend the cash, earn commission and recover their loan by discounting the bill with Bank of Scotland, which had then to wait for payment from the acceptor.[14] The overdraft limit on cash accounts to traditional customers was again reduced, to £500, but the rule was relaxed for private bankers. At the general meeting of proprietors the following year 13 directors were removed from office and replaced by private bankers and men sympathetic to them. Policies designed to protect the bank's capital were overturned. The bank now had less of a cushion against possible losses; the cautious approach of Bank of Scotland since its first days was giving way to a demand for higher returns, but at the cost of higher risk.

In 1769 a formidable new competitor arrived on the scene. Douglas Heron & Co. was started by two substantial landowners and backed by some of the wealthiest and most influential property owners in Scotland, including the 71-year-old Duke of Queensberry, who became chairman, and the youthful Duke of Buccleuch, not long back from his Grand Tour in the company of his tutor, Adam Smith.[15] More than 200 subscribers included members of the aristocracy, lairds, merchants and private bankers involved in the discount trade. Henry Dundas, a young advocate with political ambitions, invested a large part of his 19-year-old wife's £10,000 dowry.

The new bank appeared to have the highest ideals, declaring it would support trade, manufacturing and agriculture, and adopting the motto '*Pro Bono Publico*', meaning 'For the Public Good'. It intended to fill the gap left by the Edinburgh banks for finance for industrial investment and agricultural improvement and it had the firepower to do so: its nominal share capital was £150,000, of which £96,000 was immediately called up. Bank of Scotland and Royal Bank were under-capitalised by comparison, their capital and reserves after decades in business totalled £82,000 and £77,000 respectively.[16] Crucially, the new bank did not have limited liability, which would have necessitated an Act of Parliament. It was a partnership and therefore the assets of all its subscribers were at risk.

Since it was backed by some of the wealthiest men in Scotland, this was regarded as a sign of its strength and the bank had no difficulty getting credit in London.

Headquarters were opened in Ayr – so it became known as the Ayr Bank – but within days branches had been opened in Edinburgh and Dumfries, and later agencies were added in other parts of the country. Lending began immediately – including to the bank's own shareholding partners, some of whom drew down their loans before they had paid their share subscriptions.[17] The bank issued its own notes and its aggressive lending policy meant that within a short period Ayr Bank notes made up two-thirds of the currency of Scotland. Its advances soon exceeded the whole of its capital and deposits and its notes were quickly finding their way back to the bank for redemption in cash. To fund its ballooning lending it resorted to the London money market. Sir William Forbes, a rival banker, decried the debt-financed purchase of West Indies estates by some of his countrymen and the fashion for larger, more luxurious New Town houses:

> Such causes combined had induced those gentlemen to have recourse to the ruinous mode of raising money by a chain of bills on London; and when the established banks declined to continue a system of which they began to be suspicious, the bank of Douglas Heron, & Co., commonly known as the Ayr Bank, was erected. But, instead of proving a cure to the evil, they, by their improvident and injudicious management, found themselves compelled to plunge into this kind of circulation still deeper than the others, although with a more solid foundation. The fictitious paper in the circle between Edinburgh and London had thus arisen to an astonishing height.[18]

The trigger for the inevitable crash came in 1772, not in Edinburgh or Ayr, but in London where Alexander Fordyce, the former apprentice hosier from Aberdeen, had followed the bad example of his countryman Adam Fairholme eight years previously by failing to quit while he was ahead. When his personal trades turned against him, he tried to cover his debts – which had reached an astonishing £243,000 – by raiding the deposits of his bank's customers, probably under the gambler's illusion that he could trade his way out and replace the money before it was missed. However, his partners in Neale, James, Fordyce & Down were too astute and blocked payment. The Bank of England meanwhile had become alarmed at the depletion of its own reserves and stopped discounting Scottish and other dubious bills. Fordyce had nowhere else to turn; he could not cover his positions. Like Fairholme, he fled for the Continent, but survived the journey.* His bank was declared bust the following week. The collapse set off a chain of bankruptcies across London and the contagion spread to America, the West Indies and European cities as far apart as St Petersburg and Amsterdam.[19]

Among those who lost money were the unfortunate Adam brothers, who had previously suffered in the Fairholme collapse. They were involved in the hugely ambitious Adelphi project, building a grand new district of warehousing and houses along the Thames. It was already financially stretched at the time of the crisis. They were brought to the edge of ruin, but survived by selling their assets in a public lottery.[20]

A horseman supposedly brought news of the disaster to Edinburgh in 43 hours – half the time it took for the post from London to arrive – and set off a panic as depositors mobbed the offices of private banks demanding their money. Most could not pay and put up their shutters. In the days that followed there was a chain of bankruptcies, including Andrew St Clair and William Alexander, two of the banks which had been supplying Bank of Scotland with gold. Only those banks which had not indulged in the circulation of fictitious bills were spared. David Hume described the scene in a letter to Adam Smith: 'We are here in a very melancholy situation: continual bankruptcies, universal Loss of credit, and endless suspicions. There are but two standing houses in this place, Mansfield's and the Couttses[†] . . . The case is little better in London. It is thought, that Sir George Colebrooke [chairman of the East India Company] must soon stop; and even the Bank of England is not entirely free from suspicion . . . The Carron Company is reeling, which is one of the greatest calamities of the whole; as they gave employment to near 10,000 people.'[21]

Glasgow was less affected, with only one company closing, but the biggest casualty was the Ayr Bank, which was heavily dependent for continuing support from the London market. There was an immediate run – 'The labouring classes holding £1 notes crowded to the company's

---

* He stayed away for three months, then came home to face his creditors, avoided the debtors' prison and lived a reasonably comfortable life until 1789.
† Mansfield, Ramsay & Co., and John Coutts & Co.

offices demanding payment in specie [cash].'[22] But the bank's managers, dazed by what was happening around them, seemed for a time not to understand the hopelessness of its position, offering £100 reward for the conviction of anyone passing on false rumours. Not for the last time, the 'false' rumours about the weakness of a major bank turned out to be true. With the London market closed to it, the Ayr Bank had a desperate need for liquidity. Some of its leading partners, including the two dukes, went in person to beg the Bank of England for a loan of £300,000, but the terms for security and interest were considered too harsh. They then turned to Bank of Scotland and Royal Bank.

The Edinburgh banks had been unsure how to treat the new competitor. It was 18 months after the Ayr Bank began trading before they would accept its notes and allow it into the regular note exchange.[23] In the six months before the crisis broke, they seem to have decided that the newcomer was a permanent part of the new financial system and were prepared to support it. Royal Bank lent the Ayr Bank £10,000[24] and Bank of Scotland advanced £22,000 in gold and bills against the personal bond of the bank's cashier.[25] But two months later attitudes had changed. After failing to get money from the Bank of England, the Ayr Bank partners made an approach to the two Edinburgh public banks asking for an immediate £20,000 from each (later increased to £50,000 from each).[26] The request was rejected. There is no mention of it in the minute book of Bank of Scotland, so the proposal cannot even have got as far as the directors. The Ayr Bank had no choice but to suspend payment of its notes.

The Ayr Bank limped on for another year before an orderly liquidation began and the painful process of an inquiry to find out what went wrong. Although hardly impartial and independent, the inquiry report makes salutary reading even today. A management which had no experience of banking was incompetent, the directors were remote, the partners, who were the owners of the bank, were kept in the dark and the three branch offices acted independently, so that no one had a complete picture of the state of affairs.[27]

The total liabilities of the bank were £1.1 million, but its assets amounted to barely a third of this. The most difficult problem was the £200,000 in issued notes – more than the total of Bank of Scotland and Royal Bank notes combined – which were widely dispersed throughout the economy. If they became worthless the country would have been brought to its knees. Public announcements by the Duke of Argyll, the Faculty of Advocates and several Scottish burghs that they would continue to accept them in payment helped restore confidence.[28] The Ayr Bank partners, who owned between them millions of pounds worth of land, accepted their liability for its debts, which encouraged Bank of Scotland and Royal Bank to resume accepting the notes pending the winding up.

Refused credit by the public banks, the Ayr Bank partners raised £450,000 by selling annuities, but at a ruinous cost estimated at 15 per cent a year when interest rates were 4–5 per cent. Bank of Scotland bought £50,000 worth,[29] but the deal was too good to last. The partners later obtained an Act of Parliament, skilfully piloted against opposition by Henry Dundas, enabling them to buy back the annuities and replace them with cheaper stock, secured on rents from their estates. Eventually all the creditors were paid, but not without distress. Not only did the partners lose the £500 they had subscribed for each share, but they had to fund a further £2,200 per share to cover the funding shortfall.[30] The dukes, earls, large landowners and wealthy merchants were able to absorb their losses, but of the 226 partners in the bank, half were ruined. Property prices fell as estates had to be sold in a hurry to meet the obligations. As late as 1793 – 21 years later – Ayr Bank debts were being publicly auctioned in the Old Exchange Coffee House in Edinburgh and litigation lasted well into the following century.[31]

The effect of the collapse on the economy was felt first in capital projects. Work ceased on the Monklands and Forth & Clyde canals, two major engineering works, and on public buildings in several royal burghs.[32] There was also a pause in the take up of feus in the Edinburgh New Town. Youngson, in his seminal book *The Making of Classical Edinburgh*, attributes this to the problems of North Bridge,[33] but it may also have been because of lack of cash by the private bankers, lairds, lawyers and merchants who aspired to live in grand Georgian houses. The Carron Ironworks, which Hume had worried about, found itself unable to pay wages and debts, but was saved by Bank of Scotland agreeing to discount its bills and advancing £20,000.[34] Rural industries had already been hit by poor harvests, which had a knock-on effect to tax revenues and the linen industry. High prices and unemployment led to riots in Perth, Fife and Angus, chief centres of linen production, and there was a renewed upsurge in emigration from the Highlands and among lowland weavers and tradesmen.[35]

The fallout in the banking industry was more profound. At the beginning of 1772 there were 31 public, private and provincial banks operating in Scotland; by the end of the year half of these had failed.[36] Bank of Scotland and Royal Bank were shaken by the crisis. Although they held over £100,000 in Ayr Bank notes between them,[37] their survival was never at risk, but they had been tempted a short distance down the same dangerous path. Bill discounting by Bank of Scotland continued for a few years on a more cautious basis, but then tailed off.[38] In 1771 Royal Bank asked three of its directors to make a thorough examination of the state of its finances. Their report made sobering reading. Although the bank had lent £370,000 in the preceding twelve months, it had made no profit on it – in fact after exceptional items it had sustained a small loss of £605.

Worse, over the previous five years its surpluses had barely covered its dividend and expenses, its retained profits (reserves) had not increased at all. The directors identified two major defects in its management. Firstly, its readiness to grant cash accounts, where the holders could go into overdraft up to an agreed limit, meant that it had no real control over how much it lent – and these accounts were a third of its total lending. Secondly, it had no proper accounts for the cost of its London operations – discounting bills and securing gold and silver. The board resolved to tighten controls and to boost profitability by selling £122,000 in the stock of the Equivalent Company which it still owned and using the proceeds either to lend at a better rate of return, or reduce its own borrowing.[39] Nevertheless, Royal Bank's shares slumped to a new low.[40]

Both banks realised they were under-capitalised, so their refusal to help rescue the Ayr Bank may not have been a rejection of responsibility for the banking system as a whole (a *quasi* central bank role), but a tacit admission of their own weakness. After the crisis the two Edinburgh banks, led by Bank of Scotland, accepted a multi-bank system and moved to take control of it through the note exchange.[41] In this way the public banks were able to monitor the note issue and discipline any bank that was thought to be issuing more notes than the system would bear.

Bank of Scotland strengthened its balance sheet by calling up the remaining unpaid portion of its £100,000 authorised capital and petitioning parliament for consent to enlarge the capital to £200,000.[42] It also began to relax its credit restrictions. In 1773 there was a counter-revolution on the board. Out went the private bankers and bill discounters and back came the lawyers and politicians. The Earl of Leven, whose great-grandfather had been governor of the bank in the early part of the century, was elected deputy governor, to be replaced two years later by

Henry Dundas, who had recently entered the government as lord advocate, the senior Scottish minister. He was elected governor in 1790 and served until his death in 1811, when he was succeeded by his son.

Royal Bank also increased its capital, using its retained earnings to take it up to £150,000, and later petitioning parliament for a new charter to enable it to double its cushion against losses to £300,000. There had been a change of political leadership at the bank in 1764. Sir Lawrence Dundas, a self-made businessman who was a distant kinsman, but a political opponent of Henry Dundas, had been elected governor. He had previously been a director and shareholder in Bank of Scotland. A new era of political manipulation of the banks was beginning and the stage was set for a trial of strength between two ambitious men called Dundas.

11

Dundas versus Dundas

DESPITE SHARING A surname, Henry and Lawrence Dundas were very different. Henry was the son of Lord Arniston, one of the most important landowners in Midlothian. His father and his grandfather had been lawyers and politicians and he had a swift rise through the Scottish legal establishment, becoming solicitor general at the age of 24. He entered parliament in 1774, in a seat effectively in the gift of his family (although he had to elbow the incumbent out of the way), and a year later he entered Lord North's Tory government as lord advocate, the most senior government minister in Scotland. Henry was born with social position and a political career, and built his power base by uniting the landed interest.

Lawrence Dundas, on the other hand, had had to buy his place in society and politics. From modest middle-class beginnings, he had made himself one of the richest men in Britain. He had followed his success as commissary to Cumberland's army in Scotland and Flanders with huge and profitable contracts to provision the British army and its allies in the Seven Years' War. By the peace in 1763 his fortune was estimated at £600,000–800,000. A self-made man with contempt for inherited privilege, he quickly came up against establishment power when he first tried to enter parliament in 1747. He ignored the disapproval of the Duke of Argyll, who then ruled political Scotland for the Whigs, and got himself elected MP for Linlithgow Burghs after paying what the duke described as 'the greatest sum to purchase an election that was ever known in the country'. Retribution was not long coming. Argyll collected evidence against him and the following year Dundas lost his seat on grounds of corruption and bribery.[1]

He consoled himself with improving his social standing – buying more land in Scotland, England and Ireland, two slave estates in the West Indies and a baronetcy.[2] He sent his son to Eton and joined the London

Society of Dilettanti, a group of the 'great and good' supposedly founded to further the study and appreciation of Greek and Roman art. Horace Walpole, scholar son of the then prime minister, called it 'a club, for which the nominal qualification is having been in Italy, and the real one being drunk: the two chiefs are Lord Middlesex and Sir Francis Dashwood, who were seldom sober the whole time they were in Italy'.[3] This is a little unfair on Dundas, who may have been a drinker and a notorious gambler, but was also a patron of the leading designers and makers of the day, commissioning at one time or another the architect Robert Adam, the landscape gardener Lancelot 'Capability' Brown and the furniture maker Thomas Chippendale. He also collected Dutch and Flemish old master paintings.[4]

The Duke of Argyll died in 1761 and his political fixer in Scotland, Lord Milton, five years later. This was Lawrence Dundas's opportunity to restart his political career. At the general election of 1768 he made doubly sure of his place and was returned to parliament for two seats, Richmond in Yorkshire and Edinburgh. He also bought seats for his son, his brother and several friends. He gave up the English constituency to serve for Edinburgh.[5] He had spent heavily in the city to secure the votes he needed, making donations to the Merchant Company, charities and educational institutions. Since the electorate was only 33 voters,[6] it was not difficult to ensure a majority if you had enough money. His largess was lampooned in a poem addressed to him in *The Weekly Magazine, or Edinburgh Amusement*:

> Hail Generous Man! By Providence assign'd
> To distribute its favours to mankind
> On whom it smil'd that Scotia too might smile
> (Neglected corner of this glorious Isle!)
> Whose Bounty through the land diffusive flies,
> And re-ascends like incense to the skies;
> As genial show'rs to earth in mercy given
> Descend, and rise again in dew to Heav'n,
> Such, in a thousand instances expressed,
> The Lame, the Orphan and the Beggar blesst.[7]

His two sponsors in the city were the lord provost, Gilbert Laurie, a failed solicitor who made his living as an apothecary, and Thomas Simpson, a pewterer, who was a member of the Incorporation of

Hammermen and spoke for the trades vote. Both men had been under the patronage of Lord Milton (who had secured the sinecure of Engraver to the Scottish Mint for Simpson, a paid position even though the Mint had not struck a coin since 1710). But after Milton's death they were looking for a new, well-heeled and well-connected patron. Dundas had money and, even though he was not a minister, he had political influence. He helped them steer the Act through parliament which extended the royalty of Edinburgh to the New Town – an essential measure if the city was to finance its expansion. He also secured a government pension for Simpson in 1777.[8]

But he was not above going against the council to suit himself. In 1767 he managed to obtain the feu of the key site in St Andrew Square, which was marked on James Craig's plan as the location for a landmark church. The line between the two churches on the outer sides of St Andrew Square and Charlotte Square would form the axis of symmetry of his grid. Whether Dundas led the official registering the feu to believe he was going to build a church, or merely resorted to bribery, is not known, but once he secured the land he ignored Craig's intention. He built himself the most impressive house in the New Town – a three-storey classical mansion designed by Sir William Chambers, and the only one set back behind its own garden.* It is said that shortly after the house was finished, Sir Lawrence lost it in a game of cards to General Sir John Scott, and that he had to pay for a new house to be built for Scott nearby so he could retain his family home.[9] There is no documentary source for the story, but Dundas was reputed to be a reckless gambler.

His influence with Edinburgh merchants and the council probably enabled him to be elected governor of Royal Bank in 1764. With Milton gone, one of the bank's first acts was to sever ties with the British Linen Company which, although not yet calling itself a bank, had abandoned linen manufacture for lending. Through a network of branches and agents across the country it was issuing notes and becoming a serious competitor to the two established Edinburgh banks, accounting for a quarter of the total of banknotes in circulation. Bank of Scotland had called on the Royal to stop its support for British Linen,[10] which it did, closing its account and withdrawing credit.[11]

---

* It became the head office of Royal Bank in 1825, but this was long after Dundas's death.

Dundas also put his weight – and that of Royal Bank – behind the construction of the Forth & Clyde canal. This was a gigantic undertaking. With an estimated cost of £150,000 it would be the biggest financial project in Scotland since the Darien disaster, but the engineering challenges were immense. The new waterway was to be 35 miles (56 kilometres) long, connecting the River Forth near the mouth of the river Carron to the Clyde at Bowling, West Dunbartonshire. It had to be cut through 20 different rock formations and a soft bog, which kept swallowing the stones used to make the banking. It needed 16 locks on the eastern section to lift vessels 150 feet (45 metres), and 19 on the western section to take them down again. Reservoirs had to be built to keep them filled. An Act of Parliament was obtained establishing the canal company and subscription books opened in Scotland and London.

At first the fundraising went well. There was great enthusiasm for 'improvement' and economic development and examples of successful canals in England and France to inspire investors. The Duke of Queensberry was appointed chairman and many nobles and large landowners took up shares, including Dundas. He doubtless had the economic advancement of Scotland in mind, but the canal also crossed two of his Stirlingshire estates and would be useful in exporting coal and other produce. By the summer of 1768 £128,000 had been subscribed, to be paid in staged calls as the work progressed. Sir Lawrence cut the first turf and distributed five guineas to the workmen.[12] The difficulties began when the company made the first call for 5 per cent of the money, which was needed to meet the costs of promoting the legislation and acquiring the land. No fewer than 203 – around 20 per cent – of the subscribers did not respond, leaving a big gap in the financing. Despite reminders and threats of legal action some of the shares remained unpaid five years later and had to be re-offered in a rights issue to those shareholders who had stumped up. Getting cash out of the shareholders, whose initial enthusiasm had waned, proved to be a perennial problem for the project, compounded when the collapse of the Ayr Bank impoverished many of the original subscribers.

Royal Bank acted as banker to the canal company and allowed it to overdraw on its cash account at 4 per cent rather than the legal maximum of 5 per cent, provided it used Royal Bank notes for its payments. But the losses soon outstripped the amount the bank was prepared to advance without security and Sir Lawrence stepped in to guarantee the loan. By 1772 the Dundas family were liable for £19,600 owed to the bank.[13]

Construction faced many problems and at one stage the geologist James Hutton had to be recruited to advise and inspect some of the work. Although not an original subscriber, he became a shareholder and a member of the management committee.

The company decided it needed another £70,000 to complete the canal and tried to float a bond yielding 5 per cent and secured on future freight tolls, but in the aftermath of the Ayr Bank fiasco there was no take-up. In 1784 the government, which had resisted calls for state aid up until that point, finally relented and invested £50,000, enabling the canal to be completed 'sea to sea' but also becoming a major shareholder and having a decisive say in the running of the business. The Treasury's demand for regular accounts imposed a new and beneficial rigour to the company's financial management. In 1790 the fisheries sloop *Agnes* left Leith and sailed to Greenock, the first vessel to travel from east to west Scotland using the canal.[14]

In parliament Lawrence Dundas's wealth and his small group of relatives and friends brought influence with the government. In 1769 he bought £100,000 worth of shares in the East India Company in order to help candidates favoured by the government to get elected to the board.[15] He was made a member of the privy council in 1771, but never became a minister and was denied the peerage he craved. Ministers were prepared to recommend it, but the king, George III, would not sanction it. This may have led to his decision to distance himself from the Tory party and draw closer to Lord Rockingham's Whigs.

As soon as he became a minister, Henry Dundas began a campaign against his distant kinsman, trying to undermine Lawrence's support in Edinburgh council and in the merchant community and attacking his reputation by encouraging pamphlets alleging he had gained his wealth through corruption. He also tried to get him unseated, but could not match the financial muscle of Sir Lawrence who was re-elected in 1774 and 1780. The animosity appears to have been personal as well as political, but why Henry was so vindictive is not clear. Having failed to destroy his political powerbase, the new lord advocate turned to Lawrence's position as governor of Royal Bank of Scotland.

In 1776 Henry Dundas was introduced to William Ramsay of Barnton, senior partner of Mansfield Ramsay & Co., one of the leading private banks in Edinburgh. The go-between was Patrick Miller, a long-standing partner in the firm and brother of the lord justice clerk, a senior Scottish judge and an ally of Dundas. The firm had close ties to the two Edinburgh public banks and large shareholdings in both. In particular it had built up its holding in Royal Bank very rapidly over the previous two years and now held around a fifth of the total stock. What the lord advocate proposed was that Ramsay should sell the firm's substantial Royal Bank holding to himself and a group of his trusted supporters – mostly lawyers and judges – who would then have the necessary votes to unseat Sir Lawrence Dundas as chair and install the Duke of Buccleuch in his place. What was offered in exchange for this considerable concession by the firm, we do not know. Ramsay was taken aback and replied that he meant no disrespect, but he thought it improper for people in his profession to meddle in matters of this kind: 'I had never before heard of the proposal and expressed my surprise most thoroughly and told him at once plainly that I could not interfere. Also, that having been on the town council from 1761–71 and held all of the offices except one, I vowed never to return there and never to have anything to do with politics in any shape.'[16]

Miller intervened and eventually changed Ramsay's mind. It was not an easy conversation; Ramsay said that it was the first disagreement they had had in 20 years in partnership. We do not know the arguments Miller used, but it is possible he stressed the importance of keeping on the right side of the rising star of Scottish politics. More specifically he may have held out the prospect of wresting the banking of government excise revenues away from Mansfield Ramsay's great rival, Sir William Forbes & Co. Forbes had two big government contracts – remitting £250,000 a year in excise duties to London and bringing £90,000 the other way to pay government salaries in Scotland. There was a delay of 60 days in paying the excise to London, so the bank could make profitable use of it in the meantime.[17]

Ramsay reluctantly agreed to Dundas's scheme and the share transfers were made. During 1775–6, 40 per cent of the Royal Bank share capital changed hands. Henry Dundas himself bought £600-worth of stock and the Duke of Buccleuch also bought some. Sir Lawrence, ignorant of the conspiracy, helped it along by reducing his own holding from £7,700 to £2,000, selling some to his son and the rest to lawyers, who promptly resold it to associates of Henry Dundas. At a meeting of the proprietors in 1777 Sir Lawrence, realising that Henry Dundas now had a majority of the shares in his control, stood down and a short time later the Duke of Buccleuch took his place.[18]

Although he got on well with the duke, Ramsay regretted his part in the coup. The share price of Royal Bank rose substantially over the following years and he estimated that Mansfield Ramsay & Co. had lost £73,000 by selling the shares when they did. Henry Dundas, by contrast, had made more money than he had lost in the collapse of the Ayr Bank.[19] Relations between the two men never recovered. A decade later the firm tried to reclaim the considerable sum of £13,000 it had lent Henry and his son-in-law Robert Dundas, but when James Mansfield, Ramsay's partner, had tried to get some of it repaid, he had met with abuse from the younger man, who was at that time solicitor general.

But a longer running sore was the failure to win the excise banking business for Royal Bank. The tenacity with which Ramsay attempted to persuade Dundas to intervene with the government to make the switch suggests that he felt he was owed the concession. He employed agents to lobby Dundas in parliament, got the Duke of Buccleuch, Sir Archibald Hope and the lord provost to do the same and even tried to go over Dundas's head by writing directly to the prime minister, William Pitt. Had Dundas promised to get the excise business for Royal Bank in return for the ousting of Sir Lawrence Dundas? There is a hint of expectation in Ramsay's letter to Dundas of June 1789: 'To anyone less acquainted than you are with the situation of the country, with the great and disinterested exertions the bank has made and is still making for the support of the Publick Credit and useful industry, I might fairly urge if a preference is to be given, the Royal Bank is entitled to it . . . If any order to this purpose does not come in the course of two or three weeks I shall just consider it as a refusal direct and I will plainly tell them so, adding at same time I had done my duty by writing to you asking the favour.'[20]

If he had made Ramsay a promise, Dundas conveniently forgot about it. There is a haughty distain to the tone of Dundas's reply: 'It must for many reasons give me pain when I hesitate on any suggestion of yours, especially when it is put on the footing of a favour to yourself . . . I do not find any grounds to satisfy my own mind that the measure you recommend would not be considered as a violent and a partial step taken by government to deprive some individuals of the benefit they possess in consequence of a connection with government which they have done nothing by their own misconduct to forfeit.'[21]

Ramsay did not let it rest there. His next letter was more explicit: 'You cannot have forgot that the favour I requested for the Royal Bank was voluntarily made by you to Messers Mansfield & Co. during the political struggle twixt the Duke of Buccleuch and Sir Lawrence Dundas . . . I must take the liberty to repeat that our friends are dissatisfied with your answer to me and I foresee disagreeable consequences, which a few minutes conversation may prevent.'[22]

The reply from Dundas was not the one Ramsay had wanted, but promised a meeting when he was next in Scotland. Meanwhile Sir William Forbes, Ramsay's great rival, whose bank had handled the excise revenues for 40 years, wrote to Dundas releasing him from any obligation: 'We should feel a still greater degree of concern if your influence should in any shape suffer from your friendship to us.'[23]

Royal Bank did get some political concessions, including a new charter enabling it to increase its capital, which it did by transferring money from its reserves into the capital stock, leading to a corresponding increase in the share price. But Ramsay lamented: 'I find the Dundases are completely attached to Sir William Forbes & Co.'s banking shop, contra Royal Bank. Mansfield Ramsay & Co. are of course resolved to attend to their own business and will bestow no attention to the political or pecuniary interests of the Treasurer [Henry Dundas] or his son-in-law the Lord Advocate [Robert Dundas].'[24]

In 1790 Dundas ordered an inquiry into the distribution of government revenues which disclosed that Royal Bank already had the benefit of remitting the land tax and customs and stamp duties to London, worth £170,000 a year. Mansfield Ramsay & Co. also handled the Post Office's revenues of £30,000 a year.[25] Bank of Scotland, anxious not to let its rival win all the business, wrote to Dundas, who had just become its governor, pointing out that in England and Ireland all government revenues were paid through the national bank and the same should be true in Scotland.[26] British Linen also tried to win a share of the business, telling Dundas that its support for infant manufacturing businesses gave it 'a well-founded claim to a share of any favours the Lords of His Majesty's Treasury may bestow'.[27]

Six years later Dundas divided the revenues into four equal parts – through the two public banks, Mansfield Ramsay and Forbes. The four banks established a committee – the cartel had been enlarged. One of its first tasks was to prevent British Linen from gaining a share of the lucrative business, which it succeeded in delaying until 1810, when British Linen was added to the list and the revenue was split five ways. The sums were large and the 60-day lag between receiving the cash in Scotland and having to remit to the government in London became an important part of the funding of the main Scottish banks, so much so that when the

Treasury tried to shorten the time period the banks fought a fierce rear-guard action.[28]

Lawrence Dundas lost his place at the bank, but held on to his political position for a short time afterwards. At the election of 1780 he was again attacked by the Dundas–Buccleuch interest but was still able to retain control of three Scottish seats: Stirlingshire, held by his son Thomas, Orkney and Shetland, held by his nephew Charles Dundas, and his own Edinburgh constituency. James Boswell, who met Dundas during the contest, said that to his surprise he was not the 'cunning shrewd man of the world as I had imagined' but a 'comely jovial Scotch gentleman of good address but not bright parts . . . I liked him much. I even felt for him as a man ungratefully used in his old age.' He died a year later at the age of 69 and was buried in the Dundas mausoleum attached to Falkirk parish church. According to the *Annual Register* he left £900,000 property and land, plus mortgages owed to him, bonds and annuities amounting to £400,000.[29]

12

Riot and revolution

ON 14 JULY 1789 a thousand angry Parisians stormed the Bastille, the medieval fortress that had become the symbol of absolute monarchy in France. Its governor, Bernard-René de Launay, was captured and beaten. A British visitor watched horrified as de Launay was murdered and decapitated in the street and his head stuck on a pike.[1] The revolution, which had started peacefully, had now entered a violent phase, but when the news reached Edinburgh it caused no alarm and was received with mild approval. Britain had been at war with France for much of the century, most recently after the French intervention on the other side of the Atlantic in the conflict which led to the loss of the American colonies. There was little sympathy for Louis XVI and a general feeling that the French were taking for themselves the constitutional rights Britain had achieved in 1688.

The banker William Ramsay, writing his diary in his house in Barnton, did not think it significant enough to mention and there was no reference in the minutes of the directors of either of the public banks. Nevertheless, in the following few years there was a renewed interest in reform ideas. Tom Paine's *Rights of Man* sold 200,000 copies and there was another attempt to pass a burgh reform bill in the House of Commons, which was talked out in a manoeuvre orchestrated by Henry Dundas, now home secretary in Pitt's government.

The nearest Edinburgh came to a revolutionary rising was the King's Birthday Riot in June 1792, when a rowdy mob outside the home of Dundas in George Square hoisted an effigy of him on a makeshift gallows. The minister was in London, but in the house were his mother Lady Arniston, his brother Colonel Francis Dundas and Admiral Adam Duncan, who was married to Robert Dundas's daughter. Duncan, a Dundonian, was the victor of the Battle of Camperdown against the Dutch, and at 6 feet 4 inches, a man not to be intimidated: 'The crowd "huzzaed" and a piece of wood was thrown up against the window. As the mob persisted in jeering and throwing missiles, Colonel Dundas and Admiral Duncan determined to drive the crowd round the effigy from the door. Armed with Lady Arniston's crutch which he had brought down from the drawing-room, Dundas sallied forth supported by the future queller of the Nore mutiny [Duncan]. Unluckily the Colonel was seized and beaten with his own weapon, and he regained the shelter of the house, exhibiting to his companion in arms a ghastly and formidable countenance.'[2]

After a while the crowd became bored and moved to St Andrew Square, where they broke the windows in the house of the lord provost, although they returned the following day for more chanting and it was three days before the city was quiet again. Anonymous pamphleteers tried to claim the riot as the first step in a revolution and Dundas received a letter informing him that the fate of the French aristocracy also awaited him. Effigies of him were burnt in Aberdeen, Dundee, Perth and Brechin,[3] but there was no general uprising and, as Michael Fry has pointed out, rioting was scarcely novel in Edinburgh and the King's Birthday holiday conveniently provided the leisure time and the alcohol to fuel a 'rammy'.[4]

American independence in 1783 had doomed the Glasgow tobacco trade, but the blow was softened by the fact that previous bumper harvests had filled the warehouses of the Virginia Dons and the sudden end to imports boosted the price, giving them time and money to wind down and diversify into other commodities, such as sugar and cotton from the remaining British possessions in the West Indies.[5] One minor trading house failed, but the Glasgow banks survived and the Edinburgh banks were unaffected.

In the peaceful decade that had followed the economy grew strongly and the banks expanded their operations outside their traditional markets in the capital and its hinterland. In its short life, the Ayr Bank had demon-strated a demand for lending across Scotland, which was difficult to service from one office in Edinburgh, but in trying to capitalise on this expanded market the banks followed different models. Bank of Scotland opened branches or appointed agents in provincial towns. By 1795 the network had grown to 24.

The men appointed as agents were often local politicians, part of Henry Dundas's network of supporters and placemen.[6] They were given a credit allowance, typically £2,000, which was topped up from time to time, they employed their own tellers and paid their own expenses, but often the bank employed an accountant to help them and keep a check on the state of business. Crucially the final decision on whether to grant loans or credits was taken by the directors' meeting in Edinburgh and approving loans from around the country took up an increasing proportion of the time of the board.[7] This meant a big commitment on the part of the 'ordinary directors' who were required to meet every weekday, so it was decided that they should be paid more. In 1780 the fee was increased to £2 per meeting (£520 a year, rather than the previous £360), but any director not appearing before noon was fined sixpence and any director appearing after 12.15 p.m. or leaving before 1 p.m. would be 'held abont' – presumably absent and therefore forfeiting the fee.[8] Initially the agents around Scotland were rewarded on the profitability of their lending, but the bank also wanted them to increase the circulation of its banknotes, so a trial of incentives was ordered.[9] Bank of Scotland notes were becoming increasingly common across Scotland. From an average circulation of £100,000 in 1772, there were £480,000 by 1794 and £670,000 by 1800.[10]

Notable by its absence in the Old Bank's branch network was Glasgow. Whether this was a strategic decision not to compete with the Glasgow banks, or part of an agreement with Royal Bank is not known, but in 1783 the Royal filled the gap. The Glasgow office was to be its only venture outside the capital for a long time and it chose two remarkable men as its agents. The senior of the two was David Dale, at 44 already a highly successful west of Scotland entrepreneur. From modest beginnings as an Ayrshire herd boy, he had progressed by way of weaving to running his own linen business and was successful enough to commission Robert Adam to build him a house in Charlotte Street, Glasgow, costing £6,000. His connection with Royal Bank was his marriage to Carolina Campbell, whose father John had been chief cashier. Dale was only ever part-time in the agency – in the following year he persuaded the cotton magnate Richard Arkwright to be his partner in starting a cotton mill at New Lanark – but his contacts, his local knowledge and his judgement were immensely valuable. His partner was Robert Scott Moncrieff, nine years his junior, who came from a landed professional Edinburgh family and at the time of his appointment held two government posts as a tax collector. He took quickly to Glasgow business life and his drive, energy and willingness to take risks and challenge the attitudes of the Royal Bank's directors in Edinburgh, were a complement to Dale's more measured approach to business.

The pair started work in Dale's draper's shop close to Glasgow Cross and the business grew rapidly. They were not lending to the nobility, landed gentry and lawyers, who were the Royal Bank's traditional east of Scotland customers, but to manufacturers, iron founders, cotton spinners and weavers, linen and calico printers, ropemakers, carpetmakers, watchmakers, sugar refiners, brewers, glassmakers and papermakers.[11] They were financing the start of the Industrial Revolution. Within ten years they were taking over a quarter of a million pounds in deposits and lending half a million, mostly by discounting trade bills – advancing cash on invoices to be paid. It was good business: bills were normally three-to-four months, meaning that the money came back to the bank speedily, to be lent again, and the discount (the interest rate) was 5–7 per cent, much higher than could be charged for secured lending. The procedure was quaint. Customers who wanted their bills discounted posted them into a wooden ballot box. At the end of the business day the accountant would weed out those with insufficient creditworthiness and they were discreetly returned the next time the customer visited the branch. Dale and Moncrieff would decide what discount to apply to the accepted bills.[12]

The effect on Royal Bank's profits was dramatic. Through the 1780s and early 1790s the directors' minutes were recording quarterly surpluses and rising dividends. In 1783 the bank was able to boost its capital from the £111,000 it had started with 60 years before, to £150,000 by using retained profits – essentially handing the money back to shareholders. At the same time it announced an increased dividend and revalued its own stock from £175 to £200 per share. The following year it was able to double its capital, again using retained profits, and four years later it added another £100,000 to its capital. Each time it increased the dividend.[13]

The first sign that the good times were ending came in April 1792. William Ramsay noted in his diary the assassination of King Gustav III of Sweden and the subsequent fall in stock prices in London.[14] Two weeks later France's declaration of war against Hungary brought fresh falls in the market. In August Louis XVI of France was arrested and in January 1793 sent to the guillotine. Businesses were becoming distinctly nervous that the decade of peace would soon be over, a fear confirmed by the French declaration of war on Britain in February. The market froze as those who had gold hoarded it and those who wanted it were unable to redeem their bills. Four Newcastle banks suspended payments, and banks across the UK experienced runs as depositors withdrew their money in gold or silver. Many of the smaller provincial banks went bust.

An urgent appeal was made to Henry Dundas by James Stirling, the lord provost of Edinburgh: 'I had some faint hope that the threatening cloud hanging over the West would have dissipated, but going into the Royal Bank this day at 2 o'clock I found the alarming intelligence had been received of the failure of two capital houses in London with whom some principal mercantile houses in Glasgow are deeply connected, some of whom arrived here express purposely to solicit aid and support. The directors here are greatly alarmed not knowing the extent, nay fearing a general bankruptcy in that part of the country.'

The letter ended dramatically: 'For God's sake sir, let something be done and speedily or the consequences cannot be foretold.'[15] He wrote again a few days later saying that manufacturers in the west were already laying off people, but that the banks, out of self-defence and self-preservation had been forced to limit their lending.

Sir William Forbes, whose private Edinburgh bank along with Mansfield Ramsay & Co. had withstood previous crises, faced unprecedented demands for cash: 'The demand for money at Glasgow, in particular, was uncommonly great and besides obliging many of the most opulent houses there in the mercantile and manufacturing line fairly to acknowledge that they could not fulfil their engagements, it produced the failure of . . . the "Glasgow Arms Bank" [and] to the very great surprise of everybody, James Dunlop of Glasgow, who was supposed to be one of the most opulent and cautious men of business in the west, was compelled to declare himself bankrupt.'[16]

Dale and Moncrieff were facing piles of bills they had discounted remaining unpaid when they fell due. At first William Ramsay, who besides being senior partner in his own bank was a director of Royal Bank, was sympathetic: 'Mr David Dale also embarrassed, but he must be supported.'[17] But as the bank runs continued and the unpaid bills mounted up, Ramsay become nervous: 'My distress is exceedingly great because of the most dismal prospect of Royal Bank affairs with a great many bills returned this day from the Bank of England which were supposed to be good. Matters seem to be fast drawing to a crisis and I do believe the consequences will be fatal for the Royal Bank and of course to Mansfield Ramsay & Co.'[18]

In Edinburgh the private bank Bertram Gardner & Co. failed, but it was the continued bad news from London and Glasgow that troubled Ramsay. A committee of Royal Bank directors went to Glasgow to assess the situation. Dale and Moncrieff were doing more lending than any bank in Britain, with the exception of the Bank of England and the threat to Royal Bank from Glasgow was acute: the total outstanding in discounted bills and cash advances was roughly equal to the entire capital of the bank. If they could not be redeemed for cash it would not survive. In addition, it owed Bank of Scotland £150,000. In a private memorandum to Dundas, the Old Bank complained about the debt: 'It cramps our powers – it distresses us greatly – the more so that their bills being accepted [in Glasgow] will not discount in London.'[19]

The Royal Bank's two Glasgow agents resisted making their customers bankrupt and continued to insist that they could weather the crisis given time, but with cash draining out of the bank and very little coming in, the directors' patience was being stretched. Ramsay was exasperated: 'We have been ruined by Scott Moncrieff and Dale, who ought to have managed the Glasgow branch with more safety and prudence than they have done. Still, they say the debtors of the bank have real property and goods which they cannot get sale for on account of the war with France.'[20]

The pressure on Dundas was mounting. James Fraser, treasurer of Bank of Scotland wrote on behalf of the directors appealing to Dundas not only as governor of the bank, but as home secretary and secretary for India, claiming, over-dramatically, that he ought to have concern for the 'welfare of the empire'. The bank had supported businesses in the towns where it had branches, but in Glasgow 'manufacturers and traders have suffered a dreadful reverse. From the most flourishing condition, they are plunged into the depth of distress. The private banking companies early began to withdraw from the support of credit and now do nothing. The Royal Bank's branch there may be reckoned the only source of their supplies.'[21]

Representatives from Royal Bank and Bank of Scotland went to London to lobby the minister who, despite his *laissez-faire* principles, relented. The government acted to unfreeze the credit market by issuing £2 million in Exchequer bills, which would be issued to businesses that were thought to be basically sound.[22] A fifth of the money came to Scotland and Royal Bank applied for £200,000, although the bank had to put up a bond for twice this amount, guaranteed personally by its directors. Among those pledging £50,000 each were the Duke of Buccleuch, Royal Bank governor, William Ramsay, and the lord provost.[23] The intervention was enough to stave off the crisis. Royal Bank remained solvent and with the breathing space bought by the government loan, Dale and Moncrieff were able to recover most of the money they had advanced.

The respite was short-lived. In the following three years the numerous victories of the French citizen armies against the Continental monarchies heightened the fear that an attack on Britain might be imminent. In February 1797 the Duke of Buccleuch told a public meeting to prepare to defend the coast against an invasion, but the effect was the opposite to that he intended; far from calming nerves, it provoked a panic. The speech was widely reported in the newspapers, prompting a run on the banks as depositors clamoured to withdraw their money.[24]

A few days later the news that a company of French troops had landed at Fishguard in Wales brought a gold-frenzy in London. The Bank of England's gold reserves, which had been as high as £7 million, were down to £1 million and were being further drained by £100,000 a day. The Bank directors made a desperate appeal to Prime Minister Pitt, who recalled the king from Windsor for an emergency meeting of the privy council on a Sunday, which authorised the Bank to suspend payments.[25] When word reached Edinburgh there was consternation.

The heads of the leading banks, meeting in the Bank of Scotland boardroom, felt they had no alternative but to follow the Bank of England's lead in refusing to pay the 'bearers on demand' holding their notes. This was illegal under the 1765 Act: the privy council order had not mentioned the Scottish banks. The lord provost, who was himself a member of the Royal Bank board, tried to maintain confidence in paper currency by calling a meeting of the 'great and good' – the lord president of the court of session, the lord chief baron of the exchequer, the lord advocate, and the sheriff of Edinburgh – who all declared they would continue to accept notes. The pledge was printed on handbills and advertised in newspapers, but it had no appreciable effect. Sir William Forbes remembered:

> The instant this resolution of paying no more specie [cash] was known in the street, a scene of confusion and uproar took place, of which it is utterly impossible for those who did not witness it to form an idea. Our counting-house, and indeed the offices of all the banks, were instantly crowded to the door with people clamorously demanding payment in gold of their interest-receipts, and vociferating for silver in change of our circulating paper.
>
> It was in vain that we urged the order of [the Privy] Council – which, however, applied merely to the Bank of England – and the general resolution adopted by all other banks in Edinburgh. They

were deaf to every argument, and although no symptom, nor indeed threatening of violence appeared, their noise, and the bustle they made, was intolerable; which may be readily believed when it is considered that they were mostly of the lowest and most ignorant classes, such as fishwomen, carmen, street-porters, and butchers' men, all bawling out at once for change, and jostling one another in their endeavours who should get nearest to the table, behind which were the cashier and ourselves endeavouring to pacify them as well as we could.[26]

Forbes's snobbish contempt for the noisy lower orders who were his customers does at least illustrate the extent to which paper money had replaced gold and silver in the economy – even fishwives and manual workers were now being paid with notes and in turn were using them to pay their bills. Forbes and his staff did not have enough coin to satisfy the demand, but took their own bank's notes and exchanged them for notes from the public banks – Bank of Scotland and the Royal. Though grudgingly accepted, this had the desired effect. It took a few months for the dissatisfaction to die down, but eventually the non-convertibility of banknotes was accepted: 'It was remarkable, also, after the first surprise and alarm was over, how quietly the country submitted, as they still do, to transact all business by means of bank-notes, for which the issuers give no specie [cash] as formerly.'[27]

Paper money had come of age. Though illegal, no action was taken against the Scottish banks for their refusal to cash their notes and ways were found to work around the shortage of small change. Some people resorted to tearing a £1 note into two or four and using the pieces as five or ten shillings (25p or 50p in today's money), although not every bank would accept the fragments of torn notes. The Royal Mint secured a supply of captured Spanish dollars and issued them as worth 4s 6d (22.5p) each, with the head of King George III stamped over the head of King Ferdinand of Spain. This prompted the doggerel line:

> The Bank to make their Spanish Dollars current pass
> Stamped the head of a fool on the head of an ass.[28]

Eventually parliament gave the Scottish banks temporary permission to issue notes of less than £1, which had been banned by the 1765 Act.

13

Wartime austerity

IN OCTOBER 1789 Dr William Robertson, principal of the University of Edinburgh, and several of his professors were invited to breakfast at the home of the lord provost. The university was still the 'tounis colledge',[1] and the council appointed and paid its staff, so it was an offer they could not refuse, but the occasion was the announcement of good news. The council had agreed to replace the old and dilapidated buildings with a grand new college designed by Robert Adam, the most celebrated and fashionable architect in Britain. Construction was to begin immediately and the foundation stone would be laid in a month's time.[2]

The university had been expanding rapidly in size and reputation and was outgrowing its old accommodation, much of which was in an embarrassing state. Robertson had been campaigning for 20 years for a new building on the university's land at Kirk O'Field, just outside the Old Town's walls to the south of the High Street. He had proposals drawn up for a chapel, hall, library, museum, common and teaching rooms, and houses for the principal and some professors. It was not thought necessary to provide accommodation for the students; Robertson believed that to shut them away in colleges, as they did in Oxford and Cambridge, deprived them of life experience. Their education would develop in a more balanced fashion if they found lodgings in the town. But lack of money had always been a barrier to the project. James Gregory, professor of the Institutes of Medicine, had tried to persuade Henry Dundas to earmark a third of the profits of the national lottery, which the government had introduced to help finance the war, to the project, but to no avail.

The council saw the university development as part of the expansion of Edinburgh to the south, which would necessitate a bridge over the Cowgate ravine, to complement North Bridge, which connected the Old Town to the New Town to the north. In 1785 the city obtained the South Bridge Act, which enabled it to undertake the construction and pay for it by levying a local tax on houses and other buildings outside its jurisdiction to the south at the same rate as was paid by Old Town residents. It was expected that the increased revenue would more than meet the cost of the bridge and any surplus could be used to towards the new college, which was estimated would cost £40,000.

When Sir James Hunter Blair, a partner in Sir William Forbes's bank, became lord provost in 1784 he persuaded Robert Adam to draw up plans for the bridge and the college. Adam approached the project with enthusiasm: he was not merely designing a bridge, but reimagining Edinburgh as a modern city to be compared with any in Europe. It would be entered from the south along a *via triumphalist*, a broad new boulevard, passing the new university building (which he had not yet had time to design) and crossing a new south bridge aligned with North Bridge to make one continuous axis, perpendicular to the east–west line of the Royal Mile. The new street would be lined on either side with tall elegant colonnaded classical buildings and would culminate in his magnificent Register House.

It was an ambitious vision, but the drawings sent from his office in London to Edinburgh, far from inspiring the council, terrified it. Hunter Blair and his fellow councillors had not envisaged anything on this scale. Where Adam saw grandeur, they saw unaffordable cost. Without informing Adam they commissioned a more modest scheme from architect Robert Kay and started construction work.[3]

Adam was furious when he discovered and after failing to persuade the council to change its mind, sent a bill for a whopping £1,228 as compensation for his time. This led to a protracted dispute, only resolved through the arbitration of Henry Dundas after Hunter Blair had left office. Building South Bridge began in 1786 and, despite being a major engineering challenge, appears to have been completed on time and on budget, in contrast to North Bridge. It was opened to foot passengers in 1788 and to vehicles soon afterwards. The cost was £6,446, a sum which the council recovered many times over by selling the land on either side and levying rates on the new property built on each side of the new road. The bridge gave the city access to development land in the south, mirroring its expansion to the north, but one casualty was St Cecilia's Hall, an elegant small music room opened by the Edinburgh Musical Society in the Cowgate in 1763. It lost its entrance courtyard to the bridge works and was overshadowed by the new street towering above it. Fashionable society moved to the recently completed Assembly Rooms in the New

Town and the Edinburgh Musical Society slowly faded away, selling the hall to a Baptist congregation in 1801.[4]

Hunter Blair's successor as lord provost, the wine merchant Thomas Elder, persuaded Adam to end his antagonism to the council and design the new college building. He produced plans for a monumental rectangular development, with a small entrance courtyard reached through an arch from South Bridge, and a large quadrangle behind. The centre of the frontage was to be a huge portico, supported on four columns 22 feet (6.7 metres) high and each weighing 16 tons. The projected cost was more than either the university or the council could afford, so a public subscription was launched and appeared to go well. By November 1790 £20,000 had been pledged, including donations from a Scots officer in the Russian army and a group of 'respectable gentlemen' of Calcutta. There were also gifts in kind. A farmer gave two bullocks, which were sold for £35.[5]

The laying of the foundation stone by Grand Master Mason Lord Francis Napier was attended by a crowd of 30,000. The lord provost, principal, councillors and professors processed from Parliament House behind a military band, along streets lined with soldiers and the town guard. The scene was captured by the engraver David Allan. Work began, but within 18 months it had run into financial trouble. As with the Exchange building 30 years previously, the promises of subscriptions were hard to turn into cash and the council ended up going to the court of session to try to get some of them enforced.

The work was slowed down, but the trustees overseeing the project still struggled to fund the wage and materials bills. In 1792 the government gave a £5,000 grant, which enabled some parts, including a few classrooms, the anatomy theatre and an adjoining room 'for receiving corpses' to be completed, but in 1793 work stopped altogether. Adam had died in 1792 and Robertson a year later.

The war was soaking up all the available cash and the financial crises of 1793 and 1797 were compounded by bad harvests, which drove up food prices and increased poverty. In 1795 it was estimated that 16,000 people in Edinburgh were living on charity. The philanthropic foundations in the city, which might have been contributors to the cost of the college, were fully committed trying to prevent famine. A desperate petition was sent from the trustees to Dundas in 1799 saying that the half-finished buildings, most of which were unroofed, were open to the weather and deteriorating, while the students and their teachers were working in a building site and were worse off than they had been in the old buildings. An emergency grant was made to help stop the further deterioration of the works, but with government attention focused on funding the war, appeals for help in completing the building were ignored.

Unpaid tradesmen were in dispute with the council until 1809 and it was 1816, after the Battle of Waterloo had ended the Napoleonic Wars, before work on the college was restarted. The new work used a modified design by William Playfair, which substituted Adam's two yards with a single large quadrangle. Even then it was dogged by delay and cost overruns. It was substantially complete by 1827, having cost £121,000, mostly financed by the government, but the dome, which Adam had envisaged, was not added until 1887.[6]

The university was not the only development to be delayed. Construction of the New Town was dependent on the take up of feus – ground leases sold by the council – and the rate of feuing and building ebbed and flowed with the financial climate of the time. From the first feu in St Andrew Square in 1767, the building of the east end had progressed reasonably smoothly so that the square and its neighbouring streets were completed by 1780. Moving westwards, Hanover Street and Frederick Street were completed by the early nineties, and the progress of Princes Street, George Street and Queen Street kept pace with them. William Ramsay bought a house at the west end of George Street in February 1790.[7]

Building Castle Street began in 1792, but it was 1802 before Sir Walter Scott could move into the house he commissioned at 39 North Castle Street. The owners of feus engaged their own architects and builders, so although the council specified the size and scale of the houses, there was little uniformity in design. Some houses had imposing doorways or capitals over the windows – Scott's and the neighbouring buildings had bow fronts – but many were plain. To some contemporary eyes the whole development looked drab. The lawyer and diarist Henry Cockburn complained that 'every house being the exact duplicate of its neighbour, with a dexterous avoidance as if from horror, of every ornament or excrescence by which the slightest break might vary the surface'.[8]

When it came to Charlotte Square the council wanted something with more distinction and in 1791 commissioned Robert Adam to design frontages for each side. He produced strikingly elegant elevations for imposing three-storey houses, with basements and attics – and yes, they had 'ornaments and excrescences' – Corinthian columns, balustrades and recessed, arched doors. They would be the largest and grandest residences in the original New Town and the epitome of what has become known as the Adam style. Sadly, he died before any of the square was completed and without being paid. His brother submitted an invoice for 200 guineas after his death, but the council paid only half this amount.[9] The purchasers of feus would be able to add their own individual dwellings behind the elegant common façade. The first feu was taken up the following year, but then progress was slow and by 1800 the only buildings were two-thirds of the houses on the north side, the rest of the square had not been started.[10] It was not completed until 1820.

As a peacetime prime minister, Pitt had acted to bring down the national debt, which had climbed to £243 million by the end of the American Revolutionary War in 1783. By increased tax receipts and prudent management of the public finances he had reduced it to £170 million by 1792, but he had to abandon this policy a year later when France and Britain declared war on each other. Pitt and Dundas, who added secretary for war to his other titles, believed that the conflict could be won quickly and the additional borrowing needed could be paid off in peacetime by increased tax revenues. Since Britain had a relatively small army, Pitt decided to finance France's Continental enemies to do the fighting, as well as building up the British navy. The government started to issue new debt securities relatively modestly, but the pace increased as the war dragged on and by 1797 the debt had passed its previous peak, reaching £350 million. The flood of new paper depressed the price of gilts and led to a corresponding increase in yields: 3 per cent consols, one of the most popular securities, traded at £90 in 1792, yielding 3.3 per cent, but four years later they were down to £50, yielding nearly 6 per cent.[11] It was impossible to match this by ordinary lending so private individuals and banks invested heavily in gilts.

Bank of Scotland began buying exchequer bills in 1793 and the following year added Bank of England stock, 3 per cent consols and navy and victualling bills to its growing portfolio of public debt. It continued buying whenever it had spare funds, so that by 1796 its portfolio had a market value of £844,000, which was considerably more than its book cost. It lodged these holdings with the Scottish bank Coutts & Co. in London as security against its own borrowings or purchases of gold.[12] The war years were good for the Old Bank. It increased its capital to £1 million, weathered the credit crises of 1793 and 1797 more easily than Royal Bank and its branch network was becoming an increasing source of profitable business. In July 1795 the directors celebrated the bank's centenary with a dinner for themselves, their rivals from other banks, the lord provost and senior judges in Fortune's tavern – officially the 'Caledonian Coffee Room' at 5 Princes Street, but always known by the name of its patron, Matthew Fortune.

The directors decided they had outgrown the three-storey tenement in Bank Close, the narrow alley south of the Lawnmarket, which the bank had occupied since the fire at the beginning of the century. There was no suitable location for a larger headquarters in the New Town, so they bought an area of cleared land from the council for £1,350 at the foot of Lady Stair's Close and Dunbar's Close, perched on the northern edge of the cramped Old Town.[13] It was an impressive site, commanding a view over the New Town and the Firth of Forth beyond, but it was not ideal for supporting a large building. It had been used as a 'midden' – a dump for household waste – and was at the top of the 'Earthen Mound', the huge ramp constructed up to the Old Town using the spoil excavated from the foundations of the houses of the New Town.

To counter the danger of slippage, a massive retaining wall had to be built before the headquarters could be erected, but even then there were problems. A neighbouring tenement collapsed during the digging of the foundations, plunging the bank into a ten-year dispute over compensation. Inevitably costs overran, but the bank's shareholders never knew the final amount, which was £43,000. The directors diverted £30,000 of the accumulated profits to reduce the total and carried the 'Bank House' in the books at £13,000.[14] The building, a rectangular block with a shallow bow at the front and a single cupola, was not widely admired: Cockburn called it 'a prominent deformity', but it served the bank until it was extensively remodelled fifty years later.

As soon as it recovered from its credit squeeze in 1793, Royal Bank too began buying government securities. By 1802 government debt of various kinds made up over a fifth of the Royal's liabilities.[15] British Linen was also a big buyer as were the provincial banks. This may partly have been a patriotic gesture to help fund the war, but, being highly liquid (they could be turned into cash very easily) government securities were an insurance for the banks in case there was another run and heavy demand for gold. In 1796 Pitt, looking for alternatives to increasingly expensive debt issues, launched a 'loyalty loan'. He wrote to the directors of Bank of Scotland and Royal Bank asking them to contribute and, as an incentive, told them that the Bank of England had offered £1 million and its directors a further £500,000 as individuals. Both banks subscribed £100,000, although their minutes make no mention of the directors topping this up from their own pockets.[16] The loan was clearly not enough and in the following year the government imposed Britain's first income tax, as a temporary wartime measure.

In 1801 Pitt and Dundas lost power – a blow to the Scottish banks since they no longer had their direct access to the heart of government. Dundas was governor of the Old Bank and his manoeuvring had secured the governorship of the New Bank for the Duke of Buccleuch, although Dundas's record of advancing their interests was uneven to say the least. The Treaty of Amiens brought a short respite from the war, but the resumption of fighting in 1803 and another poor harvest brought fresh credit difficulties. Scott Moncrieff wrote to William Simpson, the Royal Bank's cashier: 'These are indeed perilous times and I feel my duties to be not the most pleasant – but somehow I feel much better than on former occasions and this is from a conviction that all our bankruptcies are nothing but what might have been expected and will in the end do much good in the place by cleaning the ground of noxious weeds ... We will in the end lose a few hundred by returned bills, but in the future we will be much safer.'[17]

He was still at odds with William Ramsay, who advocated a more conservative risk policy by accepting only short-dated bills for discounting. Scott Moncrieff stood his ground: 'Sure I am [that] if good Mr R understood how matters were going on here he would be perfectly satisfied of the impracticality of following out his order to discount no bills above two months' date, unless he made up his mind to put a stop at once to the whole paper circulation business here – for it would certainly have that effect if such a measure was taken without at least giving two or three months' notice ...'[18]

David Dale retired at the end of 1803 with a gift of £500 from the board and, as he acknowledged, 'your approbation of my conduct, which I value more than money'.[19] He had steered the Royal Bank's Glasgow agency through its first turbulent 20 years, built a lending business that was providing most of the bank's profits, and made a substantial contribution to financing the take-off of industrialisation in the West of Scotland. In addition to being a shrewd banker, he was a successful entrepreneur, starting cotton mills and a dye works. He was an enlightened employer, a philanthropist and, as the founding chair of the Glasgow Society for the Abolition of the Slave Trade, a campaigner. He died in 1806.

Part 2

The evolution of the Scottish system

14

Sycophants of existing power

'TALENTLESS, IGNORANT AND sucking up to authority.' The waning power of Henry Dundas – since 1802 elevated to the peerage as Viscount Melville – unleashed increasing attacks on the closed circle of Edinburgh banks and the Tory oligarchs who owned their shares and sat on their boards, and none was more virulent in his criticism than the Whig lawyer Henry Cockburn: 'No men were more devoid of public spirit, and even of the proper spirit of their trade, than our old Edinburgh bankers. Respectable men they were, but without talent, general knowledge, or any liberal objects, they were the conspicuous sycophants of existing power . . . Not that they would discount a bad bill for a Tory, or refuse to discount a good one for a Whig; but their favours and their graciousness were all reserved for the right side.'[1]

With a renewed threat from Napoleon, Pitt had been returned to power in 1804 and made Melville first lord of the admiralty, where he won admiration by building up the fleet to block any prospect of a French invasion. His triumph was short-lived. He was impeached for financial irregularities while he had been treasurer of the navy and forced to resign. Although the House of Lords acquitted him, Pitt did not take him back into the government and he retired to Scotland, bitter, financially impoverished by his legal costs and drinking heavily.[2] He remained governor of Bank of Scotland, but the bank now looked to his son Robert for advice and influence.[3] He died in his house in George Square in 1811 and was succeeded as governor by Robert, who also took the title Viscount Melville.

Cockburn's assault was not without justification. Bank directors, officers and even local agents were usually from the same political persuasion and the same narrow class of landowners. Or they were merchants who, as soon as they had accumulated enough money, joined the landed interest by buying estates from impoverished aristocrats.

David Staig, Bank of Scotland's agent in Dumfries and provost of the town, was the local fixer for Dundas, and handled some of his personal as well as government finances. Patrick Miller, a partner in Mansfield, Ramsay & Co. and director and deputy governor of Bank of Scotland, had facilitated the removal of Sir Lawrence Dundas from the governorship of Royal Bank and his replacement by the compliant Duke of Buccleuch. Staig was Miller's agent in the purchase of the Dalswinton estate in Dumfries when he used some of his banking profits to acquire landowning respectability.

For the two public banks and the two leading Edinburgh private banking companies, Mansfield, Ramsay and Sir William Forbes & Co., the reward for staying loyal to the governing Tory party was the handling of tax revenues – effectively a constant source of cheap funding which was denied to other banks outside the capital. The profits from this stream of money enabled the two public banks to maintain their dominance, not just in Edinburgh but in the rest of the country, particularly Glasgow which was fast becoming the most important lending market. They acted as reserve bankers to the provincial banks, monitored their activities through the note exchange and clipping their wings if they tried to expand outside their localities.

Shares in the public banks were very tightly held. Bank of Scotland and Royal Bank both had less than 200 proprietors and with each individual share trading between £150–£250 in the late eighteenth and early nineteenth century, they were out of the range of all but the wealthy. For the banks' own tellers and ordinary staff the price of a single share was more than a year's salary. Shares were occasionally sold by 'roup' (auction), but where possible the banks tried to match sellers and buyers to keep the shareholding within a friendly group. 'George Brown proposes to sell his Royal Bank of Scotland stock,' wrote William Ramsay in his diary. 'I refer him to Mr Simpson [bank cashier], who will dispose of it as he did of the stock belonging to Lord Elliock and observed that this mode of sale was more decent than selling by roup. He approved of it and went to Mr Simpson.'[4]

The role of the private bankers – Miller and his partner James Mansfield at Bank of Scotland and William Ramsay (and after his death in 1805 his son, also William) at Royal Bank – came in for criticism. An anonymous pamphlet of 1778 had warned shareholders in the banks against the few men who were conspiring to gain undue influence in both Bank of Scotland and Royal Bank: 'Place not your confidence in stockjobbers; beware of politicians if such men are among you; suffer none of them to have the management of your affairs,' it warned.[5]

The private bankers were accused of using the public banks as their personal reserves. Thirty years later the older generation of private banking magnates had died, but their successors still held sway over the public banks. At Royal Bank Ramsay, Bonar & Co. (successor to Mansfield, Ramsay) held at least a fifth of the shareholding and William Ramsay and Alexander Bonar were on the board, with a group of their friends and supporters.

At the annual meeting of 1815 a group of concerned Royal Bank shareholders succeeded in getting the lawyer James Ferrier elected as a director and he immediately set out to expose the way in which the private bankers had been abusing the bank. He alleged that he had 'received information from a quarter so very respectable that he could not entertain any doubt of its correctness' that Ramsay and Bonar were trying to get enemies removed from the board and their own men elected. Not only that, but with the tacit agreement of the deputy governor, Gilbert Innes, they had used their privileged position to borrow at least £130,000 at below market rates, which was never sanctioned by the directors, nor even reported to the board. Ramsay and Bonar stormed out of a meeting, stopped attending the board and an extraordinary public spat developed. The directors, against the wishes of Innes, went to the length of having the board minute detailing Ferrier's charges, printed and sent to all shareholders.[6] Ramsay and Bonar responded with their own pamphlet accusing Ferrier of 'mistaken zeal': 'The account of our house with the Royal Bank rest on much stronger grounds than the form of applying for credit and obtaining it at any decent rate from the board. It rests on the best understanding and usage of near half a century, grounded on the close connection of having been of the greatest mutual advantage to each other for the last 34 years.'[7]

As the public row continued Thomas Allen, a shareholder, issued his own printed accusations. He alleged that Ramsay, Bonar had used the money obtained from the bank to speculate in government securities, making profits which could have gone to the bank's proprietors. The bank, he said, was sitting on £300–500,000 of undistributed profits which could have been used to increase the dividend, which was much lower than that of other banks.[8] Shareholders were told very little about the bank's performance or its assets and liabilities. Allen's inside knowledge may have come from Ferrier.

Ramsay, Bonar & Co. was required to repay its unauthorised loan and had its daily £10,000 float withdrawn, but the two partners remained on the board. Ferrier then turned his attention to the rest of the bank. There had, he told the board, been 'some neglect on the part of the directors in not taking measures for ascertaining the state of the bank cash on the death of George Mitchell, the late first cashier'.[9] During Mitchell's terminal illness his brother William had assumed the role, with no oversight by directors. Ferrier questioned a loan of £16,000 granted to Mitchell in May that year: it was not a real loan, he claimed, but issued to cover up the money taken from the bank by the Mitchell brothers and their uncle, who was the previous chief cashier, again without the knowledge or authority of the directors.

Then came the story of Charles More, a teller in the bank all his working life. Questioned by the board at Ferrier's insistence, he confessed that for 30 years he had been stealing money and had falsified the ledgers to cover it up. His only excuse was his large family and small salary and that he 'always hoped that some fortunate occurrence would happen that would enable him to replace the money taken'. The fraud had been discovered by a junior clerk, and when he had alerted his superior it had been decided to hide it from the directors. More's salary had risen over the period from £70 to £150, so the total £6,200 he had stolen was more than twice his earnings. His son John, who had been promoted to become the bank's agent in Glasgow after the retirement of Dale and Scott Moncrieff, offered to refund the total taken by his father and the money was put into various cash accounts as fictitious deposits.[10] The bank dismissed Charles More instantly, but there was worse news to come.

Ferrier and another director, Alexander Duncan, also a lawyer, went to Glasgow to reconcile the totals in the branch books with the cash in the 'closet' [strong room]. The 'turning out of the bank closet at Glasgow [disclosed] the rubbish that Mr [John] More had placed there instead of the bank notes which he had abstracted'. The books showed a cash balance of £147,415, but when the directors added up the cash in the closet it was found to be £66,869 short. On top of that £103,507 was unaccounted for in discounted bills. John More, who had made himself the most important banker in Glasgow, doing more business than Royal Bank's head office in Edinburgh, had also built up a substantial personal property and industrial portfolio, using the bank's money. He was unable to account for the missing money, nor to repay it. The directors made him bankrupt.[11] Ferrier claimed Gilbert Innes had known about More's activities but had done nothing. The bank was anxious to avoid publicity, so there were no prosecutions and Innes was allowed to stay, but new checks were instituted and the directors agreed to work to the bank's byelaws, which obliged them to check balances regularly, but had been ignored for years.

Bank of Scotland did not suffer from fraud and theft to the same degree. It had produced its own manual for the conduct of branch business and carried out regular inspections, but it had other problems. Its branch network – to which Glasgow was added in 1802 – had initially proved to be a source of considerable profits. But between 1813 and 1820 branch earnings slumped from over £60,000 to less than £1,000, necessitating the closure of five of them. Shareholders were told little about the bank's trading or its real financial position, beyond the level of each year's dividend. In fact – as Thomas Allen correctly guessed for Royal Bank – the Old Bank had substantial reserves and the directors used these to conceal the bank's real performance and maintain the dividend. The board would smooth out short-term fluctuations in the price of its shares by buying in stock and releasing it slowly over time. Twice, in 1817 and 1827 it used reserves to declare a special bonus to keep the share price buoyant.[12]

Without effective competition, the public banks had become complacent – and they had used their political influence and economic power to keep their rivals down. The British Linen Company, although it issued its own notes and had a branch network across Scotland, had never been a serious competitor, yet the Royal and Bank of Scotland consistently opposed its attempts to obtain a new Royal Charter, to allow it to increase its capital. They had also blocked it from joining the magic circle of banks sharing in the handling of tax revenues. British Linen eventually got its charter, but was refused permission to call the company a bank, although it had been doing exclusively banking business for 50 years. It had to wait a further century before being able to add 'bank' to its name.[13]

British Linen had less than half the capital of either Bank of Scotland or Royal Bank. Like them it invested heavily in government stock, rather than the Scottish economy, and it too suffered from complacency and inefficiency. Of its 14 branches, several were barely profitable, and despite setting up a branch inspectorate in 1810 it suffered seven cases of default or bad management by its agents between 1813 and 1819.[14] It was run by a clique which was even narrower than the boards of either of the larger banks. There were only five directors, who served for life. When it was necessary to find a new board member three criteria were applied: the new man (it was always a man) was related to one of the board, had an association with Dumfries or Kirkcudbright, or had already done service to the bank. When, in 1836, it was suggested that one director should retire at each annual meeting to be replaced by election, the board reacted with horror; a new director 'may not coincide with [the existing directors] in the views hitherto taken and acted on by the board'. The proposal was dropped.[15]

British Linen had the distinction of being the first to employ a female member of staff, when Eleanora Hog, aged 23, was given the job of day book clerk in 1785. But this was less gender equality than nepotism and it was 130 years before the next female employee was taken on. Eleanora's father was Walter Hog, the bank's manager, who also found a post for his brother-in-law. She was in time promoted to ledger clerk and then book-keeper, at each stage being paid as much, or more than the men doing similar work. Her final salary of £200 a year was described by the bank's historian as 'princely' and when she retired in 1816 she was granted an annuity of £50 a year.[16]

In trying to stop British Linen from growing, Bank of Scotland and Royal Bank had argued in a petition to the House of Lords that: 'the business of banking in Scotland has been of late years carried to great excess – so much so that restraint, not encouragement, is now necessary, and that any addition to its number can only increase competition which, operating without check or limitation, cannot fail to expose the credit of the country to the greatest danger by adding to that excess of paper currency which is supposed to have already been carried to an alarming height.'[17]

That statement demonstrated a failure to understand that paper had already triumphed over precious metals – a fact Adam Smith had recognised 50 years before. The astonishing growth of the Scottish economy over the next century would depend on more banks issuing a great deal more paper. The two Edinburgh public banks were about to face much more effective competition.

★ ★ ★

When the Commercial Bank of Scotland launched in 1810 it promised to be everything the two establishment banks were not. It would not be beholden to a political interest, private bankers would be banned from being directors, it would lend to entrepreneurs and businessmen, rather than speculating in government stock, and it would be broadly based in its shareholding. Henry Cockburn, who was among the new bank's supporters and shareholders (see his attack on the Tories of the existing banks, above) claimed that it marked a 'growth in the public mind': 'A demand for a bank founded in more liberal principles was the natural result of this state of things [the political subservience of the established banks]. Hence the origin of the Commercial, professing to be the bank of the citizens. It was not meant and has never acted as a political engine; nor were all even of its founders, and still less of its proprietors, of the popular party.'[18]

To describe it as a 'citizens' bank', was a little strong. Its shares at £500 each were well out of the range of ordinary people, but it was to have a broad base with 672 shareholders at its first fundraising – more than Bank of Scotland, Royal Bank and British Linen combined. Its authorised capital was £3 million and the initial call for cash brought in £600,000. The list of proprietors included the usual landowners, merchants, surgeons and lawyers, but also people whose trades would not have appeared on the registers of the existing banks – hatter, grocer, farmer, stationer, tobacconist, confectioner, shipbuilder, butcher, dyer, haberdasher, hosier and brewer.[19]

The Commercial Bank was described as a joint-stock bank, but legally it was still a partnership, so its shareholders had 'joint and several' liability for its debts should it fail. Limited liability – enjoyed by the shareholders in Bank of Scotland, Royal Bank and British Linen – still required an Act of Parliament and with the Tories in government that was a political impossibility. For its headquarters the bank had been offered the old theatre at the end of North Bridge, but the asking price of 20,000 guineas was thought too high considering the building would have needed another £4,000 spent on it. Instead the bank bought a tenement in Picardy Place at the top of the road leading to Leith. A military guard was granted to secure its treasury, supplemented by a large dog. It began issuing its own notes in December 1810 and requested admittance to the note exchange run by the established banks.[20]

Almost immediately it experienced hostility. Bank of Scotland wrote 'warning this company against all the consequences of such an assumption as calling itself "of Scotland"' and threatening legal action, but the Commercial's board stood firm and the Old Bank, having been told by counsel that its prospects of winning an action in the courts were not good, quietly dropped its demand.[21] The request to join the note exchange was ignored, despite prompting, and then Royal Bank demanded to see a list of the Commercial Bank's partners. Fearing reprisals against its shareholders, the bank responded with a list of 100 who were willing to let their names be public. There was little the established banks could do to prevent the Commercial Bank from operating, but nevertheless they kept up a campaign of harassment.[22]

The bank made a few initial mistakes – its first manager, a lawyer called John Pollock, who had no banking experience, proved to be incompetent, but did not take kindly to his dismissal. A sheriff's order had to be obtained to oblige him to give up the keys, but he pursued the bank through the courts in actions lasting years.[23] The choice of London correspondent bank was also unfortunate – it went bust in 1816. But at the end of its first year the bank had a respectable £262,000 notes in issue and made a small profit.[24]

The end of the Napoleonic Wars in 1815 brought peace, but not lasting prosperity. The euphoria after Wellington's victory at Waterloo and the end to the wartime economy brought a few boom years, but they were followed by a deep slump. Prices fell, bankruptcies increased and the banks found themselves with an embarrassing surplus of money and few borrowers. Interest rates on deposits were cut and Royal Bank had to write off bad debts of £93,000 in 1821.[25] Royal Bank and Bank of Scotland were forced to cut their dividends. This hardly seemed an auspicious time to launch a new bank, but three were being planned simultaneously in Edinburgh. The promoters perhaps believed that the example of the Commercial Bank, which had weathered its first 15 years and was paying regular dividends, meant there was still an appetite for bank shares among investors.

The first to go public was the Tory lord provost of Edinburgh, Alexander Henderson, who advertised his intention to found a 'National Banking Company of Scotland' in the *Evening Courant*. Within days he had the names of 300 potential subscribers, a success which prompted a rethink by the promoters of the 'Scottish Union Banking Company' and the 'Scottish Union Commercial Banking Company'. Henderson called representatives of all three ventures to a meeting in his house and they agreed to join forces and form a committee of management.[26] At a subsequent meeting they chose the name National Bank, set the authorised capital at £5 million and called up 10 per cent immediately.

The large authorised capital was much more than any other Scottish bank and proved to be a far-sighted move. The National did not have to increase it until 1938. As an incentive to attract the widest possible shareholding, a deposit of only £1 per share was required, which would count against the first call. Subsequently the share price was set at £10, a fraction of the price of any of the other banks' shares, and one of the factors contributing to the relatively large shareholder base of 1,300 individuals, which rose in subsequent years, in contrast to the Commercial Bank, whose base was contracting after the first flurry of interest.[27]

The manager's post was offered to Patrick Borthwick, a merchant in Leith, who demanded £1,000 a year to compensate for the fact that he would have to give up his existing concessions to avoid conflicts of interest. After taking references, the board agreed, with the proviso that any shareholder who objected should be allowed to withdraw his subscription.[28] Borthwick had a strong reputation and contacts as a merchant, but no banking experience, so an accountant was recruited from Bank of Scotland. Finding an office took up a lot of the board's initial time with ultimately unsuccessful negotiations to buy the Waterloo Hotel in St Andrew Square. The asking price at £38,000 was considered too expensive, so the bank paid £13,079 for a house on the east side of the square.[29] The building, then numbered 39 (now 42), had been previously used as a hotel. The bank later bought the adjoining houses and remained on the site for the remainder of its existence. It demolished the original buildings in 1936 and constructed a new headquarters, which opened in 1942.*

Inevitably the board received a letter from Bank of Scotland objecting to the use of the term 'of Scotland', but after getting opinion from the lord advocate, the directors ignored it. They subsequently obtained an 'ammorial ensign' from the Lord Lyon King of Arms and in 1831 a Royal Charter, signed by William IV.[30] The Commercial Bank received one at the same time, but it was largely symbolic. The legal status did not allow either bank to do anything they were not already doing and they had to wait for a change in company law in 1844 before they obtained limited liability for their shareholders. In 1836 the National Bank succeeded in gaining a share of the Customs & Excise revenues from

---

* The building subsequently became the headquarters of the National & Commercial Banking Group, then the Royal Bank of Scotland Group, and is now a hotel.

Scotland – a sign that the old banks had dropped their hostility and accepted the new multi-bank world.

The National Bank quickly opened 13 branches and appointed agents around Scotland and prospered almost from its first year, paying a maiden 5 per cent dividend in 1827, but it hardly became the radical new force in Scottish banking. A landed aristocrat, Lord Roxburgh, was appointed its first governor and when Alexander Henderson died in 1827 the board looked no further than his oldest son, Eagle Henderson, to replace him.[31] Within a few years it too was investing in government stocks as the low risk alternative to backing the rapid founding of new businesses in Glasgow and the west.

Another banking venture of the early nineteenth century was very different from either the Commercial or the National. In Ruthwell, Dumfries, 80 miles from Edinburgh, the Reverend Henry Duncan was starting a genuine people's bank.[32] Commercial banks would not accept deposits of under £10, effectively excluding the working class. Duncan's idea was to encourage the habit of saving and self-improvement by providing a secure home for their money. To give his bank respectability he invited the local landowners to become honorary members, including James Farquhar Gordon, an Edinburgh lawyer and a member of the Edinburgh Society for the Suppression of Mendacity (Begging).

In 1813, seeing the success of the Ruthwell bank, Gordon and his fellow trustees decided to launch a bank. The new institution was initially very successful. In its first year it attracted more than 700 customers and £2,500 in deposits. Four branches were opened in different parts of the city,[33] but Duncan did not wholly approve. He believed that, like friendly societies, savings banks should have their depositors represented on the management committee, rather than being run by the middle classes, as was the case in Edinburgh. He also believed that customers should have a written record of their deposits (a forerunner of the bank passbook) and that the committee of management should publish an annual state-ment of the bank's assets and liabilities. These were radical proposals. As Charles Munn has pointed out, it was another 50 years before the commercial banks were routinely publishing balance sheets.[34]

Relations between Duncan and the Edinburgh bank deteriorated after another of the trustees, John Forbes, son of William Forbes, the banker, published a letter in the *Quarterly Review* in which he criticised the Ruthwell model and claimed that Edinburgh was the true pioneer of the savings bank movement. Duncan hit back with a pamphlet, rebutting some of Forbes's claims, particularly that the annual meeting of depositors was a waste of time, while Duncan believed that it promoted goodwill and wider knowledge. The quarrel rumbled on for two years before Duncan was satisfied that Ruthwell had been given its due as the 'parent bank', but relations remained strained.[35]

The Edinburgh bank lasted until the 1830s, but it struggled compared to those founded in English cities at the same time. A pamphlet published in 1836 estimated total deposits at £12–15,000 on which it was paying 2½ per cent interest, whereas a bank in Liverpool founded approximately at the same time had accumulated £265,000 and was paying nearly 3½ per cent, and one in Manchester £197,000.[36] A new savings bank Act came into effect in Scotland in 1835, allowing savings banks in Scotland to invest their funds in government debt, which English and Welsh savings banks had been able to do since 1817. Encouraged by the change in legislation, the Edinburgh Savings Bank was reconstituted along the lines of the English savings banks, rather than adhering to the stricter rules which Henry Duncan had applied. Its trustees were convinced that their savings bank would enable the working classes to emerge from 'the shadows of pauperism'. It was still headed and run by the middle classes, including the lord provost, the lord advocate and the dean of guilds on its board of trustees. The new bank made a steady start. By 1849, it held nearly £300,000 in deposits. It did not, however, open its first branch until 1870. This marked the start of a period of expansion. By 1900, the bank had six branches in Edinburgh and Midlothian, more than 80,000 accounts, and nearly £2¼ million in deposits.[37]

15

Insurance and the first fire brigade

ON A COLD November night in 1824 fire broke out in a second-floor engraver's workshop in Old Assembly Close, off the High Street. In a repeat of the conflagration that had destroyed that part of the Old Town 124 years earlier, the flames spread quickly from building to building. In the early years of the nineteenth century, several insurance companies had been founded in Edinburgh to compete with the London firms that were already represented in the city. Fire insurance was their main business and a major conflagration like this meant huge potential losses for all of them. Fire engines employed by these companies, the army and the city arrived promptly, but there was confusion and difficulties in getting access along the narrow closes. The fire spread to other tenements and the adjoining *Courant* newspaper office, part of which collapsed into the street. By morning it had consumed much of the Old Fishmarket Close and Assembly Close.

There was hope that the fire had burnt itself out, but by noon the steeple of the Tron Kirk, which had survived the fire of 1700 and was well east of the affected buildings, caught fire.

> In a short time the whole of the conical superstructure in wood was enveloped in flame. The casing of lead melted like wax and poured down in streamlets. The minute hand of the clock on the south side suddenly dropped down paralyzed and the paint of the dial face scalded off in flakes. The strength of the structure long resisted the intensity of the heat and the weathercock retained its pre-eminence among the bickering flames. At length the fierce element prevailed – the weathercock was prostrated and the fire rose in a mighty column to the sky.[1]

The main part of the building was saved by an engine belonging to the Board of Ordnance, and the fire put out. But that night fire broke out again, in the attic of an eleven-storey tenement on Parliament Square. The firefighters fought to save Parliament House and Law Courts, but the jury room, the offices of the auditor to the court of session and of the Water Company, together with several shops, were lost. The Advocates' Library and the offices of Sir William Forbes & Co., bankers, were saved. The lord advocate, Sir William Rae, was reported to have taken a turn working on the engines fighting the fire in a tenement at the head of Old Assembly Close, where he had been born.

Despite sleet and hail on Wednesday morning, the fire continued, spread by blowing embers and there were subsidiary fires for several days after the main blazed had been extinguished. More than 300 homes were destroyed, and 13 people killed, mostly by falling masonry. Many of the ruins were so dangerous that they had to be pulled down by teams of soldiers and sailors or brought down by cannon fire or mines. As with the previous fire, the homes and offices lost were mostly those of the more prosperous citizens. The Edinburgh Annual Register for 1824 recorded: 'The most distinguished characters in the city were seen voluntarily sharing in the severest manual labour and exposing themselves with the greatest intrepidity to much personal risk. In some instances persons of the lower class refused to work at the engines, or supply water with buckets, unless a bargain was struck with them, but this mercenary spirit was not general.'[2]

The insured loss was put at £200,000 and it had two main consequences for the insurance businesses operating in Edinburgh: it led to the reorganisation of firefighting and the foundation of Britain's first public professional fire service; and it ended the rate war between English and Scottish insurance companies.

In the early part of the nineteenth century insurance companies provided their own firefighting teams. The Caledonian Insurance Company founded in 1805, for example, bought its first fire engine from Bramah & Son, London, and equipped 14 firemen with blue jackets and trousers, with 'inlays, turn-ups, and a thistle of orange'. Their helmets had a thistle on the badge underlined with the word 'Caledonian'. The total cost was £32.[3] Insured premises had an emblem or 'ticket' made of tinplate or copper and displaying the symbol or name of the company fixed in a prominent place and, although firemen would rarely refuse to tackle a blaze in a building insured by a rival, they gave priority to those insured by their own companies. Army regiments and defence depots had their own brigades, as did some municipalities, although there was sometimes dissatisfaction with the way they performed.

In 1810 the North British Insurance Company suffered the first major fire one year after its formation. During celebrations in Glasgow for the king's birthday, which included a display of fireworks, a rocket entered the window of Messrs Aitken & Company, a dry goods warehouse on Glassford Street, starting a fire that caused serious damage. The company's loss was £6,463 18s 3d. It could have been much less had the firemen not been so liberal in toasting his majesty: 'The fire engines were soon on the spot, but, unfortunately, and to the great disgrace of the Glasgow Police, under whose management they were, they were in such a miserable state of disorder, and the firemen all drunk, it being the evening of His Majesty's Birthday, that they were of no use, and the fire was literally allowed to burn and thereby occasion a loss of many thousands of pounds, which otherwise could only have amounted to a few hundreds.'[4]

The fire engines, although they were steadily being improved, were still primitive machines – horse-drawn, with hand pumps which struggled to get water to the top floors of the taller Old Town tenements. Recent buildings had internal pipes installed so that water could be pumped to the upper storeys. The Old Town, with buildings huddled together, was particularly vulnerable to fire and its narrow closes and steep inclines made it difficult to haul engines into place. The various fire teams varied in the quality of their equipment, training and leadership. Some companies made no provision at all; the Insurance Company of Scotland, founded in 1821, rejected an offer to form a fire service from Francis Braidwood, a cabinetmaker and builder who had an interest in firefighting.[5]

In the Edinburgh fire of 1824 the various fire services that attended were thought to have performed bravely – and at least one fireman died – but their equipment was inadequate, there was no co-ordination between them and no overall direction of the operation. After a series of minor fires in the city, Lord Provost Alexander Henderson, had called a meeting of the insurance companies to discuss pooling their resources, but the discussions had not yet led to any action. After the November fire, six Scottish insurance companies – the Edinburgh Friendly, the Caledonian, the North British, the Hercules, the Insurance Company of Scotland and the Scottish Union – and the city council agreed to contribute £200 each towards the purchase of new equipment and the employment of a single body of firemen. They appointed as its leader James Braidwood, son of Francis Braidwood, the man who had been rejected by the Insurance Company of Scotland. The new force – the first in the UK – ordered four large and six small fire engines, plus portable firefighting equipment, water butts and hoses. Eighty firemen were recruited and outfitted with uniforms, helmets, hatchets and triangles – presumably for sounding warnings. The city agreed to supplement the existing 45 fire-cocks (hydrants) with 132 new ones and to find a fire house in the New Town, to supplement the two in the Old Town.[6] By 1828, 13 insurance companies – English as well as Scottish – were contributing to the annual cost of the Edinburgh service and the fire engine committee was making regular reports to the Police Commissioners.[7]

James Braidwood, who was only 24 at the time of his appointment, developed techniques and procedures that were widely copied. A trained surveyor himself, he recruited men with various construction skills, who could apply that knowledge to how a building might react to fire. He also hired workers – such as sailors – used to hauling heavy equipment about in poor conditions. The budgets he secured from the city council included a provision for 'exercises' – his men were trained and experienced before they had to tackle their first fire. He was also concerned that a fund should be established for the dependents of firemen killed or injured in action, arguing that they would be more likely to risk their lives in saving others if they knew their families would not face destitution if they died or were incapacitated. In 1833 he left Edinburgh to lead the first London fire service. He was killed in 1861 when a wall collapsed on top of him while he was fighting a fire in Tooley Street, near London Bridge.*

The Braidwood family played a major part in the insurance business in the city, but despite an early pioneer, local ventures were late in coming. The Edinburgh Friendly Insurance Office had been started in 1720 as a co-operative among a group of property owners who pooled their resources to provide fire insurance. The company charged a premium of 2 per cent a year of the sum insured and the proceeds were put into a fund and invested. Members were deemed to be partners in the company in proportion to the premiums they paid, but interestingly the insurance stayed attached to the building, not to the person paying

---

* A statue of James Braidwood was unveiled in Parliament Square, Edinburgh, in 2004.

the premium. In 1767 the company expanded its activities to the whole of Scotland. What is curious, given the success of the Edinburgh Friendly, is that although it was copied elsewhere in Scotland it never spawned rivals in the capital itself. Instead the English companies moved in. Sun Insurance, which had been established in London in 1706, opened an Edinburgh office in 1733 and Liverpool Insurance opened in the city in 1777, the year of its founding.[8] By the beginning of the nineteenth century there were at least eight English insurers with offices in Edinburgh, plus agencies for the Glasgow, Dundee and Aberdeen friendly societies, which were expanding their businesses into the capital.[9]

The appeal of the first indigenous Edinburgh companies for more than 80 years was to patriotism. Both the Caledonian (1805) and the North British (1809) urged potential shareholders to fund home grown rivals to the cross-border raiders. The North British was particularly strident, asserting that three-quarters of fire insurance business was going to the incomers: 'The insurance companies of England early availed themselves of our want of capital and enterprise by appointing agents in Scotland, who for more than a century, have drained from us the profits of this species of secure and useful speculation.'[10]

William Braidwood, brother of Francis and uncle of James, was one of the founders of the Caledonian. He had built up a successful ironmongery and building business and the new insurance company worked from his offices in Hunter Square, on the southern expansion of the Old Town. William became its first manager, putting up a caution of £2,000 and initially working unpaid. His partner was Forrest Alexander, son of a Leith sailmaker, who had established a wholesale leather and tanning business. It was claimed that Alexander determined to start the company after one of the English insurers refused a small fire claim on the grounds that his clerk had been one day late in renewing the premium.[11] Three years later Alexander was one of the promoters of the Commercial Bank of Scotland, again because of dissatisfaction with the service he received from his existing bank which unexpectedly refused to discount his bills of exchange.

The portrait painter Henry Raeburn was one of the early supporters of the Caledonian and became a partner and a director. He is said to have painted Braidwood and William Dickie, the Caledonian's first secretary, but if so these portraits have not survived. The picture of Braidwood in the Scottish National Portrait Gallery is by Charles Turner.

Raeburn is also said to have designed the masthead for the policies, an image of Britannia, with St Andrew bearing a cross on her shield, and Edinburgh in the background. Raeburn resigned after a year because the company was taking too much of his time.

The company offered 'common insurances on risks not exceeding £3,000 upon one subject' (although it exceed this maximum almost immediately, taking two risks of £5,000). It charged an annual premium of '2s per cent, hazardous 3s; doubly hazardous 5s' (1 per cent, 1.5 per cent and 2.5 per cent of the sum assured.) It refused foreign risks, cotton and lint mills, or the premises next to them. In 1818 with the coming of gas lighting, the company specifically excluded premises in which a gas meter was installed unless there was an exclusion clause for explosions. By the first annual meeting of its partners on 3 July 1806, it had insured risks of £1.6 million, despite having only £100,000 in called-up capital. The *Scots Magazine* reported that towards the end of 1806, subscribers totalled 400 and that 'a few days ago ten shares in this stock were purchased at a premium of 100 per cent'.[12] It paid its first dividend in 1808 and by 1833 the company had doubled its original capital and paid dividends averaging 8 per cent over its life.[13]

Where the Caledonian appealed to the merchant class for support, the North British hoped to appeal to a more traditional source of capital: 'Subscribers may include not only the most opulent and enterprising merchants and capitalists throughout Scotland, but also a considerable part of the landed interest, who are so much interested in retaining their floating capital within the country for its own improvement.'[14]

In its initial advertisement in the *Edinburgh Courant*, the company made some bold claims: 'The proprietory [sic] will be liable for all debts against the company only *to the extent of the shares subscribed for by each*, which condition will be inserted in all their policies.' Since, like all other companies, the North British was a partnership, this was of dubious legality. It also made an extravagant assertion about its future: '[The] almost certain profits of the plan in contemplation preponderate over every probable risk attached to it. It may be sufficient to state that among the various insurance companies established in England, or this country, there is no instance either of a positive failure, or even of the subscribers having ever been called upon to exceed the first instalment.'

The firm counted among its supporters Henry Brougham, a future Whig lord chancellor, the Earl of Elgin, importer of the Elgin marbles, and George, Marquis of Huntly, later Duke of Gordon, who became the first president. Brougham's younger brother, John Waugh Brougham, a partner in the firm Brougham & Moncrieff, wine merchants and insurance brokers, became the first manager.[15] Despite its overblown claims, the firm did moderately well in its first years. It moved from its initial rented office in Bank Street in the Old Town to the High Street, which overlooked the scaffold where criminals were hanged. In 1818 a mob rescued a highwayman who was about to be executed and the castle garrison had to be called out to recapture him and carry out the sentence. At least one board meeting had to be postponed because of a hanging outside the windows. Despite this, the business grew and in 1819 premium income had risen to £5,000. In 1825 the company moved to 1 Hanover Street, in the more genteel New Town.[16]

The Hercules Fire Insurance Company was also established in 1809, but then there was a gap until the Scottish Insurance Company was launched in 1821 and the Scottish Union Insurance Company in 1824. The former got off to a poor start. Its premium income in the first year was less than its losses from paying out on fire policies and the chairman had to confess to partners that £1,200 had been 'lost' by a porter. The man had been examined by a sheriff, who was satisfied that the loss was carelessness rather than theft, but the money was not recovered and the board rejected a suggestion that the manager and secretary be held responsible for the loss.

Simultaneously with launching the National Bank (see Chapter 14 above) Lord Provost Alexander Henderson started the Scottish Union and using his political and social connections he was able to set authorised capital at £500,000 in shares of £20 (later raised to £5 million with £207,000 called up) and to attract an impressive list of directors, headed by the lawyer/writer Sir Walter Scott, as governor. Such was Henderson's confidence that he rejected out of hand an offer of merger with the North British. At its first annual meeting Sir Walter apologised that 'owing to the immense accumulation of business' it had not been possible to balance the books. However, he disclosed that losses on the fire business totalled £5,000, although these were more than offset by the life assurance business the company was doing. By the following year the fire losses had been reduced to less than £1,000.[17]

The English companies reacted to the increased local competition by using their larger capital bases and more efficient clerical systems to keep their premiums low, reducing the margins for the Scottish companies and in several cases forcing them into losses on their fire risks. At their annual meeting in 1826, partners in the Insurance Company of Scotland were told that the company had sustained 'considerable losses' and that the Sun, the Royal Exchange and the Phoenix, the three leading English houses operating in Edinburgh, 'appear to have expected the ruin of existing establishments'.[18] Managers of the Scottish companies established a defensive cartel, meeting regularly to discuss the market, the sharing of abnormally high risks and the level of premiums. They made very little headway against the outside competition until after the great fire of 1824 when the losses suffered by the English companies also forced them to increase their rates. By the 1829 annual meeting, the chairman of the Insurance Company of Scotland was reporting that despite losses up to £5,400, an increase in premiums had been agreed by the Scottish offices, and he expected the English offices to follow suit.[19] By the following year premiums had been increased by all Scottish offices, 'cordially seconded by all of the leading and influential English offices'.[20]

The English, however, found other ways to compete. In 1831 the board received a letter from its Glasgow agent describing the loss of a large policy to an English rival and saying that there was a prejudice against Scottish offices, which were slower to settle claims than their English counterparts.

The Edinburgh companies depended on their own partners to bring in business, but this was a far from reliable marketing policy. Partnership contracts usually obliged those taking shares to insure their own houses, shops, factories or offices and to solicit business from their friends. Many did not and chairmen were often moaning to annual meetings. 'I regret that many partners, especially in Edinburgh, neglect to bring even their own insurances to the company,' the chairman of the Insurance Company of Scotland complained in 1828.[21] There appeared to be little loyalty among shareholders. A year earlier, amid 'unparalleled commercial and manufacturing distress', the chairman had had to report that 'the business has suffered considerably from a quarter the directors were least prepared to expect . . . the loss of policies from partners withdrawing to cover their shares in another company'.[22]

16

Wotherspoon and the Widows

NO ONE DID more to make the launch of the Scottish Widows life assurance fund a success than William Wotherspoon. He was its first manager and, since it failed to raise a loan big enough to meet its start-up costs, he worked unpaid. The fledgling company could not afford an office and so it operated for two years rent-free from his home in Brown's Square, later moving into his law office at 71 Princes Street. When a delegation of the directors went to London to seek advice from William Morgan, actuary of the Equitable Life Society, Wotherspoon was one of them and paid his own expenses for the journey, which would have taken 2–3 days in each direction, with overnight stops in inns along the way. When in November 1815 the directors decided that 'from the state of the funds and the business of the society it was impossible and, in the present circumstances, seemed quite unnecessary to employ both a manager and a secretary', he took on the role of secretary as well.[1] As manager, Wotherspoon was required to put up security of £500, as a guarantee of his probity. In January 1815 a grant of £150 was voted to him to cover all his work and expenses over the previous three years. At an average £50 this was much less than the annual wage of a lowly bank teller, but there is no record of him complaining. The new fund was a mutual from its inception – it had no shareholders and was owned by its policyholders – so Wotherspoon had no stake in the business other than a desire to see it succeed.

It may be melodramatic to say that he gave his life for Scottish Widows, but we do know that his health had been poor during the period in which he had worked to get the new life assurance society started. By March 1817 he was failing sufficiently for the society to appoint John McKean, his partner in his law firm, as co-manager. Wotherspoon died the following year. He was uninsured,[2] because while other directors had taken out policies for £500 or £1,000,[3] Scottish Widows had refused Wotherspoon's application on medical grounds.

He was not the only person to work unpaid in an effort to get the company off the ground. David Wardlaw, one of the initiators, anticipated that the board might want to pay him and forestalled them:

It is not my intention to make any claim of remuneration for any services that I have performed . . . Having been the first inventor of the scheme and, viewing it as a plan that will ensure great public advantage to the country, I am sufficiently repaid by the prosperity which it has already had, and with the prospect of increasing success which the circumstances of the Society now hold out. I beg, therefore, that you will record an entire discharge on my part for all the trouble which I have had in the preliminary part of the institution.

But while I thus disclaim any pecuniary recompense on my own account, I beg leave to add that the services of Messrs. Cockburn and Wotherspoon, which were of a more laborious and professional nature, deserve an ample recompense, and I have no doubt that their claims will therefore meet with all due consideration.[4]

Patrick Cockburn had been one of the promoters of the new firm and became its first actuary and auditor, but by 1820 when Wardlaw wrote his letter to the board, Wotherspoon was already dead. The directors allowed his family £250, a half or a quarter of what they might have received had he been insured, plus £50 in lieu of rent on the room in his home which had been used as an office.[5]

Since its lead in the creation of the Church of Scotland's widows' fund 60 years earlier, Edinburgh had neglected life assurance. In London, Equitable Life ('the Society for Equitable Assurances on Lives and Survivorships') established in 1762, had been followed by other companies, mostly proprietary, that is with shareholders rather than owned by the policyholders. By the beginning of the nineteenth century several of these London firms had offices in Edinburgh and were aggressively striving for business. It was the lack of a home-grown competitor that spurred a group of merchants, lawyers and others meeting in the Exchange coffee house in the High Street in March 1812 to consider setting up a life assurance company. A draft prospectus had been prepared by two lawyers, and a teacher of mathematics had prepared an annuity table.[6]

The meeting appointed a committee, including Wotherspoon, to obtain a legal opinion from the solicitor general on the prospectus and from John Playfair, professor of mathematics at Edinburgh University, on the suitability of the tables.[7] A couple of weeks later, the prospectus was ready and an impressive list of patrons had been recruited, including the Duke of Buccleuch, the Duke of Argyll, Viscount Melville and Lord Primrose. The extraordinary (honorary) directors included the industrialist and philanthropist Robert Owen.[8]

The decision to operate as a mutual company posed several problems. Since there were no shares, the company needed to sell policies to raise cash. But in order to sell policies it needed to set up an organisation and start a marketing campaign. Five thousand copies of the prospectus had been printed and circulated to towns and cities throughout Scotland, but they had not yet been paid for. Wotherspoon proposed to the committee – by now meeting in his house – that they write to the patrons and extraordinary directors asking for loans, which would be repaid from the first policies sold.[9] The response was not encouraging. Not for the first time the 'great and good' were prepared to lend their names to new ventures, but reluctant to open their wallets. After a few months, the committee wrote again to the Duke of Buccleuch, the biggest name on the list: 'We have sufficient encouragement to suspect that the scheme will go on and prosper, provided means can be found to defray the preparatory expenses, but if these cannot be raised, we must, however reluctantly, drop the further prosecution of it. In almost any other case I should have hesitated to send your Grace a *second* application.'[10]

The renewed appeal met with no more success than the first. Only £248 17s was subscribed – less than half of that asked for and less than had already been spent. Nevertheless, the committee decided to press on. A delegation went to London to ask for help from Morgan at Equitable Life and in July 1814, a meeting of the extraordinary court of directors – opened with a prayer from the Reverend Dr Johnston – resolved that the society was now formed. The prospectus declared that 'the association shall comprehend All Ranks' and added that 'Unmarried men might nominate at their admission sisters or other females, who shall be considered on the same footing as wives.' But there were restrictions: 'No person to be admitted a member who is above sixty years of age, or whose wife is more than twenty years younger than himself.' And 'The widows of persons committing suicide, falling by the hand of justice, or dying on the seas (except in His Majesty's packets passing between Great Britain and Ireland) shall only be entitled to annuities corresponding to the value of the interest of their husbands at the time of their deaths.'

It sold its first policies two months later. David Wardlaw, one of the founding directors, took the first policy, insuring his life for £1,000, and became the first member of the society. His fellow founder Patrick Cockburn insured his life for £500 – both men had to produce certificates of health,[11] a stipulation that excluded Wotherspoon. By the end of the year the society had 27 members and had insured their lives for £18,800, but all it had were the initial premiums paid. An unexpected death of one of the early policy-holders, resulting in a big pay out, would have severely embarrassed the fledgling business. The directors had assumed that the sale of annuities – a guaranteed annual income in exchange for an immediate lump sum payment – would be their main business. The company was named the Scottish Widows Fund and Life Assurance Society because it saw its primary purpose as providing pensions for the widows of its members. Insuring members' lives came second. If that had worked out in practice the company would have built up capital early in its life and have its liabilities – paying out the annuities – deferred. In fact by the end of the first three months only one annuity contract had been sold, the rest were life insurances, with small annual premiums. Funds were going to build slowly and the risk was substantial.[12]

By the end of 1815 Scottish Widows had an insured risk of £100,000 and was receiving little more than £1,000 in annual premiums. It was keeping its costs low and running largely on the goodwill of its directors, who guaranteed the rent when the company moved out of Wotherspoon's office and took its own premises. Although it was careful to insure only 'good lives' – making painstaking checks on the age and medical history of applicants – it was acutely vulnerable to a spate of unexpected deaths. But fortune stayed with it. When the first claim of £500 against a policy came in November of that year, the company was able to survive[13] and over the next few years its income expanded faster than the claims against it, but growth was initially slow. By 1820 it had insured fewer than 200 lives and had annual income of only £3,300, but the parsimonious way in which its directors, particularly Patrick Cockburn, squashed any proposal for unnecessary expenditure meant that it had accumulated a fund of nearly £10,000.[14] By 1821 it was able to afford £945 to buy a corner flat on South St David's Street.[15]

A spur to the sale of policies was the stipulation in its articles of association that there would be periodic quantification of the assets and liabilities of the business and that any surplus would be shared with members. By 1825 when the society conducted its first investigation assets had zoomed to £230,000, while liabilities were £210,000. From the surplus, the directors declared a bonus of £12,000 to be distributed to policyholder members.

The success of Scottish Widows prompted others to enter the market. North British Insurance, although it was suffering from heavy losses on its fire business, started a life business in 1823. The following year it doubled its capital to £1 million, raising £18,000 in new money.[16] The business went well, so that by 1830, on the accession of William IV as king, annual life premiums at £24,000 were three times the income from fire insurance. The life business was producing profits that more than offset the losses the company faced on its fire business, enabling it to pay a dividend for the first time in four years and add £7,000 to its reserves.[17] From its launch in 1824 the Scottish Union insured lives alongside fire risks. The first annual accounts showed impressive business, with life premiums of £10,000, against costs of £1,600. There were no claims.[18] The Edinburgh Life Assurance Company began in 1824, insuring the lives of lawyers, accountants and bankers. It counted Sir Walter Scott among its extraordinary directors – 'a graceful and useless appendage' as he described himself. At the annual partners' meeting of 1825 he was lined up by the board as 'light artillery' to oppose a motion from the floor: 'But my eloquence was not required, no-one renewing the motion under question: so off I came, my ears still ringing with the sounds of thousands and tens of thousands, and my eyes dazzled with the golden glean offered by so many capitalists.'[19]

He painted an interesting picture of the employees and customers of the company who attended the annual meeting: 'There were there moneyers and great oneyers, men of metal — discounters and counters — sharp, grave, prudential faces — eyes weak with ciphering by lamp-light — men who say to gold, *Be thou paper*, and to paper, *Be thou turned into fine gold*. Many a bustling, sharp-faced, keen-eyed writer* too — some perhaps speculating with their clients' property.'[20]

Other companies followed. The Insurance Company of Scotland, which had been started by the Commercial Bank in 1821 to cover fire risks, launched its life insurance business – the Life Insurance Company of Scotland – in 1825. Unlike the North British, it decided to form a

---

* Writers to the Signet – solicitors.

separate company to raise additional capital. Initially both companies shared an office and manager, although they had separate boards and shareholdings. Not all the partners in the fire company were convinced that a life assurer could work, so there was tension between the two companies from the start.[21]

One major choice any new life business had to make was which mortality tables to use to calculate the level of premiums. The Life Insurance Company employed William Wallace, a colleague of Playfair and also a professor of mathematics at Edinburgh University, to review the practice of other firms. He recommended following the Scottish Widows' policy of using the Northampton tables, which had been drawn up for Equitable Life by its then actuary Richard Price in 1783. The accuracy of the tables was already under attack, because they gave mortality statistics for the whole population, rather than the better-off classes who were likely to buy insurance policies and were likely to have a lower probability of an early death. But they were generally thought to favour the life company rather than the person buying the policy, so Wallace declared them 'perfectly safe', subject to a few modifications.[22] The new company intended to take a cautious approach to accepting business and appointed a physician and two surgeons to assess any medical risks. Unlike the Widows, it would be a proprietary company and to encourage purchase of the shares set the price of the first call at £1.

Its first few policies set the tone. Alexander Gibbon, an advocate of Aberdeen, took a £40 policy on the 'whole life without profits' of Mrs Sophia Urquhart or Munro, 44, widow of Captain Charles Munro. The directors wanted further information: 'Mrs Munro having been born in Calcutta, the manager was directed to ascertain whether she was of Indian descent and in what degree.' A week later it was reported that Mrs Munro's mother and both her parents were natives of St Helena, which had been under the control of the East India Company for a century and was the place of exile of Napoleon from 1815 until his death in 1821. The board agreed to take the insurance at the rate advertised in the tables.[23] An application for a £1,000 policy on the life of Mrs Janet Murray or Dow, 48, Springhouse, Stirling, was more problematic: 'The agent having stated that Mrs Dow was of a lusty habit, the directors considered it proper that information should be obtained more particularly in regard to this, whether she was very corpulent and if she had acquired a full habit of body suddenly. It was also thought desirable to ascertain from her medical attendant whether she had passed a period generally considered virtual in regard to the female condition.'

Inquiries must have satisfied the board and Mrs Dow was accepted. She died 13 years later, prompting a dispute over claims between the Perth Bank, to whom she had assigned the policy, and her husband whom she had married after the policy had been taken out.[24]

At the first annual general meeting of the partners, chairman William Henderson blamed unfavourable commercial conditions for low take-up of shares and policies issued. Under the partnership agreement, every partner was required to insure his own life with the company and to procure friends with 'good lives' to also insure themselves.[25] The company had the ability to fine those shareholders who did not also take out a policy, but most decided they would rather pay the fine. A year later Professor Wallace told the meeting that new business would have increased by two-thirds had partners adhered to the rule.[26]

The Life Insurance Company developed a specialism in insuring aris-tocrats and landowners[27] but this often meant laying off some of the risk with other offices. In 1828 the board received a letter from the private bankers Sir William Forbes & Co. enclosing a death certificate for the Earl of Mar and a claim on his insurance policies to meet his outstanding debt with the bank. Shortly afterwards came a note from the West of Scotland Life Insurance Company, one of the joint insurers, saying that the Earl had been insane.[28] Subsequent investigation disclosed that he had been a drug addict, taking up to three ounces of laudanum (opium) a day.[29] A joint committee with the other insurers decided to contest the claim on the grounds that the earl's habit had not been disclosed at the time he took out the policies, and the bank sued. The case dragged on for four years, made more complicated by the death of one witness and the madness of another (the earl's son). Eventually Forbes accepted the insurers' offer of an out of court settlement.[30]

Relations between the fire and life companies became strained after the death of their joint secretary. An investigation by the life company board showed that the accounts were in a mess. It wanted an immediate replacement secretary to be appointed, but the fire company, which was struggling to meet its fire losses and was trying to keep costs down, would not agree.[31] The board of the fire company had already expressed its 'disappointment' with the progress of the life business, and now called for a full account of all rent, salaries and expenses owed and paid by the life office.[32] A dispute over what was owed and what had been paid soured the atmosphere and confirmed the life company board in its decision to separate. It moved out of the shared offices and found itself a new home in North Bridge Street. In 1832, to emphasise the break, it changed its name to the Standard Life Assurance Company.[33]

A problem all life companies shared was that premium income had to be invested profitably, but the options were limited. Despite an upsurge in the number of joint stock companies in the first quarter of the nineteenth century, there was not yet a developed public equity market. Shares in the big London institutions such as the Bank of England or the East India Company were freely traded, but shares in the Scottish public banks were tightly held and some of the newer ventures being launched were highly speculative. Government stocks offered attractive rates and the Insurance Company of Scotland was already investing in Russian, Prussian, Argentinian and Columbian government securities as well as British funds,[34] but the life company appears to have made only domestic investments.

Mainly the life companies lent money on heritable bonds secured against property, and an assessment by Standard Life showed that it was achieving double the return on lending than could be had from investing in government securities.[35] In this respect they were in competition with the banks, but with one crucial difference: they did not issue their own banknotes. This was both a strength and a weakness. By not issuing notes they could not create credit and therefore were limited in expanding their lending beyond the amount collected in premiums, but they were also not tied geographically. Scottish banknotes were not generally accepted south of the border, whereas the life companies had no such restrictions and were writing policies and making loans in England and Ireland very early in their lives.

Another profitable investment opportunity was exploiting the British government's reliance on inaccurate pricing in the annuities it sold. This scandal had been going on for over a century, since Sir Edmund Halley had shown that the government was losing money on its annuities. There had been questions in the House of Commons, but the practice continued, possibly because the buyers of these under-priced annuities were politicians and civil servants. John Finlaison, a Scottish self-taught mathematician, had tried to expose the policy while he was actuary at the Treasury, but it took years before the practice was discontinued. In 1833 Standard Life spent £6,000 offsetting the cost of annuities it had sold by buying annuities on the same lives from the government.[36] The following year, having been told by its London broker that the government intended to stop the practice, it bought more annuities worth £7,000.[37] In order to buy an annuity on the life of a named individual, the purchaser did not need that person's consent or even knowledge, although Standard Life seems to have informed its policyholders since the board was told that some had decided to invest alongside the company.

The comfortable profits that the life companies were making inevitably drew competitors into the market; the Caledonian Insurance Company belatedly followed its competitors by starting a life business in 1833 and the Life Association of Scotland began in 1838. William Braidwood, an ironmonger who had been one of the prime movers in the establishment of the Caledonian, was also one of the promoters of a new mutual life assurer, Scottish Equitable, although he died before its launch in March 1831. His son, also William, became the first manager, working, as was the pattern for mutuals, unpaid. The new firm worked from the offices of the Sea Insurance Company of Scotland in Hunter Square in the Old Town, which also provided clerical support. The business got off to a reasonable start, with an insured risk of £67,000 and premium income of £2,033 in its first year, but tragically William Braidwood was not there to see it. He had lost a lot of money in other parts of his business, became depressed and committed suicide. He was insured with the new company, but taking his own life nullified the policy.[38] Growth continued so that by 1840 the company had funds of £119,000 and its first investigation the following year showed a surplus of assets over liabilities of £60,000.

Among the more unusual entrepreneurs was the unlikely combination of William Fraser, a master printer, and James Cleghorn, a Berwickshire farmer, turned magazine editor, turned actuary. Fraser had made a study of friendly societies and was convinced that the three commonly used mortality tables, the Northampton, another based on statistics from Carlisle and those produced by Finlaison, the government actuary, all favoured the insurance companies against the policyholders. He calculated that there was a difference of eight years in the life expectancy of a 25-year-old man between the Northampton and the Finlaison tables, but that the real expectation was greater still.[39] He also believed that the existing mutual offices did not share enough of the profit with their policyholders and that the method of distributing the gains was unfair.

With Cleghorn, who had acted as actuary to the widows' fund of the Faculty of Advocates and Writers to the Signet, they launched the

Scottish Provident Institution in 1837. Like Wotherspoon before him, he worked through ill health to get the society started, lent the business his own money and died uninsured. The board acknowledged his contribution, erecting an obelisk to him in Warriston cemetery, Edinburgh (even though he was buried elsewhere), and voting his dependants £320.[40]

While most of the new Scottish life assurance companies were based in Edinburgh, the West of Scotland Life Insurance Company, founded in 1826, was headquartered in Glasgow. It later changed its name to Scottish Amicable.

17

The ruin of Walter Scott
(and how he got out of it)

IN 1825 SIR Walter Scott was at the height of his powers. His day job, as a principal clerk to the court of session, paid well (£1,000 a year or more) and left him considerable time to write, since the court only sat for 4–6 hours a day and only for six months of the year. He was also a part-time sheriff at Selkirk, which paid another £300 a year. He had won fame in Britain and abroad as a poet, novelist, critic and editor. By 1825 he had published 11 epic poems, including the very successful *Lay of the Last Minstrel*, and *Lady of the Lake*. The *Waverley* series of historical novels, although published anonymously, were huge commercial successes, earning large advances and copyright fees. His productivity was impressive: in the ten years up to 1824 he published 19 novels, including some of the most famous – *Rob Roy, Ivanhoe* and the *Bride of Lammermoor*.

His discovery of the Scottish crown jewels in a locked chest in the bowels of Edinburgh Castle had been rewarded with a baronetcy. He was elected president of the Royal Society of Edinburgh in 1820 and two years later orchestrated the extravagant tartan-fest for the visit of King George IV. He was a man of property, with an elegant bow-fronted New Town house at 39 North Castle Street, which he had built for himself, his wife Charlotte and their four children. He also had a country estate in the Scottish borders on which he built Abbotsford, a grand house in the Scots baronial style. He was in demand as a businessman – chairman of the Edinburgh Oil Gas Company, Governor of the Scottish Union Insurance Company and an extraordinary director of the Edinburgh Life Assurance Company. In 1824 he was one of the promoters of the Wool Stapling Company, which intended not only to 'staple' wool, but also to make loans to sheep farmers.[1]

In January 1826 he learned that he was financially ruined.[2]

Supporters of Scott – most notably his son-in-law John Gibson Lockhart, who wrote a ten-volume memoir of his father-in-law – have tried to portray Scott as a victim, deceived by his agent, his publisher and his printer, or as one of the many innocent casualties of the financial crash of 1825–6.[3] But he was not blameless; for many years he had been living beyond his means, borrowing or forcing others to borrow to fund the advances on his books. He needed a constant flow of money to add to his country estate and he paid more than the market value to secure land next to Abbotsford – paying £4,200 for a farm in 1811. The house itself was heavily ornamented and very expensive, with Scott expanding and elaborating the plans as his social standing increased. To support his position in society, which was loftier than normal for a court clerk, he entertained generously in Edinburgh and the borders. He spent money on his children, buying his son Walter a commission in the Hussars for £3,500,[4] and paying his lavish expenses, as he described in a letter: 'I have yours with the news of Walter's rattle-traps, which are abominably extravagant. But there is no help for it but submission. The things seem all such as cannot well be wanted. How the devil they mount them to such a price, the tailors best know. They say it takes *nine* tailors to make a man – apparently, one is sufficient to ruin him.'[5]

And he was generous to his friends. When the actor Daniel Terry took the lease on the Adelphi Theatre, London, Scott stood surety for a loan of £1,250 (which he later lost).

With expenses well above what he could earn from the law, Scott tried to maximise the income he received from his writing, but in a way that hid what he was doing. Socially and professionally that would not have looked good. In 1809 he secretly became a partner in a publishing venture fronted by John Ballantyne, brother of his printer, James Ballantyne. The firm was conceived as a way of shutting Archibald Constable, his Edinburgh publisher, out of the revenues that came from his books so that he could have more of them for himself. Scott had a half share, with the two Ballantynes a quarter each. Initially it went well, with the publication of *Lady of the Lake* producing big profits.

If he had stuck to publishing his own works the business might have succeeded, but Scott made a string of poor editorial decisions that resulted in heavy losses and warehouses full of unsold books. These included the poetry and correspondence of Anna Seward, 'the Swan of Lichfield', who had died in 1807 naming Scott as her literary executor with instructions to bring out her collected works – some of which Scott himself described as 'absolutely execrable'.[6] They were a financial disaster. In 1813 the company was hopelessly in debt, mostly to James Ballantyne, Scott's printer. To preserve his reputation Scott had to quietly wind-up the business without disclosing his own half share in it and go back to Constable as his publisher.[7]

He also kept secret the fact that he was the controlling partner in James Ballantyne's printing business – and used his influence to get other contracts for the company without disclosing his interest. Like most companies at the time, Constable and the Ballantyne businesses were unlimited partnerships.

Scott was not naive and had some financial sophistication: he had been trained in double entry bookkeeping at the Edinburgh Royal High School and was a meticulous keeper of his own accounts and those of the Speculative Society, where he was treasurer. As a lawyer he would have been familiar with protested bills and promissory notes. With James Ballantyne, his partner in the printing business, he regularly reviewed the company's cashflow, borrowing and net worth.[8] He knew what he was doing. He borrowed heavily, from his brother to part-finance Abbotsford and, with the Duke of Buccleuch as guarantor, taking an overdraft of £4,000 to pay off the debts of John Ballantyne, the failed publishing company.

Scott was a formidable adversary when bargaining for the sale of his copyrights. In 1818 he negotiated £12,000 for the republication rights to 16 of his novels and poems which had already been published and which he described as 'eild kye' (cows barren from age).[9] He pioneered the 'advance' on works yet to be written and routinely spent the money before writing a word. Sometimes he pressed Constable for cash; on other occasions he accepted bills (effectively IOUs) which he could use as security to borrow from banks. He was able to command huge sums: in 1821 he received 5,000 guineas as an advance on the republication of four books on which he had already made £10,000. A short time later he exchanged contracts for four 'works of fiction': 'not one of them otherwise described in the deeds of agreement—to be produced in unbroken succession, each of them to fill at least three volumes, but with proper saving clauses as to increase of copy-money, in case any of them should run to four. And within two years all this anticipation had been wiped off by *Peveril of the Peak, Quentin Durward, St. Ronan's Well,* and *Redgauntlet.*'[10]

★ ★ ★

The crisis that triggered Scott's downfall had its roots in the victory over Napoleon in 1815. Public borrowing had soared during the war years, forcing up yields on public debt issues and thus general interest rates. Scottish banks invested their spare capital in government securities, buying and selling with fluctuations in the market and making large profits, which they distributed to their shareholders in dividends and special bonuses. When the war ended the government acted to bring down the national debt by repurchasing gilts,* interest rates fell and banks found themselves with an embarrassment of deposits which they could not invest profitably. Scottish banks, which unlike their English counterparts paid interest on deposits, reduced their rates and put limits on the amount any individual could hold with them.[11] Investors, encouraged by a succession of good harvests that reduced food prices and the need to import grain, looked for other ways to get a higher return on their money.

Some invested in debt being issued by the newly independent South American states. Bonds from Argentina, Colombia, Peru, Chile and others offering interest rates as high as 6 per cent – twice the yield on British government securities – were floated in London. Others turned to the stock market. There was a boom in companies formed to exploit new technologies like gas lighting, railways and steamship services. Some of the new concerns – such as the banks and insurance companies described in the previous chapters – were genuine additions to the economy, but such was the clamour to invest in new businesses that ventures began to appear which had no obvious merit. The Thistle Insurance Company, which advertised itself in the *Edinburgh Weekly Journal* in January 1825, appeared to have no appeal other than to enable those who had successfully applied for shares to sell at a profit to others who had failed to get any. Demand for insurance stocks was so great that the share price of the North British and the Hercules insurance companies had doubled between 1809 and 1824,[12] this in an age where share prices often remained constant for years.

Edinburgh businessman Anthony Romney, writing to his brother Richard, was sceptical about most of the new ventures: 'If some only had been proposed, which appear to be the most practical schemes, I should not have been so much afraid. But the ushering upon our little district of the world such a host of them at once and several with a view to the same

* Government securities: see Chapter 13.

objects, and then some so very visionary and chimerical, I confess makes me jealous of the whole, and almost satisfies me that they are the illegitimate offspring of the wanton demon of speculation and not the true wedlock children of an increased national capital and an augmented commercial activity.'[13]

Speculation was helped by the abolition of the Bubble Act of 1720, which had curbed stock jobbing. Henry Cockburn was characteristically graphic in his description of the sudden boom: 'The newspapers of the day contain little else than advertisements and recommendations of joint-stock associations, in not one out of five hundred of which there was either plausibility or honesty. Everything unattainable, or useless if attained, was to be made easy and valuable, provided people would only take shares; which the ignorant, the excited, and the deceived by gambling directors or by paid secretaries and agents took – to no other effect than enabling fraudulent speculators to make a gain in the market by crazy prices paid by fools for what did not exist.'[14]

The mania for shares was most marked in London, but it spread across the country. In Scotland Edinburgh, still the wealthiest city, despite being overtaken by Glasgow in population, was the main speculative centre.[15] Belatedly, some years behind London and the main provincial cities of England, Scotland began to see the emergence of stockbrokers as independent specialists, rather than being lawyers or accountants who facilitated the sale and purchase of shares as a sideline to their main business. John Robertson, a wine merchant, became a full-time stockbroker in Edinburgh, while Wardlaw and Cunninghame turned from bookselling to stockbroking in Glasgow.[16] Anthony Romney was not impressed: 'There darted forth simultaneously, as if from some hidden cavern, a race of men who proposed to act the part of golf-bearers, or bottle holders in this new game that was about to be played, under the designation of Stockbrokers.'[17]

Inevitably the eagerness of investors to subscribe for new share issues attracted fraudsters. The most notorious was Gregor MacGregor, a Scottish solider who had fought with the British army in the Peninsular War and claimed to have been a general in Simon Bolivar's army in the Venezuelan revolt against Spanish rule. In 1821 he came to Britain from Central America to raise investment and recruit settlers for the state of 'Poyais', of which he alleged he was 'Cazique', or ruler. His prospectus, which ran to 355 pages, described a land with a healthy climate, fertile soil, rivers either teeming with fish or containing 'globules of pure gold' and an indigenous population which was very pro-British. The capital was a city by the sea of 20,000 people, which housed the parliament, courts and the bank.

MacGregor floated a £200,000 bond on the London Stock Exchange and mounted an aggressive sales campaign from offices in London, Edinburgh and Glasgow. The bond was divided into £100 lots and promised interest of 5 per cent to be paid at six monthly intervals at the bank of Sir John Perring & Co., London. One of the certificates, now owned by Russell Napier (see illustrations) has two of the coupons missing, suggesting that interest was paid for a while. The bond was supposedly secured on an import duty on goods into Poyais, but since Poyais did not exist, MacGregor must have paid the initial interest from the sales of bonds. It was a classic Ponzi scheme 60 years before the birth of Charles Ponzi.

As settlers to his new colony, he targeted Scots and, in a tragic echo of the Darien disaster, a ship with 70 emigrants set sail from London in 1822 and another from Leith with 200 men, women and children on board in January 1823. MacGregor saw both ships off and exchanged the settlers' sterling for 'Poyais dollars', which he had had printed by Bank of Scotland's official printer. The settlers discovered the fraud when they landed on the undeveloped Mosquito Coast and found a land very different from the one they had been led to expect. Disease spread quickly and 180 of them died. MacGregor left Britain before the surviving settlers returned and tried another 'Poyais' fraud in Paris. He and accomplices were arrested and tried, but, incredibly, he was acquitted and came back to Britain to attempt to float yet another 'Poyais' bond, underwritten by another London bank. He continued to try variants of the same trick for 15 years, although with limited success. In 1838 his wife died in Edinburgh and MacGregor returned to South America.[18]

The boom was fuelled by easy credit. From having an embarrassment of deposits as recently as 1824, a year later the Scottish banks had increased their lending by so much that they again had to raise interest rates to try to attract new funds. Royal Bank boosted its lending by £1 million, while its deposits fell by £600,000 – it was advancing 50 per cent more than it held in deposits.[19] Most new lending for all the five major Edinburgh banks was on discounted or even re-discounted bills, rather than being secured on property or other assets, which greatly inflated the money supply.[20] While many trade bills were genuine, being lent against an expected receivable, such as payment for a shipment or delivery in say 60 or 90 days, others were what Adam Smith had described 50 years earlier as 'fictitious' – there were no physical goods or expected payments, the bills were invented for the purpose of raising credit. So-called 'accommodation bills' involved two parties each issuing bills to each other for the same amount repayable on the same date. No cash changed hands but, provided the bills were issued by respectable people or companies, one or both parties could use them as security to raise money from a bank or moneylender.

The trigger for the crash was a poor harvest in 1825, which necessitated imports of grain, mostly paid for in gold. The Bank of England, fearing a balance of payments deficit, contracted its lending, refusing to discount bills and restricting its note issue.[21] The Bank's court of directors had been accused of failing to act to restrain the boom. Now they were accused of acting too aggressively. Speculators who had bought shares using borrowed money attempted to realise their profits so they could repay their borrowing. This sparked a fall in prices and panic selling, which quickly developed into a downward spiral. Investors got back little or nothing, leaving those who had gambled on credit unable to repay. Banks which had overextended their balance sheets found themselves exposed. Although the big public banks north and south of the border were strong enough to absorb the bad debts, smaller country banks were not. Sixty English provincial banks failed, but in Scotland, the damage was less severe. Three banks – Falkirk, Fife and Stirling – failed in 1826, with three more going before the end of the decade.[22]

The subtleties of the causes of the crisis did not concern Sir Walter Scott. He resorted to anti-Semitism for a simpler explanation: 'It is hard that the vagabond stock-jobbing Jews should, for their own purposes, make such a shake of credit as now exists in London, and menace the credit of men trading on sure funds like H and R. It is just like a set of pickpockets who raise a mob in which honest folks are knocked down and plundered that they may pillage safely in the midst of the confusion they have excited.'[23]

He was wrong on both counts. Jews did not provoke the credit squeeze – in fact Rothschild, the leading Jewish banker in London, was instrumental in shoring up the Bank of England's gold reserves in order to free up credit.[24] And 'H and R' – Hurst, Robinson & Company, Scott's London agents – were not 'trading on sure funds'. Joseph Robinson had bought £40,000 worth of hops, intending to corner the market and sell at a profit, a speculation far outside the firm's normal business as publishers and literary agents.[25] To fund the purchase he had borrowed £30,000. When the crisis came and commodity prices plunged, he had to sell at a loss and could not meet the firm's obligations.

Now an interlocking chain of bills brought down not only Hurst, Robinson, but Archibald Constable, Scott's publisher, James Ballantyne & Company, his printer, and ultimately Scott himself. The three companies were all hopelessly over-trading and had guaranteed each other's bills which had been used as security to borrow from banks. Scott was liable in several ways. He had personal debts, he had guaranteed some of the debts of Constable so it could continue to pay him large advances and, as the controlling partner in the Ballantyne printing firm, he was 'jointly and severally' responsible for its debts and for the guarantees the firm had given to Constable and Hurst, Robinson. His total exposure was £121,000 – far more than his assets.[26] The three firms limped along for a few weeks, shuffling bills and raising small sums of money where they could. Archibald Constable mortgaged his home at Polton, near Edinburgh, and Scott raised a £10,000 mortgage on Abbotsford, although £3,000 of this went to pay off a previous mortgage. He gave the remaining £7,000 to Constable in the forlorn hope that it would be enough to save the firm. By Christmas 1825 he had persuaded himself that they could escape bankruptcy, but in January 1826 a bill for £1,000 due to Constable from Hurst, Robinson was returned unpaid. Constable in turn owed the money to Bank of Scotland and could not pay.

Robert Cadell, Archibald Constable's son-in-law and partner in the publishing business, wrote to his father-in-law to tell him that the firm had run out of credit with the leading Edinburgh banks: 'We are dished with Ramsays, Bank of Scotland, British Linen Co., and Sir William Forbes & Co. I leave you therefore to judge what my feelings are . . . now the tables are turned. Robinson's bills are back, which to us is death and I can see it in no other light. Alas! Alas! such is the end of all our hopes and expectations. I have struggled hard. I have fought as for my life. Last Thursday I did not expect this, but now I see no escape.'[27]

Bank of Scotland immediately informed its branches and the head offices of the other banks of the default and the house of cards collapsed.[28] The news of Scott's ruin hit Edinburgh like a thunderbolt, wrote Henry Cockburn:

Ballantyne and Constable were merchants, and their fall, had it reached no further, might have been lamented merely as the casualty of commerce. But Sir Walter! The idea that his practical sense had so far left him as to have permitted him to dabble in trade, had never crossed our imagination. How humbled we felt when we saw him – the pride of us all, dashed from his lofty and honourable station, and all the fruits of his well-worked talents gone. He had not then even a political enemy. There was not one of those whom his thoughtlessness had so sorely provoked, who would not have given every spare farthing he possessed to retrieve Sir Walter.[29]

The matter was sensitive for Bank of Scotland, partly because of its past association with Scott – it had contributed to Scott's pageant for William IV by staging a firework display and illuminating its head office on The Mound – but also because Robert Cadell was the brother of William Cadell, newly appointed as the bank's treasurer and general manager. William had allowed Robert to clear out his deposit account the day before the collapse.[30] Robert Cadell, Archibald Constable and James Ballantyne, Scott's junior partner in the printing company, were bankrupted, their homes and possessions sold at knock-down prices, but Scott was determined to avoid insolvency. There were plenty of people (including the Duke of Buccleuch) who were prepared to give 'every spare farthing' to pay Scott's debts, but his pride would not allow him to accept their generosity. Cockburn saw him in court: 'There was no affectation . . . no look of indifference or defiance; but the manly and modest air of a gentleman conscious of some folly, but of perfect rectitude, and of most heroic and honourable resolutions.'[31]

This was a desperate time for Scott. As well as the shame of his financial situation, which he felt acutely, his wife Charlotte was in declining health. She died in May 1826, a few months after he had learned of his ruin.

Scott turned to his school and university friend Sir William Forbes, son of the father of the same name and now the senior partner in the eponymous private bank. Forbes persuaded Bank of Scotland and other creditors that they would get little by forcing Scott into bankruptcy (Abbotsford had been put in trust for his son) and to accept a trust arrangement, with Scott pledging all his earnings from writing to pay off the debt.[32] All creditors except one accepted the deal, but insisted that Scott insure his life for £20,000 – a sum so large that it had to be syndicated to several companies. Scott's Edinburgh house at 39 North Castle Street was sold and he had to move into rented rooms to serve as his base while doing legal work, but he was allowed to keep his life-rent on Abbotsford, where he did most of his writing.

The recalcitrant creditor was a firm of London gold and silver refiners called William Abud & Sons, which was owed £1,500 for ingots they had supplied to Joseph Robinson. Now they insisted that either Scott be bankrupted, or they be paid in full. They threatened legal action to overturn the trust arrangement. Again, Scott sank to anti-Semitism: 'They are Jews. I suppose the devil baits for Jews with a pork griskin.'[33] Robert Gibson, Scott's solicitor, failed to persuade them to take a third of the amount[34] and Scott was prepared to fight them in court alleging a breach of the usury law, but Sir William Forbes quietly paid Abud off, adding the debt to that already owed to his own bank.[35] Scott was stoical about his fate:

> I feel neither dishonoured nor broken down by the bad – now really bad news I have received . . . But I find my eyes moistening, and that will not do. I will not yield without a fight for it. It is odd, when I set myself to work *doggedly*, as Dr. Johnson would say, I am exactly the same man that I ever was, neither low-spirited nor *distrait*. In prosperous times I have sometimes felt my fancy and powers of language flag, but adversity is to me at least a tonic and bracer; the fountain is awakened from its inmost recesses, as if the spirit of affliction had troubled it in his passage.[36]

The trust arrangement worked. Scott produced nine further books, fiction and non-fiction. He could still command large sums for his novels, securing over £8,000 for *Woodstock* – 'a matchless sale for less than three months' work' – and £18,000 for his two-volume life of Napoleon.[37] By the time of his death in 1832 the debt was reduced to less than half. It was finally paid off in 1847 by the sale of Scott's remaining copyrights.[38] Although they had to wait for their money, Scott's creditors did much better than those of either Constable or Hurst, Robinson. The total debts of Archibald Constable & Co. were £256,000, but the creditors received little over 10 per cent of what they were owed. Hurst, Robinson's creditors, who were owed £300,000, fared even worse, receiving a little over 5 per cent.[39]

★ ★ ★

While Scott toiled, 'working with his right hand', as he put it, to pay off his creditors, the Scottish banks were in turmoil and the banking system itself was being questioned. The crisis had left the main public banks

with huge bad debts, the full extent of which they hid from their proprietors and the wider public for fear of damaging their reputations for
prudence and stability. In 1828 Royal Bank directors were told that bad
debts totalled £105,000 in Edinburgh and £107,000 in Glasgow, plus
smaller losses elsewhere. An investigation by the directors of Bank of
Scotland the following year showed bad debts of £193,000 with a list of
unpaid discounted bills, some going back seven years. There was strong
criticism of the management of William Cadell, who was forced to resign
in 1832.[40] Other banks fared less badly, with British Linen coming
through the crisis relatively unscathed. To improve their profitability the
banks, acting as a cartel, increased their lending rate to the legal maximum of 5 per cent and to strengthen their balance sheets they nudged
up the deposit rate by 0.5 per cent and negotiated credits with the Bank
of England – £500,000 for Royal Bank and £200,000 for Bank of
Scotland.[41]

Meanwhile, the crisis had provoked a heated discussion in parliament
about its causes. There was a strong feeling, although without much
evidence, that the unfettered issuing of banknotes, particularly low
denomination notes of under £5, had led to the stock-buying mania by
inflating the money supply far beyond the capacity of the real economy
to use it productively. With no regulation requiring banks to keep a
specified level of reserves, there was nothing to stop unscrupulous or
inexperienced bankers from increasing their lending by issuing as many
notes as the market would take. In Scotland the two Edinburgh banks
policed the note issue through the note exchange, putting pressure on
any issuer they thought was in danger of expanding the money supply
too far or too fast. No such mechanism existed in England.

Robert Peel, home secretary, told the House of Commons that 'no less
than 800 country banks' in England were issuing £1 and £2 notes, which
'increased the tendency to speculation'.[42] He also pointed out the differences between the English and Scottish systems. South of the border the
Bank of England had maintained its dominance by obtaining political
and legal backing for the 'six-partner rule', which limited other banks to
six shareholders and therefore restricted their capital. No other bank was
able to afford a branch network or build up reserves against loss. The
result was a proliferation of small local banks and numerous failures
whenever there was a downturn in the economy.

Peel contrasted that with the Scottish system, where the six-partner
rule did not apply. Banks were much larger and better capitalised, some

with dozens of partners, others with hundreds or even thousands. Although only the three public banks, Bank of Scotland, Royal Bank and British Linen, had limited liability, other banks were able to raise enough capital to absorb shocks. Failures were much rarer and when they did occur, the losses were spread more widely, meaning that creditors were more likely to be paid in full. The role of discounted bills in the crash does not seem to have been considered by the government.

The issue was investigated by a House of Commons committee, with Peel himself chairing the first session. He wrote requesting details of the Scottish banks' note circulation and how it had changed over the previous decade, but despite his apparent support for the system north of the border, the banks refused him the information on the grounds of confidentiality.[43] Nevertheless, all the Scottish banks gave evidence, with Thomas Kinnear, an Edinburgh private banker and director of Bank of Scotland, making the point strongly that Scotland was different from England in more ways than just the banking system. As a poorer nation, with less access to gold and silver, it was more dependent on paper money which was an essential lubricant for economic development. The Scottish banks were united in their defence of the right to issue small notes, particularly £1 notes, and described the safeguards against over-circulation provided by the note exchange between banks and the fact that Scottish notes were 'protestable' – a bank could be held legally responsible if it failed to honour one of its own banknotes (see Chapter 10 above). The Scots felt they had won when the 1826 Act limiting the issue of notes under £5 applied only to England, but their euphoria was short-lived. Before the Act came into effect Lord Liverpool, the prime minister, announced his intention to introduce a similar measure for Scotland and Ireland.[44]

Aid for the Scottish cause came from an unexpected source. Sir Walter Scott, although still at the time negotiating with his creditors, mulled over entering the controversy. He wrote in his journal: 'I am horribly tempted to interfere in this business of altering the system of banks in Scotland; and yet I know that if I can attract any notice, I will offend my English friends without propitiating one man in Scotland. I will think of it till tomorrow. It is making myself of too much importance after all.'[45]

A night's sleep was enough to convince him and over the next two days he wrote the first of three polemic *Letters of Malachi Malagrowther* and sent it to the editor of the *Edinburgh Weekly Journal*, hiding behind a thin alias. Despite his well-publicised financial problems, Scott's name still carried weight in political circles and with the wider public. He was a staunch Tory and had many friends and admirers in the government and parliament. Three *Letters* appeared over the following weeks and were so successful that they were reprinted as pamphlets. Written in Scott's folksy, prolix style, the first letter was stridently nationalist in tone, describing unwarranted interference in the court and revenue-gathering systems of Scotland to bring them into line with England, in contravention of the clause in the Act of Union which guaranteed that legislation should be 'for the evident utility of the subjects within Scotland'. Only towards the end of the letter does he turn to banking, rehearsing all the arguments against the prohibition of small notes made by the banks themselves. He then turned the government's arguments against them:

> Have I argued my case too high in supposing that the present intended legislative enactment is as inapplicable to Scotland, as a pair of elaborate knee-buckles would be to the dress of a kilted Highlander? I think not.
>
> I understand Lord Liverpool and the Chancellor of the Exchequer distinctly to have admitted the fact, that no distress whatever had originated in Scotland from the present issuing of small notes of the Bankers established there, whether provincial in the strict sense, or sent abroad by branches of the larger establishments settled in the metropolis. No proof can be desired better than the admission of the adversary.
>
> Nevertheless, we have been positively informed by the news-papers that Ministers see no reason why any law adopted on this subject should not be imperative over all his Majesty's dominions, including Scotland *for uniformity's sake*. In my opinion, they might as well make a law that the Scotsman, for uniformity's sake, should not eat oatmeal, because it is found to give Englishmen the heart-burn. If an ordinance prohibiting the oat-cake, can be accompanied with a regulation capable of being enforced, that in future, for uniformity's sake, our moors and uplands shall henceforth bear the purest wheat, I for one have no objection to the regulation. But till Ben-Nevis be level with Norfolkshire, though the natural wants of the two nations may be the same, the extent of these wants, natural or commercial, and the mode of supplying them, must be widely different, let the rule of uniformity be as absolute as it will. The

nation which cannot raise wheat, must be allowed to eat oat-bread; the nation which is too poor to retain a circulating medium of the precious metals, must be permitted to supply its place with paper credit; otherwise, they must go without food, and without currency.[46]

As an aside, Scott also lavished praise on Scottish bankers, calling them good men 'manifesting, by the excellence of their character, the fairness of the means by which their riches were acquired'. This cannot have gone down badly with the men he was trying to convince not to bankrupt him. The first letter caused a sensation, galvanising Scottish public opinion behind the banks in their opposition to any new legislation restricting the note issue. Scott was delighted: 'Malachi prospers and excites much attention. The Banks have bespoke 500 copies. The country is taking the alarm; and I think the Ministers will not dare to press the measure. I should rejoice to see the old red lion ramp a little, and the thistle again claim its *nemo me impune.*[*] I do believe Scotsmen will show themselves unanimous, at least where their cash is concerned.'[47]

In a second *Letter* he called on Scottish MPs and Lords to refuse to vote on any issue, except to oppose the government – and for Irish representatives to join the campaign. The third letter highlighted the distress that would be caused during the transition from banknotes to coinage. Gold and silver would need to be purchased at a premium, and marginally profitable industries would suffer. A working system and prosperous economy would be jeopardised merely to test a theory. Scott was right about the reaction of ministers – they were furious with him – but he quoted Shakespeare to them:

I have served you ever since I was a child,
But better service have I never done you,
Than now to bid you '*Hold.*'

Scott was not the only writer to support the continued issue of small notes in Scotland. Thomas Joplin, an English banking theorist, had long criticised the banking system south of the border and compared it unfavourably with the Scottish system. It is possible Scott used some of Joplin's arguments.[48]

---

[*] A shortened form of the motto of Scotland and of the Order of the Thistle: '*Nemo me impune lacessit*', meaning 'No one attacks me with impunity'.

The campaign was successful and it is possible that Scott's intervention carried the day. The new regulations were delayed for six months, then for six years and then abandoned altogether. There were two banking Acts in 1826 and 1828, but neither mentioned the note issue. The Scottish £1 note was saved and the distinctive character of the Scottish banking system was recognised officially and in the public mind. The historian Richard Saville commented: 'It is from this decade that the old caricature of the disloyal Scot vanishes from the repertoire of the English satirist. The dominant Victorian image was of the hard working, God-fearing, intellectual Scot; the Kirk minister, the accountant, the banker, the lawyer.'[49]

As far as bankers were concerned, that prudent image was to last more than 170 years, before it was destroyed in 2008.

18

The bankruptcy of Edinburgh

ON 27 SEPTEMBER 1799 Thomas Smith rose in his place and delivered a broadside against his fellow Edinburgh town councillors, which was eventually to lead to his removal from the council as a troublemaker. In the pre-reform local authority, he had been selected four years previously by the lord provost, Sir James Stirling, who had arranged his nomination by the dean of guilds and election as 'Third Merchant Councillor' by the baillies.* He does not seem to have been particularly political, but felt it prudent to begin his speech with a pledge of loyalty to Henry Dundas, the Tory puppet-master who controlled the council. What most concerned him was the state of the council's finances. As a businessman he was well used to reading accounts and, as he watched the council approving substantial financial transactions, including large borrowings from banks, the issue of promissory notes or the sale of annuities, he wondered how the interest and the repayments were being met. What was the magnitude of the council's income and expenditure? What were its assets and liabilities?

> I inquired at some of the gentlemen then in office whether the city kept any books? They informed me they did not know. Finding that I was on delicate ground and should instantly become an object of suspicion if I were to push my inquiries farther, as well as my short standing on the council, I resolved to be quiet. I put the same question, however, to different gentlemen then *out* of the council, some of whom had served the office of magistrate, and I received the same answer. They were alike ill-informed. Not one of them had ever ventured to take it upon him to make even the slightest investigation which, I own, impressed me with ideas not the most favourable to the city's prosperity.[1]

* Senior councillors, called aldermen in England.

There was one book, the chamberlain's cash ledger, which was laid on the council table every Wednesday. Smith had often looked at it but could not make head nor tail of the columns of unexplained figures. The chamberlain, the city's chief finance officer, told him it was not meant to be understood by *every* member of council, which led Smith to wonder whether it was understood by *any* councillor, or even by the chamberlain himself. 'If there were nothing else in my knowledge upon the subject, this one circumstance is sufficient to prove that there is something in the affairs of the city that will not bear the light!'[2]

Smith's campaign for reform included drawing up a proper job description for the chamberlain, setting his salary, requiring him to put up bonds totalling £3,000 against his honest handling of the city's money. In this Smith partially succeeded, as he did with a rule requiring a magistrate (as well as their civic role, councillors also served in a judicial role as magistrates) to be present when clerks dispensed small sums of cash – a measure which he believed would save £100–200 a year.[3] But he and his supporters failed to cut the council's eating and drinking budget by dropping one or two public entertainments a year and stopping the purchase of French wine, which he estimated could save £200–300. His bigger target, however, was the gross mismanagement of the city's financial affairs: there was systematic under-collection of rents and feu duties, particularly in the New Town where the council did not have an accurate record of how much it was owed. Spending, however, went on unchecked and the council plugged any gaps by borrowing. Despite his criticisms of the city's bookkeeping, Smith made an attempt to calculate its income and expenditure and its total debt. Income in 1798 came to just under £21,000, although this included land sales as well as money raised through duties and taxes. But spending was over £26,000, including interest or repayment of borrowing of £5,800 and the cost of annuities of £2,400.[4] The total debt he estimated at over £160,000.[5]

The situation had not improved 20 years later, when a House of Commons committee investigated the affairs of Edinburgh council and estimated that the debt had increased by £90,000 in the previous decade. The lord provost and other council members who gave evidence put the best gloss on it they could, pointing to 'non-recurring items' as explanations for huge annual deficits and asserting that there was no risk of insolvency because the property the city still had left to sell to developers was worth much more than the outstanding debt. Not everyone was convinced. The city's trade guilds sent accountant John Greig to examine the books. His conclusion, published as a pamphlet, was that there did not appear to be any reasonable hope that the debt would be diminished: 'a question therefore naturally occurs, in which all the Citizens are materially interested, how is this great debt to be liquidated?'[6]

If the residents of Edinburgh were interested, the council was not. What it lacked in prudence and attention to detail, it made up for in vision and daring. It continued a breathtaking programme of public works, including a new gaol on Carlton hill (described as 'a feudal fortress of romance'),[7] a bridge from Princes Street to Carlton hill,[8] two new schools – the Royal High and Edinburgh Academy,[9] improvements to The Mound connecting the New Town to the Old and destined to be the site of the National Gallery and Royal Academy[10] and the 'southern approach', which was to become George IV Bridge.[11] Some of these, particularly the two bridges, involved major engineering challenges and were controversial because of their cost. All of the developments involved a public–private partnership, with the sale of land and subscriptions making up part of the cost, but all left the council to fund the shortfall, which it did by selling annuities (which John Greig calculated had lost the council £8,000 in the previous 12 years)[12] or borrowing from the banks. Initially it had no problem in doing so. In 1825, the board of Bank of Scotland, for example, approved an increase in the credit limit for the council from £40,000 to £50,000 without any discussion of how the city might repay.[13] The council had similar cash limits with other private and public banks.

These urban improvements were large projects, but they were dwarfed by the council's determination to turn Leith docks into a large, modern port, capable of handling trade with the rest of Britain and Europe, and with new distant markets such as Australia. Although Leith was an independent community, separated from Edinburgh by three miles of sparsely developed countryside, it came under the local government control of Edinburgh and the council looked on the docks as an important source of revenue. Enlarging both the port and the income from it had been an ambition since the end of the eighteenth century and the council had armed itself with increased borrowing powers, £80,000 in 1799, another £80,000 in 1805 and a further £80,000 in 1813. A new dock was opened in 1806 and another – the Queen's Dock – in 1817.

Leith had seen rapid growth – the population had risen from 15,000 in 1800 to 25,000 by the 1831 census, and the tonnage of goods moving through the port had increased tenfold since 1760.[14] But much of the growth had been driven by the war and after 1815 business tailed off. As port revenues fell, the council found increasing difficulty in meeting the interest payments on its huge debts. It hiked up charges, but this proved counter-productive; it was said that to avoid them merchants were landing cargoes at Grangemouth and transporting them to the capital by barges on the Union Canal, which had been opened in 1822.[15]

In 1824 the council hit upon a plan which would relieve it of the debt it had incurred on the docks in its entirety: it would take advantage of the share-buying mania which was just beginning and spin off the docks into a joint stock company. The proposal was bitterly contested by the merchants of Leith, who were strongly critical of the council's management of the docks and accused it of stifling trade by raising the port dues to unrealistic levels. They tried unsuccessfully to get the council to pledge that it would not increase dues again. The Merchant Company and Trinity House, which represented shippers and seafarers, went further, seeking legal advice on whether the council had the right to sell the docks. But the opinion was against them[16] and the council went ahead and published a prospectus for the Dock Company in the *Scotsman* and the *Edinburgh Weekly Journal*.[17] It claimed that £360,000 had been spent on the docks, including military work and improvements covered by a government loan.

The council intended to raise £300,000 by issuing shares at £100 each (£1 as an initial deposit) and to buy £50,000 worth itself. The prospectus conceded that: 'Much depression has, no doubt, been experienced at Leith . . . but better prospects open and a fair promise is now held out of the return of better times.' Controversially, the council promised a return of 4 per cent a year guaranteed for ten years – higher than could be obtained by investing in land or the public funds, it claimed. Initially the subscription did not go well, so the council increased the guaranteed return to 4.5 per cent and hinted that it could go as high as 6.25 per cent. In response, the share price climbed rapidly and immediately the shares became the object of speculation.[18] Anthony Romney wrote to his brother: 'On the very morning after the subscription was completed, the Dock scrip, as it may be termed, was in the market for sale. In the course of the day it bore a premium; it was transferred from one hand to another, and from that hand to a third at considerable expense, some who were originally in, were out – some who regretted that they were originally out, were in – and some who never intended to be in, were in and out and in again.'[19]

The privatisation provoked bitter opposition. A pamphlet war broke out between those opposing the transfer and the council, and several court actions were launched, which took years to resolve.[20] To make the transaction legal, the council had to obtain an Act of Parliament. It was not unusual for money to be raised in advance of an enabling Act being passed – the Union Canal promoters had raised over 80 per cent of their £240,000 target by the time their legislation was granted – but the Leith merchants mounted a fierce campaign against the Docks Act, accusing the council of general mismanagement and of exaggerating the amount it had spent on the port to divert dock revenues to other projects. Worse, it was alleged that the main buyers and sellers of shares in the new company were present and former members of the council and their friends. They were making personal profits from the sale of community assets.[21] Lord Archibald Hamilton MP described the proposed bill as 'the most objectionable measure brought forward by the most objectionable parties that he had ever known'. Joseph Hume MP claimed that council members had bought shares in an illegal transaction and immediately sold them for a 15 per cent profit.[22] A petition signed by 1,300 Leith businessmen was presented to parliament. Despite ministerial support engineered by Lord Melville, who had succeeded his late father as the city's political boss, the bill failed and the council had to drop its privatisation plan. It was stuck with the debt and was finding it increasingly difficult to pay the interest.

In 1825 the council was forced to go to the government for a loan. It received £240,000 in three tranches, but as security the Treasury took over all the rates and duties from the port and appointed commissioners to manage it.[23] Far from improving the council's financial position, this made it worse: it had removed most of its debt on the docks, but still had considerable outstanding loans on other projects and had lost one of its largest sources of revenue. It muddled by for a few more years, borrowing to pay the interest on its existing debt, until it ran out of credit. At the same time the Tory supremacy of the council was undermined by the reform movement. Hard on the heels of the Scottish Reform Act of 1832, which vastly enlarged the franchise for parliamentary elections, came the movement to reform local government – the burghs. The Whig lawyer Henry Cockburn had been scathing about the pre-reform council, controlled by the Dundas (Melville) dynasty: 'Almost everything in the city was under the control of the town council; not merely what was properly magisterial, but most things conducive to the public economy . . . It met in a low, dark, blackguard-looking room, entering from a covered passage which connected the north-west corner of the Parliament Square with the Lawnmarket . . . Within this Pandemonium sat the town council, omnipotent, corrupt, impenetrable. Nothing was beyond its grasp; no variety of opinion disturbed its unanimity, for the pleasure of Dundas was the sole rule for every one of them.'[24]

The council was indeed omnipotent. It controlled not only planning and development, having the power to purchase land and to sell it, but sanctioned appointments at the university, schools and churches. It had an opinion on curriculum matters, such as whether Greek grammar should be compulsory in the Royal High School and where the school of drawing should be housed; it appointed professors and paid the college cleaner. It was responsible for the police and jails and paid the stipends of kirk ministers. It also had social responsibilities. The council's Board of Health oversaw the infirmary and was preoccupied in 1832 with fighting a cholera epidemic, which had been raging in the city for nine months. The board asked the council for funds to set up soup kitchens where the destitute could get some free nourishment, presumably to make them less susceptible to the disease. The cash-strapped council declined to increase local taxes, but approved a collection at the doors of the city's churches.[25]

The report of the charity workhouse trustees in August 1832 threw another light on the conditions of the lower classes in Edinburgh. The city was growing in prosperity and had a burgeoning middle class, but at the bottom of the social scale there was destitution and starvation. The trustees reported an exceptional drain on funds because of heavy demand, which they attributed to unemployment, particularly in the collapse of the building trade since 1825; general economic depression leading many men to leave home in search of work, throwing their wives and children onto the parish; and outbreaks of cholera and typhus, which killed husbands and fathers. The trustees also delivered a long sermon on the 'habits of intoxication, producing debility, disease and premature old age. This degrading and ruinous vice has recently reigned to a degree unexampled and is daily increasing among the classes accustomed to apply for relief.'[26] This was received without irony by a council which itself had been criticised many times for the amount of public money it spent on alcohol. The workhouse trustees had exhausted their bank credit and asked for additional funds – an increase of 2 per cent on the 'poors rate', the precept on the local property tax which was currently 6 per cent. The council decided not to increase the rate, but to make a voluntary appeal to members of the College of Justice (judges), who claimed exemption from the local taxes, including that for the poor.

By the end of 1832 the financial situation of the council was becoming desperate. Creditors pressing for payment of overdue bills had to wait because the council 'resolved to decline in the meantime receiving any new loans or paying off any debts, constituted by bond or bill'.[27] University lecturers and Church of Scotland ministers had to wait for their salaries and stipends. The city's revenues were uncertain; the yield from the ale duty had been declining with the move away from drinking beer, and there was a problem finding and retaining honest and efficient local tax collectors. The council had considered selling feu duties and even lottery tickets, but had to abandon both ideas as impractical.

There was a threat to the port of Leith from entrepreneurs, including the Duke of Buccleuch, who were threatening to build a rival deep-water dock at Granton or Newhaven, two miles west along the Firth of Forth. Leith, in any case, still needed investment – the entrance to the harbour was too narrow for steamships, which had to load and unload in open water. The dock commissioners were frank: revenues would not support further borrowing, but unless the improvements were made Leith would lose trade and the dock dues which were paying the interest on the existing loans would fall further.[28] The council was supposed to pay the government 3 per cent interest on the money it had borrowed in 1825 and to save an extra 2 per cent into a 'sinking fund' to eventually pay off the debt. In fact it was having to supplement the dock revenues with extra borrowing to meet the interest charges and was putting nothing into the sinking fund. The debt, far from diminishing, was growing at an alarming rate.[29]

The Commission on Municipal Corporations, reporting in 1833, had little better opinion of the council than had Thomas Smith at the start of the century, or Cockburn a few years later. In contrast to the most recent assessment by the city's accountant of its net debt at £290,000[30] and the lord provost's assertion that the city's assets were more than sufficient to cover it, the commission calculated the city's liabilities at £407,000 against assets of only £271,000. It found 'insufficient evidence' that the disastrous state was caused by embezzlement or fraud, but blamed: 'Exaggerated expectations of the continued and indefinite increase of the city in prosperity and size may have led the managers of the corporation into an increase of expense far disproportioned to the really considerable growth of the revenue. Offices were multiplied and salaries raised, a spirit of litigation prevailed, great profusion took place in expenses of civic parade and entertainments, extravagant sums were expended on public buildings and other public works as ill-adapted in general to their object of embellishing the city as they invariably were disproportioned to its finances.'[31]

Desperate for a solution and fearful that one of the city's creditors would go to court to make the council bankrupt, Lord Provost John Learmonth invited a group of 26 heavyweight Tory grandees, including Lord Melville, Sir William Rae, the former lord advocate who sat on the Royal Bank board with Learmonth, and the banker John Kinnear to his home to discuss the council's options. Perhaps misled by his confidence that the city's assets outweighed its liabilities, they advised him to avoid legal bankruptcy by petitioning parliament to set up a trust to take over the city's financial affairs. The council agreed to do so in April 1833,[32] but it was not straightforward. At first the government offered to set up the trust only if the council surrendered the docks in payment of £150,000 of the debt owed to – leaving another £100,000 to rank with other creditors. This was rejected.[33] In June, legislation was passed sequestrating the entire revenues and assets of the city and trustees were appointed to negotiate with its creditors. The council was effectively bankrupt.

In the same year the Burgh Reform Act was passed. Edinburgh council, not surprisingly, had been against it, complaining that the creation of a new much larger electorate of '£10 householders' was being enfranchised at the expense of the 'legitimate constituency' of citizens and burgesses who had 'acquired their right either by inheritance, by service or by purchase'.[34] In November the first municipal elections were held under the new franchise, which widened the electorate to 3,500 – 1,500 of whom braved rainstorms to return a slate of radical and Whig councillors, breaking the self-selecting Tory monopoly of the council.[35] At a meeting on polling day, members of the old council passed a series of motions congratulating each other on their service to the city.[36] They continued in office for a further week before the new council was sworn in and a new lord provost elected.[37]

But this was a false dawn: the new council was virtually powerless, its financial affairs now in the hands of trustees who were mostly Tories nominated by the old council – including ex-Lord Provost Learmonth (who had not stood for re-election), Sir William Rae, and banker John Bonar. They met in the council offices and the council's staff provided their secretariat, although not their bookkeeping. Archibald Bruce, the council's accountant, was sacked after the elections and the trustees ignored his claim for compensation for loss of office.[38] Relations between the council and the trustees very soon broke down and disputes between them about how much money the council should be allowed to run services ended up in court.[39]

Discussions between the trustees and the city's creditors went slowly and there were many competing claims. One of the council's sources of income had been 'seat rents' in the city's churches: the banks wanted these classed as ordinary revenues or even sold, but the Kirk maintained that the proceeds should only be used for ecclesiastical purposes. There were disagreements about what assets and revenues should be included in the trust and what excluded, and over how much money the city should be allowed to pay for municipal services. In 1834 the government asked Henry Labouchere MP, vice president of the Board of Trade, to investigate Edinburgh's financial position and try to broker a solution.[40] He suggested that the government should forgo repayment of the loans it had made and asked the other creditors to reduce their claims by a quarter and accept a lower rate of interest on their debt. James Spittal, the new lord provost, and Adam Black, the council's treasurer, tried to persuade the five Edinburgh public banks to consolidate all the debt in one package so that other debtors could be paid off. But the banks balked at accepting less than a commercial rate of interest as well as reducing their claims.[41] It took until 1838 before a legal agreement was concluded and the council was again put in charge of its financial affairs. There was a sting in the tail, however. As part of the arrangement Edinburgh lost its domain over Leith, which became a separate burgh. Henry Cockburn was characteristically acerbic:

> The expression of this truth, that Leith had suffered from want of representation, was worth the whole struggle. The conflict raged for a long time: but its result was that, bit by bit, Leith was successful; till at last, though not a royal burgh, it, like some other places, was included in the general measures that were adopted in a few years after this for the cleansing of those chartered abominations.

Throughout the course of the dispute, the parties were fairly enough matched in point of intemperance and unreasonableness; and if Leith had the advantage in coarse violence, Edinburgh was compensated by its superiority in disdainful insolence. In the eyes of quiet observers, the true value of the affair lay in its aiding the growth of independence in Leith. The town council actually succeeded in creating a public spirit in that prostrate place.[42]

19

English money for Scottish railways

ONE OF THE first actions of Edinburgh council's insolvency trustees in 1833 had been to raise money for creditors by disposing of council assets that could be sold quickly and easily. These included the council's share-holdings in the Edinburgh Water Company, the Union Canal and the Edinburgh and Dalkeith Railway Company, an early and successful waggon way.[1] The line had been promoted by five big Midlothian mine owners – Sir John Hope, the Marquis of Lothian, the Duke of Buccleuch and two members of the Dundas family – to bring their coal into Edinburgh cheaply. The initial plan had been to use locomotives, already widely used in England – Stephenson's Rocket had entered service with the Liverpool to Manchester railway in 1829. But, perhaps because of cost, the Edinburgh and Dalkeith which began operations two years later was entirely horse-drawn, which led to its nickname, the 'Innocent Railway'. It only switched to steam in 1846.[2] Construction costs had exceeded the £57,700 start-up capital, necessitating further share issues, when Edinburgh council had bought its stock.[3] The line opened in 1831 and was quickly profitable, with the weight of coal carried rising from 90,000 tons a year in its first few years to 116,000 by the start of the following decade. It added a passenger service and by 1843 it was carry-ing 165,000 people – more than three times the number carried on the horse-drawn omnibuses. With this volume of traffic the line was able to afford reasonable dividends.[4]

Early railways were built on coalfields around Scotland, but the big prize was to link Edinburgh (population 162,000 in 1831) and Glasgow (193,000). Not only were they the two largest and most important cities, but the towns between them produced much of the country's industrial and mineral wealth too. The route had been surveyed many times (including by George Stephenson, the leading railway engineer). In 1824 the Duke of Hamilton led a tentative attempt to put together a company to build a line 'from the eastern sea to the western sea'. He commissioned a report from engineer James Jardine, which suggested a route curving southwards from Edinburgh and passing through Mid Calder, Whitburn, Bellshill and entering Glasgow from Monklands.[5] Jardine was convinced that the line could be profitable on the revenues from transporting coal alone, without counting passengers or other freight. But despite his optimism, the project did not get very far. The financial crash of 1825–6 made raising money difficult, but there was also a suspicion that the presence of many canal shareholders among the promoters meant that the real intention was not to construct the line, but to act as a deterrent to others wanting to compete with the canal companies. In 1830 a rival proposal was made public, so the Hamilton consortium asked Jardine to update his plan. He estimated the construction cost to be £450,000–£520,000, depending on how far the line was extended, but that it could earn over £50,000 a year in profits, giving a near 10 per cent return.[6]

The competition came from the Edinburgh and Glasgow Railway Company, promoted by landowners and industrialists from both cities and including on its board John Learmonth, then still lord provost of Edinburgh. Despite his less than glorious leadership of the council, Learmonth was to reinvent himself as one of the most aggressive railway promoters in Scotland. He had made his fortune with a coach building business at the east end of Princes Street and later diversified into property speculation, buying the Dean estate, to the northwest of the New Town. He planned to divide up the land and sell feus, but access to the city centre was impeded by the 100-foot-deep ravine of the Water of Leith. His solution was to commission the engineer Thomas Telford to build a huge stone bridge – the Dean Bridge, which was completed in 1831 and opened the following year to pedestrians and two years later to horses and carts. Learmonth put up most of the cost himself, intending to recoup his outlay from leasing the land on the north side, but a slump in the housing market meant that it was a decade or more before he got his money back.[7]

The Edinburgh and Glasgow Railway Company commissioned a report from engineers Grainger and Miller, who favoured a line arcing northwards through Linlithgow and Falkirk, roughly following the lines of the Union and Forth & Clyde canals.[8] This was to be much more overtly an attempt to take business away from the water transport companies, which had demonstrated the size and profitability of the market. In 1836 the Forth & Clyde canal carried a total of 177,000 passengers by day and 20,000 tons of freight by night and earned a profit of £55,000. Grainger and Miller, incorporating some modifications to their line suggested by George Stephenson, estimated that their railway would be cheaper to construct than Jardine's route at £410,000 and would earn a higher return, at 14 per cent.[9]

The new company promised that its shareholding would come one-third from 'gentlemen connected with the West of Scotland', one-third from the East, two-ninths from 'landed proprietors on the line, English capitalists etc', and one-ninth to be held back against future calls for money.[10] It took seven years to obtain an Act of Parliament, with opposition from competing commercial interests and from the owners of houses in Princes Street, who had spent considerable sums creating gardens on the land reclaimed from the drained Nor' Loch and objected to a railway running through it. Bank of Scotland, which owned land below its head office on The Mound, also refused to sell. Despite the railway company's protestations that the line would be concealed in a cutting, behind walls and embankments planted with trees and that there would be no smoke nuisance because 'owing to the improved construction of the furnaces the smoke is now scarcely seen',[11] the company failed in its first attempt and had to be content with a terminus at Haymarket, in the west of the city centre.

Raising the money from Scotland was also not as easy as the prospectus had imagined. The bankruptcy of the council had cast a chill over the commercial life of the city. It was not only the banks that were owed money; the local authority had borrowed indiscriminately and had a lamentable record in paying tradesmen. Henry Cockburn described the gloom in 1835:

Edinburgh is at present almost a mass of insolvency. Trade, except in one or two branches, has left Leith, our port; its docks are bankrupt; our college has not a shilling; the Writers to the Signet are getting so destitute that it is not easy to see how they can maintain their library and general establishment; the Faculty of Advocates is in a similar condition, but further gone; most of our charities and other institutions are dying of hunger; the law, the college, and the church are certainly destined to subside still more; and lastly, reaching, obtruding, and withering everything, the town itself is prostrate in bankruptcy.[12]

This was an inhospitable climate in which to raise capital, so the railway promoters had to turn to England: two-thirds of the finance came from investors in Manchester and Liverpool.[13] The company, it was suggested, was 'English financed, but Scottish managed',[14] and there was to be considerable tension between the two. The line was to compete with the canals on speed and cost, so it was engineered to be as straight and flat as possible, which posed engineering and financial challenges. The valley of the River Almond had to be bridged by a 32-arch viaduct and cuttings through solid rock had to be made at Philipstoun and Croy.[15]

An unforeseen difficulty came when the track entered Glasgow. It had been intended that it should bridge the Forth & Clyde canal at Port Dundas and descend gradually to a proposed station at Dundas Street (now Queen Street). But the canal company, not surprisingly, was in no mood to help their new rival and refused permission. The alternative was to tunnel one and a quarter miles under the canal, approaching the station with a steep downward slope. Descending trains had to have a brake engine in front to prevent them crashing into the buffers, but there was a bigger problem with trains leaving Glasgow for Edinburgh. The locomotives were not powerful enough to pull trains up the steep gradient, even when 'double-banked', so a stationary engine had to be installed at the top of the tunnel to haul trains on ropes. Slipping and breaking ropes were a constant hazard until 1908, when they were replaced by more powerful double-banking engines.

The line opened in February 1842 and although it had cost £1.2 million – three times Grainger's initial estimate – it was immediately successful. Running four trains a day in each direction, it was carrying 666,000 passengers within two years – double Grainger's forecast – and making £80,000 in profit. There were three classes of passengers: first class in covered, glazed carriages, paying eight shillings; second class in covered waggons, but without glass in the windows, paying six shillings; and third class standing in open waggons, paying four shillings. As journeys took over two hours, this cannot have been comfortable – but third class made up over half the number of passengers and grew as a proportion of the total. For the first time it was possible for Edinburgh people to visit Glasgow and return in a day and vice versa. In 1844 the company overcame the opposition from the Princes Street residents and obtained parliamentary consent to extend the line from Haymarket to the new station being built by the North British Railway Company under North

Bridge. By 1848 the line was carrying a million passengers a year and was returning over £100,000 to its investors.[16]

Not everyone was in favour of the railway, which provoked opposition from the start. The town of Linlithgow, citing ancient privileges, tried to levy a charge on every carriage crossing the River Avon. The company refused to pay; the town took the matter to court and won at every level up to the House of Lords, which finally found in favour of the Edinburgh and Glasgow. A more formidable enemy was the Church, which opposed the company's decision to run Sunday passenger services. Religious feeling in Scotland was running high, with the dispute between the evangelicals and the moderates in the Church of Scotland leading in 1843 to the Disruption – the breakaway of 450 ministers to form the Free Church of Scotland. Sabbatarians, who opposed any sort of work on a Sunday, were a powerful lobby and bombarded the company with pamphlets and petitions.

When despite the vocal campaign the railway board voted in favour of Sunday running, the chairman resigned and was replaced by John Learmonth,[17] who resisted the Sabbatarians' claims and ran Sunday services. But opposition continued. Passengers arriving from Glasgow were met with a hellfire and damnation sermon from a kirk minister, boycotts were organised and even a rival coach service started, but other Sabbath campaigners went further and bought shares in the company so that they could harangue the directors at annual meetings. Coincidentally, the new chairman ran foul of the English shareholders over a proposal to merge with three canal companies, which were seeing their business eroded by the new competition from rail. For the Liverpool and Manchester investors it made no sense to take over the assets of failing businesses, but Learmonth feared that if he did not do so his new rival, the Caledonian Railway, would.

The Caledonian got its Act of Parliament in 1845, after 'a long and arduous contest, which was executed, conducted and in a great measure paid for by some of the principal railway companies previously established in Scotland', J.J. Hope-Johnstone, MP for Dumfriesshire and the company's first chairman, told the first meeting of shareholders, adding 'of other opposition, there was none'.[18] The company had raised £1.8 million to lay track from Carlisle to central Scotland. At Carstairs in South Lanarkshire, the line split in two, the eastern section going to Edinburgh and the western to Glasgow. Learmonth feared that the company would not only run services to England from Scotland's two largest cities, but also start an Edinburgh–Glasgow service, which would take away traffic and make the Edinburgh and Glasgow Company service unprofitable. He pressed ahead with his proposal for a defensive merger with the canal companies. Matters came to a head in 1846 when the English shareholders formed an alliance with the Sabbatarians and rejected the board's half-yearly report,[19] putting pressure on Learmonth and his fellow directors. Two weeks later all the directors resigned, to be replaced by a board containing seven Sabbatarians, including the new chairman, who stopped the Sunday passenger service, although continuing to run mail trains on the Sabbath. This, according to one opponent, was 'committing all the sin of desecration as formerly, but depriving the public of the advantage of the conveyance'.[20]

Although landowners and merchants financed local lines, largely out of self-interest, both the cross-border lines had to rely heavily on English investors. To fund the Caledonian, Hope-Johnstone tried to persuade the English Grand Junction Railway Company to pretend it was their scheme, to make it easier to raise English finance. They declined, but he found other ways to attract funding, so by 1848 it was estimated that 90 per cent of the Caledonian's shares were held by English investors. The North British Railway, which originally planned a line from Edinburgh to Dunbar, had similar difficulties and John Learmonth, who was also its chairman, had to extend the line to Berwick, where it could join the track being laid to Newcastle, before he was able to attract money from south of the border. In 1849 it was revealed that 77 per cent of its shares were held in England.[21]

Scottish investors had many other calls on their capital from the myriad of industrial enterprises being launched in the west of Scotland, whereas English financiers were more willing to back new rail schemes. In April 1844 the committee of the Edinburgh and Hawick Railway announced that 'a spirited company in London was ready to advance the whole money necessary to complete the undertaking'.[22] Scottish banks were initially very wary about lending to railway companies, possibly frightened by the large capital costs of buying or leasing land and of engineering the track. Business models were also untested. The Edinburgh and Glasgow Railway was rare in having the canal companies already prove the size of the market. Early bank loans were made to promoters or directors on their personal security, rather than to their companies. Royal Bank was happy to lend to the Duke of Buccleuch to fund his part of the Edinburgh and Dalkeith Railway, but not to the project itself,[23] and when the directors of the Edinburgh, Leith and Newhaven Railway Company applied for a facility of £100,000 they were granted £2,000 only on their personal sureties.[24] Bank of Scotland limited its Glasgow agent to total railway-related lending to £50,000.[25]

As the enthusiasm for railway projects grew the reluctance of the main Scottish banks to put up money led to an opening for a new type of financial institution – the 'exchange companies'. Their business model was high risk and high return. They attracted deposits by offering higher interest rates than the banks and charged an even higher rate on their lending, giving them a bigger margin than the banks. They were able to get this because they would lend to individuals on the security of railway shares – something the banks initially declined to do.[26] The first exchange companies were formed in 1844 and called themselves 'banks', the North British Bank in Glasgow and the Exchange Bank of Scotland in Edinburgh, which managed to secure an incorporating Act of Parliament. Seven more quickly followed across Scotland. As the enthusiasm of investors for railway shares grew, the business of the exchange companies expanded rapidly in an unsustainable financial spiral. Speculators borrowed to buy shares, which pushed up the price of the stock, increasing the apparent value of the security on which the exchange companies were prepared to lend. So the speculators borrowed more and bought more shares. The established banks, particularly Bank of Scotland and Royal Bank, looked on the exchange companies as a threat to the banking system: since they kept no reserves, they were vulnerable to a fall in the value of railway stock.

Despite the difficult beginnings of the Edinburgh and Glasgow and the Caledonian railways, a fervour for new schemes hit Scotland in 1845. By the end of that year plans for 115 new companies had been deposited with the Board of Trade. Every small town had a railway project – Perth had four – mostly backed by local landowners or merchants.[27] It was in the interests of the big companies to extend their services into new markets, but they followed different models. The Caledonian favoured leasing track from other companies, which meant it did not incur any upfront cost. In the North British, Learmonth bought smaller companies, or promoted new lines himself to push his network south into the border country, or northwards through Fife and beyond, necessitating new rounds of fund raising.

The early 1840s saw an end to the economic depression and a new era of expansion and optimism, brought about by a succession of good harvests, which lowered food prices and imports. Depositors who had been earning low rates of interest in Scottish banks now felt confident enough to look for more remunerative uses for their money. Shares in new railway companies, even if the projects themselves looked fanciful, seemed a good bet – they could always be sold before the track had to be laid. By 1845 over 3,000 miles of line had been authorised by parliament, but only 223 miles actually built. Companies were 'scattered haphazard across the kingdom, their sole *raison d'être* being the hope of substantial profits for their promoters and proprietors.'[28]

As demand for shares expanded, so the number of stockbrokers increased to service this new market. In 1844 there were 11 individuals, partnerships or companies dealing in shares in Edinburgh. Two years later the number had risen to 35. Glasgow brokers had formed a stock exchange in June 1844 and six months later the Edinburgh Stock Exchange was founded, quickly followed by others in the cities and major towns (and rival exchanges within Edinburgh and Glasgow).[29] Seven brokers met in the Royal Hotel, Princes Street, elected J.W. Pillans as chairman, Albert Cay as secretary and gave three other brokers the task of writing a rule book. Dealing started shortly afterwards in a first floor flat at 71 Princes Street. By 1845 the number of members has risen to 26 and the following year to 36.[30] Although the exchanges traded shares in any joint stock company, railway transactions made up the largest part of their business. This activity mirrored that south of the border, where by 1845 the mania was well underway: 'The prevailing rage for gambling in railway scrip has only within the last two months seized upon the inhabitants of Scotland . . .' reported the *Bankers' Magazine* in June 1845. 'The offices of the sharebrokers in Edinburgh and Glasgow are now regularly besieged from morning to noon, from noon till dewy eve, aye and even later than that, by parties who wish to sell and parties who wish to buy – the former class being usually predominant.'[31]

Caledonian Railway shares, with £5 paid, traded at £6 at the end of January 1845, shot up to a peak of over £16 before closing at the end of October at £12 – and all before the company had completed its track laying.[32] In April the Caledonian Extension Company – which proposed to build a cross-country line from Ayr to Kelso – offered 60,000 shares for sale and got applications for 300,000. In Aberdeen three separate schemes were each oversubscribed six- or seven-fold. Speculation was encouraged by the fact that most companies required only a small deposit to secure the shares. By the end of November 94 railway companies had been promoted in Scotland with a combined capital requirement of £36.5 million, but the total actually paid was a tiny £180,000.[33]

The pin that burst the bubble was the poor harvest of 1845 which, following a run of good years, pricked the mood of optimism. Lowland Scotland was less affected by the potato blight, which afflicted Ireland and to a lesser extent the Scottish Highlands. Immigrants trying to escape the famine mostly stayed in the west of Scotland, where many found low-wage employment in factories, mines or on farms. Edinburgh was less affected, but any Irish paupers finding their way to the capital were liable to be refused poor relief or deported.[34] Gold had to leave the country to pay for imports, interest rates rose and stocks fell, forcing those speculators who had bought on borrowed money to sell, which further depressed prices. By the end of November Caledonian shares had more than halved from their peak to trade at £7. Robert Allan, who published a regular listing of shares and prices, was shocked: 'The railway mania of 1845 has terminated this month in as thorough a panic as the loudest prognosticator of evil ever contemplated; and perhaps a more suddenly heavy fall in the value of the share property never before occurred.'[35]

Some of the first casualties were the exchange companies. One of the most active, the Glasgow Commercial Exchange Company, collapsed with a loss of £657,000, the North British Bank £354,000[36] and one by one the others either failed or were taken over by the banks.[37] Bankruptcies in Scotland doubled between 1845–8 and the mainstream banks did not escape unscathed. Despite its earlier misgivings Royal Bank had lent the North British Railway £244,950 in mortgages, perhaps because of Learmonth, who was on the board of both. In 1850 repayments were overdue, but the bank had little option but to extend the term.[38]

Learmonth was still in expansionary mode in 1845 and was determined to beat the Caledonian railway with a service to Carlisle. In August of that year the North British bought the Edinburgh and Dalkeith Railway for £160,000 and converted its horse-drawn operation to steam. The company had already promoted the Edinburgh and Hawick Railway and secured an enabling Act. Now it raised £400,000 from shareholders with the intention of extending its network from Edinburgh, through the Scottish borders, with branches to all the main towns, and eventually into England.[39] But the construction and engineering costs were substantial. The track on the Edinburgh and Dalkeith had to be relaid to take the heavier engines and the undulating countryside of the borders line necessitated tunnels and viaducts. Thousands of 'navvies' – manual workers from Scotland, England and Ireland – had to be employed and lived in squalid camps along the route. There were frequent labour disputes and violent disturbances. Shareholders were becoming uneasy, but Learmonth rejected a takeover bid from England.

The first blow to his ambitions came when Edinburgh council, now led by Adam Black as lord provost, threw its weight behind the Caledonian as the preferred route to England from the capital. There may have been some residual political animosity towards Learmonth, but there were sweeteners too. The Caledonian promised it could halve the cost of importing coal into 'Auld Reekie' and offered to allow the Edinburgh Water Company, where Black was on the board, to lay its main supply pipe alongside the track.[40] The North British completed its line to Hawick, but increasing costs meant that it never fulfilled Learmonth's ambition of reaching Carlisle. In 1852 the dividend was suspended and a group of shareholders forced changes on the board and the eventual ousting of Learmonth.[41]

The Caledonian Railway began running trains to Carlisle in 1847 and a year later started an Edinburgh–Glasgow service. Its route was longer than the Edinburgh and Glasgow track, but it had faster locomotives, so it was able to offer four trains in each direction per day, taking two hours for the trip, against 1.5 hours for the E and G. To compensate it offered lower fares, sparking a price-cutting war which slashed the Edinburgh and Glasgow fare receipts. The battle lasted until September when both sides called a truce and increased fares.[42]

20

The failure of the Western Bank

DESPITE THE FINANCIAL disasters and numerous failed schemes, railways were revolutionising communications within Scotland and with England. From 1850 an alliance of the three separate companies operating the East Coast main line made it possible to go from Edinburgh to London by rail, although initially that meant changing trains twice, to cross the Tweed at Berwick and the Tyne at Newcastle on foot. In 1853 a further technological leap was made when Bank of Scotland installed the electric telegraph in its head office on The Mound,[1] followed later by Royal Bank. It was now possible to get London stock exchange and money market prices daily and communicate with Glasgow instantly.

But these advances had come at a cost: railway mania, which had persisted until 1847, had left the Edinburgh public banks seriously weakened, despite their initial caution, and had exposed the inadequacies of their governance and management controls.[2] At Bank of Scotland Alexander Blair, the experienced banker who had been recruited from the British Linen Company to take the reins after the dismissal of William Cadell, revealed the shocking state of the balance sheet to his directors. To cover the losses on railway and other loans and the increased cost of interest to match the competition from the exchange companies, the bank had been forced into a fire-sale of nearly £1.2 million of the government and other securities it held as its reserves.[3] The loss involved was equal to the whole of the retained profits and, if business continued at the same level, he foresaw the need to sell a further £600,000 of stock, putting the bank in a very precarious position.

At Royal Bank the position was no better. Directors were concerned about the level of their reserves and the discount rate – at which it lent to commercial customers – had been raised to the crisis level of 6.5 per cent on bills over four months. Even during the French wars the rate had only risen to 5 per cent.[4] Commercial Bank was seriously exposed to railway loans and elsewhere in Scotland the Town and County Bank in Aberdeen was in trouble and there had been a run on the North of Scotland Bank.[5]

Glasgow was becoming the biggest source of business and of worry for the Edinburgh banks. It had long been both the largest and the fastest growing city in Scotland, driven by the relentless pace of industrial innovation. Its population in 1801 was estimated at 77,000, but by 1851 it had more than quadrupled to 329,000. The railways had given a big boost to the coal, iron, steel and engineering industries, but the processing of cotton, manufacture of cotton goods, dyeing and chemical production were also booming, as were the sugar, building and construction industries. Glasgow was a major port and the expansion of transatlantic trade stimulated the shipbuilding and marine engineering industries. Inventors, innovators and entrepreneurs were forming new enterprises and the growth in output meant voracious demand for finance for working capital and new factories. For several decades this had mostly been supplied by Bank of Scotland, through its Glasgow branches, and Royal Bank through its agent. Between them the two Edinburgh banks discounted more bills than the nine other banks which operated in the city put together.[6] But the demand was rising so quickly that their capacity and their appetite for risk were being tested.

Frequent credit crises in the first half of the nineteenth century had made the two senior Edinburgh banks nervous. In 1833 Horsley Palmer, the governor of the Bank of England, had adopted a rule: against all 'liabilities to pay on demand' (i.e. banknotes issued and deposits, which could be withdrawn without notice), the bank should keep a reserve of a third of the total value; two-thirds of this should be in securities such as government stock, and one-third in bullion (gold and silver). This was a highly conservative position, with no statutory backing, which, by giving depositors and the holders of notes confidence that their money was always safe, was intended to ensure stability. But sometimes it may have had the opposite effect. When the bank's bullion position dropped to below one-third – as it often did when poor harvests meant that food imports had to be paid for in gold – the Bank of England applied the rule. It sold consols (government securities) to buy gold, which had the effect of increasing interest rates, and it tightened credit, restricting the number of the bills it would accept for discount, increasing the rate of interest it charged, or occasionally suspending discounting altogether. This could trigger defaults among poorly capitalised banks and commercial enterprises.[7]

Although the Scottish banks were fiercely jealous of their independence and were critical of Palmer's management, their boards also favoured a prudent policy. Bank of Scotland formally adopted the Palmer rule in 1840,[8] although it sometimes found it difficult to apply. Royal Bank directors also appear to have been cautious, but they were at odds with their chief cashier and general manager, John Thomson. He had indulged in a vigorous exchange of letters with Palmer in 1836, accusing the Bank of England of precipitately increasing its discount rate.[9]

Thomson was an expansionist and favoured a looser lending policy. He led Royal Bank to open more branches and unsuccessfully tried several times to expand by acquisition. Before becoming its chief executive, he had been the bank's agent in Glasgow during a period full of drama and danger. Not only had he witnessed at first hand the astonishing explosion of the city's population and economy, but he lived through the radical riots which erupted following the Peterloo Massacre in Manchester in 1819. Barricaded in the bank's Glasgow office, he had packed up the bills of exchange into 'field parcels' and despatched them with £56,000 in cash to head office out of harm's way.[10] Behind barricades with a company of Glasgow Sharpshooters, he waited for the 60,000-strong mob that was rumoured to be on its way to ransack the city. To meet them 5,000 troops were stationed in the streets, but the battle never came. The radicals were intercepted, there were skirmishes and arrests and later three executions.[11]

It was the freewheeling business culture of Glasgow, rather than its street politics, which most impressed Thomson. He estimated that in four years £20 million in bills had passed through his hands, financing sugar, cotton, cotton goods, timber, grain and house building. He frankly admitted that up to a third of the bills he discounted were 'fictitious' – invented for the purposes of obtaining credit rather than being backed by genuine business transactions. But they oiled the gears of the rapidly expanding Glasgow economic machine and he kept bad debts to a manageable level.[12] He was promoted to Edinburgh to lead the bank, but he never won the complete trust of his board. In 1839 a committee of Royal Bank directors, dissatisfied with Thomson's record, had investigated the rapid rise in the total of cash credits the bank was granting – up by over 60 per cent in four years. Many were discovered to be 'dead loans' rather than overdrafts, the principal was not being repaid and the interest was rolling up. To cover the risk the bank had had to sell most of its government stock, reducing its reserves to a dangerous level. The directors were dismayed: 'Hence it has happened that this great establishment has recently found itself surrounded by formidable difficulties and has been forced to scrimp its best customers instead of affording . . . substantial aid to the trade and manufacture of the country at the moment when such aid is most required.'[13]

They forced Thomson to adopt more cautious limits, but by 1845 their patience was exhausted. They accused him of trading on his own behalf with the bank's money at lower than a commercial rate of interest.[14] A special meeting of the court of directors resolved that it was 'absolutely necessary for a change of management: Mr Thomson being made aware of the feeling of the directors, shall retire from his office as cashier'.[15] He did not take the news well, expressing his 'astonishment and surprise with which I received your proposal to resign after 28 years with the bank'. It took several days to winkle him out and he handed over the keys to the 'cash closet' only under protest.[16]

Thomson's later career was no more successful. In 1850 he tried to organise a rescue of the Edinburgh and Glasgow Bank, which had been formed by the merger of the Glasgow Joint Stock Bank and the Edinburgh and Leith Bank. Disastrously, the merged institution kept two managements and two boards of directors, who refused to show each other their board minutes. The bank suffered heavy losses on loans secured on railway shares and had to appeal to the Bank of England for support. Thomson tried to bring together three banks, but the plan fell through and eventually the Edinburgh and Glasgow was taken over by Clydesdale Bank.[17]

The west of Scotland banks were the poor relations of their larger eastern sisters, and the Thistle, Ship and Glasgow banks were still partnerships with less than 30 partners between them and therefore a narrow capital base.[18] In 1830, the promoters of the new Glasgow Union Bank, a joint stock bank rather than a partnership, had higher ambitions. With 425 subscribers and a nominal capital of £2 million, of which £500,000 was called up within the first few years, the new bank aimed to be a major player in the city. It started cautiously, but within 15 years had absorbed the Thistle Bank (1836), the Paisley Union Bank (1838), the Edinburgh private bank of Sir William Forbes, Hunter & Co. (1838) and the Ship Bank (1843), which had itself taken over the Glasgow Bank Company. It issued its own banknotes and opened offices across

Scotland. In 1843 it took over Hunters & Co. of Ayr and renamed itself the Union Bank of Scotland.

Other entrepreneurs followed the Union Bank's lead. The Western Bank, which was launched in 1832 had a nominal capital of £4 million – twice that of the Union – and aimed to call up £600,000. But the bank set a dangerous precedent by allowing its subscribers to borrow against the value of their stock, so its own shareholders made up a significant proportion of its lending and it ended its first year with paid-up capital of only £219,000. From the start the bank went after new business aggressively. The established Edinburgh banks, which had been indifferent to the start of the Union, were alarmed by the Western Bank's disdain for keeping reserves. Rather than holding part of the capital in gold or government securities – which could be easily converted to cash in case of need – the Western lent virtually all its capital in discounts or cash advances.[19] There was a trade-off between safety and profit. Investing in the national debt may have been lucrative during the war with France, when the government was forced to pay high interest to borrow what it needed, but in peacetime the yield on gilts was far below what could be earned in the commercial market. Holding gold or silver earned no interest at all.

The managers of the Western took the view that they had a duty to finance the local economy of the West of Scotland and that the trade bills they received as security for their lending were perfectly safe. This position was quickly tested as the credit market tightened. Within two years its drafts were being refused in London and the Edinburgh banks were wary about accepting its notes.[20] They remonstrated with its directors and management. The authority of the Edinburgh public banks and their ability to regulate the banking system north of the border depended on coercing or persuading the Western to act more responsibly. For a while it looked as though they had succeeded. The Western changed its manager and pledged to maintain a reserve – although it never had more than 5–6 per cent of its deposits invested in government securities, where the Edinburgh banks kept a quarter to a third. But this show of prudence – given in writing to the three Edinburgh chartered banks – was enough, and its notes were accepted into the note exchange and it was given a loan of £100,000.[21]

Clydesdale Bank, which launched in 1838, was the creation of liberal reforming merchants and local politicians, led by James Lumsden, a 60-year-old printer and stationer who had been one of the moving civic spirits in the city. It began life with £375,000 in paid-up capital, quickly increased to £500,000 to match the Union. The Clydesdale also allowed its proprietors to borrow on the value of their stock, but appears to have vetted its shareholders thoroughly before allowing them to buy. It also took care in selecting its staff, recruiting from other Scottish banks and from as far afield as Sligo to find experienced men.[22] Lumsden wanted a foot in both cities and arranged for the Clydesdale to buy the business of Ramsay, Bonar, the last of the Edinburgh private bankers and one of the banks Thomson had failed to buy for the Royal. By 1840 Clydesdale had nine branches. It took over the Greenock Union Bank in 1844. It prided itself on being boring and safe and grew its business steadily and prudently.[23] The City of Glasgow Bank, which launched a year after the Clydesdale, raised £656,000 in capital from 780 shareholders, it too initially followed a gradual path.[24]

In 1845 the Scottish Bank Act, which restricted the ability of Scottish banks to issue notes and prohibited new banks of issue, required banks to make regular returns to the government on the amount of gold and silver they held and disclose the size of their note circulation. The results shocked the traditional bankers. While the five Edinburgh public and joint stock banks accounted for half the total £3 million note circulation in Scotland, the upstart Glasgow banks were expanding fast. One of the problems for the established Edinburgh public banks was that the individual Acts of Parliament which set them up prohibited them from acquiring other banks. The new joint stock banks, which operated under more modern companies' legislation, did not have this restriction. One way of building their note circulation quickly was to buy smaller rivals and consolidate their note issue. The Union Bank's note circulation of £327,000 was larger than Bank of Scotland's £300,000 and dwarfed the Royal's at £183,000. The Western Bank was not far behind its Glasgow rival with £284,000.[25] The note issue was only part of their lending, most of which was done through discounted bills of exchange, which did not show up in the figures.

By 1847 the Western Bank was again in trouble, but this time its directors went to the Bank of England, rather than the Edinburgh banks. They secured a loan of £300,000, which was enough to see the bank through its difficulties, and the money was repaid a year later.[26] In the next decade the bank did roaring business, discounting £16 million in bills in 1847 and £12 million the following year. Most galling for the Edinburgh bankers was the fact that the Western seemed to be thriving by ignoring their prudent principles. Within ten years from its foundation it had opened 26 branches and by 1857 had over 100. It attracted wealthy and influential Glasgow industrialists to its board and share register, including members of the Baird, Dunlop and Douglas ironmaking families, who were among the richest and most successful in Britain. Its shares traded at a premium on the Glasgow Stock Exchange, the £50 stock reaching £86 at one point,[27] and it paid high dividends, rising to 9 per cent in 1856. It borrowed in the London money market, pushing its credit as far as possible,[28] and was so thirsty for deposits that it adopted a policy of late-night branch opening to attract working-class customers, being willing to accept smaller sums and offering them a better interest rate than the establishment banks.[29] Such aggressive competition damaged the nascent savings bank movement in Glasgow.[30]

Alexander Blair, who considered himself Scotland's premier banker, was concerned that the rapid expansion of the Glasgow banks was endangering the stability of the banking system. In particular, the ability of the new banks to expand by acquisition had placed Bank of Scotland, Royal Bank and British Linen at a disadvantage. For 150 years they had attempted to regulate the Scottish banking market, injecting credit when the economy was constrained and curbing expansion when it was in danger of overheating. Now that calming influence was being threatened. No one bank on its own was big enough to rescue the system if it got into trouble. His solution was to merge the three Edinburgh public banks into one, producing a large, well-capitalised bank with the equivalent financial and moral authority north of the border that the Bank of England enjoyed in the south: 'If the power of junction [merger] be conceded to these three banks they, thus constituted, will be better able with safety to themselves and the public to avert any monetary crisis from Scotland, or in the event of a discredit to act with perfect consistency under the new law as settled by the Bank of England charter and other recited acts.'

His was a patrician view of the market and he managed to convince himself that creating one dominating bank would be good for competition: 'As a united body they would by the influence and example of broad and liberal principles limit the irregular actions of establishments carrying on business upon narrow views without regard to the public safety. They would also present a check to any monopolising spirit which may arise out of the present state of the law, and to novelties in banking practice, which are unauthorised both by the letter and the spirit of [the law].'[31]

On scraps of paper[32] he began to work out what the new central bank would look like, how it would be capitalised, what cost savings could be made, how much it would be able to pay in dividends and how the share-holdings would be split. He did not spend any time considering a new name; it would be Bank of Scotland, just as the leading bank in England was the Bank of England and in Ireland the Bank of Ireland. He secured the support of his directors and sent a memorandum to the chancellor of the exchequer to pave the way for a special Act of Parliament that would make the merger possible.

The other two banks were not as keen. Under Blair's plan Royal Bank proprietors would hold a majority of the shares, but this was not enough for the Royal's board. Robert Sym, Blair's opposite number, told him that his directors would not entertain the idea unless the new sharehold-ing was split in proportion to the total capital contributed – issued shares plus retained earnings.[33] Blair tried to modify his proposal, but could not reach agreement. He maintained his belief in the idea, but the creation of a central bank of Scotland was stillborn.

Whether a merged Edinburgh bank would have made any difference when disaster struck is questionable. The crisis of 1857, unlike most of the others in the preceding decades, was not ignited by failed harvests or some other domestic event, but by a series of failures abroad and has been called the first really worldwide financial crisis in history.[34] The Crimean War (1853–6) had been quickly followed by the Indian Mutiny (1857–8) which hit Indian government securities held by the banks as part of their reserves.[35] That year saw a crisis in France, and in September and October more than 1,400 American financial companies suspended payments and mobs were storming New York banks. With 20–25 per cent of all British exports dependent on America and an estimated £80 million of American stocks and bonds held by British firms, it was inevit-able that British trading companies and the banks that serviced them would be hit hard.[36]

First to go down was the Liverpool Borough Bank, but the contagion soon spread to Glasgow where the cotton merchant J. & A. Dennistoun, which had operations in London, Liverpool, New York and New Orleans, was forced to suspend payments. Several smaller houses, all indebted to the Western Bank, failed completely.[37] All Glasgow banks were affected to some extent, but the Western had expanded dramatically in the previous five years by making reckless loans to companies on both sides of the Atlantic. It now was swamped with 'hopelessly bad' debts. The Western directors appealed to the Edinburgh banks for advances on the security of discounted bills, but these bills were hardly likely to be worth any more than the loans the bank had already lost. Alexander Blair wrote in a memo to the Bank of Scotland board: 'It has been admitted that their system of business is more like that of a pawnbroker than of a banker.' He believed they needed at least £1.2 million – £200,000 from each of the five Edinburgh banks, plus the Union Bank – but he was not really interested in saving the Western. He wanted to see it brought down as a warning to others not to stray from the narrow path of prudent banking: 'An arrangement of this kind would probably sustain general credit, but would not correct the errors which have brought the bank so flagrantly into difficulty. This can only be effected by an agreement to wind up the affairs of the bank, failing any other proposition for securing the community from a further repetition of the same incompetence and danger.'[38]

A few days later in the evening of 26 October, the chief executives of Bank of Scotland, Royal, British Linen, Commercial, National and Union banks met at the home of Archibald Bennet, secretary of Bank of Scotland, in Eton Terrace, Edinburgh. They agreed to lend £500,000 provided the Western Bank directors dissolve and wind up the company. But their terms were strict: security of £750,000 in commercial bills had to be put up, plus personal bonds from the directors or 'a sufficient number of responsible shareholders'.[39] Clydesdale Bank also offered £100,000.

Blair knew that this was not enough to allow the Western to survive, but it might have bought enough time for the directors to appeal to the bank's richer shareholders. The *coup de grâce* came with a leak of the offer reported in the 'Money Market and City Intelligence' gossip column in *The Times* on 30 October confirming that a condition of the aid given by the other banks was that the bank be wound up.[40] This sparked an immediate run as depositors fought to get their money out. The directors made a desperate appeal to the Bank of England, but it was already stretched supporting banks in the north of England and refused additional credit. The Western closed its doors on 9 November. The crisis was now so serious that it was affecting all banks, which were trying to stem the loss of deposits. *The Times* reported: 'The unfortunate resolution, not to say mistake, on the part of the other banks in refusing to afford sufficient aid to the Western Bank of Scotland, notwithstanding its notoriously solvent proprietary, has produced a panic affecting more or less all of them and has given no inconsiderable blow to the confidence of the community of Scotland general in its banking system . . . Even the notes of the old chartered banks and the Bank of England itself were refused in many cases, the clamour being for gold.'[41]

The City of Glasgow Bank closed its head office, but depositors took the train to Edinburgh to try to get their money from the sub-office, until, after 'severe crushing and squeezing about the doors'[42] it too had to close. The Union Bank managed to stay open by bringing a large quantity of gold from London, guarded by military escort. The Union's official history commented: 'The bank not only met every demand, but provided special facilities for withdrawals – to the great advantage of a number of pickpockets who found the excited gold-laden crowd an easy prey.'[43] Bank of Scotland had to bring £30,000 in gold from London to meet demands from depositors wanting to withdraw their money[44] and Royal Bank sold down its reserves to increase liquidity.[45] Commercial failures across Glasgow led to fears of a breakdown in public order and the despatch of a dozen officers and 220 men of the Rifle Brigade from Edinburgh Castle to Glasgow and a detachment of lancers from Piershill barracks to Hamilton.[46]

The Bank of England increased its discount rate to a record 10 per cent, but responding to the crisis was made difficult by the legislation of the previous decade which meant that Scottish banks could only increase their note issues above their quota if the new money was backed by gold. The chancellor of the exchequer, fearing more failures in Glasgow, considered allowing Bank of England notes to be circulated in Scotland, but abandoned the idea in the face of 'national feeling in Scotland'.[47] The five Edinburgh banks, plus the Union Bank made a joint appeal to the government to suspend the Act, which was granted.[48] Slowly confidence was restored, but only at the cost of reducing reserves of all the Edinburgh banks to vulnerable levels.[49] The Western Bank had gone, but had the lessons of its collapse been learned? Blair was not convinced they had. He warned his directors:

> There is no valid reason for the assumption that in the course of a few years a similar crisis will not again produce similar effects in Scotland. One ill-conducted establishment has been removed and the banking and commercial interests have a precedent before them which should inspire caution and guide their practice. On the other

hand, confidence in a section of the banks has been shaken, not only by the discredit which attached to them for the first time, but likewise from the disclosures which have been made and from the extended knowledge of the legal liabilities to which their shareholders are exposed.* It would therefore be extremely unwise to treat the discredit of 1857 as an event arising from exceptional causes.[50]

---

* Only Bank of Scotland, Royal Bank and British Linen had limited liability at this time. The rest had unlimited liability and in the event of failure all the assets of their shareholders were at risk.

21

Bankers in the dock

THE COLLAPSE OF the Western Bank brought repercussions and accusations. As far as the Edinburgh bankers were concerned the bank had been run recklessly from the start. Its directors and managers had ignored established prudent banking principles and compounded their error with incompetence. Several post-mortem accounts by a select committee of the House of Commons and by John Gifford of the National Bank appeared to confirm this. Indeed, Gifford entitled his report *How to Mismanage a Bank*.[1] The Western kept a much smaller proportion of its assets in low yielding government securities and had fallen into the trap of being too dependent on a handful of large borrowers. Five Glasgow firms accounted for £1.6 million of its lending, which was more than its total paid-up capital. It was also heavily exposed to dubious American ventures, including railway companies. When the crash came many of these borrowers defaulted at the same time[2] and the lack of easily realised reserves left the bank fatally exposed. It was clear too that the directors had little idea of the true state of the bank and massively underestimated the extent of its deficit.

Yet the old Edinburgh banks could hardly be 'holier than thou'. John Thomson had tried to convince his board that Royal Bank was over-capitalised and that it would be easier to make a higher percentage profit with lower reserves,[3] but was slapped down by his directors. As far back as 1840 Alexander Blair had been complaining of the unfair competition from those banks which did not hold reserves in low interest-paying government stocks.[4] Bank of Scotland tried to improve the return on its reserves by diversifying away from gilts, which were yielding less than it was having to pay its depositors. It had invested in the shares of high dividend-paying banks in Newcastle and Leeds, but they were higher risk and when the crash came it lost £246,000.[5]

The Western's collapse stirred huge resentment in Glasgow and a feeling, described as 'all but universal' by the *Glasgow Herald*, that the Edinburgh banks had either stood by and watched the Western go bust, or even actively encouraged it. The difference between the two cities was not just one of banking principles; it was a clash of cultures – of modern risk-taking Glaswegian entrepreneurs against the entrenched reactionary vested interests of Edinburgh. This was most violently expressed in an editorial in the *North British Daily Mail*:

> It is really a slur upon the mercantile character of Glasgow. A direct home-thrust at all in which our strength and honour as a city consist, that the unlimited liability of the Bairds, the Dunlops and the Douglasses of the Western Bank, and of the Orrs, the Campbells and others of the City [of Glasgow Bank] should be contemptuously thrust aside for the liability, sometimes limited, of Dukes and Marquises, whose estates are mortgaged up to the hilt and almost always entailed [protected] from their creditors, of Edinburgh lawyers whose trade is daily going down, and Highland lairds whose pedigrees are a good deal longer than their purses ... Never again must the first men of Glasgow be asked to humble themselves before a parcel of Writers to the Signet in Edinburgh on a question affecting the credit and commerce of the city.[6]

The charge that the Edinburgh banks had deliberately let the Western fail had some validity. Their reticence in accepting Western notes after the crash[7] undermined trust in the bank. They were also quick to grab some of the best of its business for themselves. Days after the Western closed, a feeding frenzy broke out among the other banks to secure its best customers. John Bishop, Royal Bank's inspector of branches, told his board that Western agents were willing to transfer deposits of £633,000, and advances more than covered by deposits – effectively cost-free new business. He went on to name customers in seven branches, their business interests, assets and bank balances: 'I have learned that some of the agents are making arrangements with other banks. The applications to me are so numerous and important that I am persuaded it would be very impolitic of our directors not to give them immediate consideration.'[8] A committee met virtually daily to secure new agents before other banks got them. Royal Bank and Bank of Scotland also wrote jointly to the chancellor of the exchequer asking to be able to increase their note issues by the amount of the Western's circulation. They were refused.[9]

It was also true that the shareholders in Bank of Scotland, Royal Bank and British Linen enjoyed limited liability, meaning that in the event of failure they would lose their investment but not be required to meet the bank's debts. The 1,280 partners in the Western Bank had unlimited liability and paid heavily for its failings. The share register included the business elite of the city, the shipowners, iron and coal masters and merchants. The extended Baird family held £78,800 of stock and there were important landowners with large holdings. But there were also lawyers, accountants, bankers, surgeons, a vet, a joiner, a slater, an upholsterer, a flesher, builders and engineers with a few hundred pounds worth of shares or even just £50.[10] The shareholders lost the whole of the bank's capital and reserve of nearly £2 million and were required to pay another million to make good its deficit and repay the depositors in full. The industrial magnates among the shareholders could withstand their losses, but many of the other proprietors could not and there was a wave of bankruptcies, adding to the depression in the city caused by the commercial failures. The ripples spread far; the Caledonian Bank in Inverness had accepted Western Bank shares as security for a loan; its own shareholders were so afraid they might be liable that they caused its temporary closure.[11]

The City of Glasgow Bank had also had to close its doors at the height of the crisis in November 1857, but with support from the other banks was able to reopen in mid-December, despite being refused aid by the Bank of England.[12] By 1864 it had recovered its reputation sufficiently to be able to increase its capital from £670,000 to £850,000 by selling new shares to its proprietors at a 30 per cent premium.[13] Clydesdale secured its position as one of the leading Scottish banks by absorbing the failed Edinburgh & Glasgow Bank (1858) and buying the Eastern Bank (1863), increasing its note issue in the process. In 1864 Royal Bank took over the Dundee Banking Company.

English banks had been obliged to publish annual balance sheets by an Act of 1844. It did not apply to Scotland, but the Union and Clydesdale voluntarily published abbreviated accounts in newspapers. Alexander Blair at Bank of Scotland was not impressed. A balance sheet gave no reliable guide to solvency because the reader could not tell whether the assets were fairly stated or not – besides, publication would merely provoke speculators, he told his board.[14] The Commercial

Bank, which also clung to minimal disclosure, caused controversy in 1859 and 1864 by twice adding £200,000 to its capital from retained earnings, causing a surge in the share price each time. Shareholders had not been told the bank was sitting on such large accumulated profits and those who had sold in advance of the free issues were understandably angry.[15]

Nevertheless, for 20 years after the crash of 1857 Scottish banking prospered. There was a financial crisis in 1866 when the London discount house Overend Gurney collapsed with liabilities of £18 million, setting off a chain of failures across the City.[16] The day after became known as the original 'Black Friday' because of the violent panic in the London market.[17] The Bank of England had to raise its rate to 10 per cent, the highest it had been since the crisis of 1857, and inject emergency credit into the system. But in Scotland there was hardly a ripple and in the years that followed the leading Scottish banks were confident enough to open offices in London. In 1875 the Institute of Bankers in Scotland was founded to teach banking skills, hold examinations and issue certificates. It was the first professional banking institute in the world and a sign of the growing professionalism and confidence of the banking industry.[18] The Scottish banking system expanded by 40 per cent between 1865 and 1877.[19]

Alexander Blair had died in office in 1859, but his prediction after the Western debacle that the same thing could happen again proved to be correct. The ruin of the City of Glasgow Bank in the autumn of 1878 came almost out of the blue. Although there had been rumours in financial circles and the bank was having difficulty in getting other banks to accept its paper,[20] the most recent published accounts a few months earlier had shown an institution in apparent good health. With 133 branches, it had the third largest network in the UK, had deposits of £8.5 million and paid a dividend of 12 per cent. Its profits and reserves looked generous. Its £100 shares were trading at £236.[21] Nor was there any overheating in the economy, which had been depressed for five years and was growing at a historically low rate of 0.5 per cent.[22]

The way the crisis unfolded echoed the failure of the Western Bank 21 years before. On 30 September the general managers of the Scottish banks met for their regular meeting. The established banks operated as a cartel, co-ordinating interest rates and charges. On the agenda was a letter from the directors of the City of Glasgow Bank admitting that their last accounts had understated their exposure on bills of exchange; they were facing heavy losses and asking for an emergency loan. The other banks responded by sending an accountant to examine the City of Glasgow's books. His report, delivered the following evening, was damning: the loss could be £3 million – a figure he later doubled.[23] Any assistance was refused and when the City of Glasgow closed its offices that evening, it never reopened.

This time the other banks had learned the lessons of the Western collapse. They issued a statement to newspapers that they would continue to accept City of Glasgow notes,[24] pending liquidation, and shored up their own reserves against a run. There was no unseemly scramble to pick up the best bits of the failed bank.[25] Instead, the other banks acted to reassure customers and calm the market.

The City of Glasgow, it transpired, had itself come close to bankruptcy in 1857, but had learned nothing from the experience. It fell into all the traps the Western had succumbed to – maintaining insufficient reserves, becoming snared into continuing to support a handful of very large borrowers (four companies owed £5.5 million) and investing in highly speculative early-stage foreign ventures – but had compounded these errors with fraud. What may have started as merely trying to cover up mistakes soon became routine institutionalised lying. To support its note issue, the bank invented gold reserves it did not have and reported the false figures to the government. The accounts it gave to shareholders were works of fiction.

How had the deception gone undetected for so long? The directors rarely exhibited any interest in the real position of the bank and any who did were eased out of the company to be replaced by what one contemporary called 'men of straw'. Similarly, any staff who raised objections about what they were required to do were replaced. Lewis Potter, one of the board members, described as a 'snarling and garrulous old man', was a bully and effectively the agent of James Morton, whose wool broking company was one of the bank's largest debtors, owing £2.3 million. *The Times* reported: 'A wholesale system of fraud had been in existence for years, partly the outcome of a kind of terrorism which some of the persons who obtained control of the bank as its debtors were able to exercise over its officials. The bank had never been strong, and once before suspended payment, so that it was never in a position to face large bad debts. A firm had, therefore, merely to get deeply in its debt to become its master, and it had several masters of that kind who preyed on its resources till these were exhausted.'[26]

Following the bank's suspension, lawyers McGrigor Donald & Co. and accountants Kerr, Andersons, Muir & Main were appointed by the directors to investigate the true state of the business. What they found was horrifying. The City of Glasgow held enough gold and silver to justify a note circulation of £366,000, but its actual circulation was £604,000. Dishonest inflated returns had been made monthly to the government to make up the difference. It had lent £1.1 million more than stated in its most recent account, but had overstated the security for those loans by £926,000. The bank owned hard-to-sell assets, which were worth much less than their purchase price: a 40,000-acre sheep farm in the aptly named Poverty Bay, New Zealand, with another 11,000 acres leased, interests in farms in Queensland and New South Wales, shares and stock in the Western Union railway in the United States, some already pledged against borrowing. Bad debts were estimated at £7.3 million, three-quarters of which had been lent to just four companies against collateral worth less than £1.5 million. The balance sheet as published at 1 June showed capital at £1 million, reserves as £450,000 and profit for the year at £142,000. In fact the losses wiped out the capital and reserves and still left a deficit of £5.2 million.[27] To put this into context, it was nearly 5 per cent of Scottish Gross Domestic Product and nearly 0.5 per cent of UK GDP. Until the credit crash of 2008, this was the biggest banking failure in British history.

What makes the City of Glasgow affair unique was the speed with which the authorities acted. The McGrigor/Anderson report, completed in a fortnight, was published on 18 October 1878. The following day warrants were issued for the arrest of the directors and the general manager, charging them with false accounting and fraud. Since all but one of the directors also had overdrafts with the bank, they were later charged with theft, although this was withdrawn during the trial and the judge accepted they had not acted out of personal gain. They were remanded in Duke Street prison in Glasgow over Christmas and New Year, before being transferred to Calton gaol, Edinburgh, for the court hearings in January. Only one director was allowed bail, and that on the enormous surety of £15,000; the rest were refused.[28]

The trial, before Lord Moncrieff, the lord justice clerk, the second most senior judge in Scotland, caused a sensation. Lewis Potter, director, and Robert Stronach, general manager, were found guilty of fabricating and falsifying the balance sheets of the bank and sentenced to 18 months' imprisonment. Five other directors were convicted of issuing balance sheets knowing them to be false and sentenced to eight months. They had already served over three months.[29] The sentences were lenient and much less than common forgers could expect, but it was the last time that bank directors in Britain were sent to prison.

The action of the other banks limited the damage. They accepted City of Glasgow notes, continued to allow their own depositors to withdraw cash and allowed those City of Glasgow depositors who were not also shareholders to transfer their deposits, although only advancing them 50 per cent of the value pending liquidation.[30] Eventually depositors got all their money back, but without interest.[31] The fraud was so blatant that there were no recriminations against the Edinburgh banks. It was seen as an isolated case, not the start of a general financial collapse – although some connected firms suffered and in London there was a stigma against Scottish banking for a while. The Union and Clydesdale banks suffered 'unmerited discredit', merely by being headquartered in Glasgow and the share prices of all Scottish banks fell.[32]

The liquidation, however, had a major impact on Glasgow and the West of Scotland, where most of the shareholders lived, and to a lesser extent Edinburgh. The City of Glasgow Bank's shareholders had unlimited liability and were required to make good the full deficiency. Not only had they lost the £1 million capital they had invested, but were required to pay another £4.4 million. Unlike the Western Bank, the City of Glasgow had few rich shareholders and much of the stock was held by people of modest means. For the artisans or professionals this was an unaffordable sum of money. The problem was compounded by the revelation that the bank had been buying its own stock to support the share price, so reducing the number of shareholders liable for the losses, and that many shareholders had bought their stock with money borrowed from the bank and had few other assets. They were jointly and severally liable – i.e. they were collectively required to make up the whole sum, even if some of their number could not pay.

The first call from the liquidators was for £500 for each £100 share. This was enough to bankrupt many of the shareholders, so a second call for £2,250 per share had to be made to the still-solvent remainder. There were 1,800 shareholders, including 480 trustees holding the shares on behalf of others, often widows and orphans. By the time the depositors had been paid and the notes redeemed, only 129 shareholders and 125 trustees remained solvent.[33] The process caused such hardship and depression that an appeal had to be launched to support destitute City of Glasgow shareholders. Royal Bank contributed £20,000.[34]

The hapless Caledonian Bank, which had suffered from the peripheral damage of the Western Bank collapse in 1857, found itself in the same position again. It had accepted four City of Glasgow £100 shares as security for a loan and now found itself liable for its share of the losses. By the time this was quantified at only £11,000, many of its own shareholders had already sold their shares at panic prices to escape personal liability and depositors had withdrawn their cash. The bank had to close on 5 December 1878 and was only able to reopen eight months later after a fund was raised in Inverness to support it.[35] Other banks did not escape unscathed. Bank of Scotland had lent £340,000 to James Morton & Co. – which was City of Glasgow's largest debtor – and held debentures and shares in the New Zealand and Australian Land Company and other minor securities. These stocks were 'not at present marketable to any material extent', its treasurer reported. He hoped to hold them until the value rose sufficiently to pay off the debt 'with little loss'. It also had deficits totalling £54,000 with the Kames Gunpowder Co. and Buchanan Wilson Co., two other companies which had been City of Glasgow customers. Although it benefited from a big increase in deposits as a result of the City of Glasgow failure, Bank of Scotland had to increase its reserves against losses and reduce its dividend.[36]

The disaster forced an examination of some of the fundamentals of Scottish banking. One was the concept of unlimited liability. While the shareholders in banks were rich landowners or merchants, this reassured depositors, but increasing prosperity meant that ordinary people could afford shares and often bought them without appreciating the risk. In the words of a writer in the American *Bankers' Magazine*, unlimited liability had become 'a delusion and a snare'.[37] British banks had been allowed to adopt limited liability by an Act of Parliament of 1858, but existing partnerships had been reluctant to do so, fearing it would reduce public trust. A new Act in 1879 introduced a new hybrid 'reserved liability', which capped shareholders' risk at around £3 for every £1 invested and many banks moved to this new arrangement. Unlimited liability had meant smaller banks, more closely tied to their home cities. As more adopted restricted liability they could attract more shareholders, leading over time to a smaller number of larger banks. Limited liability banks tended to retain more capital in order to reassure depositors and this made them safer.[38]

A second consequence was audited balance sheets. Some banks adopted this voluntarily to assure depositors and investors that they were clean, but it became mandatory in 1879. Royal Bank was the first of the Edinburgh banks to increase transparency by publishing consolidated accounts in 1879, bringing together the balance sheets and profit and loss accounts of branches, agents, and cash and securities held at other banks.[39] Others slowly fell into line. Bank of Scotland issued its shareholders with a breakdown of its lending in considerable detail and an assurance that every loan over £10,000 had been fully re-examined.[40] Banks also became more conservative, keeping more of their assets in easily realised forms like government securities, increasing their 'funds for losses' and assessing the credit quality of their borrowers much more carefully.

The affair also heralded a much closer interest by government in how banks were managed and governed. A campaign by *The Economist* and the threat of private members bills from several MPs forced the government to introduce a new Companies Act in 1879. Although superseded many times since, Thomas Ward has argued that it marked a turning point in the regulation of banks: 'They were no longer regarded as being just private businesses like any other business, but were seen differently with a public interest in the stability of the banking system. The public interest in disclosure of more information, with the confidence provided by independent audit, conflicted with the private interest of bankers in keeping their affairs confidential – and the public interest prevailed.'[41]

Andrew Kerr, one of the earliest historians of Scottish banking and a bank official at the time, summed up the episode:

> This was the third of three great banking disasters in Scotland, which it is interesting to contrast. The Ayr Bank* was a high-class concern, founded on the landed interest. Although it was doubtless taken advantage of by self-interested people, there was more of ignorance and folly than of actual iniquity about it. The Western Bank, while not having aristocratic connection, was of good commercial standing; and, although its infatuation was culpable to a degree almost requiring the plea of insanity to excuse it, yet it did not descend to criminality. The City of Glasgow Bank was never

---

* See Chapter 10 above.

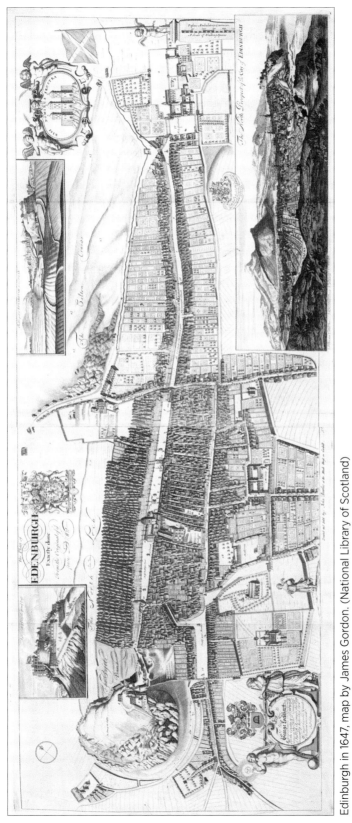

Edinburgh in 1647, map by James Gordon. (National Library of Scotland)

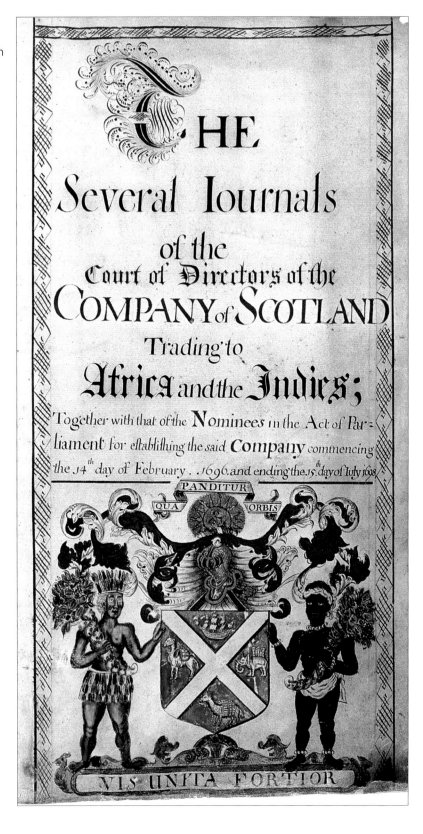

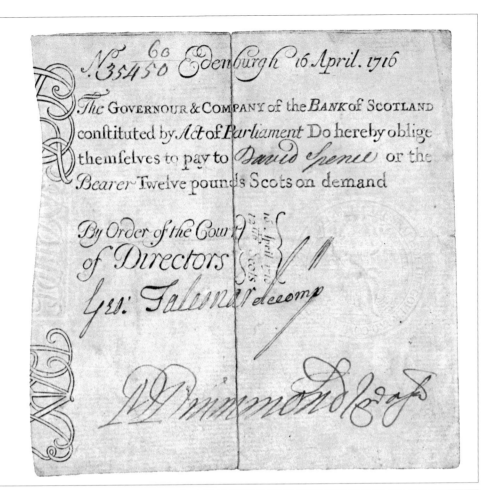

Above. Earliest surviving Scottish banknote, for £12 Scots, equal to £1 sterling. (Lloyds Banking Group © 2019)

Right. The Darien Kist, the strong box used by the Company of Scotland and passed to Bank of Scotland after the Darien disaster. (Lloyds Banking Group © 2019)

Above. An early Royal Bank of Scotland note, bearing the image of King George II, who had just acceded to the throne. (RBS © 2019)

Left. Alexander Webster packed his church with his hellfire sermons, but he was a hard drinker. He co-authored the world's first pension scheme based on actuarial principles.

John Campbell faced his first crisis as chief cashier of Royal Bank when Bonnie Prince Charlie entered Edinburgh. (RBS © 2019)

George Drummond was a visionary lord provost of the city, but also a director of the Royal Bank and the British Linen Company.
(The Signet Library, Edinburgh © 2019)

How an English lampoonist saw the credit crisis of 1772 and the collapse of the Ayr Bank.
(Lloyds Banking Group © 2019)

The Mound in 1809, with the newly completed Bank of Scotland head office behind its retaining wall on the right. In the distance the first North Bridge. (Lloyds Banking Group © 2019)

Henry Dundas, later Lord Melville, Tory fixer and Governor of the Bank of Scotland. (Lloyds Banking Group © 2019)

Above. The fraudster Gregor MacGregor floated a bond for his fictional state of Poyais. (Russell Napier)

Right. Sir Walter Scott, lawyer, writer, company director, went bust in the crash of 1825, but wrote his way out of financial ruin.

Below. An 'accommodation bill' from Archibald Constable to Sir Walter Scott. Constable was bankrupt by the time it fell due for payment. (Alistair Gibb)

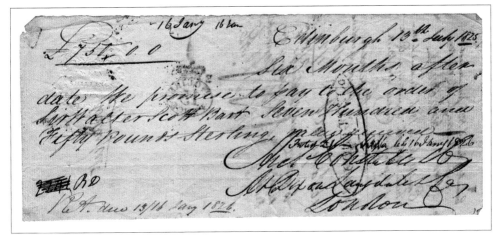

How a cartoonist saw the English and Scottish money markets during the crisis of 1825.
(Glasgow University Special Collections © 2019)

Crest for Caledonian Insurance, designed by the painter Henry Raeburn, who was a
director and shareholder.

The 'telling room' added to the Royal Bank head office in 1856. (RBS © 2019)

Trial of the directors of the failed City of Glasgow Bank in 1879. Seven of them went to prison.

Calendar for the Scottish Union & National Insurance Company for 1899. (Aviva © 2019)

Poster for Scottish Widows from 1890. (Lloyds Banking Group © 2019)

Left. Leonard Dickson, chief executive of Standard Life Assurance, died after being dragged along George Street by a runaway horse which he tried to stop. (Standard Aberdeen © 2019)

Below. National Bank of Scotland demolished several Georgian houses to make way for its American-inspired head office in St Andrew Square, opened in 1942. (RBS © 2019)

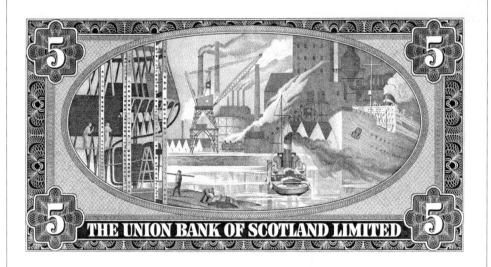

Above. Note issued by the Union Bank of Scotland, which merged with Bank of Scotland in 1955. (Lloyds Banking Group © 2019)

Right. An advertisement for the Commercial Bank of Scotland, showing its head office in George Street. (RBS © 2019)

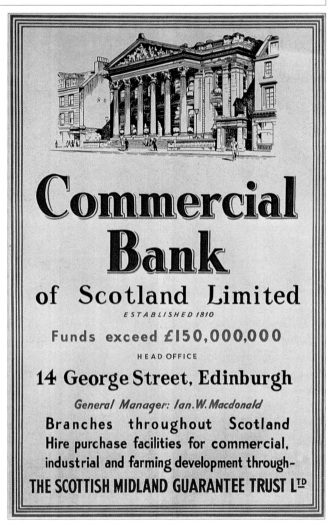

The merger of the National and the Commercial banks in 1958 made it the largest bank in Scotland at the time. Royal Bank joined it in 1969. (RBS © 2019)

Carlyle Gifford was one of the pioneers of the investment trust industry and built Baillie Gifford into a major fund management company. (Baillie Gifford © 2019)

Bruce Pattullo became treasurer of Bank of Scotland aged 41 and went on to transform the bank over the next 20 years. (Lloyds Banking Group © 2019)

Glasgow lawyer Tom Risk became governor of Bank of Scotland and formed an effective partnership with Pattullo, modernising the governance of the bank.
(Lloyds Banking Group © 2019)

George Mathewson was recruited into Royal Bank from the Scottish Development Agency and set in train major changes in culture and performance. (RBS © 2019)

George Younger gave up politics to become governor of the Royal Bank and helped Mathewson get board approval for his reconstruction of the bank. (RBS © 2019)

Charles Winter tendered his resignation as chief executive of Royal Bank in protest at the destruction of the traditional bank culture.
(RBS © 2019)

As the last chief executive of Bank of Scotland, Peter Burt thought that the merger with Halifax would secure its future.
(Lloyds Banking Group © 2019)

James Crosby became chief executive of the merged Halifax Bank of Scotland (HBOS), but resigned in 2005. He later surrendered his knighthood.
(Lloyds Banking Group © 2019)

Lord Stevenson became chairman of HBOS in 2001 and was in post when the bank failed in 2008.
(Lloyds Banking Group © 2019)

Fred Goodwin won praise for his integration of NatWest and went on to make Royal Bank briefly the largest bank in the world. He was stripped of his knighthood after the government rescue in 2008. (RBS © 2019)

Lord Stevenson, Andy Hornby, Fred Goodwin and Sir Tom McKillop apologised to the House of Commons Treasury Committee in 2009 for the failures of their banks. (PA Images)

highly esteemed outside the circle of its dupes, and seems to have been a long-continued fraud. It traded on the respectability of its neighbours and the unlimited liability of its shareholders. Blessed would it have been if, when it temporarily ceased the issue of notes in 1857, it had been held to have forfeited its right to issue. This would have practically terminated its evil career at a comparatively early stage.[42]

Part 3

Modernisation and internationalisation

22

Financing American railroads

THE COLLAPSE OF the Western and the City of Glasgow banks reinforced the conservatism of the Edinburgh banking cartel, which entered a decades-long period of complacency. Seven large banks – five in Edinburgh, which accounted for 70 per cent of the market,[1] plus the Union and Clydesdale in Glasgow – now dominated the system, moving 'more or less in step, for more than 70 years'.[2] They grew, but all were organised in much the same way, and, through the general managers' committee, agreed their interest rates and charges. Only the location and distribution of their branches differentiated them and competition between them for customers was practically non-existent.[3] The directors of these banks were reinforced in their unshakable belief that their way was the only correct way. The failed Glasgow banks had not only been incompetent, but they had invested their depositors' money in wildly uncertain foreign ventures. The establishment banks were not going to follow them.

Both the Western and the City of Glasgow banks had made substantial advances to American railway companies. The railway boom in the United States was producing massive economic benefits and there were fortunes to be made investing in shares and bonds. But it was also a fiercely competitive market, full of traps for the unwary. Predicting winners and losers was beyond the capabilities of a Glasgow-based board and management. City of Glasgow had sought to tap into local knowledge by opening an agency in New York, headed by the chairman's brother, but early investments had not gone well. As part of their support in 1857, the establishment banks had insisted City of Glasgow close its US office, but the bank was in too deep to take its losses without endangering its survival and over the next 20 years a variety of complex schemes intended to extricate it merely increased the deficit.[4] When the bank was liquidated, its losses in America were only a small fraction of its total liabilities, but it had been tempted into a faraway market in which it was ill equipped to understand the risks, let alone control them. The other banks accepted the lesson.

If banking was about to become boring, another part of the finance sector was about to become exciting. Bankers may have averted their eyes, but other individuals had seen the potential in the fast-developing US economy. Like Britain, it had experienced a railway mania, but by the last quarter of the nineteenth century the market was beginning to mature. Two Scotsman had realised independently that there was money to be made and found novel ways to mitigate the risk.

The first was Robert Fleming, a shining example of the 'lad o' pairts', a bright boy from a modest family who won a bursary to Dundee High School, where he excelled at mathematics and bookkeeping. At 13 he began as an office boy to a merchant in the Cowgate, but by his late teens was holding responsible jobs in the offices of the large world-leading Dundee jute spinning companies, and winning the trust of prosperous and influential businessmen. He was also becoming fascinated with the stock market. An early loss during the crash of 1866 took him five years to pay off, but rather than dampening his enthusiasm, it shaped his subsequent investing philosophy of tempering courage with caution. By his mid-twenties he was managing the investments of Edward Baxter, a leading Dundee textile merchant, who had extensive overseas holdings. Fleming visited America for the first time in 1870, representing Baxter, and saw an economy rebounding from the end of the civil war. He returned convinced that it offered huge opportunities for investors.[5]

Options at home for those with spare capital to invest were limited. Company shares were still tightly held by the promoters, their families and associates. The stock exchanges, which appeared in every major city, did restricted business, and when new companies were floated their shares were regarded as high risk. Bank deposits, government securities and commercial debentures – stock carrying interest, but not a share in the ownership of the company – were more common. But by 1873 Britain was entering a long period of economic depression and interest rates remained low.

Fleming's insight was to see that the risk of investing abroad in new railway ventures could be spread by adapting a new sort of legal entity, pioneered a few years earlier in London. The Foreign and Colonial Government Trust of 1868 enabled investors to pool their holdings (in this case treasury bonds) and thus spread the risk. Fleming took the idea and adapted it, issuing a prospectus that promised a 7 per cent return by investing in the mortgage bonds (similar to debentures) of American railway companies – a far higher rate than was available by investing in Britain. It seems remarkable, but aged 27 and having visited America only once, Fleming persuaded four of the richest businessmen in Dundee to subscribe to his Scottish American Investment Trust in January 1873 (soon renamed First Scottish American Investment Trust).

He had laid the ground well. The minutes of the first meeting said: 'Mr Fleming had previously brought the subject under consideration of the gentlemen present individually, giving them a sketch prospectus of the nature of the business and the working of the proposed trust.' The prospectus stirred such enthusiasm that the target capital of £150,000 had to be doubled. Fleming was appointed manager and visited America soon after the launch, but his directors were not idle.

> The founders of the First Scottish were provincial merchants and self-made men interested in the operational aspects of their company and they were closely involved in day-to-day decision-making. They demonstrated great attention to detail; meeting in Dundee on an almost daily basis during the first few months of the trust's existence, and in a typically Scottish manner, the First Scottish charged even lower fees than Foreign & Colonial. These hard-working, self-made businessmen from Dundee were very different in style from the professional men and aristocratic individuals who established Foreign & Colonial in London and gave asset management a Scottish dimension.[6]

Fleming's initiative and drive (he subsequently visited the US 125 times) established Dundee as a phenomenal source of capital. By 1890 the total invested in America was estimated to be ten times the value of all the city's property and equivalent to 20 years of the city's savings.[7] It also made him a successful and celebrated pioneer of investing, but he did not keep his lead for long. Another Scotsman who had seen the potential in America followed Fleming two months later with a second pooled investment vehicle, the Scottish American Investment Company, which quickly became known as SAINTS.

William Menzies, nine years older than Fleming, was a lawyer whose practice in Edinburgh managed the financial affairs of well-heeled clients as their 'man of business'. He also acted as law agent for the Church of

Scotland. By 1873, he had already visited America three times and recognised the potential: he was attracted by the investment trust model, but as a lawyer he saw some of its shortcomings. Foreign & Colonial and First Scottish were both trusts with limited lives (ten years in the case of First Scottish) and were subject to the restrictions of trust law. SAINTS was established as a company with a different legal basis, which gave it much more freedom and allowed it to adopt an innovative capital structure. It would issue ordinary shares of £10, but call up only £2 initially. It would also borrow by issuing debentures, paying interest of 5.5 per cent – 1 per cent more than banks paid on deposits and even more than could be obtained from insurance companies or by investing in government stocks. The debentures were secured on the unpaid portion of the ordinary shares (i.e. the shareholders would have to pay off the debenture holders if the company failed), but in return the shareholders had access to a pool of borrowed money.

This was unprecedented financial engineering and its sophistication was a considerable advance on Fleming's straightforward trust (which later converted to a company). If not the first, this was a very early example of the professional use of gearing, using borrowing to amplify the return to shareholders – £100,000 had been called up from ordinary shares, but £400,000 of debentures was issued. The whole lot could be invested in American railway mortgage bonds yielding 7 per cent, with the debenture holders receiving 5.5 per cent and the difference going to pay the company's expenses and the dividend on the shares. If the investments were well chosen, everyone would gain – the secured debenture holders receiving a higher return than they could get in Britain without incurring undue risk, the shareholders receiving a dividend which could be double that of the debenture holders.[8]

They also had the advantage of pooled investment – their risk was spread over a portfolio of investments– and the company would choose the stocks for them and collect the returns due. Since they would be investing on the other side of the Atlantic this was a substantial saving in time and uncertainty over making direct investments themselves. Even with steamship travel and the electric telegraph (and telephone from the 1890s), remote investors were at a considerable disadvantage.

On 14 March 1873 William Menzies called nine business associates to a meeting at his offices at 22 Hill Street, Edinburgh, and explained his plan in detail. Despite its complexity, they approved his scheme and 15 days later SAINTS was formed. The prospectus promised that the company would invest in the US and 'British America' (Canada), firstly in 'well-selected railroad mortgages, Government, State and Municipal stocks' and secondly, in mortgages over 'improved city or county lots'. The legal form also allowed the company to receive money on debenture, deal in American securities and act as agents in collecting interest and coupons due in America. Menzies claimed that voracious expansion and limited capital in the US meant that interest rates must remain high for years to come and he added some colour: 'The wonderful fertility of the virgin soil, the multitude and variety of its production and manufactures, the rapid development of its railroad system . . . and enormous immigration taking place in America, all combine to the development of almost illimitable resources and the creation of material wealth.'[9]

SAINTS was enthusiastically received and fully subscribed in a month. Debentures went better than expected and by 1874 the company had reached the limit of its borrowing powers. There were 461 initial shareholders, mostly from Edinburgh, the borders and Fife. They included lawyers, their clerks, merchants, bankers, ministers of religion, clerks and manufacturers, doctors, accountants, academics, school teachers, army officers, architects, engineers, publishers, printers, plasterers, booksellers, fish curers and civil servants. The debentures appealed to widows and lawyers who managed family trusts, but there is evidence that the ordinary shares in investment trusts particularly appealed to women, who were beginning to demand more say over their own financial affairs. By examining the registers of Dundee investment trusts, Claire Swan has shown that women held more than a quarter of the shares, a much higher proportion than was common in joint stock companies of the time, where female investors usually owned less than 10 per cent. The figures are reflected in English financial companies of the period, so is likely to have also been echoed in the Edinburgh trusts. These were not merely widows who had been left stock, or wives whose husbands had put shares in their own names – between 40–50 per cent of the women investors were unmarried.[10]

William Menzies became SAINTS' manager, serving on a board with seven other directors. Sir George Warrender, a director of Royal Bank, who became chairman, was described as 'a shrewd, keen man of business, inclined to be purse proud, but just in his ways and method. If a shareholder proved unruly or unduly prosy, Sir George could snuff him out in a very polite yet decided way.'[11] Other board members included John Cowan, head of a papermaking firm and prominent liberal politician; Thomas Nelson, a publisher with an office in New York, had extensive knowledge of the US and was described as 'small, physically weak, mentally a giant with a great bump of kindness in his nature'; Alexander Duncan's family ran an American bank, (although they defaulted on a loan from SAINTS in 1875); Edward Blyth, consulting engineer to the Caledonian Railway, could appraise US rail opportunities. He had 'a great bump of common sense'.

The comments came from John Clay, who did the US investigatory work on potential investments. He described Menzies as an optimist, who took a broad view of things, but failed in detail. 'Through his kind-heartedness, his judgement was often swayed, the pendulum turning the wrong way to help some friend. I lay this garland on his grave – that he had a heart of gold.' Menzies set up an advisory board of Scots business-men in the US, led by John S. Kennedy, a Glaswegian working on Wall Street, who became SAINTS' agent, providing valuable market infor-mation. The company used the sterling it raised in Scotland to buy gold, which was then sold in the US for a premium against the dollar, which was still suffering the effects of the civil war.[12]

Fleming and Menzies arrived in the US at roughly the same time in 1873 to find their first investments. A financial downturn, which had begun in Vienna that spring, forcing European holders of US stocks to sell at depressed prices, spread across the Atlantic, triggering the failure of New York banks and a market crash. Prices were low, but it took time and judgement to decide which companies would survive and continue to pay the interest on their mortgages. Both men chose well, built their reputations as shrewd investors and expanded their businesses over the next two years. Fleming floated two further trusts, taking the total under management to £1.1 million, most of it raised in Dundee.[13] SAINTS had three rights issues (offering new shares to existing shareholders), trebling the amount of ordinary capital and increased its borrowing, despite reducing the interest it had to pay to 4 per cent.[14]

Between them, the two men had in a very short time established a new way of investing with a distinctive Scottish style. Both men believed in personal research, visiting companies and investigating their finances, markets, managements and governance before they would invest. Menzies described the basic principles in a lecture to the Scottish Chartered Accountants Students Society in 1890. Foremost he empha-sised the need for first-hand research: 'You will be told that it possesses advantages superior to any other railroad in the United States, and though possibly not yet built, it has a magnificent future before it. I was once offered the bonds of a railway company in the course of construction which were recommended to me on the ground that the railway commenced nowhere and ended nowhere, and therefore was not bound to carry through traffic at unpaying rates.'

Next was the need for fundamental analysis, to look for financial results and to investigate to see that they were honest results. Third came the need for a sense of perspective and understanding of the ranking of obligations – always choose 'first mortgages to get a "front seat" and if they represent real value, don't panic at the first sign of trouble, hold onto them and they are pretty sure to come right'. Menzies, as a Church of Scotland elder, valued morality: 'Whatever crazes prevail for a while evaporate and common-sense asserts supremacy in the long-run. The will of the people of American is a more autocratic power than that of the Czar of Russia … Among businessmen in the United States you will find men whose uprightness and integrity and code of honour is not surpassed by any businessmen of this country.'[15]

Menzies concentrated on railway mortgages and bonds and would not buy shares in the companies themselves. Also, he made it a rule that no more than 10 per cent of the capital of SAINTS should go into any one security. He would only invest in trunk lines, not feeders or branches and only in companies with a reasonable debt to value ratio. Net revenue had to be more than sufficient to pay the interest and the management had to be competent and honest men, in his judgement. As a lawyer, he insisted on a good legal form for the mortgage. His investing rules served him well. SAINTS always met the interest payments on its debentures and paid a dividend of 3 per cent in 1873, its first year. By the following year it could afford to pay 10 per cent and in the following 50 years never fell below that level and reached as high as 18 per cent. By the time he retired in 1903, William Menzies calculated that he had spent a year of his life on the Atlantic.[16]

The news that Scottish money was available in America spread quickly. It was not just railway companies that needed cash. In 1871 fire had destroyed the centre of Chicago, a city of 400,000 people and the third largest in the US. A massive reconstruction programme, coupled with a shortage of domestic capital pushed up interest rates to 8 per cent – double the rate available to Scottish lenders. Two Chicago businessmen, Henry Sheldon, a lawyer, and Daniel Hale, a banker, crossed the Atlantic in search of funds. They enlisted the help of James Duncan Smith, a solicitor to the Scottish supreme courts, and together they formed the Scottish American Mortgage Company in 1874. It adopted a similar capital structure to SAINTS and declared in its prospectus that it would invest only in mortgages on heritable property and would lend no more than half the value of a property.[17] In fact, although it was registered in Edinburgh, two of its ten largest shareholders were American and another four were Dundee merchants. The company initially concentrated on the state of Illinois, but when, after five years, rates dropped to 6 per cent it broadened its geographic range in search of higher returns.[18]

Other similar companies followed in rapid succession. The North British American Mortgage Trust was founded in 1875.[19] The American Mortgage Company of Scotland, 1877, invested in first mortgages on farms, 'a class of security so safe as to be largely taken advantage of by the American Savings Banks and by law the National School funds are required to be similarly invested'.[20] The Edinburgh American Land Mortgage Company, which followed in 1878, also invested in farm loans. The United States Mortgage Company and the American Trust and Agency Company were both formed in 1884.

The Scottish Investment Trust (SIT), which came in 1887, was founded by John Dick Peddie, who, unusually, was neither a lawyer nor an accountant, but an architect. He had also been a director of SAINTS and became the new trust's first chairman. An early investment was the purchase of offices at 6 Albyn Place, in the extended Edinburgh New Town. At the time of writing SIT is still an independent trust and still in the same building.[21] Although these companies survived, they had missed the bargain prices that Fleming and Menzies had been able to obtain in their pioneering days and their returns to investors were less impressive.[22]

The next big innovation came with the launch of the Edinburgh Investment Trust (EIT) in 1889 by the lawyer Patrick Campbell and the stockbroker James Lawrie. It was unashamedly 'me too'. It listed the existing trusts in its prospectus and baldly stated 'there seems ample room for another', but it was to be different in one important respect. Whereas all the preceding companies had invested in mortgages, EIT placed half its initial capital in the ordinary shares of 209 companies – from brewers and tobacco companies, to diamond miners and shipping lines.[23] This groundbreaking preference for equities doubtless reflected the expertise of James Lawrie, but it also responded to a fundamental change in the stock market. In the second phase of industrialisation, established companies were beginning to use the London Stock Exchange to raise capital for expansion by issuing large numbers of new shares. For the first time there was an opportunity for professional investors to take stakes in successful companies with proven products and markets which were raising capital to expand.[24]

EIT took a stake in the Distillers Company, which brought together several Scotch distilleries and achieved a stock market listing in 1886. As the whisky market boomed over the next 20 years, it proved one of the trust's best investments. It also bought shares in two north of England breweries, the De Beers Mining Company of South Africa and the Broken Hill Proprietary Mining Company of Australia. This was not yet the 'cult of the equity', of which Edinburgh was to become a leading exponent in the next century, but it was a pioneering advance in the profession of investing. With half its capital in shares (and the rest mostly in railway bonds, spread across South America, Europe, the Far East and the US), EIT could be considered higher risk than some of its predecessors.

Its capital structure, with only a quarter of its capital in ordinary shares while the rest was borrowed in debentures or preferred stock, was also fairly aggressive. Its shares were £10 and had to be fully paid on subscription. At a time when a hospital surgeon might earn £50 a year or a high school teacher £100, this was an expensive speculation. Nevertheless, it attracted a wide spectrum of shareholders, including a bank teller and a nursing sister with 10 shares each and a minister of religion with 20, although the first share issue was not fully subscribed and James Lawrie had to buy £28,000 worth himself.[25] Investment trusts were firmly established as a popular choice for individual investors and Edinburgh was to make them a speciality.

23

Ivory and Gifford

THE RUSH TO invest abroad astounded the anonymous writer in *Blackwoods Magazine*:

> For a small country like Scotland to be able to spare, even for a time, tens of millions sterling, is one of the most striking paradoxes in the history of commerce. The Scotch, of all people in the world, are supposed to be best able to take care of themselves and their money. Wherever a passably honest penny can be earned, they will not be far to seek; and yet it has come to this with them, that they will face almost any risk for the sake of the difference between 4 per cent at home and $4^1/_2$ per cent across the Atlantic or at the antipodes.[1]

The author estimated that, even in 1884, before the Edinburgh Investment Trust had been formed, two-thirds of the money invested abroad by British investment companies – or about £20 million – had come from Scotland. Add in direct investments in mines, land, cattle and lumber companies, private holdings and others and the total was over £40 million.[2] The investment and mortgage companies and cattle businesses, he conceded, were making a reasonable return, but he had little praise for other forms of investment. Two-thirds of Scottish mining ventures returned nothing and the stock was worthless; only one land company returned 10 per cent, one 4 per cent and several were 'barren': 'The lumber companies have been crooked branches of the tree of know-ledge ... and their dividends require no elaborate calculation.' His conclusion was that once you netted off losses and underperformance, the capital would have been better employed at home.

And yet the enthusiasm for investing overseas seemed undimmed. American investment houses were advertising in Scottish journals for funds, and Australian banks, mostly managed by Scotsmen, recruited

Scottish lawyers to procure deposits.[3] Bank of Scotland acted as agent for the Bank of South Australia and for Australian and New Zealand mortgage companies.

The connection between Scotland and the antipodes was not new. There had been two-way trade for most of the nineteenth century and, besides money, Scotland also provided emigrants and expertise – agriculturalists, stockbreeders, land managers, bank clerks, bureaucrats and agents. The vast land holdings built up by James Morton, which had helped to bankrupt the City of Glasgow Bank, were transferred to a company headquartered in Edinburgh after the liquidation.[4] Unable to borrow from the banks, it asked Standard Life to advance £20,000. The board initially agreed, but then withdrew the offer, but within a month the life assurance company had lent £8,000 secured on a property in New Zealand and a few years later was building a large antipodean mortgage business. Scottish Widows was also active, opening an office in Sydney in 1886.[5] But Australia was headed for a crisis and new entrepreneurs were about to enter the market and to exploit it in the way Menzies and Fleming had been able to do in America more than 20 years earlier.

James Ivory came from a family of lawyers – his grandfather had been a judge, his father an advocate and sheriff – but after school at Harrow and a period in Germany he chose to train as an accountant. This was not unusual; many lawyers also performed what we would now see as accounting functions for their clients and Sir Walter Scott had pronounced accountancy 'highly respectable' as a profession.[6] The Edinburgh Society of Accountants had been established in 1853 and the following year received its Royal Charter.[7] Ivory qualified as a CA after training with a firm in the city and set up his own practice in 1887 at the age of 25. In 1895 he went into partnership with Thomas Sime, forming Ivory & Sime, but in 1907 Sime emigrated to Canada, leaving his name, but taking no further part in the business.

In the 1890s Australia suffered a severe financial and economic crisis, the result of international financial tightening, exacerbated by a prolonged drought that hit agricultural businesses. Mortgage holders began to default and provincial governments could not borrow, forcing them to cut back on spending. Gross domestic product fell 10 per cent in 1892 and a further 7 per cent the following year and did not recover until 1899. Credit seized up as more than half of note-issuing banks suspended payment and several non-bank financial institutions failed.[8] The effect on Scottish owners of Australian securities was dramatic; prices plunged and their stocks were virtually unsaleable. Those who had been attracted by high interest rates to lend to Australian banks found that their money was frozen, with no certain date when they might be able to withdraw it. James Ivory saw this as an opportunity. In 1897 he founded the British Assets Trust (BAT), raising first £15,000, later increased to £50,000, and placed advertisements in Scottish newspapers:

AUSTRALIAN BANK DEPOSITS – The British Assets Trust is prepared to purchase a limited amount of deposits of Australian reconstructed banks. Holders desirous of realising are requested to communicate the amounts held by them and the price at which they are willing to sell to James Ivory CA, 65 Castle Street, Edinburgh.[9]

As a second string, Ivory also offered to buy, or lend money against, life assurance policies and included a pre-printed form in BAT's prospectus, which included the requirement to 'state present health', and asked 'what is the surrender value?' He anticipated the market in endowment policies by nearly a century.[10] Ivory's business model was to buy distressed assets as cheaply as possible, hold them until prices recovered and sell or redeem at a profit. He was obviously gambling that the issuing companies would survive, but his faith and judgement paid off. Between 1898 and 1914 BAT's annual return to its shareholders averaged 6.9 per cent, much higher than could be obtained by investing in British government stock or depositing cash with a bank.[11]

As he sold, he reinvested the proceeds not in Australia but in the US, and by 1914 over 80 per cent of BAT's money was in American recovery stocks. He also invested in industrial companies, which were to become household names, such as Westinghouse, International Harvester, General Motors and Otis Elevator, and in oil in the US, Mexico and Canada.[12] But James Ivory was not done with the antipodes. Working with Alfred Shepherd, a partner in the law firm Guild & Shepherd, he formed the Canning Downs Estate Company in 1901, which bought 33,000 acres in Queensland for £104,000. Again the plan was to buy while prices were depressed and hold until they recovered, and again it proved successful. Over the next five years the land was sold in small parcels, netting a £31,000 profit after expenses. Ivory and Shepherd went on to form the Caledonian Assets Trust, but it was short lived and in 1905 Ivory liquidated it and folded the capital into BAT.

The liquidation notice shows that Ivory had moved his office to Charlotte Square, although to No. 43 rather than No. 1, which was much later to become the home of Ivory & Sime.[13] The move did not endear him to his neighbours. Robert Adam had designed the square as the most desirable residential location in the New Town and the other inhabitants did not appreciate the intrusion of commerce.[14] Not that it would have bothered Ivory very much. He was a motoring enthusiast and owned one of the first cars in Scotland, with the number plate S3. His own home, Laverockdale House in the leafy suburb of Colinton, was 15 minutes' drive away and he could park the car in front of his office. Ivory had commissioned the celebrated architect Sir Robert Lorimer in 1907, but it was 1912 before Laverockdale was complete. In Scots baronial style with 'mod cons', including its own electricity generator and an internal telephone system, it was designed to give him the feel of a country estate, with the convenience of proximity to the city.[15] He filled the house with his collection of Arts and Crafts furniture, of which he was a noted and knowledgeable collector.

James Ivory's grandson Ian described him as an arrogant man. 'He did what he believed to be right and to hell with the rest.'[16] But he could also be generous and was a philanthropist, supporting the Pleasance Trust, which ran a welfare centre in one of the poorer parts of Edinburgh.

The pre-First World War years were exceptionally profitable for those trusts investing in America. Periodic Wall Street panics provided buying opportunities, but the underlying economy was strong. SAINTS, for example, steadily increased its dividend year after year until 1912, but the war brought dramatic changes.[17] Exchange controls made it difficult to deal in the US and funding the war forced the government to increase the national debt 12-fold, issuing vast quantities of new securities, including war loan. Many investment trusts sold all or part of their US holdings, or deposited them with the Treasury as security for obtaining US dollars. This was initially done voluntarily, but after 1917 became compulsory. SAINTS liquidated nearly two-thirds of its £4.2 million of US assets by 1916 and bought government stock.[18] The end of the war brought austerity and a bleak investment outlook. Exchange controls were still in force, making it very difficult to reinvest in the US, or to repatriate the proceeds of those American assets that could be sold.

Where others saw barriers, James Ivory saw opportunity. He had been a shareholder in the Edinburgh American Land Mortgage Corporation since 1901 and joined the board in 1918. Since its foundation 40 years before, its record had been uneven. Its prospectus in 1878 had promised that it could borrow in Britain at 4–5 per cent and invest in the US at 8–9 per cent, but by the time it was ready to invest in 1880 the market had turned down. Rates were 7 per cent and from this it had to pay its American agent 1 per cent and a similar amount to its American broker. It had to abandon its exclusive focus on farm lending to buy what was going in the market. By the turn of the century business had picked up, but the board contemplated merging with the Alliance Trust in Dundee or being taken over by the Investors Mortgage Company, another Edinburgh fund. Neither of these possibilities came to anything.[19] Its activities in America ground to a halt during the war and immediately afterwards its long-time manager, William Wood, a nephew of the founder, died.

Edinburgh American Land had a portfolio of farm mortgages and railway bonds worth $2.8 million – or £600,000 at the then current exchange rate – but its market capitalisation (the total value of its shares) was little over half this. James Ivory saw that buying the company was a way of obtaining US assets at a time when a straight exchange of dollars for sterling was impossible. In 1919 he made an offer for the company. Although this is often described as the first contested corporate takeover in British stock market history, it was not the dramatic and acrimonious bid battle that we have become used to in the twenty-first century. It opened with a letter from Guild & Shepherd, representing BAT, to Carment, Wedderburn & Watson, solicitors for Edinburgh American Land, stating that an offer was being contemplated and politely asking for permission to examine the books 'to enable them to determine as full a price as was justified'.[20]

The board was initially uncertain, there was some haggling over the firm's reserves and Ivory had to increase his offer, but eventually he won over the directors and their professional advisers and bought the company for £337,500. He immediately changed the name (to Second British Assets Trust) and the investment style. The American portfolio was progressively sold off and the proceeds reinvested. The shareholding was simplified and the borrowing sharply increased. With high gearing the potential rewards to shareholders were magnified, but so was the risk, although this was not a problem until the Wall Street crash of 1929.[21]

James Ivory had established himself as one of the smartest and most audacious investors in Edinburgh and founded a dynasty that was to last for 80 years, with his sons Basil and Eric following him into the business and eventually his grandsons too. But he also had his reverses. With Alfred Shepherd, his close collaborator and fellow investment manager, he had launched the Electrical Securities Trust, which was to invest in electricity supply firms at home and abroad, but Ivory's enthusiasm for electricity was not yet shared by the investing public and the venture failed.[22] A much greater set back was a putative offer Ivory wanted to make for the Oregon Mortgage Company, managed by the Edinburgh law firm Murray, Beith & Murray. Before he was ready to go public, the news reached the Oregon board, which reacted with hostility, blocking the bid. Ivory blamed Shepherd for the leak and never used the firm again.[23]

★ ★ ★

While James Ivory was building his reputation and his company, a young lawyer was beginning his journey to becoming another of the most successful investors in Edinburgh. Carlyle Gifford* accepted an offer to go into practice with Colonel Augustus Baillie in 1907. It was a good combination: Gifford was an energetic and technically gifted young solicitor, Baillie was not a lawyer at all, but an old soldier and landowner who had come into the law by being a notary public. His strength was his connections among the prosperous landed gentry: Baillie got the clients and Gifford did the business.

The firm's move into fund management came fairly soon after Gifford's arrival through a chance conversation with Alastair Macgregor, son of an Edinburgh stockbroker, and home on leave from his job in the Malayan (now Malaysian) rubber planting industry. The growth of the motor industry meant there was a great prospect ahead for rubber, he said, but a slump in prices following a Wall Street panic had made it very hard to raise funds to plant new trees. Gifford saw an opportunity and the Straits Mortgage and Trust Company was established in 1909. It would raise money in Scotland to finance 'well-planted rubber estates for the purpose of maintenance and development until the tapping period is reached'. Baillie called on his circle of friends to provide both the initial seed capital and a board that included several men who were already directors of rubber companies. The 40,000 £1-shares (a quarter paid on subscription) were taken up before the prospectus was published.[24]

---

* He was christened Thomas Johnstone Carlyle Gifford, but was always known by his third name.

But events moved fast. The success of the Model T Ford heralded the start of a mass market for cars and stimulated other manufacturers to enter the market, prompting a sharp jump in rubber prices by 1910. This had a double effect on the new company. It made it easier to attract new funds and the share issue was increased to 100,000. But it also meant that planters were much more able to raise money, so the opportunities envisaged in the prospectus were harder to find. The directors had to look elsewhere, first making investments in debentures or convertible shares in established rubber companies and then buying into businesses outside the rubber industry. By 1913 the company conceded that it was no longer a specialist rubber investment vehicle, but a general investment trust. The name was changed to the Scottish Mortgage and Trust.

Scottish Mortgage was sufficiently successful to prompt Baillie and Gifford to launch a new vehicle in 1914. The Scottish & Foreign Trust was to invest in the emerging markets of the time. Russia particularly was thought to be full of potential, with vast natural resources and its troubles – the Russo–Japanese war and the failed revolution of 1905 – well behind it. Some £85,000 was invested in Russian railway and city bonds, with other investments in China and Brazil. The outbreak of war, Russia's defeat and the 1917 revolution sunk Scottish & Foreign, and when it was wound up in 1927 it owed £104,000 to banks. Shareholders got nothing.[25]

A second new venture in 1914 had a happier fate. The Edinburgh, Dundee and Aberdeen Investment Company was to have a diversified portfolio across industrial sectors and geography. Baillie again brought in influential directors and shareholders, including several Dundee jute barons, so it was not surprising that the company's initial holdings included three Scottish registered jute companies with interests in Bengal. There were also stakes in UK companies, including the engineering and defence company Vickers, Standard Life and the Edinburgh Investment Trust, as well as American railways – Union Pacific, Southern Pacific and the Aitchison, Topeka and Santa Fe. There was an investment in the Russian Commercial & Industrial Bank bought at £35 a share, which the new trust was fortunate to be able to sell at £25 in March 1917. The outbreak of war, however, brought investment activity almost to a standstill. The London Stock Exchange closed for five months and Wall Street for nine, and Colonel Baillie and the trust's chairman, also an officer, were recalled to their regiments.[26]

As was the custom at the time, both these trusts were highly geared – they increased the risk/return of their shareholders by borrowing, either from banks or by issuing debentures or preference shares. In the case of Scottish & Foreign Trust, debt meant that the losses were greater. In the case of Edinburgh, Dundee and Aberdeen, the gains were magnified. Managers and investors were prepared to face higher risk to get the prospect of higher return.

The end of the war brought a stroke of luck for Gifford. The secretary of the Scottish Canadian Mortgage Company, founded in 1913 with £164,000 to invest in western Canada, resigned through ill health. Gifford was appointed secretary (and subsequently manager) and immediately set about remaking the portfolio. Low-yielding holdings were sold and the proceeds reinvested in a range of new stocks as widely dispersed as the Assam Frontier Tea Company, the Rio de Janeiro Tramway, the Sao Paulo Electric Company and several US utilities. Scottish Canadian also made a small investment in one of Baillie Gifford's own trusts, Scottish Mortgage, and was taken over in 1926 and renamed Second Scottish Mortgage & Trust Company.[27]

The 1920s brought slow growth in Britain and Europe, still recovering from the war, but boom times in America and a rapid expansion of Baillie and Gifford's funds under management. Carlyle Gifford used the good returns for his investors to launch a steady series of new capital issues in each of the trusts.[28] To mark the growth of the investment business, Gifford split the firm in two: Baillie & Gifford WS continued offering legal services, but investment management was transferred to a new entity, Baillie Gifford & Company.

★ ★ ★

By the end of the decade Scotland had made an indelible mark on the investment trust industry. Of 209 trusts in the UK, 79 were in Scotland and the majority of those were based in Edinburgh.[29] Although there were many professional investment managers in the city, there were two dominant personalities: James Ivory and Carlyle Gifford. They shared several characteristics – they were intelligent, visionary, entrepreneurial and ready to take risks. They were also strong personalities, able to convince or cajole their boards and their employees into following their leads. Neither liked to be told he was wrong.

They also had influence outside their own companies. James Ivory had joined the board of Standard Life in 1906 and with Charles

Whigham, another accountant, who represented the New York bank J.P. Morgan in Scotland, he persuaded the company's conservative directors that the higher returns available in American farm mortgages were worth the increased risk of investing abroad.[30]

Gifford's reputation had spread to London. In 1924 he founded the Independent Investment Company, together with the economist John Maynard Keynes and the investment manager Oswald Falk. It was to have a very active investment policy, switching nimbly between asset classes, but with three such strong personalities there were inevitable disagreements. 'Falk would buy a stock one day only for Keynes to sell it the next!'[31] Gifford felt himself caught in the middle and resigned in 1931. But that year Baillie Gifford was asked to take over the management of three London investment trusts – Friars, Abbots and Monks – and in 1935 another, the Winterbottom. He was also one of the founders of the Association of Investment Trust Companies, becoming chairman in 1934.[32] Curiously, however, he resisted invitations to join the board of a bank or major insurance company.

Why Ivory and Gifford fell out is a matter of conjecture. The proximate cause seemed to be the refusal by Ivory of an invitation to sit on one of the Baillie Gifford trust boards,[33] but the enmity between the two firms outlasted Ivory's death in 1939 and was only really ended after Gifford's death in 1979. The Wall Street Crash of 1929 and the Depression of the 1930s exposed the weakness of their high-risk, high-gearing investment model. Dividends in their flagship trusts had to be slashed and were not restored to their pre-crisis levels until after the Second World War. Investors were kept in ignorance about how much their capital had been diminished by the simple expedient of not publishing valuations.[34]

24

Consolidation

JAMES IVORY AND Carlyle Gifford were typical of the new men starting and running financial companies. Whereas a century before they might have learned their business skills as merchants, now they were professionals who were adapting their training as lawyers, accountants, bankers or actuaries to managing money in investment companies, banks or insurance firms. They still looked to the aristocracy or landed gentry to give tone and old-world respectability to their boards, but political influence was less important than connections to wealth. The old rivalries of Whig and Tory, which had led to the plot by Henry Dundas (Tory) to unseat Lawrence Dundas (Whig) as governor of Royal Bank, and to the founding of the Commercial Bank (Whig) and the National Bank (Tory), were less and less relevant. The Whigs had become the Liberals, but, especially after Lloyd George's People's Budget of 1910, they had only a few adherents among the financial elite, who were mostly Tories now. Carlyle Gifford was unusual in having republican sympathies, perhaps because of his experience in the US, which made him refuse to accept an honour, while his contemporaries could expect to be made knights at some point during their careers.[1]

Financial services was Edinburgh's dominant business sector and one of the most important in Scotland. Of the 108 largest companies north of the border in 1904, a third were financial – 8 banks, 14 insurance companies, 22 investment and property companies.[2] Although the two largest companies were both railways, the North British with a capitalisation of £47million and the Caledonian with £42 million, seven banks had capital of more than £10 million – Bank of Scotland £15 million, National Bank £14 million, Commercial £14 million, Royal Bank £13.6 million, Union Bank £12 million, British Linen Bank £11.9 million and Clydesdale Bank £10.9 million. Insurance companies were also large – Scottish Widows £17.2 million, North British & Mercantile £16.3

million, Scottish Provident Institution £13.1 million and Standard Life £10.9 million. The banks held deposits totalling £96 million, while the insurance companies managed £100 million, half in the four largest. The 22 investment and property companies managed £15 million.[3]

These companies were bound together by a network of cross-shareholdings and shared directors. Of the 108 largest companies, 85 per cent had interlocking directorships – a total of 612 men held 833 director-ships. Virtually all the financial businesses were connected in this way. The average size of a bank board was 11 men, of which 7 would have more than one directorship. With investment companies, the average size was 5–6 people, 3 of whom would typically be on more than one board. Scottish Widows' board had 12 multiple directors, Union Bank 10, Royal Bank 9, Standard Life 9. The remaining banks had 8 multiples each.[4]

Two titled chairmen had led Bank of Scotland for 50 years – the Earl of Stair from 1870–1903, succeeded by Lord Balfour of Burleigh from 1904–21. The Marquis of Linlithgow linked Bank of Scotland and Standard Life by sitting on the boards of both. The sixth Duke of Buccleuch occupied the governor's seat on the Royal Bank board practic-ally by hereditary right. Since the third duke was installed by Henry Dundas in 1777, a Buccleuch had been governor of the bank continu-ously, except for a gap from 1819 because the fifth duke was only 13 when his father died. However, the place was kept for him and from 1838 he served as governor until his death in 1884. (In fact the tradition continued until the eighth duke stepped down in 1969 when Royal Bank merged with the National and Commercial, see below). The sixth duke was also on the boards of Standard Life and Scottish Equitable, where he rubbed shoulders with the Earl of Mansfield, who was also on the board of the National Bank. The Marquis of Tweeddale (who, unusually, had been a Liberal MP before succeeding to the title) was a director of the Commercial Bank, Edinburgh Life and Scottish Widows, as well as being chairman of the North British Railway.

Place holding was not uncommon. The Earl of Elgin resigned from the Royal Bank board in 1894 when he became Viceroy of India, but returned in 1904, replacing the Earl of Strathmore, who had been on the board since 1868. The old order was changing, but at a snail's pace. Of the men with multiple directorships 32 held titles, 25 of these were hereditary. Lawyers and accountants dominated the remainder of the financial companies' boards. Leonard Dickson, an accountant who was chief executive of Standard Life, joined the Royal Bank board in 1906 and served until 1919, when he died following an attempt to stop a runaway horse led to him being dragged along George Street. As well as cronyism, there was nepotism. The sixth Duke of Buccleuch sat alongside his son, the Earl of Dalkeith, on the boards of Royal Bank, Standard Life and Scottish Equitable. Members of the families of Dundas, Balfour of Burleigh, and the brewery magnates Younger and McEwan, either by direct descent or by marriage, popped up frequently. Ivory and Fleming founded dynasties.

The aristocrats met in the House of Lords, but the professional elite also had their social centres – the New Club in Princes Street and when in London, the Caledonian Club. They played golf together and in the season fished for salmon, shot grouse or deer on the estates of their board members or more affluent customers. In their day jobs they moved in exclusively male company. The First World War took many male staff away, but the banks were reluctant to employ women to replace them. By 1918 Bank of Scotland had only 39 female staff, from a total of 804, and these as clerks.[5] Similarly, the social lives of the senior managers were also spent largely in male company. It was not until 1970 that the New Club admitted women as 'associate members' confined to their own annex; they became full members only in 2010. It was 2017 before the Honourable Company of Edinburgh Golfers allowed women to join and play on its course at Muirfield. Not all men were misogynists. James Ivory's American wife Florence was an active suffragette and Emmeline Pankhurst stayed at Laverockdale House when addressing meetings in Edinburgh.[6]

The professional financiers lived well. The titled directors had to suffer in cold and draughty ancestral piles, but the new business elite built themselves mansions with all the modern conveniences. James Ivory could drive in from Laverockdale House in his motorcar, when he was not at Brewlands, the estate he bought in Glenisla. Carlyle Gifford, a keen squash player, had a private court built a short walk from his home in Rothesay Terrace.[7]

Sir George Anderson, treasurer of Bank of Scotland 1898–1916, eschewed motor transport and preferred to arrive at The Mound in his horse-drawn carriage from Beechmount, the grand house he had built in Murrayfield. Set in eight acres on the slope of the hill, it cost £30,000 and contained a library and billiard room as well as pillared public rooms. From its turrets there were, according to a contemporary, magnificent views 'to landward and seaward' – perhaps a little exaggeration, since Corstorphine Hill blocks any view to the Firth of Forth.[8] Anderson, who always dressed in a black frock coat, considered himself the doyen of Edinburgh bankers and insisted on chairing the general managers' committee meetings. He had assumed airs and graces since his beginnings as an apprentice in the Fraserburgh branch of the North of Scotland Bank. Bank of Scotland rewarded him well – £5–6,000 a year, some 40 to 50 times the salary of a clerk. In addition, the bank paid his income tax.[9]

With a board of titled amateurs above them, the general managers were omnipotent in their banks. Anderson was said to be 'a strict businessman with a will as hard as granite, he will not go back upon his decisions on any account'. At British Linen Bank, Hamilton Hotson was 'a thorough martinet and is apt to forget the monotony of banking life and how banking employees are subject to ... the malady of sameness'. Andrew Aitkman at the Commercial Bank had such an even tone of voice that if 'he kicked [an employee] downstairs [he did so] with so charming a grace ... he thought he was handing him up.' Thomas Smith at the National Bank was more mild mannered. In his career he had 'followed the line of least resistance and made no enemies on the way up'. Dean Swift's benediction 'Blessed are they who expect nothing, for they shall not be disappointed', was said to have applied to him.[10]

The general managers carved up the Scottish banking market between them. They were protected from competition from outside Scotland by a 'gentlemen's agreement', made in 1876[11] that the English banks would not open branches north of the border and the Scottish banks would not expand into England. Single London offices and a few Clydesdale Bank branches in Cumbria were overlooked. Within Scotland the general managers changed their interest rates and charges at the same time and pledged not to poach each other's customers or staff. This restriction hit bank employees hard. If a bank worker felt his (still overwhelmingly men) promotion was being blocked unfairly, he could not leave and join a rival bank. Transfers between institutions happened only at the highest levels. For lower rank staff the alternative to stagnation was either a change of career or emigration to the banking systems of the colonies, particularly Canada and the Far East. Wags said that HSBC, the initials of the Hongkong & Shanghai Banking Corporation, stood for 'Home for Scottish Bank Clerks'. Canadian banks were active in the Caribbean and advertised in the *Scottish Banker* magazine for experienced staff.

To work in a bank was seen as socially prestigious and secure, but bank clerks were underpaid and exploited. Typically, boys would enter the profession straight from school at age 16 and become indentured apprentices – bound by a legal contract which specified, among other things, that the apprentice could not marry without his employer's consent. They would be given menial jobs like filling the coal buckets and cleaning the brass plate outside the door, progressing – provided their handwriting was good enough – to writing up the branch journal and balancing the ledger. Each branch had to balance its books every evening and only then could ambitious employees go off to evening classes to study for the examinations of the Institute of Bankers in Scotland. Poor wages forced some clerks to take second jobs, working as collectors at greyhound race meetings, until the general managers issued a circular prohibiting such activities.[12]

Attempts in 1919–20 to form a union – the Scottish Bankers' Association – were headed off by the employers with a combination of intimidation and promises that were never kept,[13] but discontent rumbled on through the 1930s until in 1937 a strike was called. It was to be led by a walkout at the Union Bank, where the Association claimed 80 per cent membership, but the management moved to crush it, threatening all strikers with the sack and the loss of the employer's contributions to their pensions. The strike was over by 10 a.m. in the Glasgow head office, and by lunchtime staff in the other branches were back at work. In protest at the bank's heavy-handed measures the Co-operative Wholesale Society withdrew its account. The Union's general manager dared it to leave, believing that no other Scottish bank would accept it because of the 'no poaching' rule, but he was wrong. Commercial Bank, perhaps with some vestige of its radical roots, accepted the business.[14]

In 1920 Bank of Scotland had sought to modernise by obtaining new legislation, amending the 1695 Act of the Scottish Parliament that set it up. For the first time it was permitted to open branches abroad and carry out a range of services that were prohibited by the original Act. Notably, the provision that anyone becoming a Bank of Scotland shareholder would gain Scottish citizenship was abolished.

This had become controversial a century earlier in 1818, when George Sandy, the bank's secretary, had written in alarm to Lord Melville, the chairman, enclosing list of 49 men, who, judging from their names appeared to be foreigners and had purchased stock totalling £10,000. He suggested that 'these parties may have had other motives than merely becoming naturalised Scotchmen',[15] a sensitive subject in the xenophobic atmosphere following the end of the Napoleonic Wars. Melville discussed it with the home secretary and it was decided to try the matter in the courts. One of the new shareholders, a Chinese named William Macao, was chosen to fight a test case, with the bank paying his legal costs. Lord Alloway found in Macao's favour, but the government appealed and two years later had the ruling overturned. Macao was thus a legalised Scotsman for two years, but, since the 1695 Act preceded the Act of Union, he was never a British citizen. However, he continued to live in Edinburgh and when he died in 1831 was buried in St Cuthbert's churchyard.[16]

Scottish banking was insulated by the era of gentlemanly capitalism. Deals concluded verbally seldom needed writing down and hostile take-overs were unthinkable against honourable men, who came from the same backgrounds, shared the same attitudes and were members of the same clubs. But isolation could not withstand the pace of economic change. A wave of consolidation in England had created a 'Big Five' group of London banks, the smallest of which was larger than all the Scottish banks put together. The larger industrial companies north of the border, particularly those based in Glasgow and the west, were doing increasing proportions of their business in the south. For them, the Scottish banks lacked scale and a network. In 1918 Lloyds bought the National Bank and a year later the Treasury approved two 'affiliations', which were actually 100 per cent takeovers. Barclays bought British Linen Bank and Midland bought Clydesdale (and later the North of Scotland Bank). Scottish banks had often discussed amalgamations between themselves, but personal differences usually led to these talks going nowhere. Only the minor provincial banks were absorbed, Royal Bank taking the Dundee Banking Company in 1864 and Bank of Scotland absorbing the accident-prone Caledonian Bank in 1906.

Royal Bank made cross-border raids of its own. In 1924 it bought Drummonds, the London private bank established by the expatriot Scot Andrew Drummond in 1717. In 1930 it took over Williams Deacons Bank, which had a network of branches in the northwest of England, and in 1939 it purchased the private partnership Glyn Mills & Co, a London merchant bank.[17] Both these companies had been in trouble and the Bank of England had been actively trying to find a partner for them, but nevertheless they gave Royal Bank a meaningful presence in the much larger English market for the first time. Drummonds was integrated into Royal Bank's branch network, but the other two acquisitions remained separate from the Scottish operations. None of the English banks attempted to integrate their Scottish acquisitions, which continued to operate much as they had done previously, with their own boards, managements and seats on the general managers' committee. Ownership had changed, but very little else.

★ ★ ★

Banks fared a little better than the investment trusts during the First World War. Their assets were not requisitioned and, although they were obliged to buy war loan, it was issued on very favourable terms. Scottish banks subscribed to the first £350 million issue in 1915 up to 10 per cent of their deposits, in line with other banks. The plan had been that the commercial banks would take £60 million of the loan, the Bank of England £40 million and the remaining £250 million would be bought by the public. Recent research has shown that patriotic fervour did not extend to financing the war effort; the public fell short, buying only £91 million. To avoid a propaganda disaster, the Bank of England secretly provided huge loans to its cashier and deputy cashier so that they could make up the shortfall and the government could claim that individuals had purchased the full amount.[18] Later issues of war loan paid progressively higher rates of interest and went better. By 1916 Scottish banks held £60 million, representing 30 per cent of their deposits.[19] To fund the war effort money had been diverted from commercial lending, particularly to stockbrokers, who were important customers for the Edinburgh banks, but not considered priority borrowers by the government.

Financing the war effort was controversial. The banks were allowed to convert other government securities they held into the more favourable new loans. Bank of Scotland converted the whole of its stock of consols into war loan.[20] By the end of the war the national debt placed a huge burden on the public finances, which took many years to clear and contributed to the Depression of the 1920s and 1930s. Not for the last time, the government was accused of giving special treatment to the financial industry. The radical Labour politician Tom Johnston, who later became secretary of state for Scotland, published a blistering attack in 1934:

The war was not to be fought with interest-free money and/or/with conscription of wealth; though it was to be fought with conscription of life. Many small businesses were to be closed and their proprietors sent overseas as redundant and without any compensation for their losses, while Finance, as we shall see, was to be heavily and progressively remunerated.

As each war loan became exhausted the lenders upon the first lower-interest war loans were permitted to transfer into the later higher interest loans, and usurers' interest upon credit was added to the national burden, so that to-day that burden is insupportable and the nation staggers along, cutting the bread and cheese of its poor and starving the social services in a vain attempt to meet the charges incurred in the Great War Loan ramps.[21]

By the time the Second World War was declared in 1939 the financial system was much more ready than it had been in 1914. The government and the Bank of England had been preparing since the Munich crisis of the previous year, when Prime Minister Neville Chamberlain's agreement with Hitler started the slide towards conflict and caused a run on the pound. Emergency regulations gave the Treasury the ability to increase the money supply without reference to parliament and the Currency (Defence) Act made the banknotes of the Scottish banks legal tender for the first time. This, and the shortage of coin, meant that the circulation of Scottish notes shot up. Bank of Scotland started the war with £23.7 million of its notes in issue, but by 1945 this was £65.9 million. The demands of wartime finance meant that an increasing proportion of bank assets were channelled into buying government stock, at the expense of lending to individuals and companies that were not directly involved in the war effort. As a proportion of deposits, lending more than halved during the war years and loans that were made were directed to defence contractors, like Barr & Stroud, the Glasgow optics company which made submarine periscopes, rangefinders and binoculars, or to agriculture, which was ramping up home food production.

When the war ended the banks found their balance sheets skewed towards government stock. This was fine as long as interest rates remained low and gilt prices high, but with post-war reconstruction demanding increased investment, the government could not allow this situation to go on indefinitely.

The life assurance companies were more perceptive in seeing change coming and switched their holdings from gilts to commercial securities. The election of a Conservative government in 1951, committed to raising interest rates and cutting public debt, caught the banks off guard. Gilt prices fell, reducing the value of their reserves and leaving them weakened. All banks were in a similar position, but Bank of Scotland was particularly exposed, with a deficit on its investments of £5.2 million.[22] At the same time nationalisation of basic industries like coal and railways (and later steel) robbed the Scottish banks of some of their biggest customers, as decision-making moved to London. Automation and the need for investment also weighed heavily on the sub-scale Scottish sector. Midland Bank moved first, merging its two Scottish subsidiaries into a single entity – the Clydesdale and North of Scotland Bank, later simplified to 'Clydesdale' – to cut costs and improve marketing. It was clear to the others that they had to act.

In the early 1950s the treasurer of Bank of Scotland retired and the board broke with tradition by going outside the banking system for his replacement. The choice was William Watson, who had been a non-executive director on the bank board for several years. A qualified chartered accountant, he had spent most of his career in investment management at Baillie Gifford and had risen to be one of the most senior partners, running the company during Carlyle Gifford's years in America doing war work for the British government. But in 1947 the two men clashed so fundamentally that Watson resigned.[23] Baillie Gifford's loss was an opportunity for Bank of Scotland. To the bank staff he appeared as an aloof outsider with little understanding of day to day banking, but they were unaware of the weakened reserve position, which was where Watson's investment experience made him the ideal candidate as he began to rebuild capital strength.[24] He also opened merger talks with the Union Bank and the Commercial Bank, which also had a new chief, another outsider, Ian Macdonald, a former professor of accountancy at the University of Glasgow. After a while Macdonald pulled out, believing that a three-way amalgamation was too complicated to succeed, but the other two went ahead and the deal was announced in 1952, with the integration complete by 1955.

The two banks, which adopted the Bank of Scotland name, had complementary strengths, the Bank in the east and the Union in the west. The Union's magnificent new American-style head office on the junction of St Vincent Street and Renfield Street, became the Glasgow head office and the merged bank kept local boards on each side of the country – later adding London and north of Scotland boards. It was now unequivocally the largest bank in Scotland – but not for long.

In 1958 Ian Macdonald broke off talks with British Linen Bank and was surprised to receive an offer to merge the Commercial Bank with the National Bank.[25] Such a move made sense in the overcrowded Scottish banking market and would propel a combined bank to near the top position, but the Commercial had previously ruled out the idea, fearful of losing control. The new approach was instigated by Sir Oliver Franks, chairman of Lloyds, who told Macdonald that Lloyds was prepared to accept a minority shareholding in the combined bank and pledged not to make a bid for 100 per cent ownership.[26] The two men knew each other from their time at the University of Glasgow. Macdonald had been a part-time accountancy professor while Franks had occupied the chair in moral philosophy, which Adam Smith had held two centuries previously. Franks's assurance cleared one obstacle to the merger, but talks nearly foundered on the Commercial Bank's insistence that Macdonald become full-time executive chairman of the combined bank. This was resisted fiercely by the board of the National and only resolved by Franks's personal intervention with Macdonald, who became chairman, but conceded that there should be a general manager.[27] To clear the air, the Commercial Bank agreed that the name of the merged bank be National Commercial, rather than their own preference Commercial & National. Relations with Lloyds were restored and shortly afterwards the National Commercial announced a move into hire purchase as a joint venture with Lloyds,[28] which seemed at the time to be a sound move into a fast-growing sector of the consumer market.

The merger left Royal Bank feeling increasingly uncomfortable, as computerisation put renewed strains on modernisation budgets. In 1969 it announced its merger with the National Commercial. The new group would trade in Scotland under the name Royal Bank. In England Royal merged its two subsidiaries into one – William & Glyns – which retained a separate banking licence and management autonomy and absorbed the National Commercial's 43 English branches, the result of an acquisition of a small English bank.

As the more profitable of the two banks, Royal Bank shareholders received 55 per cent of the new entity, but it was a takeover by the National Commercial in all but name. The holding company for the whole group was the National & Commercial Banking Corporation, Ian Macdonald became chairman, with John Burke, another National Commercial man, as general manager. The head office moved from Sir

Lawrence Dundas's former house at 36 St Andrew Square to the huge square edifice of the National Bank, a few doors along at 42. The Commercial Bank's Victorian Greek temple nearby in George Street became the international office. The merger ended the near feudal reign of the Dukes of Buccleuch as governors of Royal Bank. The roles of governor and chairman of the board had been split and the eighth duke held a largely ceremonial title, but the new company dispensed with the post altogether.

The two managements promised to make significant cost savings 'without giving rise to any redundancies'.[29] There were over 1,000 branches in the combined group, with overlap affecting 850 of them; nevertheless, branch closures proceeded slowly. The merger was waved through by the Treasury and the Bank of England without a reference to the Monopolies & Mergers Commission. Lloyds was diluted down to 16 per cent and again pledged not to make a bid for the whole group, but it retained its 50 per cent share of the joint venture hire purchase firm, now called Lloyds & Scottish.

This left British Linen Bank as the wallflower. A merger with Bank of Scotland had been discussed since 1967, but it was 1971 before its board agreed a takeover proposal, with Barclays, as the owners of British Linen, accepting 35 per cent of the enlarged Bank of Scotland Group.[30] It was a very gentle merger by today's standards – for five years afterwards promotion was by turn rather than by merit, with a candidate from one bank followed by a candidate from the other bank.[31]

In 20 years eight Scottish banks had been reduced to three, but had Scotland's banking history meant that the country had become 'over-banked?' Whereas in England in 1951 there had been one bank branch for every 4,500 people, in Scotland the figure was 3,000. The average English bank branch collected £641,000 in deposits; in Scotland the figure was £429,000.[32] Even allowing for Scotland's more challenging geography, this put Scottish banks at a competitive disadvantage to their southern neighbours – it cost them more to collect deposits. Consolidation was supposed to answer this problem, but rationalisation was slow. In 1951 there had been 1,699 branches in Scotland. Ten years later the figure was still 1,683.[33] In many larger towns and the cities you could still see branches of the same bank within a short walk of each other.

★ ★ ★

In the middle of the shrinkage in the number of banks, a new one was founded. In 1969 a young advocate, Angus Grossart, who was qualified as a chartered accountant as well as in law and had a flourishing commercial practice, joined with Iain Noble, a director of the Scottish Council Development and Industry, to form Noble Grossart – a new merchant bank. In traditional Enlightenment Edinburgh style, the two men had met as members of the Speculative Society, founded in 1764, although neither of them was from the city. Grossart was from the west of Scotland and a graduate of the University of Glasgow. Noble, whose father was a diplomat, had been educated abroad and then in England at Eton and Oxford.

In his law practice Grossart had seen increasing amounts of work for Scottish companies going to London banks and did not see why much of it could not be done in Scotland. Noble's interest was much more in economic development; he wanted to see more Scottish companies founded and grow. The two men raised £300,000 from Scottish financial institutions and began corporate advisory and a modest lending business. 'Neither of us had worked in a merchant bank and I had not ever been in one,' Grossart recalled.

Iain Noble left after 18 months, selling his shares to buy an estate on Skye and beginning a career as a serial entrepreneur, starting a hotel and a whisky company and later the Gaelic college, Sabhal Mòr Ostaig. He was involved in the shipping firm Seaforth Maritime, the oil company Lennox Oil and Noble & Company, a corporate advisory business he began with his brothers. Noble Grossart, meanwhile, flourished, adding share placings and stock market introductions to its range of services and taking small share stakes in promising Scottish companies, such as the coachbuilder Walter Alexander, the Wood Group, which was expanding in oil services, and Stagecoach, the bus operator. In 1975 it won the mandate to manage a £250 million fund from the Kuwait Investment Office.

25

The slow decline of gentlemanly capitalism

ON SUNDAY 9 May 1965 Sir Alastair Blair, lawyer, chairman of three investment trusts, board member of Bank of Scotland and Scottish Widows, sat down to lunch at the long communal table in the clubhouse of Muirfield golf course. His arrival was the signal for those already dining to get up and silently move as far away as possible, taking plates, cutlery and wine glasses with them. Among the tight-knit Edinburgh financial elite of the time there was no more dramatic way than a public snub of demonstrating that a line had been crossed.[1]

Sir Alastair's sin was one of association rather than commission. He was chairman of two trusts managed by Ivory & Sime, British Assets and Second British Assets, which held a controlling interest in a third trust, Atlantic Assets. It had just been exposed as having an incentive scheme for its managers that today would be considered modest by the standards of many hedge or private equity funds, but at the time shocked the establishment. The *Daily Express*, favourite newspaper of the middle classes, had splashed across its front page: 'The secret £500,000,' with a picture of Blair in the green uniform and eagle-feather bonnet of the Royal Company of Archers, the Queen's bodyguard in Scotland, and Lord Polwarth, governor of Bank of Scotland and a director of British Assets.

Neither man stood to gain from the incentive arrangement, but they were the most visible targets for the disapproval of their peers on other boards. Having to eat alone was not the only sanction Blair had to suffer. His fellow directors of the Investors Mortgage Security Company, which he also chaired, forced him to resign. The fallout affected others. Eric Ivory, son of James and now senior partner in Ivory & Sime, was made to stand down from the chair of the Scottish Investment Trust and later to resign from the board. Blair, Polwarth and Ivory also suffered socially; dinner invitations were withdrawn and there was said to be 'much weeping' among the women of the Ivory family at their ostracism.

The end of gentlemanly capitalism is usually reckoned to date from 'Big Bang', the deregulation of financial services by the Thatcher government in 1986, but the Atlantic Assets affair showed that the seeds had been sown long before. Atlantic had been formed in 1954 with a share structure that rewarded its managers, who included Eric Ivory and Jimmy Gammell, his young nephew by marriage and the up-and-coming star of the firm. The arrangement treated all shareholders equally until such time that the capital of the trust was tripled and an income of at least £100,000 was achieved. After that, the managers were entitled to one-sixth of the increase in capital and income.[2] The trusts were quoted on the Stock Exchange, but the arrangement was not disclosed to shareholders at the time. It was only when the targets were reached and the managers started to reap the benefit of the good performance 11 years later – the £500,000 of the *Express* headline – that it became known and caused a sensation.

Harold Wincott, doyen of investment journalists, had exposed the scheme in two articles in the *Investors Chronicle*, concluding: 'We can instance many, many cases of other trusts which have done just as well for their shareholders (and their country) ... without the necessity of providing special and secret arrangements.'[3] The source of his information was rumoured to have been Ivory & Sime's rivals Baillie Gifford, particularly 84-year-old Carlyle Gifford himself and George Chiene, the firm's senior partner. They clung to the old ethos of the investment management industry, that service rather than personal enrichment was the guiding principle. Gifford attempted to write to *The Times*, saying 'a grave blow, unparalleled since investment trusts started eighty years ago has been struck at confidence in directors and managers'. The letter was not published on legal grounds, presumably because there were more personal allegations made later in the text.[4] Chiene was outraged that managers should seek to make money for themselves, seemingly at the expense of their clients. As the firm's official history makes clear: 'no-one who was an active partner in Baillie Gifford ... was at all interested in becoming personally wealthy and all were content to live comfortably but not extravagantly while doing a stimulating and intellectually satisfying job to the best of their ability.'[5]

It is likely that Eric Ivory shared this traditional view, but had allowed the incentive scheme to ensure that Gammell, who was very interested in making money, stayed with the firm. The son of a general and himself a former soldier who had been at both Dunkirk and the D-Day landings, Jimmy Gammell's family had once possessed wealth and land, but had lost both. He felt it his duty to rebuild the family fortunes.[6] He was bright, with an analytical mind and saw more quickly than most of his competitors that in an era of high income taxes, capital appreciation rather than a steady income were what investors would want from a trust. He marked the beginning of the end of the reign of the 'professional amateur' and brought a new rigour and competitiveness to investment management, favouring research over gut feel. He succeeded Eric Ivory as senior partner and over the next 20 years made Ivory & Sime the leading Edinburgh investment house, taking it into new areas such as the oil industry, first in Texas then in the North Sea, but also challenging the orthodoxies of the investment management sector and occasionally taking big risks.

★ ★ ★

By the 1970s the winds of change were sweeping through the banking industry too. The board of Bank of Scotland was faced with stagnation. The profit in 1978 was the same as five years earlier[7] and although some of the group's subsidiaries, such as the consumer credit company North West Securities, the corporate advisory business trading under the revived British Linen Bank name, and the international division were doing well, the core domestic bank was barely profitable. Of the top 200 commercial companies in Scotland, Bank of Scotland held the accounts of less than a quarter, only slightly ahead of the much smaller Clydesdale Bank. Royal Bank serviced half.[8] There was still a strong sense of 'small n' nationalism among the directors and a fear that poor performance made the bank vulnerable to a bid and the loss of its independence. The Barclays shareholding was a bulwark against takeover, but Barclays was becoming disillusioned: Bank of Scotland was neither a subsidiary it could control, nor an attractive investment.[9]

The retirement of the treasurer (as Scotland's oldest bank still called its chief executive) offered the opportunity for change. The board was still led by an aristocrat, but Lord Clydesmuir was not from the traditional landed elite; his title was only one generation old and he was a member of the Colville family, west of Scotland steelmakers. Tom Risk, a Glasgow corporate lawyer, who was the deputy governor, persuaded Clydesmuir to leap a generation and promote Bruce Pattullo, a tall, reserved and intelligent man who was only 41, and had been running British Linen.

Pattullo was unusual in having attended a Scottish prep school and Rugby before taking an economics degree at Oxford. Twenty years before when his contemporaries had looked for jobs in the city of London he had returned to Scotland and been one of the bank's first graduate recruits. Graduates had been treated much the same as people who had joined the bank straight from school. He had been required to study for the qualification of the Institute of Bankers in Scotland (having acquired the habit of individual learning at Oxford, he opted for correspondence rather than night classes) and had progressed through the traditional bank system, 'passing money over the counter' and making the tea – the essential rites of passage for a senior bank executive to have credibility with his staff – before being moved around the bank and gaining a good general knowledge of how it worked and the problems it faced. Although he played golf, Pattullo's passion was tennis and he had a court built in the garden of his home in west Edinburgh. Aspiring managers in the bank began to work on their serves.

He favoured evolution rather than revolution, but quickly began to change the corporate culture from one of top-down decision-making to empowerment. He abolished the central 'business development unit', which was supposed to find new opportunities and customers, but had not. Instead he sent a memo to every manager challenging them to come up with ways to grow the parts of the business under their control. An impressed junior manager told me at the time: 'The treasurer has let it be known that he's interested in ideas from anywhere.'

At the top, he ended the old hierarchical structure and formed a board of general managers, who met regularly to discuss their own parts of the business and the progress of the group as a whole. From 1981 it included Joan Smith as the bank secretary, the first woman to reach the executive. With Risk, who had succeeded Clydesmuir as governor, he redesigned the bank's governance – separating the role of the directors, who concentrated on strategy and acted as trustees of the interest of shareholders (no longer called Adventurers as they had been in 1695, but still quaintly called 'proprietors') and the management board, which ran the bank day to day. Younger managers were promoted, new products introduced and a new marketing campaign launched under the slogan 'A Friend for Life'. The London banks had abrogated the century-old gentlemen's agreement by beginning to open branches in Scotland, giving Pattullo the opportunity to expand into the ten times larger English market.[10]

In 1984 Barclays decided to sell its one-third stake in Bank of Scotland. Risk asked to be allowed to find a buyer, rather than have the shares put up for auction which might have been the trigger for a bid. The bank had a long-standing relationship with Standard Life, largest of the Edinburgh life assurance companies, as its principal banker and biggest reseller of its policies. Risk was also a former chairman of the insurer, so he picked up the telephone and called Robert C. Smith, the current chair, who was an old business friend from Glasgow. Quietly, in a typically Edinburgh way, the two Glaswegians arranged that Standard Life would acquire the Barclays stake for £155 million and provide a safe haven against the fear of takeover.[11] One insider called it 'a squalid Edinburgh stitch-up', but it showed that some vestiges of gentlemanly capitalism remained.

The following year Pattullo outlined to his senior executives the progress his reforms had made. Pre-tax profit was up 35 per cent on the previous period, over five years it had doubled and compared to a decade before it had increased by 474 per cent. Only Lloyds Bank had achieved a better result in the UK banking market.[12] The bank now had double protection against predators – the largest block of its stock was in safe hands and its superior performance meant that its shares were expensive.

While the Bank of Scotland directors on The Mound shored up their own defences, below them in the New Town the Royal Bank board was also feeling vulnerable. Faced with a recession at the beginning of the 1980s the Royal was finding it hard to increase its market share. There was some success in reducing staff numbers and the Royal seemed to take pride in paying its staff less than other Scottish banks, but profit per member of staff was declining compared to the Royal's competitors.[13] On top of this the new Conservative government led by Mrs Thatcher had imposed a windfall profits tax on banks, which would cost the Royal £12 million and badly deplete its reserves.[14] Lloyds Bank no longer felt itself bound by its no-bid pledge and had been making informal approaches to the board, which concluded it needed to decide its own destiny. In order to preserve its independence, it proposed to give it up.

Merging Royal Bank with a larger partner had first been mooted by board member Sir Michael Young-Herries (usually known as Michael Herries) in 1976. Herries was from a Dumfriesshire landowning family and after Eton, Cambridge and war service with the King's Own Scottish Borderers, when he won a Military Cross, he had joined Jardine Matheson, the powerful Hong Kong-based trading house, rising to become *Taipan* (managing director). There he had become friends with Peter Graham, his opposite number at the Chartered Bank, second only to the Hongkong & Shanghai Banking Corporation (HSBC) as the largest bank in the colony. Graham was now deputy chief executive of Standard Chartered (the merger of the Chartered and the Standard banks) and was keen to diversify the group's activities from its core markets of South Africa and the Far East by making a major acquisition in the UK. It had only a minimal presence in Britain, even though it was registered and headquartered in London. The early talks came to nothing, but with Lloyds pressing either to sell its stake in Royal Bank or make a bid for the whole thing, Herries, who became chairman in 1978, resumed the discussion. In March 1981 Standard Chartered made a formal offer of £334 million, which was recommended by the Royal Bank board. Sir Gordon Richardson, governor of the Bank of England, had been kept informed and gave his blessing to the arrangement.[15] It was a deal arranged between gentlemen.

It may have made sense in St Andrew Square, but when the news broke few others in Scotland saw the logic of selling out. The Royal's directors were unprepared for the hostility their announcement provoked. Individuals and institutions lined up to criticise the board for abrogating its responsibility to grow the bank and proposing to abandon the independence of one of Scotland's oldest institutions to a bank headquartered in London and chaired by a failed former Tory chancellor, Lord Barber. Pointedly George Mathewson, the chief executive of the Scottish Development Agency, went public with his opposition to the merger. It was very unusual for the head of a government body to take such a controversial stance and, since Mathewson was known to have a close working relationship with George Younger, the secretary of state for Scotland, there was a belief that he was voicing the opposition the minister could not express openly.

The gentlemen of Royal Bank were shaken. A worried Herries telephoned Richardson to discuss the fierce opposition, but much worse news came soon afterwards. HSBC made a counter offer which valued Royal Bank at £500 million – 50 per cent above the Standard Chartered bid. HSBC was led by Michael Sandberg, who would also have known Herries well. Not only had they been prominent businessmen in the colony and at the same time, but both had been stewards of the Hong Kong Jockey Club, one of the most prestigious social organisations. Sandberg, however, did not feel himself bound by the unwritten rules

of the Hong Kong expatriate elite and had built his bank by befriend-
ing and backing some of the aggressive Chinese businessmen and
property developers who were propelling the colony into the top rank
of world business centres. HSBC had been eyeing Royal Bank for some
time and was furious that Standard Chartered seemed to be about to
get the prize for 'an idiotically low price with the accompanying air of
a stitch-up'.[16]

Sandberg had also been to see Richardson, who had made it clear he
would not countenance a bid from HSBC, which he considered was not
a British bank and operated outside the UK regulatory system. Sandberg
was used to the *laissez-faire* atmosphere of Hong Kong, where the financial secretary, Scotsman Sir John Cowperthwaite, believed that the
market, not the government, should regulate banks. Despite Richardson's
disapproval, HSBC went ahead with a counter offer.[17] Sandberg's audac-
ity shocked the City of London. The governor of the Bank of England
had ultimate responsibility for the banking system and such was his
power that it was joked that he had only to raise his eyebrows to quash
any move he did not like. Now he had been defied and the authority of
the Bank called into question. A furious Richardson might not be able to
stop HSBC from bidding and could not ensure the success of the
Standard Chartered approach, but he had other means to thwart
Sandberg's ambition.

A few weeks later both bids were referred to the Monopolies and
Mergers Commission. Few doubted that Sandberg's disregard of
Richardson's opinion was the hidden reason for the investigation. Neither
offer raised competition issues, so the pretext for the investigation was
the regional interest – how the bids would affect the Scottish economy
and society. Royal Bank's submission struggled to make a convincing
case for its acceptance of the Standard Chartered offer, or to differenti-
ate it from the HSBC bid. There was more than a hint that Sir Gordon
Richardson had influenced the bank's words. HSBC, Royal Bank
claimed, did not have a good reputation for compliance with actions
which the Bank of England deemed to be in the national interest:
'Conclusions are drawn which show considerable concern about the way
in which a Royal Bank under Hongkong & Shanghai ownership would
co-operate in control of the UK banking system ... Intolerable strains
would be placed on management of a member bank of the Committee of
London Clearing Banks and the Committee of Scottish Clearing Banks
if they were "encouraged" by their Hong Kong masters to act in a way

which did not allow Royal Bank to play its proper part in co-operating with the Bank of England.'[18]

At the beginning of 1982 the Commission ruled against both bids, leaving Royal Bank without a strategy to take the company forward. John Burke, now called managing director rather than general manager, wrote to his staff to persuade them that the board was not as unprepared as it looked and implying that although the Standard Chartered bid had not won support in the country, that was not the reason the bank had faced such hostility: 'Banks in general, by the nature of their business, are traditionally unpopular in certain minds and any opportunity is taken to subject them to criticism. Additionally, in these difficult times many businesses and individuals are undergoing financial collapse and the people concerned may believe, in most cases irrationally, that their bank is at fault in not providing them with unlimited amount of financial assistance.'[19]

It was hardly an inspiring message for a staff wondering what the future held for them and one can sense Burke's disillusionment. He retired later that year, to be replaced by Sidney Procter, a Lancastrian who had been managing director of Williams & Glyn's, the group's English subsidiary, which operated independently from Royal Bank. On either side of the border the two banks had different branding, separate products, different strategies and, despite the fact that both used IBM computers, IT systems which did not talk to each other. Procter did what no Scotsman had dared to do, he set about integrating the two banks and renamed all the southern branches as 'Royal Bank of Scotland', giving the group for the first time a High Street presence across the UK under the same name, and a claim to be the fifth force in British banking (the London Big Five, having been reduced to four by consolidation). Lloyds had dropped its desire to bid for the whole group, but now wanted sole ownership of the hire-purchase business. Royal Bank dragged its feet over accepting Lloyds' offer for its 40 per cent stake in Lloyds & Scottish, but finally conceded, ending its involvement in a pioneering and successful venture.

Procter was only in post three years before retirement, but he did a lot to try to show that the bank had not run out of ideas. In a rare flash of entrepreneurialism it invested £20 million to back Peter Wood, who was to revolutionise the motor and household insurance businesses with his Direct Line telephone-only service. In 1985 Procter bought Charterhouse Japhet, a London merchant bank, in a £150 million deal said to have been concluded over dinner in New York with the financier Jacob Rothschild. To finance it Royal Bank raised £115 million by issuing new shares, so, for a brief time, it was larger in market capitalisation than Midland Bank, smallest of the Big Four, although it lagged in assets and profits.[20] It was a fitting end to Procter's career and he retired in 1985.

His successor, Charles Winter, an affable chain-smoking, time-served Scottish banker who had started as a 16-year-old apprentice in Dundee, continued to make acquisitions. Charterhouse took advantage of the 1986 deregulation of the stock market to buy the Liverpool-based stock-broker Tilney; Winter bought a travel agent chain, A. T. Mays, in the belief that it could sell the bank's personal loans to holidaymakers; and in 1988 the group made its first US purchase, buying Citizen's Financial, a New England personal bank. There was a justification for each purchase, but it was hard to discern a coherent underlying strategy and unlike Bank of Scotland, Royal Bank had not reformed its management structure or practices. There were 14 grades between the lowliest clerk and the exec-utive, and the people at the top jealously guarded their privileges – chauf-feured cars and the 'mess' – a suite of dining and reception rooms on the third floor of the headquarters where senior managers were waited on by liveried staff.[21] Winter never forgot his roots and would not have described himself as a 'gentleman' in the social sense that many of his board members were, but, especially after a heart attack, he did not have the energy or the authority to change the old order.

26

Banking: the cultural revolution

BY THE LATE 1980s several of Royal Bank's non-executive directors were becoming concerned that its poor profit performance and slumping share price could make it vulnerable to collapse or takeover. They persuaded the board that new blood was needed to bring energy and ideas. Sir Robin Duthie, chief executive of the tent maker Blacks of Greenock, had been chairman of the Scottish Development Agency (SDA), and pushed the name of its Chief Executive, George Mathewson.

Mathewson was not a career banker. He had been born in Dunfermline and after studying electrical engineering to doctoral level at what is now the University of Dundee, but was then a college of the University of St Andrews, he had worked for Bell Aerospace in the US and taken an MBA degree there. He came back to Scotland at the beginning of the oil boom to work for the investment bank ICFC,* rising to become a main board director based in London responsible for a portfolio of a thousand companies. He returned north as the second chief executive of the SDA, and transformed a bureaucratic government body into a nimble, dynamic organisation focused on industrial investment, urban regeneration and the attraction of investors from the US and Japan. At the end of his five-year term he was considering an offer to run a New Zealand electricity company when the call came to move to Royal Bank as director of strategy, but with the clear expectation that he would succeed Charles Winter as chief executive.

Unlike many of the Royal's top executives, who gave the impression they were content with the bank's performance, Mathewson was fiercely competitive and combative – he played club rugby into his fifties and once joined a tennis party at the home of Bruce Pattullo, but was not invited back: 'He always hit the ball very hard, it didn't make for very

* Now called 3i.

enjoyable games.' But he was also a team builder. He had managed the transformation of the SDA with a small group of bright young men, mostly recruited from outside the agency. When he moved to Royal Bank as strategy director he brought the team with him. These were not time-served bankers, but intelligent, ambitious people, many with postgraduate degrees and the arrogance which comes with being young and highly educated in a workforce where many of their superiors had not been to university. Their analysis of the problems of the bank showed contempt for the ponderous management structure and complacent attitudes. Society and business had changed rapidly, but banking had not kept pace with it. With a handful of like-minded second-tier executives from within the bank, Mathewson began a series of weekly meetings to plot an internal takeover and oust the senior management.

Their chance came with the recession of the early 1990s, which cruelly exposed the bank's poor lending record. At the end of 1991 the Royal's bad debts soared to £323 million and group profit collapsed by over 80 per cent. The retail bank managed a contribution of less than £6 million, but only by finding every legal means it could to flatter its accounts. Bank of Scotland also suffered from the economic downturn, but still managed to increase its pre-tax profit to £140 million. Mathewson was helped by the fact that George Younger had recently resigned from the cabinet as defence secretary to become a director, then in 1991 chairman of the Royal Bank of Scotland group. The two men had worked closely together when Younger had been secretary of state for Scotland and had given Mathewson the political cover he needed to run a successful interventionist industrial policy at the SDA which ran counter to the ethos of Mrs Thatcher's government. The move had paid off. Reversing the pattern of decades, Scotland started to do better in the league tables of economic performance and prosperity than many of the English regions. When there were riots in English cities in protest at the harsh austerity being imposed from Westminster, Scottish cities had remained calm.

Younger's relaxed manner and urbane charm disguised a decisive mind and a shrewd judge of character. The two men were to become as effective a combination as Tom Risk and Bruce Pattullo at Bank of Scotland. Mathewson and his team made a presentation to the Royal's directors and argued that only a radical transformation could save the bank. Despite reservations by some directors, the board decided in his favour. The speed and severity of the clear out of the old guard from the top jobs shocked the bank and its competitors. Charles Winter, nominally still chief executive, but whose power was fast ebbing away, felt the anger and dismay of his colleagues and offered his resignation to Younger: 'I have seen over the past few months the culture of Royal Bank being quite destroyed by a series of radical and rapid changes, all apparently generated by a feeling that the management of the bank up to this point has been typified by total incompetence and that revolutionary rather than evolutionary change was necessary.'[1]

Younger kept Winter in post for a further six months, but then he made way for Mathewson. Since Winter was still short of the bank's retirement age of 60, he was given a year-long sinecure as vice chairman, where he watched the bank he had served for 44 years changed out of all recognition. He left in 1993 and died three years later at the age of 63. He was the last chief executive to have come up through the traditional route: joining the bank straight from school, studying for the exams of the Institute of Bankers in Scotland at night classes, 'passing money over the counter' as a junior clerk and then progressing by stages through most departments. It was a system which produced rounded bankers with practical as well as theoretical knowledge. It also inculcated a strong shared belief in the values and traditions of the bank. But it bred a resistance to change and was out of sympathy with the age.

The effect on the Royal of the Mathewson revolution was dramatic, but the most radical changes were yet to come. The bank was split into three – a wholesale bank to service corporate customers, retail for smaller businesses and personal customers, and an operations division, to provide shared services such as property, computer services, now renamed 'Information Technology' and personnel, which was renamed 'Human Resources' following the fashion of the time. The 17,000 staff were also divided three ways – those whom the new management wanted to keep, those whose attitudes or skills did not fit the new regime and those who were to be given the chance to adapt.

The retail bank went through fundamental change. Under the code name Project Columbus, Mathewson's team identified numerous failings, including poor organisational design, poor-quality people in key positions, lack of vision and investment in IT, unreliable lending and pricing policies, unimaginative products and low priority given to customer service.[2] The solution, it was decided, was to reinvent branch banking and it called in the international management consultancy McKinsey to help. Hundreds of branch managers now found themselves either facing early retirement or having to be interviewed for their own jobs. 'The golf courses of Edinburgh were full,' quipped Mathewson. He was feared and despised by many of the older bank staff, but convinced of the rightness of what he was doing, he inured himself to criticism. 'They've named me "shit of the week",' he told me after one particularly pointed criticism.

Compared to the gradual evolution that Pattullo had encouraged at Bank of Scotland, the upheaval at Royal Bank was more like Mao's Cultural Revolution. It was a shock not only to the Royal's staff, but also to the whole of Scottish banking, which had regarded entry into one of the banks straight from school as being the passport to lifelong employment. From now on people 'who had done nothing wrong' could find themselves out of a job. It gave rise to a gallows humour:

Question: What is the definition of an optimist?
Answer: A Royal Bank manager whose wife irons five white shirts on Sunday evening.

The changes signalled the end of the branch manager as a territorial potentate – the local representative of the bank to any customer, whether that was a firm employing a thousand people, or a widow eking out her meagre savings. In his place came the 'relationship manager', whose geographic area was much less important than his or her understanding of the needs of the customer. It now became possible to say 'or her' because although women had been entering banking in increasing numbers, they had not progressed to branch manager status. Project Columbus cleared out a raft of older male employees and in their place promoted equally men and women, who previously had been confined to clerical or branch teller jobs. (The exception in Royal Bank being The Ladies' Branch in Edinburgh's Princes Street, inherited from the National Commercial Bank, which was entirely staffed by and exclusively for women.) In this it was liberating, although it was notable that despite the fact that women frequently topped the prize list in Institute exams, very few made it beyond middle management to the top grades of Royal Bank. The same was true of Bank of Scotland and Clydesdale Bank.

Mathewson slaughtered sacred cows. His bright young PhDs showed that Charterhouse, the upper crust London merchant bank bought a few years before, was not earning its keep. Mathewson sold it and fell out with its suave chief executive, Victor Blank, who had also been a main board director of Royal Bank and had been considered by some directors as the natural successor to Winter. The top jobs in the reorganised divisions did not necessarily go to experienced bankers. Although Mathewson put Tony Schofield, a long-serving bank executive in the Royal's English subsidiary, in charge of the retail bank, he brought in Iain Robertson to run the corporate bank, based in London. Robertson was an accountant by training, but had spent years in the civil service and had followed Mathewson as chief executive of the SDA. When he joined the Royal he had only a couple of years' banking experience at NatWest.

Changes were also occurring at head office. No longer were time-served bankers with their Institute exams acceptable as heads of specialist departments like finance, marketing, computing or personnel. In came professionals with no banking experience at all, but university degrees and professional qualifications in accountancy, marketing, information technology or human relations. The effect on the Royal's performance was rapid. From coming last in surveys of customer satisfaction, the Royal now regularly came top. With its new confidence it expanded in America, developed its insurance arm, began to innovate in technology and started to challenge Bank of Scotland in corporate lending and structured finance. As a sign of how much banking had changed, Mathewson ignored the unwritten rule that Scottish banks did not poach each other's staff and lured away Leith Robertson, a leveraged corporate lending specialist, from Bank of Scotland, much to Pattullo's annoyance. Previously bank staff had not thought of themselves as selling products; now all front-line staff had sales targets. Profits zoomed. By 1994 they were at ten times what they had been in 1991. By the end of the decade they were over £1 billion.

The staff who survived the upheaval benefited. They liked being part of a winning organisation, one lauded for its customer service rather than castigated for its failings. Their numbers increased rapidly, as did their remuneration. They were now in an environment where their progression depended on their performance, rather than length of service or 'Buggins' turn'. The non-financial benefits of working for the bank increased and care was taken to ensure that the premises in which they worked were pleasant and efficient. Staff wanted to share in the success that they were helping to achieve. Staff bonuses began to be earned regularly as targets were hit or exceeded and it began to be commonplace to take annual payments in shares rather than cash.

But other consequences were less apparent at the time. Collegiate management was now a thing of the past. Senior managers did not have time to dine together every working day, shared values and problems discussed over coffee or lunch gave way to analysis, feasibility reports and business plans. Broad experience conceded to narrow expertise. The new HR professionals wanted to control management education of new recruits, not to outsource it to an arm's length body like the Institute of Bankers in Scotland. They were looking to create competitive advantage, not to have their key managers go through the same courses as their rivals, so they began to organise their own training and education courses. Enrolments for the Institute's banking courses declined and with them its financial viability. It began to be regarded not as the bedrock on which Scottish banking expertise and reliability was founded, but as a fusty old institution which needed the dust blown off it. To survive, the Institute began to offer new shorter courses, like modules in mortgage appraisal and telephone selling. The old concept of the well-rounded banker who had studied all aspects of the craft was disappearing.

★ ★ ★

In 1988 Bruce Pattullo split the top job at Bank of Scotland in two. He took the new title of chief executive, concentrating on growing the group by acquisition. His old title, treasurer, which went back to the early days of the bank, was now effectively managing director of the UK banking and finance operation, and he gave it to his brightest lieutenant, Peter Burt.[3]

Burt, like Pattullo, was middle class, having been educated at Merchiston, one of the more academic Scottish public schools, and St Andrews, the smallest, oldest and most exclusive of the Scottish universities. After graduating he had taken an MBA degree at the prestigious US Wharton business school and started his career with Hewlett Packard, one of the new breed of successful computer companies where management style could not be more different from that of Scottish banking. Hewlett Packard had open-plan offices and its shirt-sleeved employees called each other by first names no matter how junior or senior. Even the founders were known as Bill and Dave. Chains of command were short and hierarchy was not important. Innovation and experimentation were encouraged and so was teamwork. Returning to Edinburgh, Burt had worked briefly for a high-tech spin-out company and then putting together financial deals for the North Sea oil industry in the merchant bank Edward Bates, which had been acquired by Atlantic Assets.

Bates had collapsed in the secondary banking crisis in 1975, throwing Burt and his colleagues out of work. He was unemployed for three months – not a long period by today's standards – but he had recently married and had his first child and he felt the anxiety of uncertainty and repeated rejection acutely. The experience had marked him and it was not something he wanted to hide. In his search for a new job he had been interviewed by Bruce Pattullo, then running the Bank of Scotland Finance Company, who had not had a vacancy, but had been impressed enough to send Burt up to The Mound, where he had been hired in the new 'Special Duties' department of the International Division. It was a period when the Bank of England was restricting sterling lending so Bank of Scotland was exploring ways to lend in foreign currencies. The bank's reputation in the oil industry was growing and Burt worked on some of the major North Sea field financings. Through ability and hard work he had worked his way up, becoming a divisional general manager in 1983 and general manager leading the international department two years later. His brain and drive made him the obvious successor to Pattullo.

Like his boss, Burt was a tennis player, but his sporting enthusiasm lay elsewhere. He was an exceptional amateur golfer and drove himself as hard on the tee as he did at work. An interviewer once asked him why he played golf and got a rhetorical question in reply: 'Why did I turn to banking?' The interviewer concluded: 'Despite him putting golf on the same level as banking, you get the impression that one is a passion and the other a job that enables him to follow his love. In golf, he says, "You are competing against yourself, nobody else – and every so often you hit a perfect shot and there is no reason, other than human frailty, why you shouldn't do it every time."'[4] Human frailty was not something Peter Burt allowed to hold him back in banking any more than in golf. His *annus mirabilis* came in 1993 when he achieved two personal goals – getting the bank's cost/income ratio below 50 per cent and taking the amateur record at the championship Muirfield golf course with a round of 69, which stood for many years.

He had a sharp mind and a quick wit which could sometimes wound, not always intentionally. For some this made him difficult to work with. One non-executive director remembers that although Burt was never a bully, his rigorous reasoning could intimidate subordinates into not standing up to him or putting counter arguments in case a flaw was found in them. Burt was an admirer of the Hewlett Packard style of 'management by walking around', but his own style was not exactly pedestrian. David Jenkins, the bank's economist recalled seeing him running down the first-floor corridor at the bank's international division, tripping at the top of the stairs and falling head-over-heels right to the bottom, where, to the amazement of those watching, he sprang up and continued running to his next appointment. Jenkins was one person who was not intimidated by Burt's intellect, but admired and liked him. The two men became close colleagues and Jenkins used his sense of humour to turn Burt's barbs aside and tell him home truths if the occasion demanded. When Jenkins retired (and sadly died shortly afterwards), his counsel was missed.

In 1990 Tom (by then Sir Tom) Risk retired and Pattullo took his place as governor, but continued as group chief executive. While Peter Burt ran the domestic banking business, Pattullo tried to find acquisitions to expand the bank abroad. It had opened a New York branch and had long had a representative office in the Texas oil capital of Houston. Gradually it opened small offices in other large US cities, but it hankered after a slice of the huge American domestic banking market. With over 15,000 registered banks, there was no shortage of opportunities, but Scottish caution kept getting in the way. Pattullo later regretted his hesitation: 'The Presbyterian instinct means that you don't pay top dollar at the table.'

Having made little progress in America, the bank turned to Australia. In 1987 it took a stake in Countrywide Building Society, taking full control in 1992. The country's financial markets were deregulating and the bank applied its skills and balance sheet to grow the business. It was a modest and cautious purchase, but Pattullo felt emboldened by the experience to go further. Two years later he splashed out £437 million to buy Bank West from the government of Western Australia, which had rescued it in the late 1980s. Such a bold move was out of character and the stock market reacted badly, marking down Bank of Scotland shares. But six months later Pattullo sold 49 per cent of the new subsidiary on the Australian stock market.

The year 1995 saw Bruce Pattullo receive his knighthood and the bank celebrate its tercentenary. The *Financial Times* Lex column marked the occasion by calling the company 'the most boring bank in Britain' which had made dullness a virtue. 'The business's steadiness helps explain 300 years of consistent profitability and more recently how the bank has outperformed the sector by nearly 100 per cent since 1980.'[5] The following year saw the bank again produce record profits and a return on equity of an unheard-of 36 per cent, but the market punished it for allowing its cost/income ratio to rise over 50 per cent – although it was still the lowest of any UK bank. There was no gloom for the next five years as the bank rode the boom in the UK economy and increased its profits by an average of 20 per cent a year.

If there was an outward show of optimism, it was masking deeper concerns. Despite Bruce Pattullo's exhortation to his managers to pull in the deposits, they could not keep up with the bank's success in lending. In 1978 the bank had only minor reliance on the international wholesale money market: it had been able to fund over 90 per cent of its lending from retail deposits – the savings of its customers – and a large proportion of these were in current accounts, which did not pay interest. By 1985 the amount of lending covered by branch deposits had fallen to less than half.[6] This trend had serious implications, but it would not be easy to reverse and the question mark over how the bank would fund itself in the future became a weakness. In the minds of Pattullo, Burt and the board it made the bank vulnerable to takeover and the possibility of losing its independence just as it was celebrating its 300th birthday.

These fears were heightened by the shock decision by Standard Life in May 1996 to sell the one-third stake in the bank it had acquired a decade previously from Barclays. But times were changing and the 'squalid Scottish stitch-up' which Tom Risk had been able to pull off ten years before was no longer possible. Local loyalties and the necessity of avoiding embarrassment in the New Club cut no ice with the professional fund managers running Standard Life's equity portfolio. The insurance company had done well out of its Bank of Scotland shares, but it represented a disproportionate element of its equity holdings and if the bank's performance faltered in the future, the shareholding could drag down the fund's return. The announcement came without warning and immediately promoted speculation that the shares might be sold to a potential predator, such as one of the London Big Four or a foreign bank wanting to enter the UK market. The *Financial Times* Lex column declared that the decision had 'put Bank of Scotland into play'[7] and the share price jumped on speculation of a possible future bid, which continued for a month until Standard Life placed its shares in the stock market, selling them in small lots to many different buyers rather than as a lump to a single purchaser.

There was relief on The Mound, but it did not answer the underlying problem of what to do about the increasing reliance on wholesale funding. The bank commissioned the management consultancy McKinsey to report on its strategic options, but it confirmed what was already feared. If it carried on growing at the rate it had been, increased reliance on the inter-bank market – and therefore increased vulnerability – was inevitable. The alternative of putting the brakes on growth could have the same effect: the share price would fall making the bank an easier target. The only answer was to get access to a new, large source of deposits and do it quickly.

In 1997 the bank signed an agreement with the supermarket chain Sainsbury's to create the Sainsbury's Bank, which offered savings products devised and operated by the bank, but branded and sold by the supermarket to its customers. There were no branches, customers used the telephone (and later the internet) to access their accounts and carry out transactions. It was the first such venture in the UK and within months it brought in several hundred million pounds in deposits which Bank of Scotland effectively lent to itself – useful, but not nearly enough. So Pattullo and Burt began a series of journeys through England talking to building societies, which typically had high deposit ratios, trying to interest them in being bought or entering into a merger. Burt joked that he had eaten a 'rubber-chicken' lunch or dinner in every sizeable town from Bristol to the Scottish border. But again the bank's cautiousness held it back.

It was not the only suitor looking for a mate and the bank balked at the prices being paid. Royal Bank had suffered the same series of frustrations. Mathewson had held tentative talks with the Trustee Savings Bank (TSB) in 1995 and Cheltenham & Gloucester Building Society in 1997, but both had been taken by the much bigger Lloyds Bank; in the same year Bristol & West Building Society was taken over by Bank of Ireland and in 2000 Barclays bought the Woolwich. Royal Bank had also tried to form an alliance with the Midlands-based Birmingham Midshires society, only to find itself jilted when Halifax, the largest former building society and now a retail bank, bettered its offer and made off with the prize.

Bank of Scotland already had working arrangements with Halifax – a team of 20 from the bank had been seconded to the building society for a year to help sort out problems in its commercial property lending business and the bank, through its successful credit card processing operation, provided the back office for Halifax's Visa card. Trying to build on this relationship, Pattullo and Burt had on two occasions tried to interest the building society's management in a closer tie-up, but both had come to nothing. On the first, Jim Birrell, chief executive of Halifax until 1993 and a dyed-in-the-wool building society man, dismissed any idea of a merger with any bank. His successor Mike Blackburn, a former banker, did see the logic in putting Halifax's huge savings base to work with Bank of Scotland's skill at lending, but could not get his board to see it the same way.

In the end Pattullo had to admit defeat – all the lunches and dinners had been for nothing. He retired at the annual shareholders meeting in 1998 at the normal bank retirement age of 60. In nearly two decades at the top he had transformed an inefficient and complacent company into one which was admired for the quality of its management, its talent for innovation, its growth and its prudence. The final set of results he presented to shareholders delivered another 20 per cent increase in dividends – the 26th consecutive annual increase – and showed that costs were again below 50 per cent. The bank's shares had been the best performing in the FTSE 100 over 1997 having achieved an 85 per cent rise in the year.

But the underlying problem remained and investors did not immediately see how Bank of Scotland was going to overcome its funding problem and continue its phenomenal rate of growth. The *Financial Times* Lex column had reprimanded the bank: 'If you cannot be bothered to explain, you can hardly complain if people don't understand. Bank of Scotland's sub-par rating is a legacy of years of neglecting investors when Standard Life owned nearly a third of the shares. That position has changed and the bank has been talking more, but the message still has not been getting through.'[8]

Peter Burt had assumed the role of chief executive a few years earlier and had promoted Gavin Masterton as treasurer and chief general manager. In 1997 the two began a reform of the structure of the bank, following a similar format to that adopted by its main rival, Royal Bank. The old geographic fiefdoms – east, west and London – were abolished and in their place functional divisions were created – branch banking, corporate banking and risk and compliance. The bank was still growing, but the funding worry would not go away. Having failed to buy a building society, a couple of tentative approaches had been made to London banks, essentially suggesting that a merger could inject Scottish management expertise into a much larger under-performing balance sheet. While still governor, Bruce Pattullo had met Robert Alexander, then chairman of NatWest, who had dismissed the idea as 'Scotland 4, England Nil'.

A few years later when Barclays was going through one of its recurring changes of chief executive, Peter Burt's name had been mentioned as possible leader. He had met the chairman, but it never went any further because Burt would not come alone – making him chief executive would lead to the reverse takeover of the underperforming Barclays by the much smaller Bank of Scotland. In any case, Burt was not a member of one of the founding families, who still wielded influence in Barclays. Some executives might have been frightened by his very active management style, which contrasted with their more *laissez-faire* approach. George Mathewson at Royal Bank went through the same pointless exercise, meeting the Barclays chairman for a polite brush-off over lunch at the Savoy. If the Scots were to make an impression on the City of London, brandishing their stronger managements and superior financial performance was clearly not enough.[9]

On the positive side for Bank of Scotland, Sainsbury's Bank had proved to be much more successful than expected. Six months after launch it had taken £1 billion in deposits and had 500,000 customers, most new to Bank of Scotland since Sainsbury's had predominantly a south of England network. Two years later this was up to £2 billion. Opportunities to pull the same trick again in the UK were obviously limited: other major UK retailers were already joining up with other banks (Royal Bank of Scotland had formed a similar alliance with Tesco). But having been rebuffed in its attempt to buy a bank in Texas, perhaps the US would be more fertile ground? The concept of telephone banking was still novel there and the bank began to scout for a suitable partner, one which already had a large customer base, but was not already either providing finance itself or linked to a financial institution.

The seemingly ideal partner came in early 1999 via an unlikely route. The Catholic archbishop of New York introduced the bank's head of US operations to Dr Pat Robertson,[10] who appeared to have everything the Scottish bankers could wish for. He was an established and successful businessman with a reputed personal fortune of $200 million and a law degree from Yale, and he had built up a private television channel with 55 million subscribers. He thus not only had the potential customers for the new venture, but a means of promoting financial services to them through his own programme on his own channel. On top of that he was already familiar with the UK as a non-executive director of the fashion retailer Laura Ashley.

What had not been appreciated was that Robertson was a man of divisive religious views and expressed them regularly and forcefully on his own television show. In particular he condemned homosexuals, but he was also not much in favour of feminists or members of religions other than his own evangelical Protestantism.

The bank announced the venture in a low-key press release faxed to newspapers at the beginning of March. Although it used the headline 'Moneylenders in the Temple' in its first report the *Scotsman*, the bank's local daily in Edinburgh, was broadly complimentary, calling the deal 'low risk with plenty of upside'.[11] But the news alerted gay rights groups in the US who were quickly in touch with their UK counterparts, complaining about the unsuitability of a man with Robertson's views becoming a partner of the hitherto upright bank. Before long the Jewish Anti-Defamation League had joined the protest, citing several speeches and remarks Robertson had allegedly made. By the following day the *Scotsman* was calling Robertson 'a far-right zealot' and boycotts and pickets outside bank offices were being organised.

Momentum developed with surprising speed; a day later the *Scotsman* was reporting that customers were closing their accounts. Journalists were digging up quotes from Robertson not only criticising homosexuals and Jews, but Hindus and Muslims as well. On the fourth day the newspaper carried a leading article under the headline: 'The lure of the false prophet'. It declared that Robertson was not just a maverick, but a deliberately offensive man who had equated homosexuality with satanism and nazism and believed that liberals were involved in a worldwide masonic conspiracy to subjugate mankind to the devil. 'In a British context his views are insane. It is hard to understand how a significant minority of Americans can take his views seriously.'[12]

The crisis might have passed had Robertson not decided to use his TV show to investigate the current state of Scotland. He sent a reporter to the country and commented on the unflattering picture that came back. Scotland, he said, was a 'dark land' and the contrast with the glorious history of the country was 'kinda frightening'. He went on: 'Homosexuals are riding high in the media and in Scotland you cannot believe how strong the homosexuals are. Heroes of the calibre of John Knox no longer exist, spelling possible doom for the nation ... we need to pray for them.'[13]

Clearly the game was up. Reputational damage was outweighing the potential upside and rumours began to circulate in the stock market that the deal would be killed. Peter Burt flew to the US for a showdown with Pat Robertson in a Boston hotel and Bank of Scotland shares rose modestly on the news. Two days later it was confirmed that the deal was dead; the bank bought out Robertson for a reported $10 million and chalked it up to experience.

27

Fund management: contrasting cultures

IF THE BANKS were going through a period of rapid change, so were companies in other sectors. Ivory & Sime, under the leadership of Jimmy Gammell as senior partner, powered ahead through the 1970s and 1980s. Atlantic Assets, the trust which had embarrassed the company with its management incentives in the 1960s, was in the following decades a star performer, its initial £1 million capital growing to £150 million.[1] The other trusts it managed, British Assets and Second British Assets, also had strong growth records. Among the Edinburgh fund management companies, Ivory & Sime was seen as innovative and expansive. It was one of the first into unit trusts, in a joint venture with the London bank Robert Fleming, to form Save and Prosper, which gave it an opportunity to sell directly to small investors. It had added pension fund management to its portfolio of products. In an age of technology it was seen to be technocratic, progressive and outward looking, while much of the rest of the industry looked stuck in the Edwardian age. While other companies were seen – sometimes unfairly – as being run by old men with conservative ideas, Ivory & Sime was youthful, brash and assertive. It was a company to watch.

The driving force was Gammell. His policy was to hire bright young men (women were only employed in secretarial jobs) and quickly give them huge responsibility and autonomy. He did not particularly care about their qualifications, hiring non-graduates from state schools alongside public school men with degrees from ancient universities. They received on-the-job 'training' in the office, but they were not expected, as he had been when he first joined the firm, to go through an accountancy apprenticeship. Gammell was a constant source of new ideas; he would set some of his young lieutenants the task of making them happen and leave them to get on with it. He brimmed with enthusiasm and was prepared to back his hunches with cash and commitment. Some of his ventures had been very beneficial for the firm and its client trusts. His early interest in West Texas oil and his long friendship with George W.H. Bush (who later became US president), led to a stake in companies like Pennzoil and Zapata, which repaid their investments multiple times.[2]

But on other occasions Gammell was not so fortunate. In the 1970s he decided that Ivory & Sime should not be content with being a successful fund management company, but should expand to be a financial conglomerate, adding banking and insurance to its activities. Through Atlantic Assets he bought Edward Bates & Sons, a small London merchant bank, which floated on the Stock Exchange. With oil exploration in the North Sea just getting underway, it was to look for profitable banking and investment ventures. Gammell became chairman of the banking subsidiary and a board member of the holding company. In 1973 it bought an insurance company. While the economy and the markets were buoyant the ventures seemed promising, but after the oil shocks, a market crash which saw British stocks lose 70 per cent of their value in 18 months[3] and the depression of the mid 1970s, a number of fatal weaknesses were exposed. The insurance company and then the bank had to be expensively unwound.* In retrospect he regretted the move: 'With hindsight it was 100 per cent a mistake and I am not sure now I believe in such a concept.'[4] It should have taught Gammell a lesson and for a while it seemed it had.

The next venture was equally damaging to Ivory & Sime's reputation. Hard on the heels of the Bates episode, Gammell bought a major stake in Haw Par, a Singapore trading company associated with the controversial British financier Jim Slater. The investment was again made through the investment trusts managed by Ivory & Sime, and Gammell again took an active role, becoming chairman of Haw Par. Almost immediately it became apparent that the Singapore authorities were investigating the company and they began an action in London to extradite Slater (ultimately refused). The affair became heated and complicated and was extensively covered in the Singapore press. It was clear that there was more in Haw Par's history and Slater's manipulation of it than Ivory & Sime had realised.

Having been chairman for only a few weeks, Gammell resigned and left Singapore, but the inquiry continued and his predecessor as

---

* Among those made redundant was Peter Burt, who after a period of unemployment, found a job at Bank of Scotland (see previous chapter).

chairman was jailed for accounting irregularities. Although Gammell was never implicated in any wrongdoing, the affair demonstrated an astonishing naivety, which reflected badly on Ivory & Sime. It also damaged the performance of Atlantic Assets: it had bought its Haw Par shares with £5.3 million borrowed from another Slater company, Britannia Arrow, which it had difficulty in repaying. It was left to one of Gammell's bright recruits to sort the problem out. Ian Rushbrook, who was managing Atlantic, went to see Jimmy Goldsmith, the financier running Britannia Arrow:

> I appeared at his office and started a long spiel about the background and the analysis of the loan note, what sort of price I would be prepared to pay and how he would clearly like to have it redeemed and so on. After a while he just cut me short: 'Just tell me what you are offering Ian.' I said 'well, not a penny more than £4.2 million.' He said 'fine.' I put away my pile of analytical sheets and the deal was done. Jimmy took me to a delightful restaurant where we shared half a pound of caviar and drank three bottles of champagne and I learned something about how life should be lived.[5]

In the wake of the Haw Par disaster, the board of British Assets, Ivory & Sime's largest and most important client, instructed Gammell to relinquish executive control of the fund management firm. He had taken on too many distractions and the core business and the performance of the trusts it managed were suffering. It was a decision he accepted, but there was no obvious successor. To get what he thought was the best out of his talented junior partners, he encouraged internal as well as external competition. There was no shortage of able people to choose to take over the leadership, but the culture of the firm meant that without a strong and authoritative figurehead in charge, there would always been fierce rivalries. Gammell's nominated successor, Robert van Maasdijk, was younger than many of his other recruits and had been made a partner more recently, which caused resentment. He increased the profits, but found it difficult to get his ideas for taking the company forward implemented. After a few years he resigned in frustration. The Ivory brothers, Ian and James, had also left to set up their own investment management company, specialising in private client business. This broke the family connection with the firm their grandfather had founded. For the first time since 1895, there was no Ivory in Ivory & Sime.

The 1980s saw a spate of defections, as Gammell's bright young men found it impossible to work together. Walter Scott, who had brought a lot of pension fund money into the firm, left to set up his own pensions management company, taking other staff with him. The culture in Ivory & Sime encouraged friction. 'By and large this was very creative friction, but when the firm faced difficulties it could turn in on itself and become destructive,' Scott explained. This had happened during the 1970s when the firm was having a difficult time, but reoccurred in the 1980s when performance was improving: 'For some reason, against the background of a very buoyant business, the internal structural discussions led to the normally creative energy turning in on itself and becoming uncreative. Personally, I found that an environment I no longer enjoyed working in and so I left.'[6]

Scott's firm, Walter Scott & Partners, was described by one of its directors as 'just like Ivory & Sime, without the complications'. The 'complications' included investment trusts, which added administrative and regulatory cost and had independent boards of directors to keep satisfied. The new business concentrated on managing investments for institutional clients, mainly pension funds. It left the managers with more time to concentrate on getting their performance right.

After a slow start, Scott's firm proved to be more successful than the company he had resigned from. One by one, Scott and other defectors founded businesses which eventually overtook Ivory & Sime – among them Newton Investment Management, Artemis and Aberforth Partners. Others left to join existing companies, or to move out of investment management into corporate finance like Peter de Vink, who set up Edinburgh Financial & General Holdings, or banking like James Laurenson, who became managing director of Adam & Company, a new private bank.

Ivory & Sime had changed from a partnership, which it had been since its foundation, to a limited company and in 1983 it went public on the Stock Exchange. Despite previous troubles, the firm had launched a string of new trusts and brought in more pension money to manage. It was by a long way the largest specialist investment house in Scotland, with over £2 billion under management and had a much higher public profile than its competitors. The flotation was an immediate success, with the share price more than doubling on the first day of trading. Atlantic Assets held 30 per cent of the business, but most of the rest was in the hands of the remaining directors, who all became rich as a result.

The firm continued to win business and launch new trusts. In a delicious irony, it secured the management of the £185 million Investors Capital Trust, which under its previous name of Investors Mortgage Security Company had dismissed Sir Alastair Blair as its chairman over the Atlantic affair twenty years previously.[7] North Sea oil exploration was in full swing and the firm took bold steps to establish itself as one of the financial pioneers. The share price continued to rise so that by 1985 it was 200p, against an issue price two years earlier of 22p.[8]

Jimmy Gammell retired in 1985 after 36 years with the business. Along the way he had taken big risks and made some serious blunders, but he had transformed a modest Edinburgh private partnership into a successful public company with an international reputation. Although he appeared only occasionally in the press, and then reluctantly, he had encouraged his bright managers to have high public profiles and to get the firm's name in the papers as often as possible. It was 400 miles away from London, but was on the regular calling list for the investment writers of Fleet Street. Being named in newspapers was not something other firms encouraged their managers to do, but by always being ready with an apposite quote the Ivory & Sime directors had burnished not only their own reputations, but that of Edinburgh – and particularly of Charlotte Square – as an investment centre. Gammell had much to look back on with satisfaction; he had rebuilt his family fortunes and acquired a Highland estate. He may have been more colourful than many of his contemporaries, but he had become a pillar of the Edinburgh financial establishment, serving on the board Standard Life. He had been a director of British Linen Bank, and took a leading part in its merger with Bank of Scotland, where he also joined the board.

What he had not done was to leave behind a sustainable business. The effect of the flotation had been to reward the existing managers and leave little for the next generation of talent. The rapid turnover of senior staff continued into the 1990s and some of the big risks the firm had taken in the North Sea failed to come off, dragging down investment performance. In an effort to stablise the company, Caledonia Investments, controlled by the powerful Cayzer family, bought a near 30 per cent stake and installed new management, but that failed to work and in 1997 the firm was taken over by the insurance company Friends Provident, which merged it with its own investment management arm. Symbolically, in 2001 the firm moved out of its offices at 1 & 2 Charlotte Square – one of the most prestigious addresses in Edinburgh – and the following year changed its name to ISIS. One of the most illustrious and controversial names in Edinburgh finance was no more.

The offices were bought by Walter Scott, who eventually owned ten of the houses in Charlotte Square. He installed his own investment management business in numbers 1 & 2, continuing a tradition of finance in the Robert Adam's square begun by James Ivory when he moved his business there in 1905.[9]

★ ★ ★

Around the corner from Charlotte Square, in Glenfinlas Street, Ivory & Sime's traditional rivals were also going through a period of rapid change. When George Chiene retired as senior partner in 1972, he left Baillie Gifford in a weak and vulnerable state. The business was heavily reliant on a small number of big clients and it began to lose them – some through bad luck and others through bad management. Takeovers and bankruptcies led to the loss of some pension fund contracts, leaving the firm dependent on its investment trusts. Its fixed fees insulated it for a while from poor performance, but costs were climbing. Finding new business was not a quick or easy process. Chiene had not approved of active marketing – to the extent that he had rejected a chance to bid for the management of the Glaxo pension fund because the approach had been made through a junior partner and not through the 'correct procedure' of writing to the senior partner.[10]

The firm's investment trusts were not safe. In the bear market of the 1970s they were trading at a discount of up to a third of their asset value – that is, if you added up the market value of the shares and bonds they owned, it came to much more than the market capitalisation of the trust as a whole. One way of looking at this was that the managers, in this case Baillie Gifford, were not adding value by their work, but decreasing it.

Pension funds, particularly those of the large nationalised industries that had strong cash flows from their members' contributions, could bid for a discounted trust, break it up and sell off its holdings at a profit. In 1977 the National Coal Board pension fund bid for the self-managed British Investment Trust, and the British Rail fund bid for the Baillie Gifford managed Edinburgh & Dundee Trust. The firm put up a fight, but the eventual loss of the trust – its second biggest client – left it so demoralised that the partners considered selling out. Their problem was that Baillie Gifford was not worth very much: it was only profitable by virtue of the fact that the partners had reduced their incomes to below market rates. A rebuff by the Alliance Trust in Dundee and a very low offer from a Bristol firm persuaded them that selling or merger was not a viable option – they had to go on.[11]

The firm's recovery was aided partly by the confidence some of the younger partners had gained in touring brokers and shareholders in the effort to resist the British Rail bid. But it also owed something to the Edinburgh network. Gentlemanly capitalism still had some value. The boards of the remaining Baillie Gifford managed trusts agreed to an increase in fees – helped by the fact that Scottish Mortgage, the largest, was chaired by a godson of Carlyle Gifford. Other connections helped secure the management of the Scottish solicitors' widows' fund and the Church of Scotland Trust. These small wins, together with cost-cutting, including the closure of the London office, gave the firm breathing space to reorganise and plan for the future.

Baillie Gifford had also recruited bright young men during the 1960s and 1970s, including Gavin Gemmell, Douglas McDougall, Max Ward, Richard Burns and Robin Menzies. In contrast to Ivory & Sime, their experience had pushed them together, rather than pulling them apart. 'Their experience of hard times during the 1970s, both in the markets and particularly as junior partners at a time of extreme peril for the firm, was to make them a very cohensive and effective team.'[12] In another difference with Ivory & Sime, Sarah Whitley became the first woman graduate trainee in 1980, becoming a partner in 1986.

The 1980s brought an easier investment market as world economies recovered from the turbulent 1970s, and a radical Conservative government led by Margaret Thatcher began a campaign of deregulation: exchange controls were abolished, dividend restraint ended and income taxes reduced. The decade that followed was one of rebuilding for Baillie Gifford, repairing deficiencies such as a lack of expertise in UK equities (it had always concentrated on the US) and Far East investing, particularly Japan. There were setbacks, such as the loss of the Cadbury pension fund as a result of poor performance, but slowly the firm became more confident, began to market its services more effectively and build up its reputation. Charles White, as senior partner, showed himself more willing than his predecessor to put himself in the front line in order to win new business, although not always with success.

Baillie Gifford had answered an advertisement in *The Economist* for a firm to manage $100 million for a Middle Eastern client. That led Richard Burns, one of the younger partners, to several meetings and finally to an appointment in a New York hotel suite where Burns and White met 'the Doctor', a Saudi businessman who claimed to control the funds and held out the promise of much more than the advertised amount. The two Edinburgh men were startled when the meeting started with the US and UK national anthems played on a portable tape recorder. Charles White wrote in his note of the event: 'This bizarre beginning set the tone. The two and three-quarter hours which followed represented the most grotesque encounter which I have experienced in over thirty years in the world of investment management. It took the form mainly of a monologue by the Doctor, in which bombast, boasting, irrelevant digressions, wilful obscurity and frequent references to the importance of sincerity, honesty and affection were the principal constituents.'[13]

The meeting ended with a slide show of Middle Eastern scenes in which most of the pictures were upside down or the wrong way around. A subsequent meeting in Cairo involving Burns and Gavin Gemmell, another of the new partners, was equally inconclusive and no businesses resulted from the episode.

Throughout the 1980s and 1990s Baillie Gifford, like Ivory & Sime, experienced periods of strong growth, mixed with stock market reverses and loss of some clients – 30 of them in 1995–8, taking £1.5 billion away with them.[14] But there were important differences between the two firms. Baillie Gifford lacked the strong personality of Jimmy Gammell, its senior partners encouraged innovation and initiative among the younger recruits, but fostered a culture of co-operation rather than competition. On several occasions the firm was led by joint senior partners, with no one dominant personality. Even then other partners were involved in major decisions.

A second distinction was that Baillie Gifford remained a partnership and did not seriously consider changing to a limited company, or going public. This meant it was not always in the public eye and if there were problems they could be dealt with in private. It was not subject to the same pressures to maintain its growth and, periodically, would close its doors to new clients so that it could concentrate on serving its existing clients. But being a partnership did not insulate it from the necessity of becoming more professional. There was some initial resistance when Gavin Gemmell introduced training in making presentations, but the results – a measurable increase in the proportion of new investment mandates secured – won round the doubters. Other modernisations followed. Training on the job was supplemented by courses at leading business schools, staff appraisals were formalised and technology adopted, despite an internal memo of 1993 which claimed that email was counter to the culture of the firm and in any case would never catch on.

Big Bang, the deregulation of the stock market by the Thatcher government in 1986, brought consolidation into financial services, with banks buying investment managers and stockbrokers. Baillie Gifford stood aside, preferring to remain as a niche player and determine its own destiny – in any case it was probably still too small to attract the attention of international investment banks. Expansion was not a priority and only once did the firm consider making an acquisition. When British Linen Bank decided to sell Dunedin Fund Managers, its investment management arm which numbered investment trusts and pension funds among its clients, the Baillie Gifford partners made an indicative offer of £40 million, but lost to Edinburgh Fund Managers, which paid twice the price. This confirmed them in their belief that organic growth was better than expanding by acquisition.

The firm expanded its American business and a longstanding involvement with Japan finally paid off with significant funds to manage. It increased its pensions management department. In 1987 Baillie Gifford had outgrown its offices in Glenfinlas Street and moved to a purpose-built seven-storey block in Rutland Court, but by 2000 it had outgrown this building too and moved to another new build in Leith Street. From £500 million under management in 1982, the total had reached £2 billion by 1987. By 1988 it had already surpassed Ivory & Sime, with £3.5 billion under management. Ten years later the figure was £16.2 billion. By its centenary year in 2008 the figure was over £55 billion.

28

The end of the exchange

BIG BANG AND the deregulation of 1986 merely formalised a process that was already underway – the centralisation of the stock market and share dealing in London. The Edinburgh Stock Exchange had ceased to exist in 1964, after the Jenkins committee on company law recommended that the Board of Trade should reduce the number of authorised provincial exchanges, increasing their size and efficiency. In response Edinburgh, Glasgow, Dundee and Aberdeen amalgamated to form the Scottish Stock Exchange. The Greenock exchange did not want to join and was wound up in 1965. In April 1971 all share dealings were centralised on a new trading floor in the reconstructed Glasgow Stock Exchange, in St George's Place (now renamed Nelson Mandela Place), but in the mid 1980s the Scottish exchange was absorbed into the London Stock Exchange and the daily trading of shares north of the border ceased after 140 years.

When the Edinburgh exchange had started during the railway mania of 1844, it was already 70 years behind London, Dublin (1793), Manchester and Liverpool (both 1836). It initially operated from a room in a house at 71 Princes Street rented at £25 a year, but had to move from time to time as business increased and more space was needed to accommodate the brokers, who dealt with each other face to face. Initially members paid a £10 joining fee and £5 a year subscription, but the popularity of the trading floor was such that the fee was increased to £100 in 1845 and by the end of the century it was £200. The exchange was a convenience for its members, since buyers and sellers were in the same room, but it also served as a restrictive club, much as the old craft guilds had done. New entrants had to be proposed by existing members and were elected by ballot. In addition to the fee and subscriptions they had to provide surety against defaults on their trades, which by the end of the century was £3,000, a substantial sum, usually satisfied by taking out an insurance policy. Again following the practice of the guilds, there were concessions for sons of members and experienced clerks.[1]

A year after opening, membership had reached 27 and by 1846 there were 38 broker members.[2] Publication of official lists started in 1845, with 130 stocks, but by 1871 the exchange traded 369 stocks, of which 44 were Scottish companies. The rest were quoted on exchanges all over Britain and had to be executed through arrangements with other brokers. At the start, orders outside Edinburgh had to be placed by post, although later the telegraph and the telephone speeded the process considerably. The railway sector still dominated trading and in 1871 two-thirds of the total were railway stocks. This changed over time as railway companies amalgamated and the number of other Scottish quoted companies increased – by 1940 some 808 commercial company stocks were traded in Edinburgh, of which 315 were Scottish, but railway shares were down to 31. Investment trusts made up a large proportion of the remainder (247 of which 144 were Scottish). There were also 23 insurance companies, of which 11 were local, and 19 banks, of which 7 were local. Of the Scottish financial stocks, the overwhelming number were in Edinburgh.

There were other types of interesting securities traded. Edinburgh followed Dundee's lead into cattle ranching in the US and funds were raised in Scotland by launching issues on the Edinburgh Stock Exchange. The directors of the SAINTS investment trust formed the California Pastoral and Agricultural Company with capital of £250,000 in 1881. In 1882 the same group formed the Wyoming Cattle Ranch Company, with authorised capital of £200,000. The Missouri Land and Livestock Company was formed in 1882, but was predominantly a land, rather than an agricultural, business and in 1883 Western Ranches was formed. All were quoted on the Edinburgh Exchange. Later, rubber companies in the Far East raised money in the same way. Fifteen were formed between 1907–10 and quoted on the exchange.[3]

By 1888 the exchange was prosperous enough to justify a specially designed new building on the northwestern corner of St Andrew Square.* The main market hall had seats for members and their clerks, who were connected by telephone to their offices, mostly clustered around the exchange in St Andrew Square and George Street, and to the London and Glasgow Stock Exchanges. The basement housed a clearing house

---

* It was demolished in 1966.

and post/telegraph office. In Edinburgh only one stock could be traded at a time. If a member wanted to buy or sell a share, he had to ask the secretary to call it: only then could other brokers bid. Procedure was strictly followed: 'A broker may offer stock, and his stock may or may not be taken. If rival bidders appear to call simultaneously and there is any doubt which should obtain the stock, the Chairman gives his ruling.'[4]

Initially settlement for transactions had to be made in cash on the day of sale, but later Edinburgh adopted the London principle of fortnightly settlement. The exchange acted as a cartel, determining the cost of trading. Commissions were fixed by each exchange and 'strictly adhered to' by members, but varied between exchanges – Edinburgh, with its professional investors charging less than Glasgow, where the 'punting population' posed more of a risk to brokers. Eventually Glasgow agreed commissions with other Scottish exchanges and Edinburgh fell into line: 0.5 per cent for railway and other shares, 0.25 per cent for banks. By 1878 this was still the level and strictly enforced. As were rebates – member firms could share commissions with London brokers, but not with other bodies. Edinburgh petitioned for a relaxation because law firms who acted for wealthy clients were placing increasing amounts of business directly with London brokers who could give them a share of the commission, whereas Edinburgh brokers could not. Even Scottish banks and insurance shares were being traded in London, but the system was not changed until 1941, when Edinburgh brokers were allowed to rebate solicitors, accountants, banks and investment trusts to bring them into line with London rules.[5]

The Edinburgh exchange reached its peak in 1929 with 76 members, but thereafter membership slowly declined in the face of the growth in the London market. At the end of the Second World War there were still 24 provincial stock exchanges in all of the main commercial cities in Britain (including five in Scotland), plus the Provincial Brokers Stock Exchange for everyone else. To be a member of an exchange brokers had to have their office within a ten-mile radius, meaning that they had to deal through other brokers to satisfy clients who wanted to buy or sell in other parts of the country. But instant communication via telephone or telegraph made it easy for clients to place business on the London market, where there was much more liquidity. In 1941 an agreement was made between the London Stock Exchange and the Associated Stock Exchanges, representing the provincial markets, to standardise commissions. Where once provincial exchanges might have been able to offer a cost advantage, now it was the same price to deal in London or in Edinburgh. Change took 30 years, but the end of the provincial exchanges was inevitable.

After 1973 Edinburgh stockbrokers could join the London Exchange as members and deal on the trading floor in their own right. Apprentice brokers, called 'blue buttons' because they were required to wear a blue badge with the name of their firm, circulated around the floor collecting prices from the jobbers, who made a market in the shares. Senior members were allowed to deal, but if a 'blue button' had been around long enough to be trusted, he might be allowed to place an order. This was done in an abbreviated language heavy with numbers, which would have meant nothing to an outsider. But once the brief exchange was over, the trade was done – there was no handshake and no signature on a contract. The motto of the exchange was 'My word is my bond'.

Alongside the development of the exchange came the evolution of the brokerage firms. William Bell, an accountant, started share dealing in 1841 and was one of the founder members of the Edinburgh Stock Exchange. By 1955 the firm had become Bell Cowan & Company, but then went through a rapid series of mergers – with Lawrie & Kerr, John Robertson – another firm with a history going back to the 1840s – Macgregor Walker and finally Robert White – changing its name each time. It spent three years in the ownership of Lloyds TSB, before the bank decided that owning a stockbroker was not a good business model, and in 1993 was acquired by the London broking firm Brewin Dolphin, which itself had been the product of numerous mergers and had briefly been owned by a bank.

Most Edinburgh brokers did private client work, taking orders from banks or building societies acting on behalf of their customers. They had to share commissions, but until deregulation swept away the cartel, rates were high, so there was plenty to go round.

Edinburgh's largest stockbroker in the 1980s had only a small proportion of its clients in the city. Since he had become senior partner of Wood Mackenzie in 1969, at the age of just 32, John Chiene had concentrated on institutional, rather than private client, business and had courted large financial clients, most of whom were in London. Chiene came from a family steeped in Edinburgh finance. He was a nephew of George Chiene, the former senior partner of Baillie Gifford, and his father, also John, had been secretary of Edinburgh Investment Trust, before moving into the whisky industry.

After Cambridge the younger John Chiene worked in fund management and London stockbrokers before joining Wood Mackenzie at the age of 25. As senior partner he developed a distinctive business model, producing high quality independent research that could be sold to commercial firms as well as being used to attract broking customers. The firm covered a range of sectors but, as the North Sea began to be developed, concentrated on the oil market and quickly made a name as the leading oil analyst in the UK. Its early adoption of computers also meant it was able to value portfolios quickly, a tool it could use to gain competitive advantage, but also a service it could sell to investment trusts and insurance companies.

Until the change in regulations in 1974, dealing in London meant sharing commissions with London brokers, but as soon as the geographic restriction was relaxed the firm opened in the City in its own name. By the mid 1980s Wood Mackenzie was handling nearly a tenth of the trades on the London Stock Exchange. Staff numbers had grown to 200 and revenues to £6 million,[6] but Big Bang proved a problem for the company. One of the reforms swept away the demarcation between brokers – who acted merely as agents for their clients and therefore did not take on the risk of prices moving against them – and 'jobbers', who made markets by dealing on their own accounts. If brokers were also to become jobbers, potentially cutting the cost of dealing for their own clients, they would need access to a lot more capital. Rather than raise new capital themselves, most of the big London broking firms sold themselves to banks.

Chiene and his partners anticipated deregulation, selling the company to the merchant bank Hill Samuel in 1984, but three years later Hill Samuel itself was taken over by TSB, the former Trustee Savings Bank, which sold Wood Mackenzie to NatWest. Then began an unhappy period in which Wood Mackenzie's business was damaged by the problems of NatWest, which became embroiled in the Blue Arrow share scandal, resulting in the resignation of the bank's chairman and a year-long fraud trial. Chiene left the City in 1990, but the firm he had led went on to be sold twice more – to Bankers' Trust of the US in 1998 and a year later to Deutsche Bank. In 2001 the management and staff bought out the company, in a deal backed by Bank of Scotland. After several more changes of ownership Wood Mackenzie has become very successful, but as an analyst rather than a broker.

The last independent Edinburgh stockbroker, Torrie & Co., sold out in 2002 to become the local branch of the London firm Charles Stanley.

John Torrie, who had taken over the management of the firm from his father, had been receiving takeover approaches every year for the previous 12 years. But the burden of regulation became too much for him: 'I was spending more time than I was comfortable with dealing with management issues, I wanted to return to being just a stockbroker.'[7]

* * *

The winds of change were also sweeping through the insurance industry. Increased competition, making it necessary for companies to spend heavily on marketing, information technology and opening up new distribution channels, led to a wave of consolidation in the fire and accident market during the 1950s. The predators in Scotland were the big London general insurance companies, which had always been active in Edinburgh, competing against the homegrown firms. First to go was Caledonian Insurance, founded in 1805, which was acquired by Guardian Assurance in 1957. Its magnificent 1939 art deco headquarters on the corner of St Andrew Square and George Street, decorated with bronze figures representing 'Insurance' and 'Security' by the sculptor Alexander Carrick, became the Scottish headquarters of its parent company. In 1959 the North British, launched in 1810, became a subsidiary of Commercial Union, its nineteenth-century headquarters in Princes Street making way for shops. The Hercules Fire Insurance Company, established in 1809, had a more convoluted path. It had been acquired by the Scottish Union in 1849, which in 1877 merged with the Scottish National Insurance Company to form the Scottish Union and National Insurance Company. It survived for another 80 years before being acquired by the Norwich Union Fire Insurance Society in 1959.

The life assurance companies survived longer than their general insurance counterparts. In the late 1980s Edinburgh still boasted seven life assurance companies, all except one mutually owned. The exception was the smallest, the Life Association of Scotland, which had been acquired in 1968 by the Dutch insurer Nationale Nederlanden. The mutuals claimed a competitive advantage over their proprietary rivals because not having to pay dividends to shareholders meant that they could give higher returns to their policyholders. This edge had served them well for 150 years and by 1979 Edinburgh was headquarters to three of the ten largest life companies in the UK – Standard Life, Scottish Equitable and Scottish Widows.[8] But the life sector was subject to the same pressures as the general insurance business, costs, particularly for marketing, technology and regulation were rising and competition for new customers was intensifying.

As they gained more life assurance or pensions business, the companies were required to hold more capital against potential payouts and risks. Now the disadvantage of mutuality became apparent; whereas the proprietary companies could go to their shareholders for additional capital, the mutuals could not. Staying small made them vulnerable, growing meant demutualising or finding a partner to provide capital. One by one the mutual companies began to give up their independence. Scottish Mutual was bought in 1991 by Abbey National, a former building society which had turned itself into a bank. Scottish Equitable was bought by the Dutch company Aegon in 1994. Scottish Widows sold itself to the bank LloydsTSB in 2000 for £6.7 billion and a year later Scottish Life sold itself for £1.3 billion to Royal London, a mutually owned company which was itself the product of a merger between two mutuals. Scottish Provident had a longer route to the same place: in 2000 it sold 40 per cent of its fund to Aberdeen Asset Management,[9] but was then acquired by Abbey National and eventually joined Royal London. In each case the policyholders received the sale price as a bonus to their policies. Average payouts varied, but in some cases they were substantial. With the promise of a cash windfall which they would not otherwise have received, the managements had no trouble in persuading their policyholders to accept the offers.

Only Standard Life resisted the pressure to demutualise. As the largest of the Scottish life companies (and in 1979 second only to Prudential in the UK), its management, led by the actuary Scott Bell, believed it did not have to give up its mutual status. But in 2000, following the sale of Scottish Widows, it came under sustained attack from a group led by Fred Woollard, an Australian fund manager based in Monaco. He had bought a large number of endowment policies and stood to gain from any windfalls after demutualisation. In its defence, Standard Life said that the company would be worth £12 billion on flotation on the stock market, a low valuation which was challenged by Woollard who claimed that the market capitalisation and the corresponding payouts to policyholders could be 50 per cent higher. The issue was put to a vote in a stormy general meeting attended by 2,000 policyholders and the count overseen by the Electoral Reform Society. To force demutualisation Woollard needed a 75 per cent vote in favour, but he secured less than 50 per cent.[10]

The company had won, but it proved to be a pyrrhic victory. The majority vote to remain mutual had come after a sustained period of high bonus rates for policyholders on the back of a rising market, boosted by the 'dotcom bubble'. When it reported results for the year Standard Life recorded a 25 per cent growth in new business.[11] The bubble burst soon afterwards and over the next few years market returns were much lower. Policyholders had been denied a windfall at a time when the market was at a peak. Now the company should be reducing bonuses, but the management realised that it would have to offer policyholders inducements to keep their loyalty. Bonus rates were maintained rather than cut, charges for pensions were reduced and the company offered a guarantee for customers with endowment mortgages, who feared that lower investment returns might mean that the surrender value of their policies did not meet their outstanding debts.[12]

Scott Bell had retired and his successor as chief executive, Ian Lumsden, who had previously been finance director, took a bullish view of the company's strength and prospects. It had achieved high investment returns by heavily weighting its portfolios towards equities, which in the boom years grew in value much faster than bonds. He maintained this position even though the market was turning down, believing that Standard Life had sufficient capital to withstand a short-term 'blip'. Others took a different view. Two of the company's main rivals, Norwich Union and Prudential, had sold down the proportion of equities in their funds and an independent analyst, Ned Cazalet, published research arguing that Standard Life was taking an unrealistically optimistic view of its prospects.

The regulator, the Financial Services Authority, had also had doubts and made its own calculation of Standard Life's capital position and the dangers attached to the equity portfolio. It concluded that the company risked insolvency and in 2004 it forced changes: Lumsden resigned, to be replaced by Sandy Crombie who had headed the investment division. Over the following six weeks the company quietly sold £7.5 billion of equities, taking the proportion in the 'with-profits' fund down from a 57 per cent weighting to 35 per cent.[13] The solvency position was restored, but at a cost. Bonus rates had to be cut and over the next four years 5,000 staff were made redundant. Standard Life had to renege on its guarantee for 770,000 holders of endowment mortgages. The small print had given it an escape, but the costs were nearly £400 million and the company's reputation took a hammering.[14]

Staying mutual had not benefited Standard Life. In 2005, although the same three Edinburgh life assurance companies were still in the UK top ten, Standard Life had dropped to seventh place in terms of its premium income and had been overtaken by Scottish Widows.[15] In 2006 the company announced it would demutualise and float on the London Stock Exchange. This time 98 per cent of policyholders voted in favour. The company's market capitalisation was £5 billion, a half or a third of what it might have achieved six years previously. Policyholders received windfall payments averaging £1,500 – compared to the £5,600 Scottish Widows policyholders had received in 2000.[16]

Part 4

Triumph and disaster

29

The battle for NatWest

WHILE EDINBURGH WAS losing its independent life assurance companies, the two banks faced a dilemma: they had been growing quickly, but having to rely on Scotland for most of their deposits limited their growth in the much larger English market. Both Bank of Scotland and Royal Bank had tried and failed to find building society partners and attempts to forge a friendly alliance with one of the London Big Four banks had come to nothing.[1] Their superior performance insulated them from a bid by underperforming NatWest or Barclays, but a large American or European bank looking for a foothold in the UK market might think the cost worth paying. To maintain their independence, they had to find a means of growing.

A dramatic way out of the impasse was suggested by Will Samuel, who as head of corporate finance with the long-established and revered London merchant bank Schroders, was an adviser to Bank of Scotland. He also had a personal link; his sister Lesley Knox was a non-executive on the bank board. If NatWest could not be interested in a friendly merger, suggested Samuel, why not launch a hostile bid?

This was a radical suggestion. Hostile bids were never easy in any industry, but especially not in banking. The Bank of England, which had overall responsibility for the banking sector, was known not to look kindly on such moves and the last openly hostile full bid – by HSBC for Royal Bank of Scotland 18 years before – had been blocked by the government. There was also the difference in scale. Bank of Scotland was less than half the size of NatWest. There was no way it could raise the resources for a cash bid, so it would have to persuade NatWest's institutional shareholders – the professionals who managed investments on behalf of pension funds and insurance companies – to accept Bank of Scotland shares in payment.

Samuel argued that NatWest's management record had been so awful for so long that shareholders would be ready to take the risk. The London bank had lurched from crisis to disaster with amazing regularity. After nearly going bust in the secondary banking crisis of the 1970s, during the following decade it had become embroiled in a financial scandal which resulted in an investigation by the Department of Trade and the resignation of several board members, including the chairman. Ill-judged acquisitions in Canada and the US had not worked and been sold at a loss, and the domestic banking business in the UK was slow and inefficient. In an astonishingly arrogant move, the bank had built the NatWest Tower, an ostentatious headquarters in the City of London, which until the development of Canary Wharf was the tallest building in Britain. The building had a footprint in the shape of the bank's logo and an art gallery at the bottom, which housed its extensive picture collection. (It was only occupied for a few years before Irish terrorists severely damaged it with a bomb in 1993.) The latest disaster, losses uncovered in the investment banking business, had again led to calls for top resignations.

By 1999 NatWest had a new chairman in Sir David Rowland, who had made his name leading the Lloyds of London insurance market, but also a long-serving chief executive, Derek Wanless. He was regarded by the City as undoubtedly clever – he had studied maths at Cambridge and was a qualified statistician as well as a banker – but far too nice. He lacked the ruthlessness to deal with the bank's inflated costs. Peter Burt was convinced that Bank of Scotland's management could run NatWest and that he had a sporting chance of convincing the City to back him, but the London bank would be a huge mouthful to swallow. Samuel suggested a plan which he thought would halve the risk and double the chances of success, so in August 1999 Burt walked down The Mound from the Bank's headquarters in the Edinburgh Old Town, crossed Princes Street into the New Town and called on his main rival, the chief executive of Royal Bank of Scotland – now Sir George Mathewson, after his knighthood in the New Year's Honours List. Burt's proposal was that they should co-operate in a joint attack.

On paper the plan looked watertight. Both Scottish banks were much smaller than NatWest, with Royal Bank being slightly larger than Bank of Scotland, but together they were roughly equal to the London bank. The plan was to capture and dismember NatWest, injecting a double dose of strong Scottish management to drive down costs and boost sales. Mathewson was sufficiently interested in Burt's joint bid idea to want to explore it further and small groups of top executives from both banks started meeting in secret to plan the attack and the division of the spoils.

At the same time, each bank individually began to work out how it would manage its share of the acquisition. Gavin Masterton, for Bank of Scotland, was already planning his moves and for the Royal, Mathewson's new recruit, Fred Goodwin, was doing the same. Masterton had worked his way up through banking in the time-honoured fashion. He had joined the old British Linen Bank straight from school, taken a correspondence course to get his certificate from the Scottish banking institute and been moved around by the bank to gain experience. He had joined Bank of Scotland when it acquired British Linen and progressed quickly up the management chain. Recognising his potential, the bank had put him through Harvard University's Advanced Management Programme.

Goodwin, still only 41, by contrast, was one of the new breed of late entrants to banking from other professions. The son of an electrician, he had been born and brought up on a council estate in Paisley, and had been the first of his family to go on to higher education. He had read law at Glasgow University and then trained as an accountant, rising quickly to become a partner in the international firm Touche Ross. While there he had worked on the liquidation of the Bank of Credit & Commerce International and came to the attention of National Australia Bank when he had done consultancy work for them. His sharp forensic mind had convinced them to hire him to head their two UK banking operations, Clydesdale and Yorkshire Bank. His record of improving the performance of both banks was impressive, but his cost-cutting and aggressive style had earned him the nickname 'Fred the Shred'. He was reluctantly considering a move to Australia and the top post in NAB when Mathewson lured him to Royal Bank as his number two.

Both Scottish banks were ambitious to continue their expansion, but to do that they needed access to the vast deposit base which NatWest had garnered through its 1,700 branches. Royal Bank had 200 English branches, but Bank of Scotland had only 25. Dividing the NatWest total between them would enable each of them to leap decades of organic growth. The talks continued for a few weeks but as they began to work out the detail it became clear to both sides that the joint bid idea had a fundamental flaw – they both wanted the same parts of NatWest and neither was willing to allow the other to take the largest share or the best bits. However united they might be during the bid battle, afterwards they had to become competitors again. The talks ended in failure. Mathewson wanted Burt to agree not to bid alone; Burt was unwilling to do so, but he still faced the problem of convincing his own non-executive directors to go ahead with a lone bid.

At the next meeting Burt told his board that Bank of Scotland was too small to survive on its own. It lacked the scale necessary to invest enough in technology, marketing or management to be able to compete and would sooner or later be swallowed up by a larger predator. Despite misgivings by several directors, opinion was moving in his direction when NatWest made the decision for them. At the beginning of September 1999 the London bank announced an agreed takeover of the insurance giant Legal & General at the high price of £10.7 billion. This was a now-or-never moment for Bank of Scotland. NatWest at twice the size was already a big pill to swallow; if it were to succeed in acquiring the insurance company it would become more than three times Bank of Scotland's size and well out of reach.

The announcement also created an opportunity. Institutional investors did not like the NatWest proposal and began to criticise it openly: the London bank was paying too much, previous acquisitions had not been well managed and had destroyed value rather than creating it, and NatWest's management should be concentrating on getting their existing business right before taking on new ones. They showed their displeasure by selling NatWest shares and over the next two weeks the value of the bank on the stock market fell by more than a quarter, making it more digestible for Bank of Scotland.

If they were going to move, the team on The Mound did not have much time. NatWest had called a special shareholders' meeting for early October to approve the Legal & General deal. To persuade NatWest's investors to reject it, Bank of Scotland had to be ready to make a public announcement of a credible and detailed alternative proposal. The bank's internal team had done some work, but there had been little thought about the technical aspects of an offer and the bank would not have Will Samuel on its side. Schroders was acting for Legal & General and so was compromised.

The clock was already ticking. Peter Burt virtually moved into the Canary Wharf offices of Credit Suisse First Boston, the international investment bank which was to be one of the lead advisers. As it happened, an ideal opportunity to launch a bid was coming up at the end of September 1999. The annual meetings of the International Monetary Fund and the World Bank in Washington are usually attended by the chairmen and chief executives of all major commercial and central banks and the events that go on around them, dinners and receptions, are fertile ground for informal networking and deal-broking. Everybody who is anybody in banking would be there. Peter Burt and Sir Jack Shaw, governor, were due to attend, but quietly they cancelled their air tickets and persuaded Sir Bob Reid, one of the deputy governors of the bank, to go instead. Discreet inquiries were made to find out when Sir David Rowland and Derek Wanless, NatWest's chairman and chief executive, planned to cross the Atlantic: Sunday 26 September.

Initially the announcement of the Bank's bid was planned for Thursday 23 September, but the supporting documentation was not ready and it had to be put back for a day. There followed 24 hours of intense nail-biting waiting to see if the news leaked, but the security held fast. Takeover announcements have to be made before the Stock Exchange opens in the morning and dealers get to their screens. Traditionally, the first news is delivered in a call from chairman to chairman. At dawn on Friday 24 September Sir Jack Shaw dialled Rowland's home, only to be told by his wife that Rowland had gone out for an early morning run and would call back. The *Financial Times* later reported that in fact Rowland was still in bed, trying to decide whether to go for a run or not, but in any case a few minutes later he returned the call and Shaw delivered his bombshell.[2]

By 6.45 a.m. Rowland had called Wanless, who called his senior executives and summoned them into the office for an urgent meeting. For most it was merely an early commute, but for Bernard Horn, NatWest's head of group operations, it meant a scrambled return from Lake Como, where he was celebrating his wife's birthday. Also called was Terry Eccles, the senior executive of the investment bank J.P. Morgan, which was advising NatWest on the Legal & General deal. At 7.15 a.m. first news of the bid hit dealers' screens.

At 9 a.m. there was a hastily arranged meeting between Bank of Scotland's senior team and their NatWest counterparts. The Scots outlined their proposal, the English listened politely, but were noncommittal and the meeting ended quickly. Bank of Scotland's timing was impeccable. The IMF and World Bank meetings would not start until the Monday, but many senior bankers were either already in the US on Friday 24 September or on their way. Royal Bank's Sir George Mathewson had taken a few days off and crossed the Atlantic early to watch the opening of the Ryder Cup, the annual golf tournament between Europe and the United States. That morning he was among the crowd on the edge of the green at the Country Club, Brookline, near Boston. Club rules dictate that all mobile telephones must be switched off during play, but Mathewson had never been one to follow rules and took the call telling him of Bank of Scotland's bid. He cut short his vacation and flew back for a hurriedly arranged meeting with Royal Bank's City advisers, Goldman Sachs and Merrill Lynch. They were, he told his colleagues later, 'gagging for us to make a counter bid'. Mathewson, however, decided to hold his fire. He was not the only one to catch an early plane home. Peter Ellwood, LloydsTSB's chief, abandoned the IMF meetings and flew back that Sunday.

The bid sent a shockwave through the City. An early morning flash from Reuters declared: 'Bank of Scotland has torn up the handbook on how to achieve a British financial services merger and thrown the pieces to the wind.' An unnamed analyst was quoted as saying: 'This is about as hostile as you can get without going up and punching the other side in the face. The law of the jungle now presides.'[3] Most comment, however, favoured Bank of Scotland. Reuters added that the bid had 'stunned and delighted' the City. 'A David of British banking has taken on one of its Goliaths and the delighted spectators think it can win.' The following morning's newspapers were equally enthusiastic. *The Times* said the bid had been timed to perfection and the paper contrasted the return shareholders had received from Bank of Scotland over the past decade with that from NatWest. A hundred pounds invested in the bank at the beginning of 1989 was worth £1,515 a decade later, whereas had it been invested in NatWest it would be worth less than half that at £745.

Over the next few days Bank of Scotland gave details of how it would transform the performance of its target. A massive £1 billion a year was to be taken out of costs by eliminating duplication between the two banks and reducing the number of processing centres from 54 to 9. Most of NatWest's branches were to be moved from Victorian or Edwardian buildings to shopping malls and there was to be a much more aggressive sales policy. The message was clear: under Scottish management NatWest would be driven much harder. Brandishing his Scottish credentials, Peter Burt said that NatWest's bloated and expensive head office would be reduced to a brass plate in London. The combined bank would be run from Edinburgh.

There was a feeling of *déjà vu* about NatWest's response. It was now promising to sell exactly the same subsidiaries as Bank of Scotland had said it would sell; it would give its branches a makeover, cut costs by freezing recruitment and salary rises; the art gallery in NatWest Tower was to be closed and the bank would end its sponsorship of an annual art prize. To answer criticism of its management, it would recruit a number two to chief executive Derek Wanless. Burt described the new strategy as a 'copycat' defence and the City was distinctly underwhelmed. It was too little, too late and it left Wanless in charge – a man associated in the City with NatWest's years of underperformance.

The special meeting to approve NatWest's purchase of Legal & General was a mournful affair. Professional investors holding the vast majority of NatWest's shares did not bother to turn up and the handful of small shareholders who did attend heard the formal announcement of what the City had known since the morning of the bid – the L&G deal was dead. After the meeting the NatWest non-executive directors met with David Mayhew, senior partner at Cazenove, stockbroker to the Queen and adviser to many of the top 100 largest companies. Executive directors were pointedly excluded. Wanless was to be thanked for his service and summarily sacked. Rowland assumed the role of chief executive as well as chairman, and as his number two he was to bring in Ron Sandler,[4] who had fulfilled the same role in Lloyds of London. The City was again unimpressed. Wanless had gone, but now there were two insurance men running the bank, with not a banking qualification or a year of banking experience between them. Yet not everything was going Bank of Scotland's way. Since the bid had been announced its share price had been rising, but NatWest's price had been rising faster. This meant one, or possibly, two things: Bank of Scotland would have to raise its bid and/or another bidder would enter the contest.

NatWest's share price stayed ahead of the value of the bid and at the end of November the bank bowed to the inevitable. Jack Shaw again telephoned David Rowland before dawn to tell him that Bank of Scotland had made an improved offer, there was to be more cash, meaning higher borrowing, there was to be a special dividend of £2 billion for shareholders as an extra inducement and crucially NatWest shareholders were to get more of the combined group; now they would own 70 per cent as against 68 per cent under the first offer. The whole package now valued NatWest at £24.3 billion – a colossal sum – but it was not enough. NatWest's share price continued to rise and by the end of the day was above even the value of this increased offer. The market was expecting even more and Bank of Scotland would be stretched to breaking point to provide it.

Royal Bank launched its attack on NatWest on Monday 29 November. This time Sir David Rowland received his pre-dawn call from Sir George Younger. It hardly came as a surprise to Rowland or to anyone else. The weekend papers had been full of stories of talks between George Mathewson and Rowland, with the Royal trying to win approval from the NatWest board so that its offer would be friendly and recommended, rather than a second hostile attack. The talks had broken up on the previous Friday and Rowland had gathered his board together on Saturday for a brief meeting, but there was not much to discuss. NatWest had decided it wanted to remain independent; there was to be no deal. The fight would now be a three-cornered contest.

The Royal Bank's team, which had been working on the detail of their offer for weeks, had had to do some last minute tweaking when Bank of Scotland announced its increased offer; nevertheless, the new bid had a very familiar shape. The headline value was slightly higher and the promised cost savings were £165 million more, but otherwise the recipe was the same. Non-core subsidiaries were to be sold, there was to be a closer focus on the core business. The Royal contrasted its financial performance against the record of NatWest and compared NatWest's management to its top team – chairman Sir George Younger, chief executive George Mathewson and Fred Goodwin, who was designated as the man who would run the bank. One of the factors which may have discouraged Rowland from endorsing the bid was that Royal Bank had made it clear that if it won there was to be no place for Rowland or Sandler in the merged group. George Younger had announced the date of his retirement and Royal Bank's board had agreed that Mathewson would succeed him as chairman, with Goodwin becoming chief executive.

Mathewson's caution in not rushing into a bid had given him a number of advantages. He had seen how the City had greeted the Bank of Scotland bid, he knew the size and structure of the competing offer and, crucially, he had waited until the Office of Fair Trading had ruled that a takeover would not have to be referred to the Competition Commission. Although the Royal Bank team had been working intensively on their bid before going public, they were now coming fresh to the fight, whereas Peter Burt and his team had already been at full stretch for more than two months. Also, the delay had given the Royal's PR team time to leak out favourable news, such as the decision by the Spanish banking giant

BSCH,* which was a shareholder in Royal Bank, to back the bid and contribute cash.

In public Burt was philosophical: 'I would prefer not to enter into a pitched battle with a company so close to home, but the Royal will do what it believes is in the best interests of its shareholders and so will we.' But the Royal's move was a bitter blow. At one time the team from The Mound might have hoped to declare victory before Christmas and go home to their families; now it would continue at least until February and they would be fighting on two fronts. Even for a man of Burt's prodigious energy, this was a sapping experience and it was tying up around 150 senior employees in the company. It is a tribute to the depth of management that Bank of Scotland was still able to turn out double-digit growth and announce new ventures, but it was a big distraction.

For the first time Burt had to acknowledge publicly the possibility of defeat when he was asked whether failure would lay Bank of Scotland itself open to takeover. He dismissed the question, adding that if the price of NatWest rose too high, he would walk away 'without a backward glance'. But the tension was obviously getting to him and, against the advice of his public relations managers, he succumbed to the temptation to attack the Royal Bank's management, recalling Fred Goodwin's nicknames of 'Fred the Shred' and 'Fred the Impaler', and drawing attention to the fact that many of the Royal's top executives had been brought in from outside, without much banking experience. 'I'm struggling to think of an executive of RBS who came up through the ranks. If Fred Goodwin falls under a bus, who is going to run the bank?' George Mathewson briefly replied in the same negative style, drawing attention to the age of Burt's number two, Gavin Masterton (58, less than two years from normal bank retirement age) and Fred Goodwin, 41. It was left to Goodwin to bring the temperature down. 'We think logic and fact will win this. It needs to be done on a more professional footing, rather than slagging each other off.'

As the contest ran its course, both bidders added refinements to their offers in the hope of making them more attractive to shareholders, and NatWest announced that it had poached Gordon Pell, a senior executive at LloydsTSB, to join them. This went part way to answering the criticism that, however able Rowland and Sandler might be, they lacked banking experience. Pell had it in spades. Rowland's defence tactics,

---

* Now Santander.

which had previously looked piecemeal and borrowed from his tormentors, now began to look plausible. By adopting virtually the same programmes as Bank of Scotland and Royal Bank – sell peripheral businesses, concentrate on core banking and reduce costs – he had removed strategy as a basis for deciding the bid. If all three banks – the Royal, Bank of Scotland and NatWest – had the same strategy and were roughly offering to return the same value to shareholders, it was a question of which management team could best deliver. His argument was that the incumbents had the best chance, since they knew the business best.

As the bid moved into its final days in mid-February opinion swung between the three possible outcomes. One or two analysts now suggested that NatWest might – or indeed should – remain independent and it began to look possible that both bidders might fail. There was a fillip for Bank of Scotland as the influential *Financial Times* Lex column recommended that shareholders accept its bid, but slowly large institutional shareholders began to declare themselves for Royal Bank. Now the peculiar logic of the stock market began to show itself. As Royal Bank began to look the likely winner, its share price fell, whereas the price of Bank of Scotland shares rose on the prospect of it being the loser. By the Thursday of the last week Royal Bank's shares had fallen 18 per cent from the level at which it had made the offer, meaning that its bid was now worth less than the bank's bid and less than the value at which NatWest shares were trading on the stock market.

At lunchtime on Friday there was enough good news to convince Peter Burt that he had won, but the afternoon was still taken up with a hectic round of investor meetings. In the evening the Bank of Scotland's team – Burt, Masterton and George Mitchell, head of corporate banking – were invited for champagne by Richard Lambert, editor of the *Financial Times*, which had been a consistent supporter. As they filed into his office Burt asked Lambert what was it to be: congratulations, or commiserations? The latter, replied Lambert. Enough institutional shareholders had now declared for Royal Bank to guarantee it at least 51 per cent of NatWest shares. The three men drained their glasses, cancelled their remaining scheduled meetings with investors and caught the last flight to Scotland. The Royal Bank team met in a Holborn pub, then Mathewson and Goodwin headed for the Savoy Grill.

In the following week NatWest gave up the fight and Royal Bank mopped up the remaining shares. George Mathewson felt strangely deflated after his stunning victory. A decade before, his bank had been on the edge of falling into loss, now he had tripled its size and made it a major force in UK banking. He had fought a short, but extremely hard campaign, tirelessly presenting to investors, not only in London and Scotland, but flying to New York to woo NatWest's American shareholders. After months of lack of sleep and living on adrenalin, fatigue and depression overcame him. 'It took me weeks to recover,' he told friends, 'and I won!'

30

Into the arms of Halifax

THE LOSER SUCCUMBED to flu and had to take a week off work – an almost unheard of event for Peter Burt – but he knew he could not afford to give way to exhaustion. A week after conceding defeat, and after numerous post-mortems, he admitted to being bitterly disappointed, but determined to carry on. 'We must do something. We don't necessarily have to acquire something, but we must drive the business forward because if we don't we will not only be seen to be vulnerable, we will be vulnerable and deservedly so.' It was a sentiment widely shared. Despite Bank of Scotland continuing to report sparkling profits growth, in the harsh judgement of the City Burt was now seen as having had two failures in a row, the Pat Robertson affair and NatWest. 'The next thing he does has got to work, otherwise he's toast,' one unnamed banker told the *Financial Times*.[1]

The feeling of despondency in the bank extended from the boardroom to the branches. Six months' work had crumbled in 24 hours and there was no alternative to swallowing hard and carrying on, but the concern that Bank of Scotland could now become a victim persisted. Takeover rumours swirling around for the following six months were enough to keep the share price at a premium level, but they were baseless and when Burt reported a 14 per cent rise in profits for the half-year he commented that despite the stories, there had been a 'distinct lack of bids'. Slowly the speculation died down and the share price subsided. The old problem, however, would not go away. Bank of Scotland's growth was being propelled by its success at lending, which was expanding at 20 per cent a year, but it was only generating new capital at 13 per cent a year.[2] To fill the funding gap it was increasingly being thrown back on the wholesale funding market, which was short-term and capricious. It badly needed access to a larger deposit base. Burt had received a tentative approach from National Australia Bank, owner of Clydesdale Bank, and had spent some weeks talking to them but the discussions had come to nothing.

Another opportunity was not long in coming. A call came from Abbey National, a former building society which had demutualised and turned itself into a bank. The fit looked reasonable. In contrast to Bank of Scotland, Abbey had deep roots in the north and south of England, with only a small branch presence north of the border. It was predominantly a deposit taker and a mortgage lender, with only a modest corporate or small-business lending book, although it had moved into pensions and life assurance. Abbey was headed by another Scot, Ian Harley, whose insistence that he be the chief executive had scuppered previous deals, according to press reports. He was not an easy man to talk to – even Abbey's own chairman, the former Tory politician Lord Tugendhat, described him as 'a bit dour', before adding, 'but he does deliver'. But Burt got on quite well with him and did not feel he was an obstacle to a merger.

Talks continued with Tugendhat urging them on enthusiastically, but more than personalities were getting in the way. Peter Burt favoured a merger of equals – Abbey was bigger, but Bank of Scotland was better, a more comprehensive organisation with a broader range of skills and superior performance. Abbey, however, was unimpressed and saw it as a straight takeover. Recognising that a takeover by an English company, of a bank which had been part of the Scottish firmament for 300 years, might not go down too well north of the border, Abbey's PR department tried to make some conciliatory noises, promising extra shareholder gatherings and board meetings in Scotland. There would also be Scottish directors – 'it will be a pretty tartan board'. Despite this patronising tone, the negotiations progressed, with Tugendhat and his deputy Charles Villiers meeting Sir Jack Shaw and Sir Bob Reid for Bank of Scotland. A deal looked doable. Bank of Scotland thought it could generate £400 million more in profit from Abbey National's branch network and estimated that £350 million could be taken out of costs. Abbey began to talk enthusiastically about becoming a fifth force to challenge the hegemony of the Big Four London banks. However, Abbey's corporate lending book did not look good, and the Bank of Scotland team was not allowed to see the figures.

Bank of Scotland was on the verge of walking away when LloydsTSB announced an offer for Abbey. The predator was now the prey and although there was a certain referral of the bid to the Competition

Commission on monopolies grounds, meaning a six-month delay, investors put pressure on the Abbey board to end its ambitions to tie up with Bank of Scotland and support the LloydsTSB bid. Lloyds' branch network had considerable overlap with Abbey. If it could hold on to the customers while closing branches it would be able to make massive cost savings. It was a trick it had pulled off twice before with its acquisition of TSB (the Trustee Savings Bank) and the former building society Cheltenham & Gloucester.

In the spring of 2001 Gavin Masterton retired as group managing director of Bank of Scotland and was succeeded by George Mitchell who, like Masterston, was a bank lifer, having joined straight from school. A quick learner and a safe pair of hands, he had led the bank's operations in Hong Kong and New York before being given a mess to sort out in the international treasury department and then heading corporate banking. Life had to go on and the bank pressed ahead with an acquisition in Ireland and a deal with insurance company Zurich to offer loans and credit cards to its customers.

Peter Burt, tired after years of trying to solve the bank's strategic problem, had taken his family for a skiing holiday to Chamonix in the French Alps when he took a call from David Mayhew, senior partner at Cazenove. The Old Etonian had been against the bank in the NatWest battle; now he was asking whether Burt would be willing to meet James Crosby, chief executive of Halifax. The former building society had undergone a transformation since Bank of Scotland had last approached it to discuss a possible merger. Mike Blackburn had retired as chief executive to be succeeded by the man he had brought in to run Halifax's insurance business. Yorkshireman James Crosby was young (45 in 2001), energetic and fiercely intelligent. After reading mathematics at Oxford he had trained as an actuary with life assurance company Scottish Amicable, before moving into fund management with Rothschild Assurance. He looked the archetypal egghead and it was joked that he was bald because his brain was so big it had pushed his hair out.

In the six years since he had taken over the top job he had made a series of bold moves designed to transform Halifax from being a one-product mortgage bank to a more rounded financial institution. He had spent £1 billion buying the life assurance business of Equitable Life to add to Halifax's Clerical Medical subsidiary; he had poached Scotsman Jim Spowart from Standard Life to set up a new telephone and internet bank named Intelligent Finance; he had bought into the wealth management business St James's Place Capital; and he had gone into partnership with Peter Wood, the man who had set up Direct Line insurance. To manage Halifax's retail business, Crosby had recruited Andy Hornby, who was even younger (34 in 2001) and just as bright. He had followed a First in English at Oxford with an MBA from Harvard, where he graduated top of his year. His brief working career had seen him make a rapid ascent, from the Boston Consulting Group, to Blue Circle Cement to the supermarket group Asda, where he had become retail managing director, overseeing 36 stores and 14,000 employees, and joined the management board at the age of 32.

Halifax was the biggest mortgage lender in the UK and had a truly gigantic deposit base, with over 11 million saving customers. For decades it had been run very conservatively, with the result that its vast mortgage book was solid and secure (in the jargon of the industry it had a low loan-to-value ratio). It was also very profitable. Until Mrs Thatcher's government started deregulating the mortgage business in the 1980s, building societies, of which Halifax was the largest, could charge virtually what they liked, knowing that there was little price competition and that customers, once signed up, were unlikely to leave. Now all that had changed. Borrowers were being enticed away from traditional providers like Halifax by banks that were keen to get mortgage business and were prepared to offer cut-price deals. New competitors were also entering the market, offering loans over the telephone or the internet. Hornby, using the retail skills he had learned at Asda, had taken the fight to the enemy, offering existing customers new incentives to stay and trying to extend Halifax's market-leading share further by competing fiercely for new loan business.

Together Crosby, Hornby and Edinburgh-born Lord Dennis Stevenson, who had become chairman in 1999, had revived investor confidence in Halifax. For years the share price had languished below the level at which the company had first floated on the Stock Exchange when it demutualised; now it was rising strongly again.

For Bank of Scotland, Halifax made a much more attractive partner than Abbey National. It was bigger and appeared to have few of the management hang-ups that had dogged the Abbey negotiations. It had no corporate lending to speak of, but its problem was the reverse of the bank's. It had 'deposits coming out of its ears'; the difficulty was where to lend them profitably. Peter Burt played it cool with David Mayhew on the telephone, but conceded that, yes, he thought it might be worth making time to speak to James Crosby.

When he arrived at Halifax's London corporate flat in St James's, he was surprised to find James Crosby with his foot in plaster after a fall, but the meeting went well enough. Secondary to finding an escape from the bank's strategic straightjacket, one of Burt's objectives was to keep the headquarters in Scotland, which he believed was key to retaining the organisation's independent spirit and keeping together the formidable management team he had built up. A fear always in the back of his mind during the NatWest bid had been that, despite the intention, the economic pull of the larger organisation would have steadily moved the focus of decision-making to London. That was much less of an issue this time. Whatever the merits of the Yorkshire town, if it came to a choice between Halifax and Edinburgh from which to run a UK financial services group, the Scottish capital would come out top on most criteria.

The shape of the deal proposed by Mayhew was that Halifax would provide the chairman, and Bank of Scotland the chief executive. Although variously described in the press as 'excitable' and 'eccentric', Dennis Stevenson had an established reputation in the City and was an assidu-ous networker with fingers in many pies. Peter Burt was to be chief exec-utive, although on the understanding that he would not go on beyond his 60th birthday, which was less than three years away, and that he would be succeeded by Crosby. Not to lead the new group from the beginning was a blow to the younger man, who had been chief executive of Halifax for only two years, but one he was prepared to accept to get the deal done. The problem was what to do with him in the meantime – there was no obvious job description for an 'heir apparent.' Bringing the two management teams together would mean that the key divisional posts would go to able and strong-minded men who would not take kindly to having Crosby floating around without a clear role.

To further the discussions Burt organised a dinner for the top manage-ment teams from both companies in the dining room of Bank of Scotland's head office on The Mound. The room has one of the most impressive views in Britain, taking in Edinburgh Castle, with the city spread out below it. But the diners' minds were on other things and the meeting did not go well. Crosby was ill at ease and there were personality clashes across the table. The Bank of Scotland men, on their home ground surrounded by history, were older, more experienced, and confi-dent that they understood what was possible and what had to be done. The Halifax team seemed younger, smarter and in a hurry. There was a danger that disagreements might derail the discussions, but it was Andy

Hornby, the most junior in age by a decade, who worked to calm tempers and find common ground.

Burt was insistent that, despite Halifax's larger size, the deal should be seen as a partnership of equals. They would form a new holding company and carry out what was known in the City as a 'nil premium merger' – shares in the new group would be swapped one-for-one with existing shares in Halifax or Bank of Scotland. The two brand names would be retained, although Halifax would conduct its retail business under the Bank of Scotland name north of the border. In the corporate market, the brand name would continue to be Bank of Scotland. Unlike Abbey, which thought it should have the upper hand, Halifax was content with this arrangement, which was simpler and meant that its shareholders would end up with most of the combined business, 63 per cent against 37 per cent for Bank of Scotland shareholders.

Top posts would be allocated on merit, but the split was roughly equal. Mike Ellis, Halifax's chief operations officer, would fill the role as finance director of the new group, Andy Hornby would take charge of retail and personal banking, and Phil Hodkinson, who was brought in from Zurich Financial Services, would look after the insurance and investment business. From the bank, George Mitchell would run corporate banking, Colin Matthew business banking, concentrating on the smaller end of the market, and Gordon McQueen would merge the two treasury operations. It all looked pretty straightforward; there was very little overlap either in skills or branch network. There would be few redundancies: costs could be saved, but that was not the basis for the merger. Seizing opportunity was to be the driving motivation.

Burt and Crosby, joking that Yorkshire thrift had met Scottish parsimony, spent little time and no money on deciding the name of the new holding company, which was to be Halifax Bank of Scotland. Since it would inevitably be shortened to initials, Burt had no hesitation in agreeing that the Halifax name should come first – HBOS may not be elegant, but it was preferable to BOSH. The choice of name upset the Herne Bay Operatic Society, which had called itself HBOS for years, but the PR men straightened that one out. The corporate logo, sketched out on a piece of paper, was a combination of Halifax's 'X' and Bank of Scotland's saltire and coins.

Internally in Bank of Scotland the merger was being sold as an equal partnership, but a different impression was being given to Halifax's top management. At an away day at Bolton Abbey, Wharfdale, a handful of top managers were told about the talks, but not given the name of the intended partner. 'It was referred to as "Project Linwood" and there was great speculation at dinner as to who it might be, but it was obvious from the way they spoke that Stevenson, Crosby, Ellis and Hornby were to get the top jobs. No one else mattered,' one Halifax manager remembered. The Bank of Scotland board could see the logic of the union but was still nervous at giving up its independence and of Halifax's true intentions. 'They always used soft language,' said one director, 'they talked all the time about merger but there was always the implied threat that if our board didn't agree, they would bid for us.' At the end of April 2001 the news that the two companies had been talking leaked and both share prices leaped up. Comment was generally favourable.

Newspapers calculated that the merged group would have a combined market value of nearly £28 billion and be the 11th largest bank in Europe, employing 61,000 people and making £2.8 billion in profits. It would still be smaller than the London Big Four (with Royal Bank now being in control of NatWest), but it would be able to give them a run for their money. In contrast to the Abbey National talks, which had dragged on for months without getting very far, the courtship between Halifax and Bank of Scotland was positively whirlwind; the two sides had been talking for only a few weeks.

Halifax had made a point of moving its annual general meeting around the country to give its customers who had taken shares at the time of demutualisation the chance to hear and question the board. By coincidence it was due to hold its AGM in Edinburgh on Tuesday 1 May. On the Sunday evening before the meeting, Stevenson, Crosby and their adviser from Lazards, met Burt and Mayhew for dinner in a private room in the Caledonian Hotel, Edinburgh. In the last few days Peter Burt had been thinking hard about his position. He was tired, not physically, but years of mental strain wrestling with the problem of Bank of Scotland's future and dragging up and down the country to proposition potential suitors had been draining. He had had fruitless talks with a dozen companies and come close to securing NatWest, only to have the prize taken from him. Now at last he had found a solution. Bank of Scotland had been growing at 20 per cent compound for 20 years – it was a record no other bank had equalled – but it was a tiger from which it was impossible to dismount. If its performance was seen to falter, its share price would fall and it would be vulnerable to takeover. More than

300 years of independence and the unique culture which the bank had fostered would be lost. With access to Halifax's large balance sheet and capital strength, Bank of Scotland could continue with its phenomenal lending growth.

He wanted to see the merger through, to oversee the integration and then to retire, having achieved what he set out to do. After a dozen years leading a FTSE 100 company he had no will to go on indefinitely. The more he thought about it, the more it seemed logical that he should not become chief executive of HBOS. He talked to David Mayhew about stepping down altogether, but Mayhew warned him that if he did that the whole deal might fall apart. At dinner, Burt announced his decision: he would take the title executive deputy chairman and concentrate on making the integration of the two companies as smooth as possible, leaving the way open for Crosby to become chief executive immediately. When news of the meal leaked out, cynics in Bank of Scotland described it as 'Peter's Last Supper'.

Speculation was now so strong that a deal would be done that there was pressure to get the final details agreed and an official announcement made to the Stock Exchange. The bank postponed the announcement of its annual results and the two management teams met again. The following day the two boards met separately to approve the deal in principle and teams of lawyers and brokers met in London with Crosby and Burt to work through the night on the detailed agreement. It was 6 a.m. on Friday 4 May before the work was finished; the statement was issued and a press conference was called for noon.

The merger was mostly well received inside the two companies. Only 2,000 jobs would be lost through reducing duplication, a fraction of those already lost in the Royal's takeover of NatWest, and these were to be achieved by natural wastage rather than compulsory redundancy. Yorkshire would retain the headquarters of the retail bank, but the corporate head office was to be in Edinburgh and Burt had secured a safeguard – more than half of the board would have to vote in favour before the HQ could be moved. Since the board was to be made up equally of directors from each side, it looked like an effective Scottish veto.

Bank of Scotland published its results on the same day, revealing that profits were up 12 per cent and had topped £1 billion for the first time. The share price of both companies rose, taking their combined worth over £30 billion, but the argument that the new bank would succeed by boosting sales rather than cutting costs did not please everyone in the

City. One analyst was doubtful that the strategy could succeed: 'We like slash-and-burn deals. The more people who get fired the better.'[3]

A few weeks later the Office of Fair Trading cleared the merger on competition grounds. HBOS would have a market-leading share of 20 per cent in mortgages and not far short of that in savings accounts, but its position in other markets such as current accounts, business and corporate accounts was tiny compared to the Big Four – underlining the fact that there was a lot to go for. As far as the balance of power in the new organisation was concerned, it was fairly clear where the weight lay. Not only were Halifax providing the chairman, chief executive and finance director, but nearly half the profit would be generated by the retail business controlled by Andy Hornby and a further quarter from the insurance activities run by Phil Hodkinson. Taken together, these five top executives had no banking qualifications and only a few years of banking experience between them. Little more than a year earlier, Peter Burt had criticised the top management of NatWest for the same failing. Now he had handed over his bank to them.

31

The 'Haliban'

IT WAS ANNOUNCED that James Crosby and Mike Ellis would have offices on The Mound and both men rented flats in Edinburgh. Ellis worked out of his office except when group business took him elsewhere and quickly won respect from the Bank of Scotland management for his professionalism, experience and the hard work he put into mastering the new business. Crosby was seen in his office much less often. He admitted to the *Independent* that he would only visit once a week and was immediately branded the 'once a week Scot'. He would continue to live in Yorkshire, where three of his four children were at school. He was recognised as very intelligent, but not an easy man to talk to or to read. With Hornby based in Halifax, the days of the close corporate collaboration of the Bank of Scotland general managers with offices grouped together on the same floor of The Mound were gone. It was much more difficult to get an overview of the business or a sense of shared values and mission.

Non-executive directors for the combined board were chosen by the executives – who issued invitations to five from each side. Bank of Scotland provided deputy governor and former Shell executive Sir Bob Reid; Sir Ron Garrick, former chief executive of the engineering group Weir; John Maclean, an accountant who had been in shipping; Brian Ivory, who had run a whisky company; and Lord Simpson of Dunkeld, whose stewardship of the electronics group Marconi, which was facing collapse, was coming under sustained attack by workers and investors alike. He lasted less than a year before resigning under shareholder pressure. Notable among those not asked to serve as an HBOS director was Lesley Knox, who had a reputation for asking pointed and difficult questions on the bank board. She also had experience in corporate finance and asset management, working for an investment bank. In the years to come her expertise would be missed.

There was also a lack of banking experience among the former Halifax directors. They were Charles Dunstone, the founder of Carphone Warehouse; Tony Hobson, who had been finance director of the life assurance company Legal & General; Coline McConville, who was in advertising; Louis Sherwood, whose background was television and retail; and Philip Yea, from the drinks industry.

Bank of Scotland had got by without ex-bankers among its non-executives, but the process of 'homologation' – the cross-examination of executives on specific initiatives, including major lending decisions – meant that they had built up a detailed picture of how the bank ran and where the pitfalls might be hidden. Those directors who moved to HBOS found that the board was expected to operate in a very different way. 'Stevenson didn't see the point of close questioning the executives,' one director recalls, 'but there was a point. Over time you could see a growing over-confidence: we lent money and we were never wrong. The board lost the habit of challenge.'

HBOS was on a different scale to Bank of Scotland and a much more complex organisation. The formal governance demands on boards had also grown, with new regulations and new City codes. 'Board papers were inches thick and if you asked a question at a board meeting an executive could always point to a report of 156 pages and tell you that your question was answered on page 144. You had never got to it – there just wasn't time to read it all.' Another director recalls: 'The HBOS governance structure was well thought through, they had taken external advice and on paper it looked very strong. In practice Dennis, James and Andy were a very tight team and they ran the company. We thought Peter [Burt] would be part of it, but he wasn't.'

Yet despite the misgivings there was a feeling that Bank of Scotland had found a way out of its long-standing funding dilemma. But had it? Despite the fabled strength of its balance sheet, Halifax had not completely eliminated the reliance on wholesale funding markets. In its last year as an independent company, Bank of Scotland had lent £66 billion and been able to cover 54 per cent from customer deposits. Although HBOS could cover 66 per cent of its lending from deposits, it was still reliant on the wholesale market for a third of its advances and that proportion would rise; there was no significant business area where deposit growth was keeping up with the rise in lending.

Responsibility for keeping the group funded fell to Gordon McQueen, who had merged the two treasury operations. Bank of Scotland had always been conservatively run, never venturing into proprietary trading, seeing itself only as a service department for the bank and its customers. Since demutualisation Halifax had started a small trading business, which, although it involved some risk, was well run and profitable, but McQueen closed it. Treasury was expected at least to cover its costs from the prices it charged corporate customers and the lending businesses within the group for the capital they needed, but McQueen wanted to go further and use higher internal pricing to force the retail, business and corporate banking operations to target deposit growth as well as lending increases. If they brought in more deposits, the bank would be less reliant on the wholesale money market and therefore safer. The proposal was vetoed by Crosby. To do so would hold the whole business back, he said.

However, there seemed nothing to fear from the wholesale funding market. The combined group had a strong balance sheet and was viewed as low-risk by those who lent to it. The rating agencies graded 99 per cent of its investment portfolio as 'A' or better, and 86 per cent was graded 'AAA' – the highest level. For Bank of Scotland's continued growth in corporate lending the outlook was good: following the merger its senior debt had been upgraded from 'A+' to 'AA' by Standard & Poors, one of the leading ratings agencies.[1] This was a mark of approval and meant that the bank would be able to borrow at lower rates, making it more competitive in its drive to take business from its London rivals.

HBOS's first annual report laid heavy stress on partnership. The cover, with the caption 'The New Force', showed two shirt-sleeved arms with hands clasped in friendship. One set of cufflinks bore the cross of St George, the other the saltire of St Andrew. In his chairman's introduction, Lord Stevenson promised 'shared values, shared vision and an ambition to seek out new opportunities'. The speed at which the merger had been agreed and concluded was testimony to the closeness of view of the two sides. 'This was a merger of equals where relative size was always secondary to the shareholder value that teams with a shared vision can create.'

In his narrative, James Crosby emphasised the bank's solidity and its intention to be a consumer champion. For personal customers he promised realistic pricing and transparent charging coupled with 'pro-consumer PR work'. For corporate banking he described the 'old world' character of the lending book – and indeed Bank of Scotland portfolio was old world. It had avoided the excesses of the new economy's dotcom boom and bust and preferred to lend to traditional industries like engineering, manufacturing, construction and property and have its loans backed by real world assets like land, bricks and mortar. In an echo of the traditional Bank of Scotland philosophy of 'staying at the table', he promised 'we also pride ourselves on having the flexibility, whenever realistic, to see customers through the bad times as well as the good. After all a bank that pulls back at the first whiff of trouble does not deserve the partnership we seek with each of our corporate customers.'

You had to look deeper into the accounts to spot some of the less satisfactory aspects of the group's performance. In retail, the area run by Andy Hornby which made up half the total group business, profits had declined despite increased lending. Costs and provisions against bad debts were up and interest margins were lower. The group's growth was being provided by insurance, which was benefiting from the acquisition of the Equitable Life salesforce a year earlier, and corporate banking, which saw lending increase by a third and profits by even more.

Deep inside the report, it was revealed that the merger had been the occasion for substantial increases in salaries for the top management. James Crosby saw his total remuneration (salary plus bonus) leap from £690,000 to over £1 million – a rise of 56 per cent and a sum which made him better paid than the chief executive of LloydsTSB, which was larger. Peter Burt was not far behind, seeing a rise from £682,000 to £994,000. Mike Ellis received 55 per cent more, Andy Hornby 64 per cent more, and the three former Bank of Scotland executives, Gordon McQueen, Colin Matthew and George Mitchell more than doubled their total takings. Even the part-time chairman, Lord Stevenson, saw his remuneration jump from £265,000 to £363,000. The extra pay would not stop with the end of employment. Since bank employees enjoyed pensions based on their final salary at age 60, the HBOS executives could look forward to retirements considerably more comfortable than they had been expecting before the merger.

A simple and crude calculation illustrates how the pay of top executives had changed. In 1990 Bruce Pattullo, as the highest paid director in Bank of Scotland earned £176,000, 16 times the average salary of all staff in the bank. There was no bonus, although these began to be introduced a few years later. By 2000 Peter Burt's salary as chief executive and highest paid director had risen to £426,000, some 18 times the average. One year later James Crosby's basic pay was 25 times the average. If you add in his bonus – which nearly doubled his total remuneration – he was paid more than 43 times the average HBOS employee.

The job of integrating the two organisations had now begun in earnest and was felt in some areas much more than in others. In corporate banking it was almost business as usual. Most of the staff and management had come from Bank of Scotland and they were still trading under the same name, with the only difference being that they had more firepower at their disposal, but in branch banking the difference was felt acutely.

Bank of Scotland staff had been though a half-revolution of their own. With Gavin Masterton as treasurer and chief general manager there had been much more emphasis on sales, with counter staff being expected to ask customers what more the bank could do for them, rather than waiting for the customer to volunteer the information. But the transformation had only been partially completed. 'We were trying to downsize the branch network because of the costs and the old idea of customer service had to change, we had to move to relationship banking. But people were used to having the same manager for three or four years – when they found they had three different managers in 12 months, they got pissed off,' recalls one executive I interviewed. 'Everyone realised that things had to change, that our network was old-fashioned, but a lot of people were steeped in their ways and didn't like change with the result that the transformation was not done as well as it should have been. There were teething problems – we would have got them fixed, but before we knew it we were into the merger.'

Bank of Scotland employees had not been prepared for the sales-driven culture which Andy Hornby, using the retail experience and skills he had learned at Asda, had introduced into Halifax. Staff were expected to sell products rather than provide a service; they were given targets to reach, and training in how to achieve them. Branch premises were also undergoing a makeover, doing away with mahogany counters and bandit screens and making them into bright, modern retail outlets. If they weren't in the right locations they were closed and new premises opened in shopping malls and other high footfall areas.

Older, more traditional bank customers were unsettled and to make matters worse, the switchover of computer systems did not go smoothly. Personal customers had their accounts moved from the bank system to the Halifax network, being given a 'roll number', a traditional building society identifier, in the process. Business customers stayed with the Bank of Scotland system. This was a physical severing of the old bank principle of seeing the business relationship as an extension of the personal relationship and created problems where customers had personal and business accounts with HBOS. There were teething troubles and a personal apology from Hornby was sent to all Scottish account holders and staff, but by that time it was too late. Many loyal customers had left.

The determination with which the Halifax way of working was imposed on Bank of Scotland was reflected in the nickname given to the men from Yorkshire, which compared them to the religious fanatics of Afghanistan – the 'Haliban'. Some senior personal banking managers from Bank of Scotland transferred to the Halifax retail headquarters in Yorkshire, but found they had little or no influence in determining direction. 'Andy had four or five people around him who were clones of Andy Hornby. They didn't have much latitude. They could hear us bleeting about things, but they weren't going to change the model for one little bit of the market north of the border. Back in Scotland we couldn't go out socially because of the constant complaints from friends.'

The differences in the new approach went deeper than style. Experienced retail bankers were at a loss to understand the logic behind Hornby's strategy. With its history of being a building society only a few years behind it, Halifax was still predominantly a home loans and savings institution. It had a dominant market share in mortgages. This was a low-risk and solid business on which it made an excellent return – in fact almost half the profit from the new group came from mortgages. But it was under sustained assault from other banks, building societies and new entrants to the market, such as the telephone and internet banks Egg, Direct Line and Standard Life Bank. They were offering much finer deals, not only to new borrowers, but to existing homeowners to persuade them to switch.

It made sense to hang on to as many mortgage customers as possible by offering those who showed signs of wanting to leave a better deal. However, the original intention of the merger, as far as Bank of Scotland staff were concerned, was to lessen the group's dependence on this big, but threatened, market share by diversifying away from mortgages, particularly into corporate and business banking. Hornby showed no signs of allowing this to happen. As the corporate lending book grew, he expanded the mortgage book, competing hard, going head to head with rivals to offer the best deals. Each new loan was less profitable than an old one, but would also eat up some of the bank's capital and liquidity (funding), meaning that it couldn't be used to support lending elsewhere.

The drive also upset existing Halifax customers, many of whom had been loyal for a long time. They now saw new borrowers being offered interest rates lower than they were paying. Complaints began to be received and the Financial Ombudsman stepped in, fining HBOS as well as other banks for treating existing customers unfairly. The bank agreed to pay £7 million compensation to 30,000 customers who had complained, but said it would not similarly recompense a further 400,000 who had not yet registered a complaint. This grudging attitude, which contrasted with that of competitors like the building society Nationwide which had put up £200 million to compensate all its customers, brought a torrent of criticism. So much for Crosby's promise in the annual report of being the consumer's champion.

To compound matters, Halifax had also started its own internet and telephone bank, called Intelligent Finance (IF). To lead it the bank had poached Jim Spowart, a veteran banker who had started his career with Royal Bank of Scotland, but already had done two start-ups with the insurers Direct Line and Standard Life. IF had been phenomenally successful in its first year, gaining 155,000 customers, grabbing a 9 per cent share of new mortgages and lending £5.2 billion. Add this to the success of the main bank and HBOS was winning nearly a third of all new mortgages. Its dependence on the housing market was becoming more rather than less.

Another puzzling aspect of the strategy was the campaign to win more current accounts. As a former building society, Halifax had a relatively small share of this market but traditional bankers from both sides of the merger were not over-keen to increase it. Current accounts were the necessary evil of retail banking – in supermarket terms they were loss leaders. Cheques, still the main form of bill payment in 2002, were expensive to process and although customers might have high cash balances on pay day, the average in an account over the month was much less and canny customers withdrew spare cash to put it into interest-earning deposit accounts. At one time banks had charged fees on current accounts in order to break even, but competition and government pressure had forced them first to introduce free banking and then to pay a grudging amount of interest on credit balances. The going rate was one-tenth of 1 per cent. Halifax went all out to grab a larger share of this business, with a market-beating promise to pay 40 times as much interest – 4 per cent.

Traditional bankers looked on in disbelief. No wonder retail profits were down, it was estimated that paying the extra interest cost Halifax

£100 million a year.[2] Extending that to customers of Bank of Scotland, which already had a much larger share in its own market north of the border, could increase this cost by £50 million – and all to gain accounts on which it would be hard to earn any profit. The theory was that once acquired, current account customers could be sold other products – insurance, savings, loans – but that was in the future.

To make things worse from the traditionalists' point of view, Hornby was undeniably superb at marketing and selling, and even the former Bank of Scotland board members were impressed, one told me: 'Hornby was a most able and most likeable marketing person. His ability to get things on TV and to sell was amazing. When you saw him in action with his people and his charts and all his modern thinking, it was difficult to believe there was anything he could not do.'

Meanwhile the bank was trying to boost its presence in the small and medium-sized business market under a new department headed by Colin Matthew. This was a lucrative sector, with profit margins more than twice those in personal banking. Bank of Scotland led this market in Scotland, but without a branch presence in the south had found it difficult to break the stranglehold of the London banks. The plan was to pilot new business banking services in 15 Halifax branches in England and then roll them out to 100 more. Matthew announced that he would recruit 1,500 experienced staff – mostly from other banks – and HBOS would match its offer to personal customers by paying interest on cash held in business accounts.

The initiative got off to a disappointing start. Branches were geared towards personal customers and business people were not keen to discuss their company's problems in busy, noisy retail malls. Halifax branch staff were unused to dealing with commercial customers and did not under-stand their needs. They were also not equipped to handle large volumes of cash, particularly coins. The campaign received a major setback when, after a training session in an open-plan branch in the Trafford shopping centre in Manchester, a flip-chart was left in full view of customers. It listed all those businesses that Halifax did not want and that staff should discourage. They included new business start-ups, taxi drivers, window cleaners, market traders, shops and supermarkets. *The Sun*, the largest selling daily newspaper in Britain, got hold of a photograph of the chart and ran a story on its front page under the heading 'Halifax couldn't give a XXXX.'[3] It went on to quote affronted taxi drivers and window clean-ers and carried a cartoon, which Bank of Scotland staff felt 'captured all our frustrations'. The *Daily Mail* called HBOS 'The bank that likes to say "no" to small business.'

The flip-chart incident was bad enough, but there was a starker illustration of the change in culture to come. A cabbage was placed on the desk of a cashier who had not hit targets in a branch in Glasgow, while in Paisley a cauliflower was the brassica which was chosen to represent underachievement. The banking union was horrified and the incident provided another reason for the press and broadcasters to criticise selling methods in financial services. The company's apology looked lame.

32

Masters of integration

WHILE BANK OF Scotland was searching for a future, Royal Bank was consolidating its new purchase. The victory in the battle for NatWest had propelled the Royal from the second division in the UK to being the third largest bank in Britain and within the top ten in Europe. Its number of branches had nearly quadrupled to 2,400, its staff had grown from 22,000 to 94,000 and its balance sheet now boasted assets of £320 billion.[1] This was by far the most significant event in Scottish banking since its beginnings three centuries earlier. An Edinburgh bank had achieved national scale without losing its identity – and Mathewson and Goodwin made sure that was the case. Despite predictions by some commentators that they would not be able to run the bank from Edinburgh, NatWest's London headquarters was closed and its functions (and its wine cellar) moved to Scotland. Of the NatWest board directors, only Gordon Pell, who had recently been recruited from LloydsTSB, was kept on; the rest were all fired. Although the NatWest name was kept for the English branches, the holding company was Royal Bank of Scotland plc.

Just as the Bank of Scotland merger with Halifax had been the excuse for large salary rises, the NatWest triumph had led to massive increases in salaries at Royal Bank, supplemented by 'special bonuses'. Goodwin's total remuneration quadrupled to £2.3 million, Mathewson's more than doubled to £2.2 million. Even the non-executive directors got more: Lord Younger's fee climbed by a third to £379,000 and the two deputy chairmen, Sir Angus Grossart and Sir Iain Vallance saw their remuneration rise by half, to £88,000. Faced with criticism of the size of the awards, Mathewson commented dismissively that 'they wouldn't have given you bragging power in a Soho wine bar'.[2] More worryingly, Goodwin fired the accountancy firm PWC as Royal Bank's auditors over its refusal to sign off a treatment of the NatWest acquisition that would have had the effect of flattering the group's profits. The new auditors were Deloitte, successor to Touche Ross, the firm where Goodwin had worked for 16 years.[3]

At the beginning of 2001 Sir George Mathewson stepped down as chief executive and was succeeded by Fred Goodwin who, at 42, became the youngest man to lead a British bank. Mathewson occupied the ill-defined post of 'executive deputy chairman' before taking over from Lord Younger as chairman at the annual meeting in April. Younger had initially opposed the idea that Mathewson would succeed him, but accepted the argument that Mathewson would be a moderating influence on Goodwin, whose reputation for brutal cost-cutting and verbal abuse of his senior staff while he was running Clydesdale had preceded him. The new chief executive had the right skills for the task in hand, integrating the two banks and delivering the cost savings and profit enhancements that would justify the £21 billion price Royal Bank had paid. Goodwin had a sharp intellect and a determination to succeed.

He set about the job with forensic precision, demanding of each item on the agenda at the morning meetings of senior executives: 'Is it an integration issue?' If the answer was 'no' the item dropped to the bottom, no matter how important. NatWest's culture went through the same violent transformation as Royal Bank's had done a decade previously. Branch managers were given new priorities, illustrated by a triangle: at the top was 'sales', in the middle was 'control', at the bottom came 'people' and 'service'. Sales were measured daily, control and employee satisfaction and engagement weekly, and service assessed monthly.[4] A top-heavy management structure was pruned drastically, sales were prioritised over customer service, and frontline staff in all departments were given demanding targets. Within a year 18,000 employees had been made redundant.

A major achievement was integrating the two information technology systems, which took two years and seven months, but passed off without interrupting the business. Early on, the decision had been made to move the much larger NatWest system onto the Royal Bank platform, which complicated the job, but was necessary to bring NatWest's working practices in line with Royal Bank's. Greenwich Capital Markets, a bond and derivatives trading operation in Connecticut, had been scheduled for disposal in the merger plan, but after a visit by Iain Robertson, Royal Bank's head of Corporate Banking and Financial Markets, the proposal was dropped. Greenwich was a proprietary trader, meaning that it took the risk that markets would turn against it onto its own books, rather than only dealing on behalf of customers. This was new to Royal Bank, but Robertson was impressed by the quality of the local executives and the risk management systems – besides, as markets recovered from the dotcom crash of 2001, it was making good profits.[5]

When it published its annual review for 2001, the first complete year since the takeover, Royal Bank was able to report that the integration was going so well that expected savings would be £2 billion a year, against £1.7 billion promised to investors at the time of the bid.[6] The following year Goodwin was able to announce the successful completion of the integration and to give a detailed timeline of how it had been achieved.[7] After so many failed banking mergers around the world, Royal Bank's absorption of NatWest was literally a textbook example of how it should be done: Harvard Business School published a case study written by the Dean, under the title: *Royal Bank of Scotland: Masters of Integration*.[8] Around the same time *Forbes*, the influential US business magazine, named Goodwin as its Businessman of the Year. Under the headline 'Brisk and brusque', the accompanying profile was largely laudatory, although it did refer to his 'Fred the Shred' nickname and 'the acid just below the surface' of his 'cool and witty' exterior.[9]

To many of Goodwin's senior colleagues, however, the acid was not below the surface, but too often splashed on them. He appeared to take a perverse delight in denigrating and humiliating his key executives, subjecting them to sudden tirades. Managers began to fear the daily gathering to discuss current business, wondering whose turn it was to be the object of the chief executive's withering scorn. The 'Morning Meetings' became known as the 'Morning Beatings' and had the effect of inhibiting open discussion of problems. Senior executives would not admit to mistakes or pass on bad news for fear that they would be subject to a blistering public assault.

For a man who prided himself on his strategic vision, Goodwin also appeared to want to micro-manage all parts of the group, down to choosing the colours of carpets and curtains, designing the annual report – even to selecting the corporate Christmas card.[10] Some of his decisions appeared capricious and could be reversed without warning. He also developed a liking for the trappings of corporate power – a fleet of chauffeur-driven Mercedes S600 cars, specially painted in the bank's shade of blue, and an executive jet, a Dassault Falcon, with a private bedroom for overnight travel.[11] The aircraft, which cost £17.5 million to buy and over £7,000 an hour to operate, was an extravagance which contrasted so strongly with the cost-conscious image the bank tried to project that the Royal Bank public relations department tried to deny its existence.[12] When in London Goodwin stayed in his permanent suite at the Savoy Hotel, while his family home in Edinburgh had round-the-clock security, paid for by the bank.[13] Huge amounts were lavished on sponsorship of Goodwin's favourite sports – golf and motor racing. The veteran American golfer Jack Nicklaus and the former Scottish driving world champion Jackie Stewart were made 'brand ambassadors' and paid £1 million a year each. The bank sponsored the Williams Formula One motor racing team and Goodwin attended Grand Prix, standing at the trackside. In total the bank spent £200 million a year on sports sponsorships.[14]

After the NatWest takeover, Gartmore, its fund management subsidiary, was sold for £1 billion, but it was not long before the group began to make acquisitions. Citizens, Royal Bank's modest American subsidiary, had been quietly buying small regional banks in its New England home territory, but in 2001 Goodwin allowed Larry Fish, Citizens' chief executive, to pay $2.1 billion for the branch banking business of Mellon. This broadened the group's geographic area, taking it into Philadelphia, and doubled the number of branches. The following year Fish acquired Medford Bancorp in its home city of Boston for $273 million and in 2003 bought Commonwealth Bancorp for $450 million and Port Financial Corporation for $285 million. Other smaller deals followed, consolidating the bank's position in its two separate markets, New England and Pennsylvania, but Citizens began to get the reputation of paying over the odds to win competitive bids.

Closer to home, Royal Bank paid £1.1 billion for the insurance company Churchill and £620 million for the Irish mortgage lender First Active, which was integrated with Ulster Bank, acquired as part of NatWest. The economy of the Irish Republic was growing strongly, driven by a commercial and residential property boom fuelled with debt. Goodwin wanted to dominate this market and pushed the local management to lend aggressively. Not all purchases worked for the bank. In 2002, at Goodwin's insistence, the bank bought Dixon Motors, a family-owned car dealership for £118 million. Senior executives were at a loss to understand the logic behind the deal and it quickly went wrong. Huge amounts of management time were wasted trying to pull it round before it was sold back to its management in 2005 at a substantial loss.[15]

Goodwin craved a larger presence in the US and pushed Fish to do bigger deals. This was not easy in the heated American banking market unless you were prepared to pay a premium price. After several false starts in 2004 Royal Bank bought Chicago-based Charter One for $10.5 billion (£5.9 billion at the prevailing exchange rate), its biggest acquisition since NatWest, financing the transaction with a rights issue to shareholders to raise £2.5 billion. The move took the bank into six new states and on paper looked like a promising prospect, but it soon became clear that Royal Bank had overpaid and, in its eagerness to do the deal, had overlooked multiple problems. The purchase never fulfilled its expectation (in fact Royal Bank took a £4.4 billion write-off in its 2008 accounts) and helped to sour relations between major investors and Goodwin. The feeling grew that he was pursuing size for its own sake and, despite strongly growing profits, was neglecting the retail bank. It did not, however, prevent his knighthood for his 'services to banking' in the same year. In the summer of 2005 Royal Bank, which was now calling itself RBS, announced the purchase of a 5 per cent stake in Bank of China, the state-owned international bank, which the Chinese leadership was anxious to modernise. Goodwin had wanted to take 10 per cent, but the board had persuaded him that with growing shareholder unease about the bank's appetite for acquisitions, it would not look good.

Royal Bank's share price was stagnating and lagging behind those of its major competitors. Several board members were concerned and Peter Sutherland, a former EU Commissioner, had asked a City public relations firm to investigate how the bank and Goodwin were perceived by major investors. The report was damning. It portrayed him as out of touch, arrogant and refusing to listen. Goodwin listened in silence as passages were read out by Sutherland at a private meeting. Shocked, the board instructed Goodwin not to chase more acquisitions, but to concentrate on organic growth. For a while it looked as though he had taken the criticism to heart. He made public statements that he was not contemplating new deals, but not everyone was convinced. Some analysts talked about a 'management discount' – the share price was marked down because of doubts about Goodwin's intentions. On a conference call for analysts, James Eden of the investment bank Dresdner Kleinwort Wasserstein was direct: 'I think there is a perception among some investors that Fred Goodwin is a megalomaniac who pursues size over shareholders value.'[16]

At the same time Goodwin was being criticised for the lavish new headquarters he had built for the Royal Bank group at Gogarburn, close to Edinburgh airport. A campus-style suite of buildings costing £350 million, it moved the leadership of the bank out of its traditional base in St Andrew Square. Mathewson had favoured a redevelopment of St James Centre, a tired, ugly concrete shopping centre behind Royal Bank's headquarters, which included the abandoned Scottish civil service head-quarters. Built in the 1960s after the demolition of the Georgian St James Square, the building had been insulated with asbestos. After difficult negotiations with the owners and tenants of the shopping centre, Goodwin abandoned the plan in favour of an out-of-town development, which he personally oversaw, again taking an obsessive interest in seem-ingly trivial details.

The resulting head office had a lot to commend it – bringing together 3,500 staff who had previously been scattered around the city and giving them clean, efficient modern working conditions. But the size of Goodwin's office, with its adjacent 'scallop kitchen', the bridge over the nearby dual carriageway, dominated by the RBS logo and the elaborate opening ceremony, with the Queen, Prince Philip and a fly-past of RAF Tornado jets, drew accusations of hubris. Shown pictures of the building and the corporate jet, Lord Younger, dying of cancer, quipped to his daughter: 'Time to sell the shares.'[17] Others were equally sceptical: 'Fred spent £350 million on his HQ, but didn't put a penny into the branches,' one director said. 'That was a warning sign.'[18]

Goodwin was demoralised by the criticism he was receiving and the RBS share price, which traded at a discount to other banks despite apparently strong profits. During the Christmas and New Year holidays he contemplated his own future – was it time to do something else? But after a month's break he returned with renewed enthusiasm: if investors wanted organic growth, that is what he would give them. The retail bank's performance was sluggish, but the investment bank, now known as Global Banking and Markets (GBM) and, after the retirement of Iain Robertson, run by Johnny Cameron, was a money-making machine. It would be made to run faster.

After the Gogarburn opening Mathewson retired as chair, handing over to Sir Tom McKillop, who had previously been chief executive of the pharmaceuticals firm Astra Zeneca. McKillop had an exemplary business record. Born in Ayrshire in 1943, after school at Irvine Academy he had taken a first degree and PhD in chemistry at Glasgow University and then joined the chemicals conglomerate ICI as a researcher. By 1994, when the decision was taken to spin-off the pharmaceuticals division as Zeneca, he became chief executive of the new firm, subsequently steering it into a merger with Astra to form one of the world's leading pharma groups. He had the reputation of being a tough operator and, despite his experience of banking as a non-executive director of LloydsTSB, took some persuading to take the RBS chair, but after doing his own due diligence he accepted in 2006. McKillop had his own concerns about Goodwin, but decided not to remove him, partly because of the pledge to concentrate on organic growth.

When he presented his first set of results in the spring of 2007, the new chairman was able to point to a 16 per cent rise in pre-tax profit to £9.2 billion and, to placate disaffected investors, a 25 per cent increase in the dividend and a £1 billion share buy-back. A look at the divisional breakdown of the figures showed GBM increasing its contribution by nearly £1 billion, while all other divisions barely nudged ahead.[19] McKillop's faith in Goodwin's pledge of acquisition abstinence temporarily wavered when in January 2007 he read newspaper reports that RBS has been talking to Rijkman Groenink, chief executive of the Dutch bank ABN Amro, but was restored by Goodwin's assurance that, although of course he kept in touch with Groenink as he did with many other bank chiefs, a full-scale bid was not in his mind.[20]

In fact Goodwin had done more than 'keep in touch'. He saw ABN Amro in much the same way that Royal Bank had viewed NatWest a decade earlier: a vast underperforming, poorly managed collection of businesses, where costs could be slashed and a hard-sell culture imposed. He could turn it around: after all, wasn't he the 'Master of Integration'? He was particularly interested in LaSalle, ABN's US bank, based in Chicago. Combining that with Charter One could make sense of Goodwin's biggest and least successful acquisition so far. The problem was ABN's size; it would be a huge mouthful for Royal Bank to swallow.

A solution was suggested by the US investment bank Merrill Lynch, which had advised Royal Bank on the NatWest takeover and several acquisitions since. Alive to the possibilities of a big fee, the Merrill team came up with a plan: Royal Bank could buy ABN together with two partners, which they had already lined up: Santander, the Spanish bank which had previously been a shareholder in Royal Bank, and Fortis, a Dutch–Belgian retail bank. Unlike the Royal Bank–Bank of Scotland combined bid for NatWest, which had fallen apart because both partners wanted the same bits, this time there was a clear separation of interests. Santander would take ABN's Italian and Brazilian subsidiary banks, Fortis the branch network in Belgium and the Netherlands, leaving RBS with LaSalle, ABN's widely admired global money transmission business and investment banking, which seemed a good fit with GBM and was headquartered in London, just across the street from Royal Bank's offices in Bishopsgate. In RBS, only Goodwin knew of this plan.

The consortium made an unofficial approach to ABN Amro, but Groenink gave them short shrift. Then, in March 2007 ABN announced it was in merger talks with Barclays. This was an event like NatWest's announcement of its intention to buy Legal & General 12 years before – a now-or-never moment. If RBS had any hope of acquiring all or parts of ABN, it had to act fast. At a subsequent board meeting, Royal Bank's director of strategy, Iain Allan, gave a presentation which balanced the advantages of acquiring the Dutch bank with the risks, but the general feeling was that other considerations were secondary; the cost – €60 billion or more – would put it out of reach. Then Goodwin produced his rabbit from a hat: RBS could acquire ABN with its partners. The contagion of 'deal fever' spread from the chief executive to the board. Allan, who remained sceptical, was sidelined. 'From that day on, literally from that day on, every board meeting was dominated by "can we do this?" Insufficient attention was paid to "should we do it".'[21] Challenge from the directors was muted. Peter Sutherland and Sir Steve Robson, a former Treasury official, raised objections, but did not feel strongly enough to resign.

Goodwin's motivation to snatch ABN Amro from Barclays appeared to be similar to Mathewson's decision to bid for NatWest against Bank of Scotland: maintaining independence. Then the reasoning had been that the loser would make itself vulnerable to takeover by a big London bank, while the winner would make itself impregnable. Now the reasoning was that the loser would make itself vulnerable to takeover by a big American bank, while the winner would make itself one of the largest banks in the world. Despite his protestations to the board that this was not a 'must do' deal, in his heart Goodwin saw it as 'do or die'. His board did not stop him and, although some of his senior executives, such as Allan and Johnny Cameron at GBM, had reservations, criticism within the group was muted. Goodwin's scathing condemnation of any views which did not concur with his own – 'Fred's hairdryer', as it was known in the bank – had extinguished any challenge.

The consortium was legally constituted at a meeting in Geneva, with Santander and Fortis insisting that RBS should lead the deal and that Goodwin should front it. Groenink was formally notified of the intention to bid against Barclays the following day. He was dismissive and a short time later announced the sale of LaSalle to Bank of America for $21 billion. One of Royal Bank's principal reasons for making the bid was now gone. Some senior executives now expected the bid to be abandoned, but it was not. RBS was committed and although Goodwin contemplated withdrawing, he decided he had no option but to proceed, convincing himself that the deal made sense even without the Chicago bank as a prize. But what was the consortium buying? Since the bid was hostile, with no endorsement from the ABN board, Royal Bank and its partners had only limited access to ABN's books and Goodwin relied on the assumption that since Barclays was making an agreed bid, it had already done due diligence and decided that the bank was clean. Even when warned by John Cryan of Union Bank of Switzerland, who had been an adviser to RBS, but was now working with ABN, that ABN's investment banking division was heavily exposed to US sub-prime debt and that 'there is stuff in here we can't even value', Goodwin pressed ahead, replying 'Stop being such a bean counter.'[22]

The consortium published its proposal in July 2007, offering €71 billion, largely in cash. The price was well above Barclays bid, which was two-thirds in shares. Even when Barclays increased its offer, its own falling share price meant that it could not match the consortium. Meanwhile the credit market was in turmoil (see next chapter). Goodwin and McKillop did briefly consider pulling out or reducing the value of the bid, but decided that legal and reputational damage would be too great. At a board meeting Johnny Cameron presented revised projections about the potential of combining the two investment banking operations and the board endorsed continuing with the bid. Cameron's previous reservations had been forgotten: there was a new rationale for continuing. At a London dinner for 40 senior RBS investment bankers, Goodwin told them: 'You guys in GBM have convinced me this is something we should do. This is a potentially transformational acquisition for us and that is why I have bid for it.'[23]

RBS had to put its offer to its own shareholders for approval and at a meeting in Edinburgh in August McKillop revealed that 94.5 per cent of shareholders had voted in favour. If investors had doubts, they were prepared to subdue them to back Goodwin's judgement. In September the Dutch regulator approved the consortium bid, provided RBS took the whole of ABN Amro onto its balance sheet while the group was being dismantled and parcelled out to the other members of the consortium. It also insisted that the group obtain regulatory clearance at each stage, adding time and cost to the integration process. In the UK the Financial Services Authority raised no objection. This was a major failure of regulation. Allowing a systemically important UK bank to take on large unquantified risks at a time of market uncertainty should have merited a thorough investigation, but as the subsequent FSA inquest report pointed out, clearance was not required and the prevailing philosophy was of 'light touch' regulation.[24]

In October Barclays conceded. Fred Goodwin had just pulled off the biggest deal of his life.

33

2007: 'We don't do sub-prime'

WHILE GOODWIN WAS fixed on RBS becoming the largest bank in the world – a feat he achieved briefly when ABN's balance sheet was added to that of RBS, making a total of £1.9 trillion, a sum bigger than the UK's Gross Domestic Product – something profound and unsettling was happening to financial and property markets.

It started in the US, where a long period of low interest rates following the dotcom crash and the terrorist attacks of 2001 had stimulated the American economy, but had left banks with a problem – where to lend profitably. Their answer was 'sub-prime mortgages'. Sub-prime borrowers were those who, by definition, were below 'prime' – they did not meet the normal criteria for being given a loan. This could be because their incomes were too low, or they had poor credit histories, or they could not or would not provide proof of their earnings. Sometimes they had no regular income at all. They were considered bad risks, but banks found a way around this drawback. Using the magic of portfolio theory, a lot of clever financial engineering and some advanced mathematics, risky loans could be sliced up, and the slices packaged together, mixed with slices of lower-risk mort-gages. The package could then be sold to investors as sound investments paying an above average yield – people with poor credit scores were willing to pay higher rates of interest for the chance of owning their own homes.

The sales pitch was that risk could be diversified away. If a package of loans was spread across the vast United States, containing different classes of borrower with mixed credit ratings, it did not matter if a few of them defaulted on their mortgage payments. It was impossible (wasn't it?) that they would all default at the same time. And even if they did, house prices were not going down, so there would always be security to fall back on.

So enticing and successful was this new business that a whole industry grew up to service it. Small banks and loan companies 'originated' the

loans – selling mortgages to people who never before would have qualified for one, often by offering an initial period of perhaps three to five
years at low interest, after which the rate would rise sharply. Sometimes
there was also an initial period when the capital did not have to be repaid,
just the interest. The loans were then aggregated and packaged by
specialist financial companies and given euphemistic names that
disguised the quality of the underlying asset – MBS (mortgage backed
securities), ABS (asset backed securities), CDOs (collateralised debt
obligations). They were rated by the credit rating agencies (for a fee) and
traded by big investment banks, which looked to make a margin on the
trades. To demonstrate how safe they were, big insurance companies like
the US giant AIG, would offer to insure the new securities against default
(again, for a fee). At its height, trillions of dollars were changing hands in
this market, with UK and European banks participating alongside the
Americans.

The first warning signs began to emerge towards the end of 2006. As
the low interest periods came to an end and their monthly payments
increased substantially, some borrowers began to default. At first it was
a trickle, then a stream. Only those who were watching the property
markets closely noticed. CDOs, MBS and ABS had become so much
part of mainstream financial markets that few people realised that their
value rested on the earning power of the poorest and most vulnerable
members of US society, whose incomes were not rising in line with the
profits of big financial companies.

If Goodwin was aware of all this, he did not show it. When asked, he
repeatedly stated: 'We don't do sub-prime.' Up to a point this was true.
Citizens, RBS group's US high street bank, prided itself on being a traditional lender and so its mortgages were only granted to qualified borrowers. What he had not said, or perhaps did not know, was that GBM
bought and sold CDOs and other property-related securities in huge
quantities – in fact they were the heart of the money-making machine on
which RBS was increasingly reliant for its profits growth.

Not only that, but Greenwich Capital Markets, the Connecticut
subsidiary RBS had acquired with NatWest (renamed RBS Greenwich
after the acquisition), was a leading aggregator, packager and trader of
CDOs. When Fred Goodwin commanded the money machine to run
faster, RBS Greenwich had ramped up its activities – hiring a top CDO
trader and his team from Citigroup. The addition of ABN Amro increased
the group's exposure to this market. When Goodwin had been told that

the Dutch bank's balance sheet contained assets which 'could not be valued' it was a warning that no one knew how many of the mortgage holders who provided the income on which the value of these securities depended would default. 'Could not be valued' was another euphemism for worth less than their book value, or possibly for 'worthless'. The warning was ignored.

The RBS board was not completely unaware of the sub-prime problem. In February 2007 it was briefed on the market and its implications for GBM, but the minutes recorded that the tone was 'positive'. There was no mention of the $2.6 billion of exposure to 'super senior' securities in RBS Greenwich. 'Super senior' were rated 'better than AAA' by the ratings agencies and so were not thought to be at risk. The following month the board was informed that 'A full review of the RBS Greenwich sub-prime lending book had been carried out and no material concerns had been identified.' But if there was nothing to be worried about, why was GBM not achieving its monthly profit targets? Johnny Cameron asked his deputy Brian Crowe: 'How much leakage of sub-prime is there into the CDO business?' Crowe's answer came as a shock to Cameron: 'CDO is all sub-prime.' Cameron later admitted to the Financial Services Authority: 'I don't think, even at that point, I fully . . . I had enough information. Brian may have thought I understood more than I did . . . And it's around this time that I became clearer on what CDOs were, but it's probably later.'[1]

Cameron, with his imperfect understanding, then attempted to explain CDOs to Goodwin, drawing him a diagram on a sheet of A4 paper. But the chief executive, deep in planning for the ABN Amro bid, did not appear to be interested.[2] Throughout the rest of 2007 the RBS board was given regular briefings on the CDO position and the group took some write-offs as values of securities in its balance sheet were marked down, but the hits, although in the hundreds of millions of US dollars, were not material when seen against the gigantic size of Royal Bank's balance sheet.

By the middle of 2007, the stream of sub-prime mortgage defaults in the US had become a river and lenders in the international money market began to get worried about some of the institutions which were borrowing: how much sub-prime did they hold? In August 2007 the French bank BNP Paribas had to suspend three of its sub-prime funds and the following month the international money market froze as lenders decided that it was better not to lend at all, than to risk not getting their money back. Hit hardest were those banks most dependent on the market rather than on retail and corporate deposits. In the UK it was the former building society Northern Rock, which had been aggressively selling UK mortgages but had no US activities, which was hit first. It had fuelled its rapid expansion with borrowed money, and was dependent on borrowing from other banks in the wholesale market for 75 per cent of its funding. When the markets froze in August 2007 it found itself with only enough cash to make it through to the end of the month and very little chance of getting any more. It had to appeal to the government for emergency funding.

A blog post by Robert Peston, then the BBC's economics correspondent, revealing that the management had approached the Bank of England for emergency financial support triggered the first bank run in Britain since the nineteenth century.[3] Television pictures of queues of depositors outside Northern Rock branches spooked bankers around the world. Alistair Darling, chancellor of the exchequer, was on holiday in Majorca and Mervyn King, governor of the Bank of England, was watching cricket at Lords when they heard the news coverage. They returned in a hurry and Darling was forced to guarantee deposits in Northern Rock to restore confidence. Slowly the money markets returned to regular trading.

By the autumn the river of US mortgage defaulters looked like becoming a flood. RBS Greenwich was in a state of panic about how to value the huge stock of CDOs and other property-backed securities in its balance sheet. They were trading in the market at a fraction of their book value and prices were continuing to fall. In October the ratings agencies began downgrading AAA rated securities. By the end of 2007 GBM was £1.5 billion behind budget, two-thirds of which was down to RBS Greenwich, which was sitting on losses of £1 billion on its 'better than AAA' 'super senior' securities.[4]

When RBS took control of ABN it began the integration process, which by now followed a familiar and hitherto effective pattern. RBS managers moved in and attempted to 'inoculate' ABN with the virus of RBS culture. But this time it was different. The Dutch were much more resistant than NatWest employees had been. Cursory due diligence had meant that when the Scots took control of NatWest they uncovered surprises. The same was true of ABN, but in NatWest the surprises had been mostly good – the bank was in better shape than they had assumed. In ABN they were mostly bad – things were much worse than they feared. Goodwin had been lulled into believing that ABN was a sound bank by its last trading statement before the takeover, which specifically stated: 'ABN Amro has a very limited exposure to the sub-prime segment.' This impression had been reinforced by Merrill Lynch in a report to RBS. But ABN had an interest in maintaining the consortium bid price.[5] In fact ABN had substantial holdings of CDOs and other mortgage-related securities in its balance sheet and had been as reluctant as RBS to mark down their value as the market deteriorated. (The full cost of this would not become apparent until 2009, when RBS wrote off £16.6 billion on its acquisition of ABN.[6])

Goodwin, always an optimist, was resistant to a further write-down in the values of CDOs, believing that the collapse of the market was only temporary and that values would come back. At the end of 2007, Deloitte, RBS's auditors, recommended additional provisions of £686–£941 million – two-thirds of which related to ABN. In fact the group made only an £188 million provision.[7]

★ ★ ★

While RBS was grappling with CDOs and ABN, HBOS was facing problems of its own. At the beginning of 2006 James Crosby had resigned. His leaving, which had been discussed only with the chairman, Lord Stevenson, took everyone else inside and outside the bank by surprise. He was not yet 50, had no other job to go to and was leaving on an apparent high: the HBOS share price had hit a peak. The *Financial Times* commented: 'Barring a complete change in HBOS's fortunes in the coming year, [Crosby] is likely to be remembered as the chief executive who walked away from his job long before anyone asked him to leave.'[8] There were two possible internal candidates to replace him. George Mitchell, at 55, had nearly 40 years of solid banking experience behind him and had worked in almost every department of Bank of Scotland. Personable, but usually undemonstrative in public, he was viewed by those who thought he should be the heir apparent as the safe bet, a practical banker who could consolidate the gains the group had made.

Andy Hornby was almost the exact opposite. Still only 38, he had achieved academic brilliance at Oxford and Harvard, whereas Mitchell had joined the bank straight from school. Hornby's only banking experience had been in the six years he had been at Halifax/HBOS and then only in the personal banking market. Mitchell's post-school education

– studying for the certificate of the Institute of Bankers in Scotland – had been narrowly focused on one industry: banking. Hornby's postgraduate education at the world's foremost business school (where he had passed first out of 800 students) had taught him that management was a generic skill that could be applied in any industry. At HBOS he had used techniques he picked up in retailing, such as weekly sales and service updates.

He was described in glowing terms by the managers he had worked for in the supermarket group Asda. Alan Leighton, Hornby's former boss, said: 'He has brought a lot of Asda stuff into HBOS. He is focused and I know spends a lot of time in the branches talking to people about what is going on and is very good at strategy. As well as being super-bright, he is also likeable.' City analysts were even more complimentary. One said: 'His overall record in the retail business has been exemplary.' Another described him as a 'superstar'. With verdicts like these, it was a surprise to find that Hornby had spent only three years at Asda, his previous jobs being at the Boston Consulting Group and Blue Circle Cement.

Hornby – young, dynamic, energetic, successful and likeable – was the board's favourite, but some of the former Bank of Scotland directors worried about his lack of all-round banking experience and knowledge. They suggested to Lord Stevenson and James Crosby that Hornby should be made chief executive of BankWest, the group's Australian subsidiary. In a few years in a smaller institution and a more benign competitive environment he would encounter a broad range of typical banking problems and be able to return with more experience and enough time still to become one of the youngest chief executives in the UK. The suggestion was rejected without discussion. Hornby was named as the new chief executive. He had no training in banking and had never experienced the sort of crisis he was about to face. Mitchell resigned shortly afterwards. His experience and willingness to raise his voice (and lose his temper) when he thought the bank was being pushed in the wrong direction would be sorely missed.[9]

Although the sub-prime scandal was a US phenomenon, loans of 125 per cent of the value of the house they were secured on, buy-to-let, self-certified mortgages and high multiples of salary had left many UK homeowners dangerously exposed to a rise in interest rates. Investors began to regard all mortgage banks with suspicion, but attention, inevitably, settled on Northern Rock as the most vulnerable. Inside HBOS the television images of queues outside Northern Rock branches sent a chill through the bank. 'It was a huge blow to us and a real confidence shaker,' remembers one senior manager. Like the Rock, HBOS had been living with the consequences of the freezing of the market for weeks. Securitisations – selling packages of mortgages to investors – had stopped and other funding, where it could be obtained, was much more expensive. Lending had to be curtailed. It was outside the experience of even the most seasoned bankers. 'Up until then we had always thought that you would always be able to fund a lending book, no one had ever seen a situation where you couldn't. We couldn't just withdraw from the mortgage market because we had deals in progress and in corporate lending some companies had facilities on which they were able to drawn down money. Also we were trying to secure our good, reliable clients,' said one senior executive.

HBOS reduced the cash flowing out of the business by closing down as much of its new business activity as it could. 'We effectively pulled out of the SME* market. Royal Bank of Scotland was circulating internal emails to say that we had stopped lending and this was a good opportunity for them to step in.' Regular reports were going to Andy Hornby and finance director Mike Ellis, who in turn briefed the board. Everyone knew the situation was serious, but until Northern Rock no one believed it might be terminal. 'The feeling inside was that this was something we had to work through, sooner or later things would get back to normal – but they dragged on and on.'[10]

HBOS was heavily exposed to the property market. At the end of 2007 it had £430 billion outstanding in loans to customers, more than half of it (£235 billion) in residential mortgages. Another £35 billion was lent to construction firms or commercial property companies and a further £8 billion to the hotel and retail trades. Home loans in Ireland and Australia added another £27 billion and lending to construction, property, hotels and retail in those countries and elsewhere another £24 billion. Add them all together and three-quarters of all lending was secured on land, bricks and mortar. The board was not unduly alarmed. Nearly half the mortgage book had a loan-to-value ratio of 28 per cent – house prices would have to fall by more than three-quarters before the size of the loan was higher than the value of the property. Of the remainder, only 3.5 per cent was over 90 per cent. The asset cover was there, but what about the lenders? Would they still be able to meet their

---

* Small and medium-sized enterprises.

repayments if there was a downturn? Here there was a worry. A quarter of all mortgages were classed as 'specialist', either buy-to-let or self-certified mortgages – over £60 billion.[11]

The UK housing market, which had shown rises of 4–5 per cent a quarter at the height of the boom in 2004, had slowed considerably by 2007, but up to the end of the summer prices had still been rising. The first fall in the October–December quarter was a little over 1 per cent, followed by a similar decline in the first quarter of 2008. A few doomsayers were claiming that prices could fall by 10–20 per cent, following similar plunges in the US, but there were plenty of people taking a more optimistic view. They included Martin Ellis, chief economist at HBOS, who told *Money Marketing* magazine 'A robust UK economy and the accompanying sound health of the labour market continue to provide strong underpinnings for the housing market . . . there is a fundamental supply and demand imbalance in the UK that simply does not exist in the US.'[12]

Unlike its Edinburgh neighbour, HBOS did not have an investment bank – or at least it did not appear to have one – and did not trade CDOs, but it was not entirely clear of the sub-prime collapse. At the end of August 2007 the bank issued a short statement to the Stock Exchange, which came as a shock to many of its shareholders: they discovered that it was an investor in US home loans on a massive scale. The statement revealed that HBOS had been forced to provide credit for Grampian Funding, a Jersey-registered fund wholly-owned by HBOS, which held $36 billion (£18 billion) of assets, $30 billion of which were invested in the US. It was a 'conduit', in the jargon of the finance market. Grampian was not a recent invention; it had been formed in 2002, but no word of it had ever appeared in the annual reports or statements to shareholders. To find any reference to it you had to obtain a copy of the report of HBOS Treasury Service plc, a subsidiary of the bank. It was, however, no secret in the international securitisation market, where it had a conservative reputation, despite some lurid press reports.

Grampian's main business was arbitrage – exploiting the difference between the low interest rates it paid by borrowing short-term and the higher rates it could obtain by lending long-term, thus turning on its head the old banker's rule 'borrow long and lend short'. It was prepared to do this because the world had changed since Bank of Scotland experienced its first cash crises 300 years before and in the twenty-first century the global inter-bank market had made the rule obsolete – or so everyone believed. The range of lenders was so wide, encompassing practically the whole developed world, and the pool of liquidity so deep – trillions of dollars – that there would always be someone, somewhere willing to lend. The worse that could happen to you was that the price would go up.

Grampian raised credit by issuing Asset Backed Commercial Paper (ABCP), essentially borrowing over a short term, anything from 90 to 270 days. Investors were willing to take Grampian's paper because, although it was a separate legal entity, it was consolidated into the HBOS balance sheet. Most of the time it would act as if it were an autonomous company, but if there ever came a crisis the bank would stand behind it. With the money it raised, the conduit bought other securities, mostly packages of American mortgages which paid a good rate of interest. To protect itself Grampian only invested in AAA-rated paper and that ruled out sub-prime (although it later revealed that it did have a very small amount, less than 1 per cent of its assets).

A year after its launch Grampian had become the largest conduit in Europe and the third largest in the world. Later it overtook the others to become the biggest player in this market. For five years it performed very well and the HBOS treasury team used its skill at buying and selling debt securities to generate hundreds of millions of pounds in profit for the bank. But when the scale of the sub-prime scandal became known, the inter-bank market started to seize up. Despite its AAA portfolio, Grampian found the interest rates it was having to pay to borrow shooting up. To meet Grampian's obligations HBOS had to lend it money. This was an embarrassing and costly exercise, but HBOS saw it as a temporary problem which would right itself once the market thawed. The bank issued reassuring statements saying that it fully expected to get back the money it had advanced to Grampian and that it would have 'no material impact' on the results. By October 2007, two months after the Northern Rock bank run, the worst seemed to be over and HBOS was able to issue a press release saying that the conduit was again self-funding.

But it was not quite that easy. Grampian did not hold many sub-prime securities, but it had the next worst thing – Alt-A mortgages. These were loans issued to Americans who on paper at least had the wherewithall to repay, but included categories of borrower increasingly seen in the UK during the house-price boom years. There were borrowers of self-certi-fied mortgages (who did not have to provide evidence of their income, called 'liar loans' in the US), those with poor credit histories, buy-to-let landlords and those borrowing on high loan-to-value ratios. HBOS tried to play down its exposure to these mortgages, but when its accounts for 2007 were published they showed that it had £7 billion at risk, plus billions more in other debt securities. But, like RBS, when the market began to drop HBOS was resistant to making a write-down. At the end of 2007 it marked the value down by only £180 million.[13]

The Alt-As were, however, the least of the issues causing stress to its inexperienced chief executive. Throughout the autumn of 2007 HBOS, along with most other banks, was finding it increasingly difficult and expensive to fund its own lending and pay off the money it had borrowed when loans fell due. 'Spreads', the extra interest payments lenders demanded to compensate for increased risk, increased five-fold between June and September. From 2001 the HBOS treasury department had been raising £10 billion a year by selling securitisation issues. The money went back into the bank to fund yet more mortgages. Alongside this it had been an active issuer of covered bonds, another form of borrowing, but considered safer and more conservative than securitisations. HBOS used the bonds to lengthen the maturity of its borrowing and on occasion had issued 20-year covered bonds. Now both the securitisation and the covered bond markets were seizing up. In September, HBOS managed to issue a new bond, but at a greatly increased price. In November, the covered bond market was briefly suspended because prices were rising so fast, making it even harder for banks to fund themselves. This was not a problem peculiar to HBOS. All mortgage lenders were suffering and some much more acutely.

34

2008: Market meltdown

A FATEFUL YEAR for both banks started reasonably optimistically. In February RBS announced another set of record results. Operating profit for the group was up 9 per cent to £10.3 billion, mainly because of a near halving of central costs and a big contribution from retail banking and corporate lending, which more than offset the fall in profit from GBM. The group made comforting noises about liquidity – its ability to fund itself – and said that its Tier 1 capital – a measure of its ability to absorb any potential losses – was 7.3 per cent, comfortably higher than the regulatory minimum of 4 per cent. Delve deep into the numbers and, although 'impairment' charges, the provision against bad or doubtful debts, had risen slightly in money terms, as a percentage of the total lent by the group the figure had actually fallen. The impression was that the acquisition of ABN had made the group not only bigger, but safer. Against this financial background the group felt comfortable enough to recommend a 10 per cent increase in the dividend to shareholders.[1]

Of course, such good figures meant substantial rises in executive pay for Fred Goodwin, whose total remuneration rose by £200,000 to £4.19 million. Johnny Cameron saw his total dip to £3.2 million, reflecting GBM's lower contribution. Tom McKillop received £750,000 for his part-time role, well up from the £471,000 in the previous year when he had only served for nine months.

The confident tone of the report was not shared by either Fred Goodwin, when he presented the results to analysts from other banks, or in the tone of their questions to the executive. The analysts were concerned that RBS seemed to be marking down its CDOs a lot less than other banks had done. In fact, Deloittes had again recommended that another £200 million be taken off of the value of the 'super seniors', but again, the Group Audit Committee and the board decided not to do so.[2] The effect of this refusal was to raise questions in the mind of lenders about how much they could rely on RBS's own assessment of its worth and its potential liabilities. Three months later the group would be forced into making a £1.9 billion provision, far more than it had done previously, but still not enough to recognise the real damage to its balance sheet that had been done by the collapse of the sub-prime market. At the results presentation doubts were also raised about the group's capital position. Analysts did not believe it was as strong as RBS claimed and vague answers from the financial director and the chairman did nothing to reassure investors.[3]

In reality the ABN deal had severely weakened RBS, which was already under strain from the problems in GBM and RBS Greenwich. Goodwin had chosen to fund RBS's share of the purchase price of the Dutch bank by short-term borrowing, rather than raising new money from shareholders, arguing that the combined group's strong cashflow would enable the debt to be paid off quickly. Similarly, he had run the group's capital down to 4 per cent and below, reasoning again that strong profit growth would enable him to rebuild capital. Goodwin had an aversion to retaining more capital than the bank needed and often talked of 'capital efficiency'. The regulator specified the types of security that could be counted as capital and these were safer and thus earned less. He preferred to keep this type of holding to a minimum so that more of the group's resources could be channelled into higher earning assets.

Following the completion of the ABN purchase, RBS's dependence on short-term funding from the wholesale money market shot up, increasing by 15 per cent in three months. It was the second largest of any of the UK banks. In addition to its normal borrowings, it had to fund its part of the price of the acquisition. Because Goodwin was confident that RBS could earn its way out of the additional debt, more than half of the new borrowing had to be repaid in a year or less and a substantial part of it was due after periods as short as five weeks. Some was even borrowed overnight.[4] RBS's total payment for ABN AMRO comprised €4.3 billion in RBS shares and €22.6 billion cash, most of which was borrowed, with €12.3 billion having a term of one year or less. Goodwin had counted on the cash paid by Bank of America for LaSalle being received in three months, but in the event this money was held up in the Netherlands, increasing the need to borrow.[5]

One of the bad surprises to come out of Amsterdam was the liquidity position of ABN's 'conduits', which traded ABCPs. RBS had to stand behind the conduits in the same way HBOS was forced to support

Grampian, at a cost of £8.6 billion.⁶ All this put a strain on the treasury team, which had to fund the stretched group balance sheet at a time when the market was freezing up and lenders were uncertain that they could rely on RBS's protestations of strength.

HBOS also announced its financial figures for 2007 and, although profits were down, the decline was a modest 4 per cent and the bank was still making over £5 billion in profit. The accompanying statement struck a confident tone, despite the financial market problems. The housing market was expected to be 'flat' in 2008, but the bank said it was 'well positioned to deliver good growth in shareholder value over the next few years'. Bad debt provisions had been increased in the corporate banking division, but had actually fallen in residential mortgages, unsecured loans and credit card debts. The credit crunch was causing it some problems, but steps it had taken in recent years to lengthen and diversify its whole-sale funding had paid off in the more turbulent credit markets of the second half of the previous year, the bank claimed.⁷

As a precautionary measure, HBOS had written down its investment in the US Alt-A mortgages by £227 million. This was more than the £180 million it had expected to have to provide when it had briefed investors at the end of 2007, but the bank was confident it would eventually get the money back. It was optimistic enough to increase the amount of cash it was paying to its shareholders, announcing an 18 per cent rise in the dividend.⁸ Investors, however, were as sceptical about HBOS as they were about RBS and the shares fell 5 per cent.

Despite the fall in profits, total pay and bonuses for the top directors went up. Andy Hornby received £1.9 million, up from £1.5 million, and Peter Cummings, who had succeeded George Mitchell as head of corporate banking, £2.6 million, up from £1.4 million – his rise including a cash incentive of £1.6 million reflecting the big boost in profits in the corporate banking division, which was being driven hard to make up for the slowdown in profits from the retail bank. Five executive directors earned more than £1 million and the part-time chairman, Lord Stevenson, saw his remuneration rise from £628,000 to £821,000. Generous though these payments were, they were not as high as they might have been. A long-term incentive plan did not pay out any cash because the target, beating the average total return to shareholders of the banking sector, had not been achieved. There was incredulity among shareholders when the bank responded by halving the targets, but it brushed off criticism: 'These targets are just as stretching as before, they simply recognise that earnings growth will be more modest,' said the HBOS spokesman.[9] As an example of Orwellian doublespeak it was hard to beat.

Across the Atlantic the severity of the sub-prime crisis was brought home forcefully in March by the collpase of the 80-year-old investment bank Bear Sterns. A year previously its shares had been trading at over $130 each. A rescue package put together by the US Federal Reserve Bank and J.P. Morgan initially priced them at $2, but after threatened legal action from shareholders this was raised to $10. An already nervous market was shaken further – no one seemed safe.

In March rumours began to circulate in the UK that HBOS was having to seek emergency funding from the Bank of England. Within 20 minutes of the stock market opening its shares plunged by 17 per cent. They had now lost half their value in a year. To stop a full scale collapse, the Bank of England was forced to issue a strong denial that HBOS had sought a loan. The last time it had been forced to do that was in 1974 when NatWest was in danger of collapse from its property lending. The FSA warned traders against spreading untrue allegations. HBOS itself described the stories as malicious and Andy Hornby issued a statement saying they were 'utterly unfounded'. There was a suspicion that 'short sellers' – speculators who gamble on a share price falling by selling shares they do not own – were deliberately forcing the price down, a practice known in the City as 'trash and cash'. An FSA investigation, which included listening to the taped telephone conversations of traders, found no evidence of criminal rumour-mongering, but did uncover some hedge funds with large 'short positions'. They were placing big bets against HBOS, calculating that its share price had further to fall.

To show their faith in the business HBOS directors, led by Stevenson, Hornby and Cummings, spent £6 million buying more shares and the price began to rally, giving them a paper profit, but it was a false dawn. When the bank published its annual report at the end of April it revealed that far from being able to shrug off the threat to its Alt-A mortgages, it was having to take serious pain. Hornby could not bring himself to use the word 'losses' so fell back on the accounting jargon by saying that a 'negative fair value adjustment' of £2.8 billion was being made to the bank's reserves. This, the bank tried to claim, was not a loss, but a prudent accounting step. Mike Ellis, the finance director, said that in order for the securities backed by Alt-A mortgages to suffer an actual loss, six out of ten of the borrowers would have to default, and the loss on those loans would have to be more than 50 per cent. 'We consider that a remote possibility,' he said.

★ ★ ★

RBS had its own problms. To make up the shortfall in profits from GBM, corporate banking, headed by Leith Robertson, the man George Mathewson had poached from Bank of Scotland, had been lending at an accelerated rate, much of it into the commercial property market. As the UK housing and commercial property slowdowns in 2007 turned into a precipitous plunge in prices in the spring and summer of 2008, lending covenants began to be breached. These were agreements between lender and borrower which specified, among other things, the level and frequency of repayments to be made and the loan-to-value ratio. A generation previously banks would have been able to fudge the numbers by tucking away problem loans into suspense accounts and trying to help the borrowers work through their difficulties. But new international accounting standards left no hiding place – banks now had to write down loans and make provisions from their capital against default, so every-thing was on display to the market. Each time they did so their credit ratings suffered and they found it harder to obtain funding.

The price of Credit Default Swaps – a means of insuring lending to RBS – gives a graphic illustration of how difficult RBS was finding to fund itself. At the start of 2007 lenders could insure RBS debt for just over 4 basis points – a basis point is one hundredth of 1 per cent, mean-ing that for an investor to insure £10 million of the bank's debt against not being able to repay would cost little more than £4,000 a year. By November, the price had risen to over 50; by March 2008 it was over 100 basis points and briefly touched 200 as the market reacted in shock to the Bear Stearns collapse. It now cost over £100,000 to insure £10 million of RBS debt – a prohibitive price for most lenders.[10]

At the beginning of April, Goodwin felt relaxed enough to fly to Bahrain in the RBS corporate jet to watch the Grand Prix motor race. He was reported standing at the trackside, sharing jokes with Sir Jackie Stewart and Peter Phillips, son of the Princess Royal, who had been recruited to RBS. All were wearing trousers in the RBS tartan. A hard landing on earth awaited Goodwin on his return to the UK as he was summoned to see Hector Sants, chief executive of the FSA. Under ques-tioning, Goodwin admitted that Royal Bank's capital was weak, perhaps even less than the 4 per cent regulatory minimum, although he was unsure of the exact figure. This was only a few months after the bank had told the market that its capital was comfortably above this level. Sants insisted that RBS must obtain more capital, by selling assets, issuing new shares, or preferably both and raise as much as it possibly could.[11]

The financial services regulator was clearly getting worried about the solvency of the banks, but the bank chief executives clung to the belief that their growing bad and doubtful debts were not a major problem. They would be able to work through them provided they could maintain liquidity. They wanted the Bank of England to lend them enough to keep them going until the international money market got back to normal. But the Bank did not share this view and Governor Mervyn King, was worried about 'moral hazard': if he bailed out reckless banks, what was to stop them carrying on in the same way and continuing to come back for more?

On 15 April Prime Minister Gordon Brown called bank chief executives to a meeting at 10 Downing Street where, almost unanimously, they demanded that more money be pumped into the inter-bank market. According to Brown most of the men present were suffering 'quiet anxiety', except for Andy Hornby, who sounded very worried. The unthinkable was happening: HBOS was running out of money. The following week at a meeting with chief executives of the leading banks Mervyn King, who had been under pressure from Brown and Darling, chancellor of the exchequer, relented and announced a Special Liquidity Scheme of £50 billion. It was time-limited, but by enabling banks to exchange assets they could not value, such as their mortgage-related debt, for gilts, it would give them solid collateral against which to borrow.

The government still had not appreciated the threat to the banks and was more worried about the mortgage freeze and the effect it would have on homebuyers, particularly young couples who were being denied a home of their own because they could not get loans. After stepping down from HBOS, Sir James Crosby, who had been knighted in 2006 for his service to the financial sector, had become a deputy chairman of the FSA – a poacher turned gamekeeper. Now Brown and Darling asked him to take on an additional role, investigating what measures could be taken to get the mortgage market moving again.

In late April RBS announced the biggest rights issue in British stock market history. It was asking its shareholders to have enough faith that they were prepared to subscribe £12 billion for new shares.[12] At the same time it was also trying to sell its insurance division to raise a hoped-for £8 billion.[13] The price of the new issue stunned the market. The new shares were offered at 200p, compared to a closing price on the Stock Exchange the night before the announcement of 372.5p – a discount of 46 per cent that smacked of desperation. A year previously they had been 600p. If the move was designed to restore confidence in RBS, it failed: the ratings agencies downgraded the bank's creditworthiness, making it more expensive for it to borrow. But the rights issue was a success. Over 95 per cent of the shares were taken up by existing shareholders, and the underwriters – three investment banks which had guaranteed the issue – were able to sell the remaining shares in the market.[14]

To show faith in their own bank, Goodwin, McKillop and the rest of the board bought shares and they urged the group's 110,000 employees, many of whom routinely took their annual bonuses in shares rather than cash, to do the same. Goodwin, speaking at the annual NatWest pensioners' lunch, even urged retired bank staff to buy.[15] Former chairman Sir George Mathewson bought several million pounds worth.[16] But not all shareholders were supportive. RBS's Edinburgh neighbour Baillie Gifford had sold more than ten per cent of its holding in the bank before the rights issue and did not take up its allocation of new shares.

In May HBOS made a tentative return to the securitisation market, offering a package of home loans valued at £500 million for sale to investors. It was a timid toe-in-the-water compared to the £5 billion twice-yearly packages it had been used to issuing, but it worked – it got its money, in fact it found so many lenders that it was able to up its target and take in £750 million. What shocked investors was the price it was having to pay, which was a huge margin over the interest rates being charged in the inter-bank market and more than the cost of borrowing from the Bank of England, which was supposed to be charging a 'penalty rate'. Some analysts saw the achievement of the issue as proof that the credit crunch was easing, others as evidence of the desperation of HBOS. A move that was seen as a confidence raiser further sapped morale.

Liquidity was not the only problem the bank faced. Like RBS it was also running short of capital. Since its share issue in 2002 HBOS had been steadily shrinking its capital, spending £2.5 billion to buy back shares from its investors and cancel them. It had also regularly increased its annual dividend. The effect of both had been to boost its share price and flatter its return on equity, but to reduce its capital. It announced that it was asking shareholders to give it £4 billion in a rights issue, but following RBS it also had to offer a steep discount. Its share price, which had once topped £11, had dropped to less than £5 before the announcement. Now it was offering new shares at £2.75. It looked like a fire sale and did nothing to bolster the confidence of shareholders, more than a quarter of whom were individuals who had acquired shares when Halifax demutualised and changed from being a building society to becoming a bank.

As a further move to conserve money, the dividend was being cut and half of it would be paid by issuing new shares to shareholders rather than cash. Hornby tried to portray the issue as one of good management, rather than desperation. But no one was convinced.

In June HBOS published its rights issue prospectus, and again tried to put an optimistic gloss on what were depressing facts. Specialist mortgages – buy-to-let and self-certified – accounted for a quarter of the £250 billion mortgage book and over 3 per cent of these were already in arrears – they had missed their mortgage repayments for three months or more. The figure did not include repossessed houses, so the real picture may have been worse. Overall the bank had £5 billion-worth of souring home loans. In the commercial market HBOS had lent more than £4 billion to housebuilders, who were facing a crunch of their own, as homes they had completed failed to find buyers. Corporate banking's 'nest egg' equity stakes in this sector had been valued at £200 million, but half of that had now had to be written off.[17] The ratings agencies also marked down the bank's creditworthiness.

Investor confidence was severely shaken by the revelations. The share price had fallen since the rights issue announcement and had briefly dipped below the issue price. If it kept falling the share issue was bound to fail: why would shareholders pay £2.75 for new shares when they could buy existing ones cheaper on the stock market? To guard against this, HBOS had spent £160 million on underwriting fees with financial institutions, which would guarantee to buy any shares that were not wanted by HBOS shareholders. The rights issue in July was the biggest flop since the stock market crash of 1987. Less than 9 per cent of the shares were bought by HBOS shareholders, leaving the underwriters to take over 90 per cent. As the price fell even further they were left with an immediate paper loss. Small shareholders were angry that the bank had bought back shares between 2005 and 2007 at prices from £8.55 to £10.70, yet now it was trying to sell new ones at £2.75. There were calls for Andy Hornby to resign, but they went unheeded in the boardroom.

To Gordon Brown the lesson was clear: 'I interpreted this as meaning that the markets did not believe that HBOS had come clean on its toxic assets and future right-offs. At the same time the RBS share price was at 197.6p, while its rights price was at 200p, and the Qataris had been left with most of the Barclays [rights] issue as there was only a 20 per cent take up. The whole market was simply walking away. They did not believe the banks; neither did I.'[18]

It did not take long for Brown's pessimism to prove justified. HBOS revealed its half-year results at the end of July – profits were halved after a loss of £1 billion on its investments, a further £2 billion write-off to its reserves, and bad debts up again. To save liquidity the dividend was being cut and would be paid by issuing new shares, rather than in cash. Andy Hornby also announced that the bank was putting some of its best subsidiaries up for sale – BankWest in Australia, the insurance company Clerical Medical and the fund manager Insight Investment. Like RBS, HBOS was desperately short of capital to absorb growing losses. Alistair Darling was sceptical about its future: 'There was a whiff of death surrounding the whole operation. Two once solid institutions, the Halifax Building Society and the Bank of Scotland, were heading for the rocks.'[19]

Royal Bank followed a few days later, announcing a pre-tax loss of £691 million, after credit market write-downs of £5.9 billion.[20] This was a massive turnaround from the previous year, when the bank had posted profits of over £5 billion for the first half of the year. Goodwin professed himself to be 'disappointed, numbed, but galvanised' and McKillop apologised for the 'pain caused to shareholders'. Shareholders and analysts were not impressed, wondering how long the chairman and chief executive could last and criticising the lack of succession planning – there were no obvious replacements from within the bank.

In the market RBS was squeezing its smaller business customers hard, trying to extract as much revenue from them as possible. In particular it was selling interest-rate swaps, credit derivative products, to business owners who did not understand what they were buying and trusted their bank managers. They were a good deal for the bank, but many businesses were ruined when interest rates turned against them.[21]

Both banks were now on a downward spiral, but their published figures would not have given that impression. Royal Bank's loss and the write-offs HBOS was posting should have been easily affordable, given the long run of record results and the annual profits both had announced six months previously. But the market had grown sceptical about published statements and no one was taking at face value Goodwin's *sangfroid*, far less Hornby's nervous protestations that everything would right itself shortly. Depositors had formed their own judgement about the prospects of RBS and HBOS. There were no queues outside branches to withdraw money as there had been with Northern Rock a year earlier, but during the autumn of 2008 there was a silent run on both banks as individuals, companies and financial institutions withdrew their cash. HBOS lost £30–35 billion within a few weeks,[22] while at Royal Bank companies withdrew £10.4 billion in corporate deposits and individuals moved £8.7 billion to a safer place.

35

'They are going bust this afternoon'

THE *COUP DE grâce* for both companies was delivered from across the Atlantic. On 7 September 2008 the US government announced it was taking the Federal National Mortgage Association and the Federal Home Loan Mortgage Corporation, commonly known as Fannie Mae and Freddy Mac, into public ownership. This was a huge step for a right-wing Republican administration led by President George W. Bush, which could not bring itself to call it nationalisation, preferring the term 'conservatorship'. The two companies were essentially mortgage wholesalers and had been wrecked by the sub-prime disaster, losing £14 billion in a year. Their bailout would eventually cost the US taxpayer more than $150 billion.

A few days later Lehman Brothers, one of the elite group of Wall Street investment banks, disclosed that it had lost $3.9 billion on mortgage debt in the previous three months alone. There were now severe doubts over the future of even the largest banks and these were reinforced when Bank of America, under strong pressure from the US government, rescued Merrill Lynch, one of Lehman's competitors, which had lost $20 billion in a year. Through the next few days the future of Lehman hung in the balance as politicians and regulators on both sides of the Atlantic tried to find a way to save it. Barclays showed interest in acquiring it, but the US government would not guarantee Lehman's losses and Alistair Darling refused to suspend UK company law to let a deal go through without it first being put to Barclays shareholders. The decision to allow Lehman to go bust destroyed any remaining confidence left in mortgage banks on both sides of the ocean.

On 15 September, a day the newspapers called 'Black Monday', 'Meltdown Monday' or 'Panic Monday', 5,000 Lehman employees in London lost their jobs and were pictured on television, streaming out of the offices with their personal possessions in cardboard boxes. The

FTSE 100 share index tumbled 200 points and bank shares went into freefall. The *Financial Times* described a macabre prediction game in progress: who will be next? The market had already decided – it would be HBOS.

HBOS posed a massive problem for the government. It had not yet found a permanent solution to Northern Rock's difficulties and HBOS was much bigger – any collapse would destroy the savings of 20 million people and create havoc in the banking system. The FSA was already searching for options and the Treasury began to work on a contingency plan. Worries focused on HBOS's capital and liquidity. A further big fall in the value of its reserves following a massive write-off in 2007 suggested that its capital was progressively crumbling away and with it the bank's capacity to absorb losses. It was also running short of cash. Hornby had tried to play down suggestions that HBOS was having problems raising money on the inter-bank market, but the credit rating agency Standard & Poors downgraded HBOS, increasing the costs it had to pay to borrow.

On the other side of the balance sheet money was not coming back as quickly as it had done. As the economy turned down, householders could not sell their homes, so they were not moving and paying off their mortgages. Credit card debt was not being paid off as quickly. Companies were taking longer to reduce their borrowings and were unable to refinance deals with other banks. Many of those firms which had over-borrowed in the days of low interest rates and high economic growth were now in trouble. HBOS corporate teams were fighting fires all over the country. Retirement home specialist McCarthy & Stone, bought by HBOS and the entrepreneur Tom Hunter in 2006 for £1.2 billion, was struggling to refinance its £800 million debt. Housebuilder Crest Nicholson was trying to get banks to exchange half of the £1 billion they were owed for shares in the company. Retail chain JJB Sports and property groups Kandahar and Kenmore had breached their lending covenants. The secondary market was also drying up. Recent deals were remaining on the books of HBOS as other British and foreign banks, which once would have snapped up portions of HBOS corporate loans, withdrew from the market, meaning that the whole debt remained with HBOS.

To keep the bank afloat, Alistair Darling had to authorise the Bank of England to make exceptional loans to HBOS, Royal Bank and other troubled banks, including Bradford & Bingley, another mortgage lender. In view of the severe fall in the HBOS share price caused by the false rumour six months before, the arrangement had to be kept secret from the market, but in confidence Darling told John McFall MP, chairman of the House of Commons Treasury Committee. The full extent of the loans did not become known for a year, when Mervyn King told MPs that, acting in its capacity as lender of last resort, the Bank of England had lent £62 billion to the troubled banks.[1] Over a third went to HBOS, which, with Darling's approval, was also borrowing $18 billion from the US Federal Reserve through Bank of Scotland's American branch.[2]

Darling estimated that HBOS was having to borrow £16 billion overnight, every night, just to keep going.[3] The figure may have been an overestimate, but the timescale was not. The market had become very short term. After the collapse of Lehman every bank wanted to conserve as much cash as possible, so lending for 24 hours was as long as they were prepared to let it out of their sight. HBOS had borrowed £278 billion on the wholesale money markets, 60 per cent of this for periods of less than a year. In the next 12 months it would have to refinance £164 billion as its loans fell due and had to be repaid, yet it was living from day to day. The strain on the treasury department was immense, but it remained calm and professional and took each day as it came.

The atmosphere was much more tense in the group's City executive suite. Andy Hornby was feeling the stress of the constant pressure and uncertainty. His easy likeability was being replaced by irritability, and the lack of sleep and continual worry were showing on his face. HBOS could not survive on its own. After Northern Rock, Brown and Darling were reluctant to nationalise another bank, so a private sector solution seemed the neatest answer. Of the possible candidates as acquirer, LloydsTSB was the obvious first choice. It was conservatively run, with a strong balance sheet (dependent on the wholesale markets for only 25 per cent of its funding) and had come through the sub-prime crisis largely unscathed. It also had the most to gain. A takeover of HBOS would give it coverage in the north of England and Scotland, where it was weak, and provide scope to make massive cost reductions by cutting out duplication in back office functions and the branch networks.

The HBOS board had often considered a merger between the two banks at strategy planning sessions, but the obstacle in the way had always been the Competition Commission. A combined bank would have a dominant market share in mortgages, personal savings and current accounts and would never be allowed in normal times. But these were not normal times. Hornby knew the LloydsTSB chairman Sir Victor

Blank well because they both served on the board of Home Retail Group, the Argos and Homebase retailer. He had also encountered Eric Daniels, Lloyds' chief executive, many times at bank meetings. Daniels, known as the 'Quiet American' in the City because of his unAmerican love of understatement, was a career banker. He had served with Citibank in Latin America and met his wife in Panama, where they still had a house with views from the Atlantic to the Pacific. He spent three years in London in the late 1980s running Citi's private bank during a previous property crash. He joined Lloyds in 2001 as head of retail and moved into the top job two years later. According to the *Guardian*: 'With his slow American drawl, Daniels is the perfect foil to the bank's go-getting chairman, Sir Victor Blank. Although he admits to a love of "over-wrought" Italian opera, Daniels is not a man given to histrionics. He even smokes with an air of quiet contemplation – leading journalists to describe him as the Marlboro man . . . When asked last month [August 2008] whether he would do any more deals he replied: "Don't hold your breath. I don't buy a pair of shoes just because they are cheap."'

Hornby and Daniels had held tentative discussions over the summer; on 16 September they began urgent negotiations. Hornby, his finance director, Mike Ellis, and main adviser Simon Robey of Morgan Stanley, met Daniels, Tim Tookey, Lloyds' finance director, and their adviser Matthew Greenburgh from Merrill Lynch, in the HBOS corporate flat in St James's. Seven years before it had been the venue for the meeting between Peter Burt and James Crosby when the merger between Halifax and Bank of Scotland had been hammered out. Then the air had been light with optimism and excitement. Now it was heavy with dejection and resignation.

Daniels knew he had the upper hand and Hornby knew he could not leave the room without a deal. According to the *Daily Telegraph*: '"Andy was in a state of panic," one person at the meeting said. There was a lot of aggression between the two teams. You always get that in a bid but this was compressed into a few moments and the stakes were enormous. Obviously, it got heated.'[4] The talks dragged on into the early hours of the following morning before the outline of a deal was agreed. HBOS would be bought by Lloyds TSB at 'around' £2.85 a share, a much higher level than the current share price on the Stock Exchange, but less than half of the value at the time the company had started life in 2002. The two sides broke up expecting to meet later that morning, but someone at HBOS leaked the news to Robert Peston at the BBC who wrote on his blog at 9 a.m. that a deal was close at near to £3 a share. Daniels was furious and an hour and a half later Peston blogged: 'maybe I've slightly over-egged the price that Lloyds TSB will pay for HBOS. Perhaps it will be nearer £2 than £3.'

News of the deal did nothing to steady the HBOS share price and the value of Lloyds TSB's shares also dropped as investors worried about what the bank was taking on. All bank shares were tumbling and in a desperate attempt to steady the market the FSA imposed a three-month ban on short selling and the Bank of England announced an extension of its special liquidity scheme, which was keeping several banks afloat. There was still the competition issue to overcome and later that day Daniels met Darling to ask the government to suspend competition law to allow a takeover to go ahead. Darling agreed to discuss it with Gordon Brown, but he was still not convinced that Lloyds knew what it was getting into or that a deal was possible at all. He instructed his officials to prepare two alternative statements, one welcoming a takeover by Lloyds TSB, the other explaining the nationalisation of HBOS.

Blank, who had once been an RBS director, had already raised the competition issue with the prime minister while they were flying back from a trade mission to Israel and Palestine, but had not got a final answer. The collapse of HBOS, with millions of customers, was unthinkable, but neither of the alternatives was appealing for the government either. It had taken nearly six months to decide to take Northern Rock into public ownership and, apart from the political opposition and practical problems, it was also threatened with legal action by some shareholders for expropriating their investments. It did not want to go through that again on a much larger scale with HBOS if an alternative could be found. But allowing Lloyds to acquire HBOS had the potential to create a fearsome monopoly. The combination would give Lloyds market leadership in key product areas: in current accounts and mortgages it would have over 30 per cent of the market; in savings, credit cards and small businesses it would have over 20 per cent and it would also lead the personal lending and home insurance markets too.[5]

The prime minister's final consent to suspend competition law was signalled to Blank during cocktails before a dinner both men were attending during the week of the final negotiations, but a picture of the two in deep conversation published in the *Financial Times* on the day the deal was finally announced gave the impression that it was a political stitch-up conceived over glasses of champagne. Later that day Daniels agreed to an offer at £2.32, some 20 per cent less than his sighting shot a few hours earlier. At their peak the shares had exceeded £11. Hornby had little option but to accept.

For the government it also looked like a good deal. Brown and Darling had not had to pledge any guarantees in exchange for LloydsTSB taking a problem off their hands and the strength of Lloyds' balance sheet would make it that much more likely that the money lent to HBOS by the Bank of England would be repaid. As an added bonus Lloyds made unsolicited pledges to keep the headquarters in Edinburgh, to keep printing Bank of Scotland banknotes and to try to safeguard jobs in Scotland. This last point pleased the Scottish Labour Party which was fighting a tough by-election in the constituency next to Gordon Brown's, but angered the MP for Halifax, where no such promise had been given.

The deal may have satisfied the two banks' boards, but it changed nothing in the real world. In the following weeks more US banks went bust and the Federal Reserve had to inject $85 billion into the giant insurance company AIG, which had insured sub-prime securities. Icelandic banks, which had expanded massively in the UK, were also collapsing, nearly bringing down their country with them. So were banks in Ireland. On the London Stock Exchange shares in LloydsTSB and HBOS continued to fall, the latter touching 90p at one stage. With each piece of bad news, the capital of banks was being erroded, the economy was getting weaker and their potential losses were climbing.

Gordon Brown realised before the banks that they needed capital as well as liquidity. Some might be able to raise it from their shareholders, but the experience of HBOS in its summer rights issue clearly showed it could not. The LloydsTSB takeover appeared to have provided a solution – although that illusion did not last long. No such answer was available for RBS. Only American banks would be large enough to take it on, but its problems were now so well-known in the market that no one would touch it.

Darling met the chief executives of the major banks in the Treasury at the end of September and again a week later. They wanted the Bank of England to lend them more money, but they were in denial about the need for more capital. The meeting broke up inconclusively and the following morning, 7 October, Darling flew to Luxembourg for a meeting of finance ministers. Uncharacteristically for the normally parsimonious chancellor, he hired a private aircraft: had he not appeared at the meeting it would have been interpreted as a sign of crisis, but he knew he had to be back in London quickly if the situation deteriorated. Barely had the meeting started when he was called out by his officials who told him that the RBS share price had collapsed. At its peak the bank's market capitalisation had been nearly £70 billion; now it was worth £15 billion, not much more than the £12 billion it had raised four months earlier. That money had been eaten up by increasing losses. It desperately needed more capital, but it was clear its own shareholders and the market generally were not going to provide it.[6]

At the same time in London, Fred Goodwin had been making an optimistic speech to a conference of investors. When it came to questions one fund manager demanded: 'In the time that you have been speaking your share price has fallen 35 per cent. What is going on?' Goodwin went pale, fumbled for an answer, then hurriedly left the meeting.[7]

A short time later McKillop called Darling in Luxembourg: 'He sounded shell-shocked. I asked him how long the bank could keep going. His answer was chilling: "a couple of hours maybe". At the end of the brief call, I put down the 'phone and told my officials: "It's going bust this afternoon." I felt a deep chill in my stomach. If we didn't act immediately the bank's doors would close, cash machines would be switched off, cheques would not be honoured, people would not get paid.'[8]

Darling was the member of parliament for an Edinburgh constituency. He lived in the city and knew the place the banks held in its life and economy: 'I remember thinking that this was once the small, conservative Scottish bank where I had opened my first bank account in Edinburgh forty years earlier. Now it was on its knees.'[9]

Darling called Brown and then Mervyn King: the Bank of England would keep RBS going until a rescue plan could be agreed. He then flew back to London and called the bank chiefs together. Despite the banks' scepticisim, a plan was being hammered out by teams from the Treasury, Downing Street, the FSA and the Bank of England. To keep confidentiality the banks had been given codenames: Jupiter, Lapwing, Badger, Elvis. An apprentice spy would not have taken long to crack the code, thought Darling, but it often confused him. The eventual plan would involve gigantic sums of money, which the government could only raise by additional borrowing. A further £100 billion was to be added to the Bank of England's Special Liquidity Scheme (making a total of £200 billion), £250 billion would be provided in loan guarantees and £50 bilion in new capital for those banks which could not raise it privately. The FSA would determine how much each bank needed to raise.

Darling explained the deal to the bank chief executives in a meeting at the Treasury which went on into the early hours of the morning. They did not like it, but they could not reject it. Royal Bank was in the worst position, but Fred Goodwin remained impassive. He was still in denial, insisting that he only faced a funding problem, not a capital shortfall. To force banks to take public money would make people think the crisis was worse than it was, he said. HBOS was next, but Hornby was unable to hide his terror and sat with his arms tightly clutched around himself. 'He looked as though he might explode,' said Darling.[10] 'I wouldn't put my money in his bank,' remarked one Treasury official, 'just look at his body language.'

The bank executives were reluctant to accept the government package. Darling remembered: 'For the first time I began to feel worried. It crossed my mind not only that the banks had failed to appreciate that there could be no negotiation, but also that they might be daft enough to take up the option of suicide – and I simply couldn't afford a row of dead banks in the morning.'

As the talks dragged on late into the night, Darling sent a car to Gandhi's Indian restaurant, close to his London flat before he had become chancellor. When the meal arrived, £245-worth of curries was spread out in his private office for hungry Treasury ministers and officials. The bank advisers and chief executives, who had been surviving on tea and biscuits, were invited to share it but declined: one poked his head round the doorway and turned away – they were used to much better food than takeaways. When the news of the meal leaked to the press, it became known as the 'Balti Bailout'. At 1.45 a.m. Darling went to bed, telling his private secretary that as long as he stayed the bank chief executives would continue to argue. Once he had gone they would give in. At 2 a.m. they conceded.[11]

On 8 October, before the markets opened, the government announced its funding package. Royal Bank of Scotland was the first to agree to take more capital, then HBOS and finally Lloyds TSB, which had committed itself to taking on the liabilities of HBOS without fully understanding their enormity. The scheme was portrayed as voluntary, but in fact it was mandatory and there were conditions: executive remuneration was to be cut, dividends suspended and the chief executives and chairmen of the Scottish banks were to be sacked. At HBOS Hornby accepted his fate, but Lord Stevenson, the HBOS chairman took it badly.[12] 'He was absolutely furious,' a government source told me. 'He didn't see what he had done wrong and why he couldn't stay.'[13] The takeover of HBOS was finally agreed later that month after the terms had been reduced again. Now HBOS shareholders would get fewer Lloyds shares in exchange for their old ones. The government would be the largest shareholder, subscribing £17 billion and owning 43.5 per cent of the merged company, next came Lloyds' shareholders with 36.5 per cent and finally HBOS with 20 per cent – less than half what they would have received with the initial offer. Since the Lloyds' share price was also falling, the cash value of HBOS was dropping by the day. The HBOS board was booted out without compensation. It subsequently emerged that in addition to borrowing from the Bank of England, Lloyds had secretly lent HBOS £10 billion to keep it going until the takeover was completed. HBOS also borrowed a further $14.5 billion (£11 billion) from the US Federal Reserve.[14]

At RBS, Fred Goodwin also accepted that he had to go, but McKillop dug in, insisting he would stay until the annual general meeting. Darling was exasperated: 'The bank's board appeared to be right behind him. They seemed to have no sense of responsbility for what had happened to RBS and were more concerned with saving face. We would not budge. In the end Sir Tom went and the others followed him a few weeks later.'[15]

The government injected £15 billion of new capital into RBS in ordindary shares, giving it a 70 per cent stake, but it also subscribed £5 billion in preference shares, paying a penal 12 per cent 'coupon' (interest rate). The £600 million annual cost of this proved too much for the bank and the preference shares were converted into ordinary stock, taking the government holding up to 84 per cent. The bank also borrowed £75 billion from the Bank of England's credit guarantee scheme, £36.6 billion in emergency liquidity assistance and $84.5 billion (£52 billion) from the US Federal Reserve.[16]

36

The end of an 'Auld Sang'

AT THE FINAL meeting of the old Scottish parliament before the Act of Union swept it away in 1707, the Earl of Seafield remarked sadly: 'Now there's ane end o' ane auld sang.' It was an event bound up with the history of the two Edinburgh banks. The old parliament had given Bank of Scotland its first charter. Royal Bank of Scotland arose from the financial settlement of the Union. As competitors or collaborators they had dominated Scottish banking for most of three centuries. In the first decade of the twenty-first century they had shaken up British banking. Now their 'auld sang' was coming to an end. The prudent management, which had come to be the defining characteristic of Scottish banking and had enabled them to survive credit crashes in the eighteenth, nineteenth and twentieth centuries, had gone. Their recklessness during the boom years of the early part of the twenty-first century had led to catastrophic failure when the credit market froze.

Both banks set records of the wrong kind. Royal Bank posted a record loss of £40 billion (£24.3 billion after tax) for 2008, a large part of it a write-off from its disastrous acquisition of ABN Amro,[1] described by the new chairman as 'the wrong price, the wrong way to pay, at the wrong time and the wrong deal'.[2] It was followed by a succession of smaller deficits in the next eight years, bringing its accumulated losses to over £58 billion, before it turned a small profit in 2017.[3] Total HBOS losses absorbed by Lloyds amounted to nearly the same, at £54 billion. At the time of the crash directors of both banks had tried to claim that their demise was entirely the result of the freezing of the market, that factors beyond their control had defeated them. But an analysis of their results showed that bad lending – lending to people who could not afford to pay it back, a feature of bank failures through the ages – was a major contributory cause. 'Impairments' (provision against bad debts) for HBOS totalled £45.8 billion between 2008–11, and for RBS £37.5 billion. As a proportion of the total loan book, RBS lost 5 per cent, but HBOS a staggering 10 per cent.[4] Set against their core regulatory capital at the time (4 per cent of total lending), it is not hard to see why they could not survive without taxpayer support.

In the last 15 years of the twentieth century and the opening years of the twenty-first, those running Edinburgh banks had detached themselves from the history of their institutions. They used the longevity of their banks only as a marketing tool to sell new products. They believed themselves smarter than their rivals and that their cleverness made the need for experience redundant. Training was on a 'need to know' basis, not the rounded education that the Institute of Bankers in Scotland* sought to give its student managers. The questions the *Financial Times* Lex column asked of Royal Bank and other banks in 2008: (1) does it have sufficient liquidity? (2) Does it have sufficient capital? (3) How good is its asset quality?[5] Might well have been asked of William Paterson more than 300 years ago and numerous careless or reckless bankers since.

There is a depressing familiarity about the reasons banks fail, whether they are operating in the Scottish market in the eighteenth or nineteenth centuries, or global credit markets in the twenty-first. The immediate cause is the bank running out of cash (question 1), and that occurs because its depositors and those it needs to borrow from lose faith that they will get their money back. That loss of trust is caused by a perception (usually correct) that the bank has been lending to people who will be unable to pay off their loans (question 3) and that the bank has insufficient capital to withstand its losses (question 2). As one bank director described it to me, a big contributor to the fall of HBOS and Royal Bank in 2008 was 'old-fashioned bad lending'. That was nothing new – banks have always misjudged the prospects of some of the people and businesses to whom they have advanced money. But the skill of banking is to put in place systems and procedures that will keep those mistakes to a minimum, and to maintain sufficient capital to absorb the resulting losses without endangering the savings of depositors and therefore not forfeiting their trust. That skill and prudence, learned through centuries of experience, became the hallmark of Scottish banking in the late nineteenth and the twentieth centuries. It was abandoned in the twenty-first century.

---

* Now the Chartered Institute of Bankers in Scotland.

Is the modern world so different? Another contributor to the failures of the 2008 credit crunch was the loss on so-called 'derivatives' – CDOs, ABCPs, ABS, MBS, Alt-As and the rest. They were certainly more sophisticated and more complicated than the 'accommodation bills' of the eighteenth and nineteenth centuries, but had Adam Smith been writing *The Wealth of Nations* now, rather than 250 years ago, he would have recognised them for what they were and classed them as 'fictitious bills' – paper with little or no intrinsic value, useful only for obtaining credit.

A study of why banks went bust in the past is no guarantee that disaster can be avoided in the future, but some understanding of history might have instilled a sense of caution in directors and managers. Powerful, arrogant and reckless chief executives were a feature of banking in the twenty-first century – but they were not the first. The boards which did nothing to curb their excesses might have learned from the way Bank of Scotland forced William Cadell to resign in 1832, or Royal Bank acted against John Thomson in 1845, after his expansionary strategy led to a dangerous rise in bad debts.

Credit markets froze in 2008 – but this was not the first time that had happened, nor the first time that bankers had lobbied politicians to intervene to save them. Royal Bank avoided disaster in 2008, as it had in 1793, only because of extraordinary emergency loans from the government. Modern bank directors might have learned some humility from their predecessors. As a condition of the first bailout, four non-executive directors, led by the governor, stood surety for the taxpayers' loan. The twenty-first century directors were not required to put their personal wealth at risk. Modern executives also got off lightly. In previous centuries it was common for senior officers of banks and insurance companies to have to pledge personal bonds against their honesty and competence. Their twenty-first century counterparts did not even have their bonuses clawed back.

Not only banks and bankers might have something to learn from the past. Entrepreneurs and property speculators who were actually or nearly bankrupted in the credit crunch could have learned from the railway mania of the 1840s, or the experience of Sir Walter Scott, who was ruined in 1826. His modesty in accepting his guilt and working to pay off his creditors might have taught them something too.

★ ★ ★

With the failure of Bank of Scotland and Royal Bank of Scotland came the end of Edinburgh's two largest concerns as independent

Scottish-headquartered companies and a demotion of the city as a corporate capital. Bank of Scotland, subsumed into HBOS and in turn swallowed by Lloyds Banking Group,[6] would become a mere brand name with little substance. Its head office on The Mound, where the bank's chief executive and top managers had worked for 200 years, demoted to a venue for corporate entertaining. Royal Bank of Scotland, already diminished by its rebranding as 'RBS', would lose its autonomy, not to a London or foreign bank, as previous boards had feared, but to the UK government, which would be forced to all but nationalise it. Fred Goodwin's grandiose office at Gogarburn would become an incubator for 80 entrepreneurs starting up companies.[7] Henceforth both banks would be run from London.

Immediately after the crisis, Royal Bank board meetings were fairly evenly split between Edinburgh and London, but the bias towards London increased as time went on. Occasionally meetings were held in the US or Eire, where the group had significant operations and problems. The Audit and Risk Committees also went overseas to review specific problems. The two chairmen during the ten years since the crash, Sir Philip Hampton and Sir Howard Davies, the chief executives, Stephen Hester and Ross McEwan, and the group finance directors were careful to keep offices in Gogarburn, but mostly they operated from the RBS London office in Bishopsgate. In contrast to previous top men at the bank, who lived in or near Edinburgh, all had their homes in the south of England. Some senior executives continued to be based in Edinburgh, but again, most of their time would be spent in London, near to the regulators, the Bank of England, government and their partners and competitors.

There was not even this much Edinburgh presence for Bank of Scotland. Its ultimate parent was unequivocally run from London. That trend had started with HBOS, which maintained The Mound as a head-quarters in name only. In reality the bank was run from England.

Millions of shareholders saw the value of their holdings in either or both banks decline by as much as 90 per cent. They included individual customers of Halifax who had gained shares in its demutualisation, staff and pensioners of RBS and Bank of Scotland who took their annual bonuses in shares or bought as part of share-save schemes. Many lost not only their savings, but their jobs too. Tens of thousands of employees were made redundant.

Both banks ceased to play such an important part in the life of Edinburgh. Sponsorship of arts, sports, civic and community events was curtailed drastically. The impact on the city was not nearly as bad as it had been on Glasgow following the collapse of the City of Glasgow Bank 130 years earlier: as FTSE 100 companies, quoted on the UK Stock Exchange, their shareholdings were much more widely dispersed and limited liability protected the holders from losing more than their investment. But it did have an effect. Unemployment in Edinburgh, although still low by national standards, jumped by nearly 50 per cent, from 11,000 in 2007 to 16,200 in 2009.[8] An inquiry by the House of Commons Treasury Committee in 2009 also found a large rise in people asking the charity Citizens Advice for advice on consumer debt and arrears of rent and mortgage payments.[9]

The change in location of top decision-making meant a rapid loss of opportunity for the professional services firms that had depended on the banks for high value work – lawyers, accountants, management and IT consultants, advertising and public relations companies, even contract caterers, taxi companies and events organisers. Many firms downsized, merged or closed. The social life of the city also felt the change. Previous Scottish-based chairmen and senior executives had played major roles in the Edinburgh International Festival, in cultural institutions like the national galleries and museums, the Royal Botanic Garden, and in business groups such as Scottish Financial Enterprise (the body which represents the finance industry in Scotland), the CBI, Institute of Directors, the Chambers of Commerce and the Scottish Council for Development & Industry. That was less possible when all the key people were based in London.

There was widespread public anger across the whole of the UK, not only in Scotland. Yet the men most responsible for the plight of two once great institutions went largely unpunished. The FSA took enforcement actions against only two people – Peter Cummings, head of corporate banking at HBOS, and Johnny Cameron, head of Global Banking and Markets at RBS – fining them and banning them from financial services for life. At the time of writing, more than ten years later, no regulatory action has been taken against either chief executive, chairman or key directors. Fred Goodwin lost his knighthood and, after resisting for months, grudgingly accepted a cut in his £700,000 a year pension. James Crosby, first chief executive of HBOS, voluntarily surrendered his knighthood and took a cut in his pension. No action was taken against the auditors, who had approved accounts for both banks that only a few months before their collapse appeared to show they were in good health.

The banks were the most visible manifestations of the decline of Edinburgh as a financial centre, but there were others. From 1999–2004 when I was chief executive of Scottish Financial Enterprise, Edinburgh could reasonably claim to be not only the second most important financial city in Britain, after London, but among the top financial centres of Europe. It was home to two banks in the European top ten, seven large life assurance companies which ranked highly nationally and internationally, all but one of which were independent. It had a fund management sector which controlled more assets than most European capital cities. The presence of headquarters for many of these leading firms ensured a flourishing corporate services sector. Legal partnerships like Dundas Wilson, McGrigor Donald and Maclay Murray & Spens could trace their histories back to the nineteenth century and owed their prosperity to the work they did for banks and other financial companies. All have now been taken over by UK law firms. Although others, such as Shepherd & Wedderburn, Burness Paull, and Murray Beith & Murray, have maintained their independence, the sector has shrunk.

The decline in the life assurance activity was apparent long before the 2008 crash and was a consequence of the centralising forces unleashed by deregulation in the 1980s. The last independent company in Edinburgh, Standard Life, merged with the fund management group Aberdeen Asset Management in 2017 and in 2018 sold its insurance business to London-based Phoenix, becoming a purely asset management company. This broke Edinburgh's link with independent life assurance firms, which had started with Scottish Widows in 1815. The loss of the stock exchange and independent stockbroking firms predated even the consolidation of the life offices, as activity was drawn south by the magnetic attraction of London. The banks had stood out against that force, but in the end were brought to their knees by their own hubris.

However, a decade after the crash financial services companies remain the largest private sector employers in the city with the two banks, RBS and Lloyds, plus Standard Life and Scottish Widows, ranking only after the National Health Service, the city council and the University of Edinburgh, in the size of their labour forces.[10] The city remains in the top ten for earnings in the UK, although in the lower half of the table and second in Scotland, behind Aberdeen.[11] Financial services still tends to pay well – a third more than the Scottish average – although less than the energy industries.[12] Where once it was qualitatively as well as quantitively superior, Edinburgh can no longer claim a more important banking presence than, say, Manchester or Leeds. It is a regional banking capital, not a national one. It is difficult to see this situation ever reversing. Most 'challenger banks', encouraged by the government to provide competition for the oligarchy of the Big Four London banks, are themselves based in London.

There is one area where Edinburgh can still boast that it is second only to London. Fund management has continued to grow, despite the market crash and subsequent economic depression. Aberdeen Asset Management mopped up several of its smaller Scottish rivals to become a major player and then in 2017 merged with Standard Life to become Aberdeen Standard (the name reverses for the asset business) and moved its headquarters to Edinburgh. It now manages more than £500 billion. Baillie Gifford – still an independent partnership – has approaching £200 billion.[13] Large international firms such as Blackrock and Franklin Templeton are represented in the city, as are a number of smaller businesses, including several spin-outs from the defunct Ivory & Sime, such as Aberforth and Artemis. Walter Scott & Partners was sold to the US corporation BNY Mellon Investment Management in 2006, but continues to work from Charlotte Square and has continued to grow. Stewart Ivory was acquired by First State of Australia in 2000, but remained in Edinburgh and in 2015 became Stewart Investors. Martin Currie was acquired by Legg Mason of the US, but also remains in Edinburgh. Dunedin Fund Managers was spun out of Bank of Scotland in 1996 and is still owned by its directors. Dundas Global Investors was started in 2010 by Alan McFarlane, who started in fund management with Ivory & Sime before becoming chief executive of Walter Scott & Partners.

Pressure on fees in fund management – and the move towards 'passive funds' chosen by computer to mirror the stock market indices – has meant that income continues to decline. Although some smaller 'boutique' fund management houses may survive, larger firms are being pressured to amalgamate in order to reduce costs.

In banking, Noble Grossart remains an independent Edinburgh-headquartered company, which celebrated its 50th anniversary in 2019. Its profits have grown steadily over the years, reaching £52.2 million in 2018.

The city also retains professional institutes, which have played a major part in the development of Edinburgh – the Chartered Institute of Bankers in Scotland, the Institute of Chartered Accountants in Scotland and the Law Society of Scotland. All are independent of their London counterparts. After 156 years of autonomy, the Faculty of Actuaries, the first of the UK professional bodies in the field to be granted a Royal Charter, merged with its London counterpart in 2010.

One intangible victim of the crash has been the relationship between banks and their customers: trust in banks has collapsed. Even in 2018, a decade later, two-thirds of those asked in a survey did not trust banks to work in the best interests of UK society, nearly three-quarters believed banks should have faced more severe penalties for their role in the financial crisis and 63 per cent were worried that banks may cause another financial crisis.[14] How can this trust be rebuilt? The banks themselves have largely sought to do it through advertising slogans, but their efforts have been undermined by scandals such as the miss-selling of PPI (Payment Protection Insurance) and the falsifying of LIBOR (London Interbank Offer Rate), the index on which many interest rates are calculated. In addition, Royal Bank and Lloyds (as the inheritor of HBOS) have faced particular criticism of their treatment of small businesses that have been damaged by their policies or management failures.[15]

Long-term observers of the industry believe that a restoration of trust can only come about through a change in culture – but that will take time. Dr Charles Munn, banking historian and former chief executive of the Chartered Institute of Bankers in Scotland: 'The financial crash was a long time coming. You could see the culture of banking deteriorating even before the deregulation of 1986. The forces of commercialisation had been growing since the 1950s with the rise of hire purchase companies that put sales before customer service. Then the banks bought those companies and internalised their culture. Big Bang accelerated that process and in the booming markets leading up to 2008 the culture was distorted to a dangerous extent.'

Munn, who chaired the Church of Scotland's special commission on the purposes of economic activity, added:

> For many years we have been creating an economy and society based on greed and fear. We have embraced Adam Smith's *The Wealth of Nations* and forgotten about his *Theory of Moral Sentiments* in which Smith argued that people have a natural sympathy for one another which helps them to moderate their behaviour and promote harmony. Smith went on to say, 'The disposition to admire, and almost to worship, the rich and the powerful, and to despise, or, at least, to neglect persons of poor and mean condition is the great and

most universal cause of the corruption of our moral sentiments.' Nothing much seems to have changed since that was published in 1759.

If our objective is to avoid economic crises in the future, we need to re-connect with Smith's moral sentiments which are themselves based on the Christian practice of loving our neighbours. The real danger is that we will just get back to business as usual and, in so doing, set ourselves on the track to repeat the crisis sometime in the future.

In 2016 the Church of Scotland and the Islamic Finance Council UK, meeting in Edinburgh, signed a partnership agreement to work towards the restoration of ethics in finance. Inspired by the work of Reverend Henry Duncan, founder of the savings bank movement, who influenced Islamic as well as Christian bankers, the partnership produced the 'Edinburgh Finance Declaration',[16] which sought to develop and promote shared values and to build on the growing interest in stewardship, sustainable investing and finance as a service of a wider communal good.

Omar Shaikh of the Islamic Finance Council described 2008 as a 'catalyst':

Once people had dealt with the immediate fallout they were prepared to look at doing things differently, to move away from short-termism, profits and bonuses linked to sales, shorting the market with innovative products to make money on the way down as well as on the way up. They were prepared to look at concepts like stewardship, not doing things which cause harm, not cheating or stealing – these are some of the principles which underpin Islamic finance, but they are also common to Christianity and Judaism.

We want to bring more people to Edinburgh to discuss these things: our aim is to make the city the Davos of the ethical finance world.

It is a lofty ambition. But Edinburgh is a city that has never lacked ambition.

Glossary

Annuity: This is a lump sum of money paid in exchange for a regular income – often for life. In the seventeenth and eighteenth centuries selling annuities was used by city administrations and governments to raise money, often with disastrous results if they got their calculations wrong (see Chapter 6). From the nineteenth century they were used by insurance companies to provide pensions (see Chapter 16).

Bills of exchange: A forerunner of paper money, these were signed IOUs exchanged by merchants in lieu of payment in gold and silver. They usually had a limited life of, say, three or six months, but could be traded. If there was a default at the end of the period they were 'protestable' – a court action could be raised to enforce repayment.

Discounted bills: Banks or other lenders would advance money against the security of a bill signed by a reputable person, but the amount advanced was 'discounted' – it was less than the face value of the bill. The 'discount' represented the interest charged and its size depended on the prevailing interest rate and the creditworthiness of the bill issuer. Advances were for a limited period and the full face value was repayable to the lender at the end of the period.

Accommodation bills: Trade bills were related to physical goods, but accommodation bills were issued purely for the purpose of borrowing money. One person would give a bill to a second person for a specified sum of money repayable after a period of, say, three months. The second person would then issue a similar bill for the same amount repayable at the same date to the first person. Both would then use these bills as security for borrowing from a bank. Adam Smith called these 'fictitious bills' (see Chapter 10).

Chain of bills: When accommodation bills became due, they could either be paid off in cash or, if the issuer did not have ready money, paid for by issuing new bills. Sometimes the chain, with old bills being paid off by issuing new bills, could go on for some time, with interest rates rising each time.

CDOs (collateralised debt obligations), **MBS** (mortgage backed securities), **ABS** (asset backed securities), **ABCP** (asset backed commercial paper) etc., were tradable financial securities invented by investment banks during the years leading up to the 2008 crash. In theory their price was underpinned by the value of the homes on which mortgages had been granted. In practice much of this security turned out to be worthless.

Cash credit: Current accounts invented by Scottish banks in the eighteenth century with the ability of the holder to overdraw – borrow up to a specified amount without prior authorisation or additional security. This was the invention of the overdraft (see Chapter 5).

Cautioners: Persons of standing who would guarantee a loan.

Consols: Public debt in the form of perpetual bonds, redeemable at the discretion of the government, and paying a fixed rate of interest. The name is a contraction of consolidated annuities. They can be traded and their price in the market after issue determines the rate of interest paid. If a consol (or other government stock) paying 5 per cent is initially sold for £100, it pays interest of £5 per year. When subsequently sold to another buyer for, say, £90, it still pays £5, but now the effective interest rate has risen to 5.5 per cent.

Debentures: These are tradeable securities issued by companies or the government as an alternative to borrowing from banks or other lenders. Unlike shares they do not confer any part ownership, but do have the right to interest payments at a rate fixed at the time of issue as a percentage of the issue price (see Consols, above).

Equivalent: The Equivalent was the money paid as part of the settlement of the Act of Union by the British government to Scotland to compensate for Scottish taxpayers taking on the servicing of a share of the English national debt. It was intended for a variety of uses, but mostly went to those who had lost money in the Darien disaster (see Chapter 4).

Feu duty: Under the Scottish system of feudal land tenure, the feudal superior (landowner) could feu (grant a lease on) land, typically for building, in return for a lump sum payment and an annual feu duty (ground rent). The system was abolished in 2004.

Heritable property: Land and buildings (as opposed to moveable property), which could be used as security for borrowing.

Specie: Physical money, usually gold and silver coins.

Sources

ARCHIVES

Minutes of the Town Council of Edinburgh (TCM)

Bank of Scotland directors' minute book (BSM)

Royal Bank of Scotland directors' minute book (RBSM)

National Records of Scotland (NRS)

Commercial Bank of Scotland directors' minutes and letters (CS)

Scottish Widows, directors' minutes (NRAS)

National Bank of Scotland, directors' minutes (NS)

Standard Life board minutes (SLBP)

A. & T. Fairholme papers, University of Edinburgh Research Collections, LA III.507

The Darien papers: being a selection of original letters and official documents relating to the establishment of a colony at Darien by the Company of Scotland trading to Africa and the Indies. 1695–1700, Constable, 1849

Letters and diaries of William Ramsay, NRS

Melville Papers, NRS and Bank of Scotland archive

Papers of the Innes family of Stow, Peeblesshire, NRS

Scott Moncrieff letters, Royal Bank of Scotland archive

The Correspondence of Adam Smith, Glasgow Edition, https://www.libertyfund. org/books/the-glasgow-edition-of-the-works-and-correspondence-of-adam-smith

The Walter Scott Digital Archive, Edinburgh University Library, http://www. walterscott.lib.ed.ac.uk/home.html

OFFICIAL AND COMPANY REPORTS

Sibbald, Robert *Provision for the Poor in Time of Dearth and Scarcity; where There is an Account of Such Food as May be Easily Gotten*, 1699

The Precipitation and Fall of Messrs Douglas, Heron and Company, late Bankers in Ayr, by a Committee of Inquiry appointed by the Proprietors, Edinburgh, 1778

Labouchere, H. *Report to the Right Honourable the Chancellor of the Exchequer, regarding the Affairs of the City of Edinburgh and Port of Leith*, Edinburgh, 1836

Report by Kerr, Andersons, Muir & Main CA and McGrigor Donald & Co. solicitors, balance sheet of the City of Glasgow Bank, 18 October 1878

Monopolies and Mergers Commission, *The Hong Kong and Shanghai Banking Corporation. Standard Chartered Bank Limited. The Royal Bank of Scotland Group Limited. A Report on the Proposed Mergers,* 20th Century House of Commons Sessional Papers, 1981/82, 1981

The failure of the Royal Bank of Scotland, Financial Services Authority Board Report, December 2011

RBS annual report and accounts 1999–2009

RBS rights issue prospectus, https://investors.rbs.com/~/media/Files/R/RBS-IR/corporate-actions/rights-issue-june-2008/prospectusfinal.pdf

HBOS annual report and accounts 2001–10

Bank of Scotland annual report and accounts 1980–2000

Lloyds Banking Group annual report and accounts 2008–10

House of Commons Treasury Committee:

Banking Crisis: dealing with the failure of the UK banks, HC 416, 2009

Banking Crisis: Vol. I, HC261-I, 2010 Banking Crisis: Vol. II Written Evidence, HC144, 2009

Parliamentary Commission on Banking Standards: *'An accident waiting to happen': The failure of HBOS*. HL Paper 144 HC 705, 2013

Financial Conduct Authority, Prudential Regulation Authority, *The failure of HBOS plc*, 2017

ARTICLES AND PAMPHLETS

A Letter to the proprietors of the Bank of Scotland and Royal Bank, 1778

Address to the Town Council of Edinburgh by Thomas Smith, 2nd edition, Mundell & Son, 1799

Button, Richard and Knott, Samuel *Desperate adventurers and men of straw: the failure of City of Glasgow Bank and its enduring impact on the UK banking system*, Bank of England *Quarterly Bulletin* Q1 2015

Campbell, R.H. *Edinburgh bankers and the Western Bank of Scotland*, Scottish Journal of Political Economy, Vol. 2, issue 1, February 1955

Cullen, Karen J. *Famine in Scotland – the 'Ill Years' of the 1690s*, Scottish Historical Review, Monograph Series 16, 2010

Dalrymple, John *Memoirs of Great Britain and Ireland*, Strahan & Cadell, 1740, retrived from https://archive.org

Fisher, Chay and Kent, Christopher *Two depressions, one banking collapse*, Research Discussion Paper 1999–06, Reserve Bank of Australia

Gifford, John *How to Mismanage a Bank, A review of the Western Bank of Scotland*, 1859, reprinted in Saville, appendix 9c.

Greig, John *Report on the Statements of the Lord Provost & Mr A. Bruce, Respecting the Affairs of the City of Edinburgh, Humbly Submitted to the Committee of the Guildry*, J. Hay & Co., 1819

Hamilton, Henry *The Failure of the Ayr Bank, 1772*, The Economic History Review, New Series, Vol. 8, No. 3, 1956

Holland, John *A short Discourse on the present temper of the nation with respect to the Indian and African Company; and of the Bank of Scotland. Also of Mr Paterson's pretended Fund of Credit*, 1696

Johnston, Thomas *The Financiers and the Nation*, 1934 https://archive.sustecweb.co.uk/past/sustec12–6/extract_from_the_financiers_and.htm

Leaves from the Diary of John Campbell, an Edinburgh Banker in 1745, Miscellany of the Scottish History Society. Vol. I, Scottish History Society, First Series, 15 (1893)

McKinstry, Sam and Fletcher, Marie *The personal account books of Sir Walter Scott, Accounting Historians Journal*. 29.2 December 2002

Meikle, Henry W. *The King's Birthday Riot in Edinburgh, The Scottish Historical Review*, Vol. 7, No. 25 (Oct. 1909), http://www.jstor.org/stable/25518146

Murdoch, Alexander *The Importance of Being Edinburgh: Management and Opposition in Edinburgh Politics 1746–1784*, The Scottish Historical Review, Vol. 62, No. 173, Part 1 (April 1983), Edinburgh University Press

Murray of Broughton's *Memorials*, Scottish History Society, Vol. XXVII

Mutch, Alistair *Religion and Accounting Texts in Eighteenth Century Scotland*, Accounting, Auditing and Accountability Journal, Vol. 29, Issue 6

Mutch, Alistair *The Business of Religion: Lending and the Church of Scotland in the Eighteenth Century*, Journal of Scottish Historical Studies, Vol. 37, Issue 2

Oram, M. and Wellins, R. *Re-engineering's Missing Ingredient: The Human Factor*, IPD, 1995

Rosenblum, Leo *The Failure of the City of Glasgow Bank*, The Accounting Review, Vol. 8, No. 4 (December 1933), American Accounting Association

Ross, Duncan *Savings bank depositors in a crisis: Glasgow 1847 and 1857, Financial History Review*, Cambridge, Vol. 20, Issue 2, August 2013

Scott, Walter *Letter to the Editor of the Edinburgh Weekly Journal from Malachi Malagrowther Esq*, 2nd edition, William Blackwood, 1826

Scottish Capital Abroad, Blackwoods Magazine, October 1884

Silberling, Norman J. *British Financial Experience 1790–1830,* https://Fraser. Stlouisfed.Org/Files/Docs/Meltzer/Silbri19.Pdf

Tennent, Charles *The structure of Scottish banking, Scottish Bankers Magazine,* January 1952

The Edinburgh Annual Register, January 1824, Vol.17

The Financial System of the early 19th century, Three Banks Review, No. 45, March 1960

Vamplew, Wray *Sources of Scottish railway capital before 1860,* Scottish Journal of Political Economy, 1970

RESEARCH PAPERS AND THESES

Gunning, Alan *War, the Central Government and the Scottish economy 1750–1830,* PhD thesis, University of Strathclyde, 1984

McCann, Jean E. *The Organisation of the Jacobite Army 1745–6,* PhD thesis, University of Edinburgh

Michie, R.C. *Scottish Stock Exchanges in the 19th Century,* PhD thesis, University of Aberdeen, 1978

Noble, M.J. *The Common Good and the Reform of Local Government: Edinburgh 1820–56,* PhD thesis, University of Edinburgh, 2016

Shaw, J.S. *Civic leadership and the Edinburgh lawyers in 18th century Scotland,* PhD thesis, University of Stirling, 1979

Smout, T.C. public lecture, *Provost Drummond,* Edinburgh University Press, 1978

Swan, Claire *Scottish-American business networks: The development of the Dundee investment trust industry, c.1873–1914,* PhD thesis, University of Dundee, 2009

Ward, Thomas *The regulatory response to the collapse of the City of Glasgow Bank 1878–79,* dissertation, University of Edinburgh, 2009

BOOKS AND CHAPTERS

Arnot, Hugo *The History of Edinburgh, from the Earliest Accounts to the Present Time,* Willam Creech, 1788

Bacaër, Nicholas *A Short History of Mathematical Population Dynamics,* Springer, 2011

Balfour-Mellville, Barbara *The Balfours of Pilrig,* Wm Brown, 1907

Bennett, Rachel *Capital Punishment and the Criminal Corpse in Scotland 1740–1834,* Springer, 2017

Blair, Alexander *Edinburgh American Assets, a brief history 1878–1978*, Ivory & Sime, 1979

Boase, C.W. *A Century of Banking in Dundee*, R. Grant & Son, 1867

Braidwood, James *On the Construction of Fire-engine and Apparatus, the Training of Firemen, and the Method of Proceeding in Cases of Fire*, Bill & Bradfute, 1830

Brown, Gordon *Beyond the Crash*, Simon & Schuster, 2010

Burns, Richard *A Century of Investing, Baillie Gifford's first hundred years*, Birlinn, 2008

Caledonian Insurance Company, History of a hundred years 1805–1905, T&A Constable, 1905

Cameron, Alan *Bank of Scotland 1695–1995*, Mainstream, 1995

Carlyle, Alexander *Autobiography*, Blackwood, 1860

Carter, Robert L. and Falush, Peter *The British Insurance Industry Since 1900: The Era of Transformation*, Springer, 2009

Chambers, Robert *Notices of the Most Remarkable Fires in Edinburgh: From 1385 to 1824*, C. Smith & Company, 1824

Chambers, Robert *Traditions of Edinburgh*, W. & R. Chambers, 1847

Chancellor, Edward *Devil take the hindmost, a history of financial speculation*, Plume, 2000

Checkland, S.G. *Scottish Banking, A History 1695–1973*, Collins, 1975

Clapham, John *Bank of England, A History Vol. 1*, Cambridge, 1966

Cockburn, Henry *Memorials of his time*, James Thin, 1977

Darling, Alistair *Back from the Brink*, Atlantic Books, 2011, Kindle edition

Davis, Jonathan *Money Makers: The Stock Market Secrets of Britain's Top Professional Investment Managers*, Harriman House, 2013

Devine, T.M *The Golden Age of Tobacco*, in *Glasgow, Vol. I, beginnings to 1830*, Manchester University Press, 1995

Devine, T.M. *The Scottish Nation 1700–2000*, Allen Lane, 1999

Devine, T.M. *The Tobacco Lords*, John Donald, 1975

Dingwall, Helen *Late Seventeenth Century Edinburgh, a demographic study*, Scholar Press, 1994

Dunlop, A. Ian, ed. *Scottish Ministers' Widows' Fund 1743–1993*, St Andrew Press, 1992

Emerson, Roger. L. *An Enlightened Duke, the life of Archibald Campbell (1682–1761)*, Humming Earth, 2013

Forbes, William *Memoirs of a Banking House*, W & R Chambers, 1860

Forrester, Andrew *The man who saw the future*, Thomson Texere, 2004

Fransman, Martin *Edinburgh City of Funds*, Kokoro, 2008

Fraser, Ian *Shredded: Inside RBS, the bank that broke Britain*, Birlinn, 2015

Fry, Michael *The Dundas Despotism*, John Donald, 2004

Gaskin, Maxwell *The Scottish Banks; a modern survey*, Routledge, 1965

Graham, Henry *The Social Life of Scotland in the 18th century*, A. & C. Black, 1901

Graham, Roderick *The Great Infidel*, John Donald, 2005

Graham, William *The One Pound Note*, James Thin, 1886

Gray, W. Forbes *A brief chronicle of the Scottish Union & National Insurance Company 1824–1924*, Pillans & Wilson, 1924

Hamilton, Henry *An Economic History of Scotland in the Eighteenth Century*, Clarendon Press, 1963

Haynes, Nick and Fenton, Clive B. *Building knowledge: an architectural history of the University of Edinburgh*, Historic Environment Scotland, 2017

Hutton, Richard. H. *The life of Sir Walter Scott*, Macmillan, 1878

Jackson, W. Turrentine *The Enterprising Scot, Investors in the American West after 1873*, Edinburgh University Press, 1968

Kerr, A.W. *History of Banking in Scotland*, A. &. C. Black, 1908

Kosmetatos, Paul *The 1772–3 British Credit Crisis*, Palgrave, 2018

Kynaston, David and Roberts, Richard *The Lion Wakes, a modern history of HSBC*, Profile Books, 2015

Kynaston, David *Till Time's Last Sand: A History of the Bank of England 1694–2013*, Bloomsbury, 2017

Lewin, H.G. *Railway Mania and its aftermath*, David and Charles, 1968

Lockhart, John Gibson *Memoirs of the life of Sir Walter Scott Bart.*, 1837 http://www.gutenberg.org

Macmillan, David *Scottish Enterprise in Australia 1798–1879*, in Payne, Peter *Studies in Scottish Business History*, Frank Cass & Co., 1967

Malcolm, Charles *History of the British Linen Bank*, Constable, 1950

Marshall, James Scott The *Life and Times of Leith*, John Donald, 1986

Martin, Iain *Making it Happen, Fred Goodwin, RBS and the men who blew up the British economy*, Simon & Schuster, 2013

Maxwell, Herbert *Annals of the Scottish Widows Fund*, R & R Clark, 1914

McInroy, Charles *Scottish Equitable Life Assurance Society 1831–1981*, 1981

Michie, R.C. *Money, Mania & Markets*, John Donald, 1981

Mills, Stella *The Collected Letters of Colin Maclaurin*, Nantwich Shiva, c.1982

Moneta, E. *Scottish Banks and Bankers*, North British Publishing, 1904

Morecroft, Nigel *Robert Fleming and Scottish Asset Management, 1873–1890*, in *The Origins of Asset Management from 1700 to 1960, Palgrave Studies in the History of Finance*, Palgrave Macmillan, 2017

Moss, Michael *Standard Life 1825–2000*, Mainstream, 2000

Munn, Charles *Clydesdale Bank, the first 150 years*, Collins, 1988

Munn, Charles *Minister of Money*, John Donald, 2017

Munn, Charles *Scottish Provincial Banking Companies*, John Donald, 1981

Munro, Neil *A History of the Royal Bank of Scotland 1727–1927*, R & R Clark, 1928

Nairn, Alasdair *Engines that move markets, technology investing from the railways to the internet and beyond*, John Wiley, 2002

Newlands, John *Put not your trust in Money*, Chappin Kavanagh, 1997

Newlands, John *The Edinburgh Investment Trust PLC 1889–2014*, EIT, 2014

North British and Mercantile Insurance Company, Centenary 1809–1909, 1909

Perman, Ray *HUBRIS: How HBOS wrecked the best bank in Britain*, Birlinn, 2012

Pittock, M. *Material Culture and Sedition, 1688–1760: Treacherous Objects, Secret Places*, Palgrave Macmillan, 2013

Pugh, Peter *Number One Charlotte Square*, Ivory & Sime, 1987

Quayle, Eric *The Ruin of Sir Walter Scott*, Hart-Davis, 1968

Rait, Robert *The History of the Union Bank of Scotland*, John Smith, 1930

Rayor, Laura in *Scotland in the Age of Two Revolutions*, ed. Adams & Goodare, Boydell Press, 2014

Reed, J.W. and Pottle, F.A. *Boswell: Laird of Auchinleck, 1778–1782*, Edinburgh University Press, 1977

Robertson, C.J.A. *Early Scottish Railways and the Observance of the Sabbath*, The Scottish Historical Review, Vol. 57, No. 164, Part 2, October 1978

Robertson, C.J.A. *The Origins of the Scottish Railway System 1722–1844*, John Donald, 1983

Romney, Anthony *Three Letters on the Speculative Schemes of the Present Times*, Bell & Bradfute, 1825

Saville, Richard *Bank of Scotland, A History 1695–1995*, Edinburgh University Press, 1996

Scott, John and Hughes, Michael *The Anatomy of Scottish Capital*, Croom Helm, 1980

Skempton, A.W. *A Biographical Dictionary of Civil Engineers in Great Britain and Ireland: 1500–1830*, Thomas Telford, 2002

Smith, Adam *The Wealth of Nations*, ed. Edwin Cannan, Methuen, 1950

Smout, T.C. *Scottish trade on the eve of union, 1660–1707*, Oliver & Boyd, 1963

Smout, T.C. *Where had the Scottish economy got to by 1776?*, in *Wealth and Virtue*, Cambridge, 1983

Steuart, M.D. *The Scottish Provident Institution 1837–1937*, 1937

Swan, Claire *Female investors within the Scottish investment trust movement in the 1870s,* in Laurence, Anne, Maltby, Josephine, Rutterford, Janette (eds) *Women and Their Money 1700–1950: Essays on Women and Finance,* Routledge, 2008

The Edinburgh Stock Exchange 1844–1944, Committee of the Edinburgh Stock Exchange, 1944

The Journal of Sir Walter Scott, Vol. 1, David Douglas, 1891

Thomas, John *A Regional History of the Railways of Great Britain. Vol. 6, Scotland, the Lowlands and the Borders,* revised by J.S. Paterson, David and Charles, 1984

Thomas, W.A. *The Provincial Stock Exchanges,* Cass, 1973

Torrance, David *George Younger, a life well lived,* Birlinn, 2008

Turner, John *Major and minor British banking crises since 1800,* in *Banking in Crisis: The Rise and Fall of British Banking Stability, 1800 to the Present,* Cambridge Studies in Economic History, Second Series, 2014

Tweddle, Ian *Maclaurin's Physical Dissertations,* Springer, 2007

Tyson, R.E. *Scottish Investment in American Railways: the case of the City of Glasgow Bank 1856–1881,* in *Studies in Scottish Business History,* ed. Peter Payne, Frank Cass & Co., 1967

Walker, Stephen and Lee, Thomas *Studies in early professionalism, Scottish Chartered Accountants 1854–1918,* Taylor & Francis, 1999

Wallace, William *The Trial of the City of Glasgow Bank Directors,* Sweet & Maxwell, 1905

Watt, Douglas *The Price of Scotland: Darien, Union and the Wealth of Nations,* Luath Press, 2007

Weir, Ronald B. *A History of the Scottish American Investment Company Ltd 1873–1973,* Scottish American Investment Company, 1973

Whatley, Christopher A. *Scottish Society, 1707–1830: Beyond Jacobitism, Towards Industrialisation,* Manchester University Press, 2000

Whatley, Christopher A. *The Scots and the Union: then and now,* Edinburgh University Press, 2014

Whyte, Ian *Scotland before the Industrial Revolution: an economic and social history,* Longman, 1995

Youngson, A.J. *The Making of Classical Edinburgh,* Edinburgh University Press, 1975

Notes and references

PREFACE

1. http://www.didaskoeducation.org
2. https://www.libraryofmistakes.com
3. https://www.nationalarchives.gov.uk/currency-converter/#currency-result

1 FAMINE AND FINANCE

1. Robert Sibbald, *Provision for the Poor in Time of Dearth and Scarcity; where There is an Account of Such Food as May be Easily Gotten*, 1699
2. Christopher A. Whatley, *The Scots and the Union: then and now*, Edinburgh University Press, 2014, p.156
3. Karen J. Cullen, *Famine in Scotland – the 'Ill Years' of the 1690s*, Scottish Historical Review, Monograph Series 16, 2010, p.2
4. T.C. Smout, *Scottish trade on the eve of union, 1660–1707*, Oliver & Boyd, 1963, p.246
5. Laura Rayor in *Scotland in the Age of Two Revolutions*, ed. Adams & Goodare, Boydell Press, 2014, p.202
6. Richard Saville, *Bank of Scotland, A History 1695–1995*, Edinburgh University Press, 1996, p.19
7. Whatley, *op. cit.* p.164
8. Saville, *op. cit.* p.18
9. Smout, *op. cit.* p.244
10. Whatley, *Scottish Society, 1707–1830: Beyond Jacobitism, Towards Industrialisation*, Manchester University Press, 2000, p.36
11. https://en.wikipedia.org/wiki/Pound_Scots
12. Scotland produced silver, but not copper
13. Edward Chancellor, *Devil take the hindmost, a history of financial speculation*, Plume, 2000, p.32

14. Whatley, *op. cit.* p.8

15. Sterling. The official exchange rate at the time was £1 sterling for every £12 Scots. For simplicity all figures are given in sterling unless otherwise stated. Bank of Scotland raised its initial capital in both £ Scots and sterling, but adopted sterling for its lending. The Company of Scotland used sterling from its inception.

16. Douglas Watt, *The Price of Scotland, Darien, Union and the Wealth of Nations*, Luath Press, 2007, p.83

17. Said by Saville, *op. cit.* p.2, to be 'a long standing opponent of the Stewarts', although others describe him as a Jacobite sympathiser and later opponent of the Union – see for example M. Pittock *Material Culture and Sedition, 1688–1760: Treacherous Objects, Secret Places*, Palgrave Macmillan, 2013. It is possible that there was more than one Cross-Keys and more than one Patrick Steill, since the spelling of his name varies.

18. Bank of Scotland archive, BS 1/92/1A, Adventurers' ledger, 1696–, folio 1–72

19. Watt, p.48

20. *ibid.* p.51

21. Chancellor, *op. cit.* pp.35–8

22. John Clapham, *Bank of England, A History Vol. 1*, Cambridge, 1966, p.19

23. John Dalrymple, *Memoirs of Great Britain and Ireland*, https://archive.org/details/memoirsgreatbri01dalrgoog

24. Scott, *Tales of a Grandfather*, 1831

2 BRITAIN'S FIRST COMMERCIAL BANK

1. https://www.reddit.com/r/europe/comments/4kdvo1/the_thirty_largest_cities_in_europe_by_population/

2. Helen Dingwall, *Late Seventeenth Century Edinburgh, a demographic study*, Scholar Press, 1994, p.11

3. https://www.undiscoveredscotland.co.uk/usebooks/defoe-scotland/letter11–2.html

4. For a discussion of inequality in seventeenth-century Edinburgh see the excellent study by Dingwall *op cit*. For equality in the twenty-first century see *Poverty and Income inequality in Edinburgh*, City of Edinburgh Council, 2015

5. *ibid.* pp.319–22

6. David Kynaston *Till Time's Last Sand: A History of the Bank of England 1694–2013*, Bloomsbury, 2017, p.1

7. *ibid.* p.11

8. Saville, *op. cit.* p.16

9. Alan Cameron, '*Holland, John (1658–1721)*', *Oxford Dictionary of National Biography*, Oxford University Press, 2004, online edn, Jan 2008 [http://www.oxforddnb.com/view/article/13531]

10. Paterson to Lord Provost of Edinburgh, 15 August 1695 in *The Darien papers: being a selection of original letters and official documents relating to the establishment of a colony at Darien by the Company of Scotland trading to Africa and the Indies. 1695–1700*, Constable 1849.

11. BSM: BS1/5/3 14 February 1696

12. BSM: BS1/5/3 30 April 1696

13. Saville, *op. cit.* p.25

14. BSM: BS1/5/3 9 April 1696

15. BSM: BS1/5/3 14 February 1696. It was 1711 before Holland is mentioned in the accounts as receiving payments. Saville, p.932

16. BSM: BS1/5/3 12 June 1696

3 THE FIRST BANK WAR

1. Andrew Forrester, *The man who saw the future*, Thomson Texere, 2004, pp.43–50

2. *ibid.* pp.75–6

3. David Armitage, '*Paterson, William (1658–1719)*', *Oxford Dictionary of National Biography*, Oxford University Press, 2004, online edn, Sept 2010 [http://www.oxforddnb.com/view/article/21538]

4. Watt, p.1

5. *ibid.* p.17

6. Forrester, p.87

7. Barbara Balfour-Mellville, *The Balfours of Pilrig*, Wm Brown, 1907, pp.58–9

8. *ibid.* pp.121–6

9. *ibid.* p.134, Watt, *op. cit.* p.2

10. Watt, *op. cit.* p.76

11. *ibid.* p.72

12. Saville, p.27

13. Watt, p.140

14. Saville, p.861

15. BSM: BS1/5/3 18 June 1696

16. Bank of Scotland letter book, quoted in Saville, p.34

John Holland, *A short Discourse on the present temper of the nation with respect to the Indian and African Company; and of the Bank of Scotland. Also of Mr Paterson's pretended Fund of Credit*, 1696, p.11

17. BSM: BS1/5/3 6 August 1696
18. BSM: BS1/5/3 15 October 1696
19. BSM: BS1/5/3 9 July 1696
20. Company of Scotland cash book, quoted in Saville, p.862
21. *Darien papers*, 1 October 1696, https://archive.org/stream/darienpapersbe-9000compuoft/darienpapersbe9000compuoft_djvu.txt
22. Watt, p.141
23. Forrester takes a very lenient view of Smith. Watt is more sceptical.
24. Saville, p.31
25. *ibid.* p.41

4 THE EQUIVALENT AND THE BEGINNING OF PAPER MONEY

1. Robert Chambers, *Notices of the Most Remarkable Fires in Edinburgh: From 1385 to 1824*, C. Smith & Company, 1824, p.13
2. Forrester, p.289
3. BSM: BS1/5/3 5 February 1700
4. Saville, p.31
5. BSM: BS1/5/3 6 February 1701
6. Saville estimates that in the period 1696–1701 the discount on Scottish bills in London varied between 8–17.5 per cent, p.842
7. BSM: BS1/5/3 1 May 1701
8. BSM: BS1/5/3 11 June 1701
9. *ibid.* pp.42–3
10. *ibid.* pp.50–2
11. https://www.parliament.uk/documents/heritage/articlesofunion.pdf
12. Although there have been various explanations, see Watt, p.231
13. Forrester, *op. cit.* p.306
14. Watt, *op. cit.* p.233
15. *Edinburgh Courant*, 6 August 1707
16. Kynaston, 2017, p.18
17. Neil Munro, *A History of the Royal Bank of Scotland 1727–1927*, R & R Clark, 1928, p.24
18. Saville, p.76
19. *ibid.* p.81
20. Whatley, p.360

5 ROYAL BANK AND THE SECOND BANK WAR

1. Ray Perman, *HUBRIS: How HBOS wrecked the best bank in Britain*, Birlinn, 2012, p.14
2. Saville, pp.86–7
3. Munro, pp.37–45
4. RBSM: RB/12/1 5 September 1727
5. RBSM: RB/12/1 30 September 1727
6. Saville, p.84
7. RBSM: RB/12/1 21 December 1727
8. Saville, p.96
9. Roger. L. Emerson, *An Enlightened Duke, the life of Archibald Campbell (1682–1761)*, Humming Earth, 2013, p.236
10. *ibid.* p.75
11. S.G. Checkland, *Scottish Banking, A History 1695–1973*, Collins, 1975, p.45
12. J.S. Shaw, *Civic leadership and the Edinburgh lawyers in 18th century Scotland*, PhD thesis, University of Stirling 1979, p.223
13. BSM: BS1/5 16 December 1727
14. RBSM: RB/12/1 15, 22 December 1727
15. RBSM: RB/12/1 15, 9 April 1728
16. Checkland, p.60
17. RBSM: RB/12/1 5 March 1728
18. *ibid.*
19. Robert Rait, *The History of the Union Bank of Scotland*, John Smith, 1930, p.12
20. BSM: BS1/5 27 March 1728
21. *ibid.* 1 April 1728
22. Emerson, *op. cit.* p.238
23. BSM: BS1/5 21, 27 March 1729
24. RBSM: RB/12/4 19 July 1745
25. *Leaves from the Diary of John Campbell, an Edinburgh Banker in 1745*, Miscellany of the Scottish History Society. Vol. I, Scottish History Society, First Series, 15 (1893)
26. RBSM: RB/12/4 19 July 1745
27. William Graham, *The One Pound Note*, James Thin, 1886, p.16
28. *ibid.* p.17
29. RBSM: RB/12/5 3 November 1749
30. Munro, pp.75–6
31. Rachel Bennett, *Capital Punishment and the Criminal Corpse in Scotland 1740–1834*, Springer, 2017, pp.49–50

6 HARD DRINKING MINISTERS FOUND THE PENSIONS INDUSTRY

1. https://en.wikipedia.org/wiki/Cambuslang_Work
2. Henry Graham, *The Social Life of Scotland in the 18th century*, A. & C. Black, 1901, p.358
3. Not the moneylender, who had died in 1707 (see Chapter 2), but since they both came from Clackmananshire, she may have been a relative.
4. Alexander Carlyle, *Autobiography*, Blackwood, 1860, p.238
5. A. Ian Dunlop, ed, *Scottish Ministers Widows Fund 1743–1993*, St Andrew Press, 1992, p.xi
6. *ibid.* p.5
7. Ian Tweddle, *Maclaurin's Physical Dissertations*, Springer, 2007, p.11
8. Alexander Carlyle, *op. cit.* p.32
9. http://rstl.royalsocietypublishing.org/content/17/196/596
10. Nicholas Bacaër, *A Short History of Mathematical Population Dynamics*, Springer, 2011, p.6
11. *Waardije van Lyf-renten naer Proportie van Los-renten* (*The Worth of Life Annuities Compared to Redemption Bonds*).
12. *ibid.* p.7
13. Stella Mills, *The Collected Letters of Colin Maclaurin*, Nantwich Shiva, c.1982, pp.105–6
14. *ibid.*
15. https://web.archive.org/web/20081202054943/http://www.actuaries.org.uk/__data/assets/pdf_file/0020/37082/ELAS_catalogue_final_Oct_2007B.pdf
16. Graham, p.358
17. https://www.nrscotland.gov.uk/research/guides/census-records/webster's-census-of-1755

7 JACOBITES DEFEATED BY BANKERS

1. Murray of Broughton's *Memorials*, Scottish History Society, Vol. XXVII
2. Devine, 1999, p.42
3. Jean E. McCann, *The Organisation of the Jacobite Army 1745–6*, unpublished PhD thesis, University of Edinburgh, p.158
4. *ibid.* p.160
5. Colin Maclaurin to Lord President Forbes, 9 December 1745
6. RBSM: RB12/4 27 August–2 September 1745
7. BSM: BS1/5/5 6 September–13 November 1745
8. RBSM: RB12/4 14 September 1745

9. McCann, p.161

10. *Leaves from the Diary of John Campbell, an Edinburgh Banker in 1745,* Scottish History Society

11. RBSM: RB/12/4 1 October 1745

12. RBSM: RB/12/4 3 October 1745

13. RBSM: RB/12/4 24 October 1745

14. Diary of John Campbell, *op. cit.* 3 October 1745

15. Kynaston, 2017, p.35

16. http://www.caithness.org/history/articles/eighteenthcenturyseabattle/eighteenthcenturyseabattle.htm

17. The copper plate is now in the West Highland Museum in Fort William, along with the story of the aborted attempt to create a Jacobite currency.

18. BSM: BS1/5/5 10 January 1746

19. RBSM: RB/12/4 22 November 1745

20. Munro, pp.103–4

21. BSM: BS1/5/5 3 April 1746

22. RBSM: RB/12/4 11 December 1747

23. RBSM: RB/12/5 10 August 1748–20 July 1750

24. Munro, p.117

25. RBSM: RB/12/6 2 September 1753

8 DRUMMOND'S VISION FOR A CITY ON A HILL

1. Hugo Arnot, *The History of Edinburgh, from the Earliest Accounts to the Present Time,* Willam Creech, 1788, p.338

2. A.J. Youngson, *The Making of Classical Edinburgh,* Edinburgh University Press, 1975, p.14

3. *ibid.* p.548

4. Roderick Graham, *The Great Infidel,* John Donald, 2005, p.140

5. T.C. Smout, *Where had the Scottish economy got to by 1776?,* in *Wealth and Virtue,* Cambridge University Press, 1983, p.58

6. Arnot, pp.662–3

7. T.C. Smout, public lecture, *Provost Drummond,* Edinburgh University Press, 1978

8. *ibid.*

9. Youngson, p.8

10. Arnot, pp.520–2

11. TCM 6 May 1752

12. Youngson, p.55

13. BSM: BS1/5/5 2 February 1744

14. BSM: BS1/5/5 1 February 1753
15. RBSM: RB/12/6 26 January, 4 September 1753, TCM 29 August 1753
16. TCM 29 August 1753
17. TCM 15 September 1756
18. TCM 25 July 1764
19. TCM 11 June 1766–6 August 1766. Youngson, in *The Making of Classical Edinburgh* and Buchan in *Capital of the Mind* state that the debt to the council remained unpaid, but it appears to have been cleared by 1769.
20. North Bridge Committee minutes 1764–70 31 October 1764
21. Chamberlain's accounts, 1st series 1766–8
22. North Bridge Committee minutes 1764–70 March, 21 May 1765
23. *ibid.*
24. *ibid.* 4 August 1769
25. A. W. Skempton *A Biographical Dictionary of Civil Engineers in Great Britain and Ireland: 1500–1830*, Thomas Telford, 2002, p.472
26. Arnot, p.244
27. Robert Chambers, *Traditions of Edinburgh*, W. & R. Chambers, 1847, p.11

9 GLASGOW RIVALRY AND THE UNFORTUNATE MR TROTTER

1. Devine, 1999, p.105
2. Devine, 1975, p.3
3. Saville, pp.65–6
4. See *Legacies of British slave-ownership,* https://www.ucl.ac.uk/lbs/
5. Devine, 1975, p.230
6. Checkland, p.69
7. BSM: BS1/5/5 6 July 1749
8. RBSM: RB/12/5 6 October, 3 November 1749
9. *ibid.* 7 September, 23 November 1750
10. *ibid.* 20 March 1752
11. BSM: BS1/5/5 19 July 1751
12. Munro, in his authorised history of the Royal Bank describes the secret agreement as 'representing the dawn of common sense in business rivalry' (p.119). In fact the two banks limited their competition and colluded on many important issues until the third quarter of the twentieth century.
13. BSM: BS1/5/5 2 January 1752, RBSM: RB/12/5 20 March 1752
14. Saville, *op. cit.* pp.136–7
15. Charles Munn, *Scottish Provincial Banking Companies*, John Donald, 1981, p.6

16. Details of the negotiations are given in John Stuart Shaw, *Civic Leadership and the Edinburgh Lawyers in 18th century Scotla*nd, PhD thesis, University of Stirling, 1979, pp.235–8

17. *ibid.* p.5

18. BSM: BS1/5/5 18 February 1757

19. RBSM: RB/12/7 4 March 1757

20. NRS GD113/315 9 August 1758

21. *ibid.* 16 August 1758

22. *ibid.* 23 August 1758

23. Forbes, p.6

24. BSM: BS1/5/6 15 December 1763

25. *ibid.* 20 December 1763

26. *ibid.* 31 January 1764

27. *ibid.* 13 February 1764

28. NRS GD113/315 9 August 1758

29. BSM: BS1/5/6 4 July 1764

30. The Bank of England had issued £5 notes with an option clause in 1730.

31. Munn, p.19

32. BSM: BS1/5/5 25 June 1760

33. BSM: BS1/5/6 30 December 1763

34. *ibid.* 6 January 1764

35. See Chapter CVII, *Selections from the Family Papers of Baron Mure*, Maitland Club, Glasgow, 1854

36. Quoted in Saville, p.230

10 COLLAPSE OF THE AYR BANK

1. Sir William Forbes, *Memoirs of a Banking House*, Chamber, 2nd ed., 1860, p.8

2. A. & T. Fairholme papers, University of Edinburgh Research Collections, LA III.507

3. *Oxford Dictionary of National Biography.* Fordyce, Alexander.

4. Forbes, p.20

5. Adam and Thomas Fairholme were listed as directors in the Bank of Scotland directors' minutes until 1769. Adam Fairholme was re-elected in 1770. This is perhaps the son of the man who drowned in 1764. The bank also held the account for the Fairholmes' trustees in bankruptcy.

6. DNB *op. cit.*

7. Henry Hamilton, *The Failure of the Ayr Bank, 1772,* The Economic History Review, New Series, Vol. 8, No. 3 (1956), p.408

8. RBSM: 4 December 1771

9. Checkland, p.122

10. BSM: BS1/5/6 8 March 1764

11. BSM: BS1/5/6 19 June 1764. The prohibition in the 1765 Act did not come into force until 1766.

12. Adam Smith, *The Wealth of Nations*, ed. Edwin Cannan,1950, p.293.

13. BSM: BS1/5/6 11 July 1765, 24 May 1769

14. Saville, p.153

15. Smith was paid £300 a year for his tutoring – twice his salary at Glasgow University. He also received a pension of £300 for life. The financial writer Merryn Somerset Webb (*Financial Times* FT Money 18 August 2018) has pointed out that since he worked for only three years to earn the equivalent of £60,000 a year in 2018 money, this was one of the best defined benefit pension schemes in history. It also provided the income he needed to devote himself to writing *The Wealth of Nations*.

16. Checkland, pp.124–5

17. Hamilton, p.409

18. Forbes, p.39

19. Paul Kosmetatos, *The 1772–3 British Credit Crisis*, Palgrave, 2018, p.5

20. https://blogs.ucl.ac.uk/survey-of-london/2017/01/13/the-rise-and-fall-of-the-adelphi/

21. David Hume to Adam Smith, *The Correspondence of Adam Smith*, Letter 131, 27 June 1772, p.162, quoted in Kosmatatos, *op. cit.*

22. Checkland, p.130

23. BSM: BS1/5/6 15, 25 May 1771

24. RBSM: RB/12/10 4 December 1771

25. *ibid.* 25 March, 8, 15 April 1772

26. Saville, p.161

27. *The Precipitation and Fall of Messrs Douglas, Heron and Company, late Bankers in Ayr, by a Committee of Inquiry appointed by the Proprietors,* Edinburgh, 1778

28. Saville, p.165

29. *ibid.* 15 June 1774

30. Munn, *op. cit.* p.34

31. Checkland, p.133

32. Hamilton, p.415

33. Youngson, p.91

34. Saville, p.164
35. Hamilton, p.414
36. Checkland, p.134
37. Saville, p.165
38. Saville, Appendix A1
39. RBSM: RB/12/10 4 December 1771. The Equivalent Company was dissolved by Act of Parliament in 1851 and the debentures redeemed – Munro, p.234
40. Checkland, p.123
41. Checkland, p.141. It included all the Scottish banks and two Newcastle banks.
42. *ibid.* 1 September 1773

11 DUNDAS VERSUS DUNDAS

1. *Oxford Dictionary of National Biography.* Sir Lawrence Dundas
2. DNB *op. cit.*
3. https://en.wikipedia.org/wiki/Society_of_Dilettanti#Membership
4. Francis Russell, Grove Art Online, Sir Lawrence Dundas
5. History of Parliament 1754–90, Sir Lawrence Dundas
6. Devine, *The Scottish Nation,* p.197
7. Wal. Ruddiman, *To Sir Lawrence Dundas, Bart., The Weekly Magazine, Or, Edinburgh Amusement, 1768–1779,* 1, 1–2. Retrieved from https://search-proquest-com.ezproxy.is.ed.ac.uk/docview/5578427?accountid=10673
8. Alexander Murdoch, *The Importance of Being Edinburgh: Management and Opposition in Edinburgh Politics 1746–1784,* The Scottish Historical Review, Vol. 62, No. 173, Part 1 (April 1983), pp.1–16, Edinburgh University Press. http://www.jstor.org/stable/25529503
9. https://www.undiscoveredscotland.co.uk/usbiography/d/lawrencedundas.html
10. BSM: BS1/5/6 15, 5 June 1766
11. Saville, pp.149–50
12. Hamilton, p.406, T.J. Dowds, *The Forth & Clyde Canal,* Tuckwell Press, 2003, p.31
13. Dowds, p.55
14. *ibid.* pp.58–61
15. http://blogs.ucl.ac.uk/eicah/aske-hall-yorkshire/aske-hall-case-study-east-india-company-connections/#_edn4
16. Letter from William Ramsay to Duke of Buccleuch, 22 July 1790, NAS GD113/4/164 36

17. Michael Fry, *The Dundas Despotism*, John Donald, 2004, pp.134–5
18. *ibid.*, pp.80–1
19. Letter from William Ramsay to Duke of Buccleuch, *op. cit.*
20. Melville Papers GB1830 MEL/2/4 20 June 1789
21. Letter from Henry Dundas to William Ramsay, NAS GD113/4/164 9
22. Melville Papers GB1830 MEL/2/7 25 September 1789
23. Melville Papers GB1830 MEL/2/6 4 July 1789
24. Diary of William Ramsay, 11 November 1789
25. Fry, p.135
26. Letter from directors of the Bank of Scotland to Henry Dundas 3 May 1790, NAS GD113/4/164 39
27. Melville Papers GB1830 MEL/3/7 5 December 1791
28. Melville Papers GB1830 MEL/28/1–15
29. Reed and Pottle, *J. Boswell: Laird of Auchinleck, 1778–1782*, Edinburgh University Press, 1977, p.251

12 Riot and revolution

1. https://en.wikipedia.org/wiki/Storming_of_the_Bastille#Storming_the_Bastille_(14_July_1789)
2. Henry W. Meikle, *The King's Birthday Riot in Edinburgh*, The Scottish Historical Review, Vol. 7, No. 25 (Oct. 1909), pp.21–8, http://www.jstor.org/stable/25518146
3. Devine, *The Scottish Nation*, p.204
4. Fry, pp.167–8
5. T.M Devine, *The Golden Age of Tobacco*, in *Glasgow, Vol. I, beginnings to 1830*, Manchester University Press, 1995, pp.174–5
6. Saville, p.179
7. BSM: BS1/5/7 1780–1790
8. BSM: BS1/5/7 28 February 1780
9. BSM: BS1/5/7 14 September 1790
10. Saville, p.179
11. Checkland, pp.232–3
12. *The Financial System of the early 19th century*, Three Banks Review, No. 45, March 1960
13. RBSM: RB/12/14 various dates
14. Diary of William Ramsay, 10 April 1792
15. Melville Papers GB1830 MEL/11/2 20 February 1793
16. Forbes, p.77

17. Diary of William Ramsay, 11 March 1793

18. *ibid.* 16 April 1793

19. Melville Papers GB1830 MEL/11/6 17 May 1793

20. *ibid.* 4 May 1793

21. Melville Papers GB1830 MEL/11/4 27 April 1793

22. *ibid.*

23. RBSM: RB/12/14 15 April 1793

24. Henry Hamilton, *An Economic History of Scotland in the Eighteenth Century,* Clarendon Press, 1963, p.336

25. Kynaston, *op. cit.* p.82

26. *ibid.* p.83

27. *ibid.* p.85

28. *Three Banks Review*, No. 45, March 1960, p.22

13 WARTIME AUSTERITY

1. The university did not become self-governing until the Universities (Scotland) Act of 1858.

2. Youngson, p.124

3. Nick Haynes and Clive B. Fenton, *Building knowledge: an architectural history of the University of Edinburgh*, Historic Environment Scotland, 2017, pp.33–5

4. https://en.wikipedia.org/wiki/St_Cecilia per cent27s_Hall

5. Haynes, p.50

6. Youngson, p.202

7. Diary of William Ramsay, 17 February 1790

8. Henry Cockburn, *Memorials of his time*, James Thin, 1977, p.287

9. Youngson, p.96

10. *ibid.* p.97

11. Norman J. Silberling, *British Financial Experience 1790–1830*, https://Fraser.Stlouisfed.Org/Files/Docs/Meltzer/Silbri19.Pdf p289

12. BSM: BS1/5/7 various dates; Saville, p.204

13. BSM: BS1/5/7 29 March 1796, Youngson p.161

14. Alan Cameron, *Bank of Scotland 1695–1995*, Mainstream, 1995, pp.89–90

15. Checkland, *op. cit.* p.738

16. Melville Papers GB1830 MEL/15/16 December 1796

17. Scott Moncrieff letters 10 July 1803

18. *ibid.* 29 July 1803

19. Dale letter 24 December 1803

14 SYCOPHANTS OF EXISTING POWER

1. Cockburn, p.252
2. http://www.oxforddnb.com/view/10.1093/ref:odnb/9780198614128.001.0001/odnb-9780198614128-e-8250
3. Melville Papers GB1830 MEL/28
4. Diary of William Ramsay, 17 November 1788
5. *A Letter to the proprietors of the Bank of Scotland and Royal Bank*, 1778. Checkland attributes this pamphlet to Peter Miller, but this seems inconsistent with his support for Dundas in removing Sir Lawrence Dundas from Royal Bank.
6. RB 12/16 21 February 1816
7. Letter to the Proprietors of the Royal Bank of Scotland 2 Mar 1816
8. Thomas Allen, 30 March 1816
9. RBSM: 12/16 23 October 1816
10. RBSM: 12/16 18 November 1816
11. *ibid.* 25 September 1816, 21 November 1816
12. Cameron, p.107
13. *ibid.* p.142
14. Checkland, p.303
15. Malcolm, p.106
16. *ibid.* p.95
17. Malcolm, p.109
18. Cockburn p.253
19. CS/13/1 7 December 1810
20. *ibid.* 30 November 1810
21. *ibid.* 7 December 1810
22. CS/13/1 2 April 1811
23. *ibid.* 17 December 1812
24. Checkland, p.290
25. Checkland, p.405
26. NS 22/1(1) 27 January 1825
27. *ibid.* 5 February 1825
28. *ibid.* 27 January 1825
29. *ibid.* 26 July 1825
30. *ibid.* 3 June 1825, 11 August 1831
31. *ibid.* 6 Dec 1827
32. Charles Munn, *Minister of Money*, John Donald, 2017, pp.46–58
33. https://www.lloydsbankinggroup.com/Our-Group/our-heritage/our-history/tsb/edinburgh-savings-bank/

34. Munn, p.58

35. *ibid*, pp.62–6

36. *Rules of the National Security Savings Bank of Edinburgh*, Neill & Company, 1836

37. https://www.lloydsbankinggroup.com/Our-Group/our-heritage/our-history /tsb/edinburgh-savings-bank/

15 INSURANCE AND THE FIRST FIRE BRIGADE

1. *The Edinburgh Annual Register for 1824*, Constable, p.240

2. *ibid*. p.242

3. *Caledonian Insurance Company, History of a hundred years 1805–1905*, T&A Constable, 1905, p.19

4. *North British and Mercantile Insurance Company, Centenary 1809–1909*, 1909, p.22

5. NRS GD354/1/1 Directors' minute book, the Insurance Company of Scotland, 13 June 1821

6. James Braidwood, *On the Construction of Fire-engine and Apparatus, the Training of Firemen, and the Method of Proceeding in Cases of Fire*, Bill & Bradfute, 1830, p.107

7. *ibid*. p.125

8. Arnot, pp.413–14

9. *Caledonian Insurance Company, History of a hundred years 1805–1905*, T&A Constable, 1905, p.10

10. *North British and Mercantile Insurance Company, Centenary 1809–1909*, p.8

11. *Caledonian Insurance Company, History of a hundred years 1805–1905*, T&A Constable, 1905, p.12

12. *ibid*. pp.17–18

13. *ibid*. pp.20–1

14. *North British and Mercantile Insurance Company, Centenary 1809–1909*, p.8

15. *ibid*. p.10

16. *ibid*. p.28

17. W. Forbes Gray, *A brief chronicle of the Scottish Union & National Insurance Company 1824–1924*, Pillans & Wilson, 1924, p.121

18. NRS GD354/1/2 15 June 1826

19. *ibid*. 15 June 1829

20. *ibid*. 15 June 1830

21. *ibid*. 11 June 1828

22. *ibid*. 15 June 1827

16 WOTHERSPOON AND THE WIDOWS

1. NRAS 3413/1/1/1 Ordinary Court Minute Book, Vol. 1, 1812–20, 20 November 1815
2. Herbert Maxwell, *Annals of the Scottish Widows Fund*, R & R Clark, 1914, p.50
3. NRAS 3413/1/1/1 10 October 1814
4. Maxwell, *op. cit.* p.51
5. *ibid.*
6. NRAS 3413/1/1/1 25 March 1812
7. *ibid.* 6 April 1812
8. *ibid.* 21 April 1812
9. *ibid.* 11 July 1812
10. *ibid.* 23 October 1812
11. *ibid.* 10 October 1814
12. *ibid.* 31 October, 19 December 1814
13. *ibid.* 6 November 1815
14. Maxwell, *op. cit.* p.55
15. NRAS 3413/1/1/2 10 September 1821
16. *North British and Mercantile Insurance Company, Centenary 1809–1909*, p.28
17. *ibid.* pp.36–7
18. W. Forbes Gray, p.122
19. *The Journal of Sir Walter Scott,* Vol.1, David Douglas, 1891, p.49
20. *ibid.*
21. SLBP/1/1 30 March 1825, Minutes of the Insurance Company of Scotland NRS GD354 1/1 23 March 1825
22. *ibid.* 11 July 1825
23. *ibid.* 12, 19 September 1825
24. SLBP/1/4 15 October 1838
25. SLBP/1/1 15 December 1826
26. *ibid.* 15 December 1827
27. Michael Moss, *Standard Life 1825–2000*, Mainstream, 2000, pp.18–19
28. SLBP/1/1 6 October 1828
29. Moss, p.27
30. SLBP/1/2 2 January 1832
31. *ibid.* 22 November, 13 December 1830
32. GD354/1/2 16 March 1831
33. SLBP/1/2 24 Jan 1831, 19 December 1831, 23 April 1832

34. NRS GD354/1/1 Insurance Company of Scotland Fund Committee 17 April 1824, GD354 1/2 8 August 1825
35. SLBP/1/1 5 January 1829
36. SLBP/1/2 4, 11 March, 10, 26 June, 15 July 1833
37. *ibid.* 23 December 1834
38. Charles McInroy, *Scottish Equitable Life Assurance Society 1831–1981*, 1981, pp.2–4
39. M.D. Steuart, *The Scottish Provident Institution 1837–1937*, 1937, p.3
40. *ibid*, pp.12–13

17 THE RUIN OF WALTER SCOTT (AND HOW HE GOT OUT OF IT)

1. *The Edinburgh Annual Register*, January 1824, Vol.17, pp.361–73
2. http://www.oxforddnb.com/view/10.1093/ref:odnb/9780198614128.001.0001/odnb-9780198614128-e-24928
3. Lockhart's allegations against the Ballantynes provoked a pamphlet war of accusation and counter accusations.
4. Richard. H. Hutton, *The life of Sir Walter Scott*, Macmillan, 1878, p.148 https://www.gutenberg.org/files/18124/18124-h/18124-h.htm#CHAPTER_XV
5. Letter to John Ballantyne, 26 July 1819, quoted in *Lockhart's Life of Scott*, http://www.gutenberg.org/files/37631/37631-h/37631-h.htm#page69
6. http://www.walterscott.lib.ed.ac.uk/biography/finance.html
7. Eric Quayle, *The Ruin of Sir Walter Scott*, Hart-Davis, 1968, p.52
8. Sam McKinstry and Marie Fletcher, *The personal account books of Sir Walter Scott*, *Accounting Historians Journal*. 29.2 December 2002, p.59
9. *Lockhart's Life of Scott*, Chapter LIV
10. *ibid.*
11. R.C. Michie, *Money, Mania & Markets*, John Donald, 1981, pp.27–8
12. Michie, p.29
13. Anthony Romney, *Three Letters on the Speculative Schemes of the Present Times*, Bell & Bradfute, 1825, p.3
14. Cockburn, p.432
15. R.C. Michie, *Scottish Stock Exchanges in the 19th Century*, PhD thesis, University of Aberdeen, 1978, p.90
16. Michie, 1981, p.43
17. Romney, p.3
18. https://en.wikipedia.org/wiki/Gregor_MacGregor#Venezuela,_under_Bol per centC3 per centADvar

19. Checkland, p.408
20. Saville, p.290
21. Kynaston, p.119
22. Michie, 1981, p.35
23. *Journal of Sir Walter Scott*, Vol. I, David Douglas, 1891, 26 November 1825
24. Kynaston, 2017, p.121
25. John Buchan in his biography of Scott put the figure at £100,000.
26. *The Walter Scott Digital Archive*, Edinburgh University Library, http://www.walterscott.lib.ed.ac.uk/home.html
27. Quoted in Quayle, p.204
28. Quayle, p.203
29. Cockburn, p.430
30. Cameron, *op. cit.* p.110
31. Cockburn, p.430
32. *Walter Scott Digital Archive, op. cit.*
33. *Journal of Sir Walter Scott*, 9 October 1826
34. Scott to Lockhart, 2 November 1827, 11 November 1827, Scott Letters, http://www.walterscott.lib.ed.ac.uk/etexts/etexts/letters10.PDF
35. Quayle, p.213
36. *Journal of Sir Walter Scott*, 22 January 1826
37. Hutton, p.154
38. *Walter Scott Digital Archive, op. cit.*
39. Quayle, p.210
40. Saville, pp.292–4
41. Checkland, pp.410–11
42. Saville, p.296
43. BSM: 1/5/12 10 April 1826
44. Saville, p.298
45. *Journal of Sir Walter Scott*, 17 February 1826
46. Walter Scott, *Letter to the Editor of the Edinburgh Weekly Journal from Malachi Malagrowther Esq*, 2nd edition, William Blackwood, 1826
47. *Journal of Sir Walter Scott*, 24 February 1826
48. See Munn, 1981, Chapter 5
49. Saville, p.294

18 THE BANKRUPTCY OF EDINBURGH

1. *Address to the Town Council of Edinburgh by Thomas Smith*, 2nd edition, Mundell & Son, 1799, p.5
2. *ibid.* p.6
3. *ibid.* p.13
4. *ibid.* pp.31–5
5. *ibid.* p.30
6. John Greig, *Report on the Statements of the Lord Provost & Mr A. Bruce, Respecting the Affairs of the City of Edinburgh, Humbly Submitted to the Committee of the Guildry,* J. Hay & Co., 1819, p.4
7. Youngson, p.138
8. *ibid.* p.147
9. *ibid.* p.156
10. *ibid.* p.162
11. *ibid.* p.174
12. Greig, p.25
13. BSM: 1/5/12 3 Sept 1825
14. James Scott Marshall, The *Life and Times of Leith,* John Donald, 1986, p.188
15. Youngson, pp. 259–60
16. James Campbell Irons, *Leith and its antiquities from the earliest times to the close of the nineteenth century,* Morrison & Gibb, 1898, pp.207–8
17. *Edinburgh Weekly Journal* 21 July 1824, p.231
18. The *Scotsman,* 17 November 1824
19. Romney, p.5
20. The *Scotsman,* 5 March 1825
21. Irons, p.210
22. Hansard, 20 May 1825
23. TCM 7 November 1832
24. Cockburn, p.95
25. TCM 7 November 1832
26. TCM 22 August 1832
27. TCM 21 November 1832
28. TCM 7 November 1832
29. TCM 2 January 1833
30. TCM 6 March 1833
31. Youngson, p.261
32. TCM 13 April 1833

33. TCM 29 May 1833
34. *ibid.*
35. The *Scotsman,* 6 November 1833
36. TCM 6 November 1833
37. TCM 14 November 1833
38. M.J. Noble, *The Common Good and the Reform of Local Government: Edinburgh 1820–56,* PhD thesis, University of Edinburgh, 2016, p.122
39. *ibid.* p.123
40. H. Labouchere, *Report to the Right Honourable the Chancellor of the Exchequer, regarding the Affairs of the City of Edinburgh and Port of Leith,* Edinburgh, 1836
41. RBSM: RB/12/23 3, 31 August, 21, 30 September 1835
42. Cockburn, p.429

19 ENGLISH MONEY FOR SCOTTISH RAILWAYS

1. Noble, p.120
2. C.J.A. Robertson, *The Origins of the Scottish Railway System 1722–1844,* John Donald, 1983, p.74
3. *ibid.* p.64
4. Michie, 1981, p.57
5. Robertson, p.100
6. *ibid.* pp.106, 111
7. Youngson, pp.271–2
8. John Thomas, *A Regional History of the Railways of Great Britain. Vol. 6, Scotland, the Lowlands and the Borders,* revised by J.S. Paterson, David and Charles, 1984, p.61
9. Robertson, pp.106, 111
10. The *Scotsman,* 30 October 1830
11. Youngson, p.276
12. Henry Cockburn, *Journal .Volume I,* Edmondson & Douglas, 1874, p.85
13. Wray Vamplew, *Sources of Scottish railway capital before 1860,* Scottish Journal of Political Economy, 1970, p.429
14. Thomas, 1984, p.62
15. https://www.railscot.co.uk/locations/C/Cowlairs_Incline/
16. Thomas, 1984, p.63
17. C.J.A. Robertson, *Early Scottish Railways and the Observance of the Sabbath,* The Scottish Historical Review, Vol. 57, No. 164, Part 2, October 1978, p.153

18. *Bradshaw's Railway Gazette*, 17 September 1845, p.543
19. Despite Learmonth's fall, the Edinburgh and Glasgow Railway Company bought the Union Canal Company in 1849 for £209,000, against the wishes of the English investors.
20. Robertson, 1978, pp.155–6
21. Vamplew, *op. cit.* p.431
22. *ibid.*
23. RBSM: RB/12/25 21 November 1838
24. *ibid.* 19 December 1838
25. Cameron, p.121
26. Checkland, pp.342–3
27. Michie, 1981, p.83
28. H.G Lewin, *Railway Mania and its aftermath*, David and Charles, 1968, pp.1–2
29. *ibid.* pp.102–4
30. W.A. Thomas, *The Provincial Stock Exchanges*, Cass, 1973, p.285
31. *ibid.* p.101
32. *ibid.* p.81
33. *ibid.* pp.95–7
34. W.W. Knox, *Poverty, income and wealth in Scotland 1840–1940*, https://www.scran.ac.uk/scotland/pdf/SP2_5Income.pdf
35. *ibid.* p.81
36. C.W. Boase, *A Century of Banking in Dundee*, R. Grant & Son, 1867, p.506
37. Checkland, p.344
38. RBSM: RB/12/30 18 December 1850
39. Robertson, 1983, p.295
40. *ibid.* p.296
41. The *Scotsman*, 15 May 1852
42. Thomas, p.74

20 THE FAILURE OF THE WESTERN BANK

1. Cameron, p.123
2. It was 1858 before Bank of Scotland decided that the railway industry was mature enough to provide safe investments for its capital. BS20/1/19 11 December 1858: Alexander Blair memorandum to directors on time to invest in railway debentures.
3. Checkland, p.415

4. RBSM: RB/12/30 16 June 1847
5. Checkland, p.415
6. Saville, p.471
7. Checkland, p.411, see also Clapham, p.205
8. On 30 November 1840, see BSM: 1/5/24 13 October 1857
9. RBSM: RB/12/23 25 October 1836
10. Checkland, p.301
11. Munro, pp.180–1
12. *ibid.* p.418
13. RBSM: RB/12/26 18 June 1839
14. RBSM: RB/12/28 19 February 1845
15. *ibid.* 22 January 1845
16. *ibid.* 24 January 1845
17. Checkland, pp.340, 466
18. Checkland, p.326
19. R.H. Campbell, *Edinburgh bankers and the Western Bank of Scotland*, Scottish Journal of Political Economy, Vol. 2, issue 1, February 1955, p.138
20. A.W. Kerr, *History of Banking in Scotland*, A. &. C. Black, 1908, p.216
21. RBSM: RB/12/22 3 November 1834, RB/12/25 8 August 1838: BS 1/21/ 10 Private and Confidential letters: 20 October 1857 Alexander Blair memorandum to the Court of Directors of Bank of Scotland on Western Bank.
22. Charles Munn, *Clydesdale Bank, the first 150 years*, Collins, 1988, p.15
23. Checkland, p.336
24. *ibid.* p.327; Boase, p.432
25. Boase, p.432
26. Campbell, p.138
27. Letter to *The Spectator*, 28 December 1857, http://archive.spectator.co.uk/ article/2nd-january-1858/19/the-western-bank-of-scotland
28. Checkland, p.467
29. Campbell, p.139, John Gifford, *How to Mismanage a Bank, A review of the Western Bank of Scotland*, 1859, reprinted in Saville, appendix 9c
30. Duncan Ross, *Savings bank depositors in a crisis: Glasgow 1847 and 1857, Financial History Review*, Cambridge University Press, Vol. 20, Issue 2, August 2013, pp.183–208
31. BSM: 20/2/10 letters and notes
32. Now in the Bank of Scotland archive BS20/2/10
33. *ibid.* Letter from Robert Sym 16 March 1847
34. Clapham p.226

35. BSM: 1/5/24 13 April 1857 Bank of Scotland held £19,700 of India bonds and £10,000 of India stock: these were sold 5, 7 August and reinvested in 3 per cent consols. 29 September: 100 guineas was donated to the India Relief Fund.

36. Clapham, pp.226–7

37. Saville, p.392

38. BSM 1/21/10 Private and Confidential letters: 20 October 1857 Alexander Blair memorandum to the Court of Directors of Bank of Scotland on Western Bank.

39. RBSM12/35 28 October 1857

40. Money Market and City Intelligence, *The Times*, 30 October 1857

41. *The Times*, 13 November 1857

42. *ibid.*

43. Robert Rait, *The History of the Union Bank of Scotland*, John Smith, 1930, p.291

44. BSM: 1/5/24 1 October 1857

45. RBSM: 12/35 12 November 1857

46. *The Times*, 13 November 1857

47. Clapham, p.230

48. BSM: 1/21/10 Private and Confidential letters: 11 November 1857

49. BSM: 20/1/19 Bank of Scotland reserves had fluctuated between £2,669,000 and £1,212,000 in 1857. Between February and December the bank sold nearly £1.5 million of stock. To meet the 'one-third rule' it needed £1.8 million, but by the end of the year held only £1.53 million.

50. BSM: 20/1/19: Blair memorandum September 1858

21 BANKERS IN THE DOCK

1. Gifford, *op. cit.*

2. WB/10 Appendix to Mr Dickson's report on the Western Bank, WB/7 Western Bank of Scotland abstract of liabilities, Campbell, p.141

3. Munro, p.181

4. BSM: Acc2003/072/22: memo from Blair 14 September 1840

5. BSM: 20/1/19 Statement of reserves at 1 January 1857: £1.3m in Government stock, yielding 3.25 per cent where deposit rate was 3.5 per cent. To increase the yield, loans were made to Newcastle and Leeds banks, which were considered safe until the collapse of the Northumberland Bank, which lost £246,000.

6. *North British Daily Mail* 13 November 1857, quoted in Campbell, p.146

7. See *The Times*, 13 November 1857, RBSM: 12/35 12, 20 November 1857

8. RBSM: 12/35 11 November 1857

9. *ibid.*

10. WB/9 Register of Shareholders of the Western Bank

11. Kerr, p.300

12. Clapham, p.309

13. *ibid.* p.270

14. BSM: 20/1/19 3 December 1858: memorandum on bank reports

15. Kerr, p.270

16. Kerr, p.275

17. John Turner, *Major and minor British banking crises since 1800.* In *Banking in Crisis: The Rise and Fall of British Banking Stability, 1800 to the Present* (Cambridge Studies in Economic History, Second Series, pp.66–101). Cambridge University Press, 2014, p.81

18. Kerr, p.279

19. *ibid.* p.291 From £77 million in total liabilities (deposits and the note issue) in 1865, to over £108 million in 1877.

20. *ibid.* p.294, Clapham, p.309

21. Leo Rosenblum, *The Failure of the City of Glasgow Bank*, The Accounting Review, Vol. 8, No. 4 (December 1933), American Accounting Association, p.285

22. Turner, p.84

23. Saville, p.422, Rait, p.311

24. *The Times*, 3 October 1878

25. North British Railways offered to transfer its account to the Bank of Scotland, but was declined. BSM 1/5/37 3, 7 October 1878

26. *The Times*, 31 December 1878

27. CS/491/77 Report by Kerr, Andersons, Muir & Main CA and McGrigor Donald & Co. solicitors, balance sheet of the City of Glasgow Bank 18 October 1878, RB/114: Liquidators report 1882

28. William Wallace, *The Trial of the City of Glasgow Bank Directors*, Sweet & Maxwell, 1905, p.10

29. *ibid.* p.407

30. BSM: 1/5/37 25 October 1878

31. BSM: Acc 01/132/33 General Circular 24 December 1879

32. BSM: 1/70/6 Treasurer's annual reports, 28 February 1879

33. Saville, p.423

34. RBSM: 12/45 23 October 1878

35. Saville, p.423

36. BSM: 1/70/6 Treasurer's annual reports, 28 February 1879

37. George Walker, *The Glasgow Bank Failure. The Bankers' Magazine and Statistical Register (1849–1894)*, *13*(5), p.331. Retrieved from https://search -proquest-com.ezproxy.is.ed.ac.uk/docview/124433327?accountid=10673

38. Richard Button and Samuel Knott, *Desperate adventurers and men of straw: the failure of City of Glasgow Bank and its enduring impact on the UK banking system*, Bank of England *Quarterly Bulletin* Q1 2015, pp.29–30

39. RBSM:/12/46 12 November 1879

40. BSM: 1/70/6 Treasurer's annual reports, 28 February 1879

41. Thomas Ward, *The regulatory response to the collapse of the City of Glasgow Bank 1878–79*, dissertation, University of Edinburgh, 2009, p.19

42. Kerr, p.303

22 FINANCING AMERICAN RAILROADS

1. BSM: 1/70/6 Treasurer's annual reports, 28 February 1879

2. Checkland, p.501

3. R.E. Tyson, *Scottish Investment in American Railways: the case of the City of Glasgow Bank 1856–1881*, in *Studies in Scottish Business History,* ed. Peter Payne, Frank Cass & Co., 1967, p.388

4. http://www.oxforddnb.com/view/10.1093/ref:odnb/ 9780198614128.001.0001/odnb-9780198614128-e-47576

5. Nigel Morecroft, *Robert Fleming and Scottish Asset Management, 1873–1890* in *The Origins of Asset Management from 1700 to 1960, Palgrave Studies in the History of Finance*, Palgrave Macmillan, 2017, pp.103–42

6. Swan, 2009

7. http://www.oxforddnb.com/view/10.1093/ref:odnb/ 9780198614128.001.0001/odnb-9780198614128-e-47813?rskey= Odm93g&result=3

8. Weir, 1973, p.5

9. Swan, 2008

10. Weir, p.7

11. The US had come off the gold standard during the civil war. When it resumed in 1987 Scottish investors made a further currency gain. W. Turrentine Jackson, *The Enterprising Scot, Investors in the American West after 1873*, Edinburgh University Press, 1968, p.16

12. Oxford DNB *op. cit.*

13. Weir, p.11

14. Quoted in Alasdair Nairn, *Engines that move markets, technology investing from the railways to the internet and beyond*, John Wiley, 2002, p.32

15. Weir, p.11
16. The *Scotsman*, 5 August 1874
17. Jackson, p.19
18. The *Scotsman*, 6 March 1875
19. The *Scotsman*, 4 March 1878
20. John Newlands, *Put not your trust in Money*, Chappin Kavanagh, 1997, pp.85–6
21. Jackson, p.21
22. Newlands, pp.87–8
23. Morecroft, *op. cit.*
24. John Newlands, *The Edinburgh Investment Trust PLC 1889–2014*, EIT, 2014, pp.8–10

23 IVORY AND GIFFORD

1. *Scottish Capital Abroad, Blackwoods Magazine*, October 1884, p.477
2. *ibid.* Total bank liabilities in 1886 were £105 million – Checkland, table 20, p.530
3. Newlands, p.91
4. David Macmillan, *Scottish Enterprise in Australia 1798–1879*, in Payne, p.341
5. Moss, p.116
6. Stephen Walker and Thomas Lee, *Studies in early professionalism, Scottish Chartered Accountants 1854–1918*, Taylor & Francis, 1999, p.26
7. The Edinburgh, Glasgow and Aberdeen societies merged in 1951 to form the Institute of Chartered Accountants in Scotland.
8. Chay Fisher and Christopher Kent, *Two depressions, one banking collapse*, Research Discussion Paper, 1999–06, Reserve Bank of Australia
9. The *Scotsman*, 26 April 1899
10. Newlands, p.93
11. *ibid.* p.94
12. Peter Pugh, *Number One Charlotte Square*, Ivory & Sime, 1987, p.15
13. *Edinburgh Gazette*, 23 June 1905
14. Pugh, *op cit.* p.25
15. https://laverockdalehouse.com/history-2/
16. Pugh, *op cit.* p.25
17. Weir, p.15
18. *ibid.* p.18
19. Alexander Blair, *Edinburgh American Assets, a brief history 1878–1978*, Ivory & Sime, 1979, p.10

20. Weir, p.170
21. Blair, p.11
22. Pugh, *op cit.* p.12
23. *ibid.* p.18
24. Richard Burns, *A Century of Investing, Baillie Gifford's first hundred years,* Birlinn, 2008, pp.6–7
25. *ibid.* p.15
26. *ibid.* p.17
27. Martin Fransman, *Edinburgh City of Funds*, Kokoro, 2008, p.67
28. Burns, pp.23–30
29. Fransman, p.43
30. Moss, pp.170, 197
31. Morecroft, pp.191–219
32. Burns, p.38
33. Pugh, p.26
34. Pugh, p.20, Burns, p.32

24 CONSOLIDATION

1. Burns, p.78
2. John Scott and Michael Hughes, *The Anatomy of Scottish Capital*, Croom Helm, 1980, p.18
3. *ibid.* pp.56–65, Table 1A
4. *ibid. p*p.20–1
5. Cameron, p.171
6. Her grandson Ian Ivory says she broke with Pankhurst over the use of violence.
7. Burns, p.187
8. E. Moneta, *Scottish Banks & Bankers*, North British Publishing, 1904, p.11
9. Checkland, p.505
10. Moneta, *passim*
11. Saville, p.719
12. Checkland, p.588
13. *ibid.* p.584
14. Cameron, p.184
15. Melville Papers GB1830 MEL/36
16. https://www.historyscotland.com/articles/scottish-history/new-research-uncovers-the-story-of-the-first-chinese-scotsman
17. Checkland, pp.578–9

18. https://bankunderground.co.uk/2017/08/08/your-country-needs-funds-the-extraordinary-story-of-britains-early-efforts-to-finance-the-first-world-war/
19. Checkland, p.559
20. Saville, p.519
21. Thomas Johnston, *The Financiers and the Nation*, 1934. https://archive.sustecweb.co.uk/past/sustec12–6/extract_from_the_financiers_and.htm
22. Cameron, p.196
23. Burns, pp.77–8
24. *ibid.* p.198
25. CS/14/35 31 July 1958, Checkland, p.243
26. NS/335/3 Special minute book: Record of private discussion at board meeting 17 October 1957
27. NS/335/3 Letter to Franks, 9 January 1958, board minutes *passim*
28. CS/14/35 21 August 1958
29. RBSM:/1608/1 Royal Bank of Scotland, National Commercial Bank of Scotland, Explanatory Statement
30. Cameron, p.222
31. *ibid.* p.225
32. Charles Tennent, *The structure of Scottish banking, Scottish Bankers Magazine*, January 1952
33. Maxwell Gaskin, *The Scottish Banks; a modern survey*, Routledge, 1965, p.38

25 THE SLOW DECLINE OF GENTLEMANLY CAPITALISM

1. Pugh, p.62
2. *ibid.* p.65
3. *ibid.* p.67
4. *ibid.* p.76
5. Burns, p.88
6. Obituary, The *Herald*, 24 April 1999
7. Saville, p.718
8. *ibid.* p.719
9. *ibid.* pp.738–9
10. Ray Perman, *HUBRIS: How HBOS wrecked the best bank in Britain*, Birlinn, 2012, pp.28–37
11. Saville, p.779
12. Perman, p.33
13. RB1869/206 Board papers 17 June 1981; RBSM:1869/207 Staff reports

14. RBSM:1869/206 Board papers 17 June 1981; RBSM:1869/207 1 July 1981
15. The Monopolies and Mergers Commission, *The Hong Kong and Shanghai Banking Corporation. Standard Chartered Bank Limited. The Royal Bank of Scotland Group Limited. A Report on the Proposed Mergers,* 20th Century House of Commons Sessional Papers, 1981/82, 1981
16. David Kynaston, Richard Roberts, *The Lion Wakes, a modern history of HSBC,* Profile Books, 2015
17. *ibid.*
18. RB1869/205, Submission to the MMC, para 8.2
19. RB1869/217, Circular to staff, 19 January 1982
20. *The Times,* 10 May 1985
21. Ian Fraser, *Shredded: Inside RBS, the bank that broke Britain,* Birlinn, 2015, p.17

26 BANKING: THE CULTURAL REVOLUTION

1. Charles Winter to George Younger, 1 July 1991, George Younger papers, quoted in David Torrance, *George Younger, a life well lived,* Birlinn, 2008, p.267
2. M. Oram and R. Wellins, *Re-engineering's Missing Ingredient: The Human Factor,* IPD, 1995
3. Perman, Chapters 6, 7
4. *Management Today,* 1 October 2001
5. *Financial Times,* 27 April 1997
6. Saville, p.800
7. *Financial Times,* 14 May 1996
8. *Financial Times,* 26 April 1997
9. Fraser, p.63
10. *Financial Times,* 2 March 1999
11. The *Scotsman,* 3 March 1999
12. The *Scotsman,* 5 March 1999
13. BBC News, 3 June 1999

27 FUND MANAGEMENT: CONTRASTING CULTURES

1. Pugh, p.193
2. *ibid.* p.154
3. https://moneyweek.com/473003/the-brutal-global-stockmarket-crash-that-hit-britain-hardest/
4. Quoted in Pugh, p.108

5. Quoted in Jonathan Davis, *Money Makers: The Stock Market Secrets of Britain's Top Professional Investment Managers*, Harriman House, 2013

6. Pugh, p.170

7. *ibid.* p.85

8. *ibid.* p.186

9. https://www.scotsman.com/news/the-man-behind-the-square-deal-1-593066

10. Burns, p.89

11. *ibid.* p.99

12. *ibid.* p.63

13. *ibid.* Appendix I

14. *ibid.* p.153

28 THE END OF THE EXCHANGE

1. W.A. Thomas, *The Provincial Stock Exchanges*, Cass, 1973, p.293

2. *The Edinburgh Stock Exchange 1844–1944*, Committee of the Edinburgh Stock Exchange, p.9

3. Jackson, pp.77–9

4. *The Edinburgh Stock Exchange 1844–1944*, p.15

5. Thomas, p.293

6. https://www.ianfraser.org/taking-stock-of-a-long-career/

7. https://www.scotsman.com/business/companies/financial/torrie-reaches-end-of-an-era-1-942972

8. Robert L. Carter & Peter Falush, *The British Insurance Industry Since 1900: The Era of Transformation*, Springer, 2009, p.76

9. *The Times*, 1 September 2000

10. *Sunday Times*, 2 July 2000

11. *The Times*, 12 December 2000

12. *Sunday Times*, 1 October 2000, *The Times*, 30 September 2000

13. *The Times*, 19 February 2004

14. *Sunday Times*, 10 October 2004

15. Carter & Falush, p.76

16. The *Guardian*, 15 June 2006

29 THE BATTLE FOR NATWEST

1. Much of the following three chapters is adapted from Perman, *HUBRIS*, 2012

2. *Financial Times* 2 October 1999

3. Reuters, 24 September 1999
4. Sandler was later to lead Northern Rock after its nationalisation.

30 INTO THE ARMS OF HALIFAX

1. *Financial Times* 18 February 2000
2. *Financial Times* 28 September 2000
3. *Daily Telegraph* 5 May 2001

31 THE 'HALIBAN'

1. HBOS annual report and accounts, 2001
2. *Daily Telegraph* 4 May 2001, *Financial Times* 7 May 2001
3. *The Sun*, 27 February 2002

32 MASTERS OF INTEGRATION

1. Fraser, p.108
2. *Financial Times*, 27 March 2001
3. Fraser, p.131
4. https://www.slideshare.net/DSAdiPratomo/royal-bank-of-scotland-case-study
5. Fraser, p.118
6. http://www.rbs.co.uk/Group_Information/Investor_Relations/Financial_Results/2001/review2001.pdf
7. http://www.rbs.co.uk/Group_Information/Investor_Relations/Financial_Results/2002/review2002.pdf
8. https://hbsp.harvard.edu/product/404026-PDF-ENG
9. https://www.forbes.com/global/2003/0106/034.html#2b1879927cde
10. Iain Martin, *Making it Happen, Fred Goodwin, RBS and the men who blew up the British economy*, Simon & Schuster, 2013, p.157
11. Fraser, p.106
12. https://www.telegraph.co.uk/finance/2882151/Revealed-Royal-Banks-secret-jet.html
13. Fraser, p.187
14. Martin, pp.151–3
15. *ibid.* p.139
16. *Goodwin's undoing, Financial Times*, 24 February 2009
17. Martin, p.149

18. *RBS investigation, Chapter 1, The Telegraph*, 11 December 2011
19. RBS *Report and Accounts* 2006
20. Martin, p.228
21. *ibid.* p.232
22. *RBS investigation, Chapter 2, The Telegraph*, 11 December 2011
23. *ibid*
24. *The failure of the Royal Bank of Scotland*, Financial Services Authority Board Report, December 2011, p.161

33 2007: 'WE DON'T DO SUB-PRIME'

1. *The failure of the Royal Bank of Scotland*, FSA, p.387
2. Martin, p.244
3. http://www.bbc.co.uk/blogs/thereporters/robertpeston/2007/10/the_rock_and_me.html, https://www.economist.com/leaders/2007/09/20/the-bank-that-failed
4. Martin, p.388
5. Fraser, p.296
6. *The failure of the Royal Bank of Scotland*, FSA, p.38
7. *ibid.* p.150
8. *ibid.* p.116
9. Perman, pp.136, 140–1
10. *ibid.* Chapter 16
11. HBOS Report & Accounts, 2007
12. Quoted at http://www.ianfraser.org/a-brief-history-of-halifax-bank-of-scotland/
13. Perman, p.150

34 2008: MARKET MELTDOWN

1. https://investors.rbs.com/~/media/Files/R/RBS-IR/annual-reports/rbs-group-accounts-2007.pdf
2. *The failure of the Royal Bank of Scotland*, FSA, p.150
3. Martin, p.261
4. *The failure of the Royal Bank of Scotland*, FSA, p.46
5. *The failure of the Royal Bank of Scotland*, FSA, p.100: the money never arrived; it was absorbed by losses at ABN.
6. *The failure of the Royal Bank of Scotland*, FSA, p.55
7. HBOS annual report and accounts 2007

8. *Financial Times*, 27 February 2008

9. *The Times*, 13 March 2008

10. *RBS investigation, Chapter 3, The Telegraph*, 11 December 2011

11. Fraser, p.330

12. *RBS rights issue prospectus*, https://investors.rbs.com/~/media/Files/R/RBS-IR/corporate-actions/rights-issue-june-2008/prospectusfinal.pdf

13. It did not find a buyer at that price, but later did sell Angel Trains for £3.6 billion and its share of Tesco Bank for £950 million.

14. *RBS completes rights issue, Financial Times*, 9 June 2008

15. Fraser, p.343

16. Martin, p.266

17. HBOS rights issue prospectus, 2008

18. Gordon Brown, *Beyond the Crash*, Simon & Schuster, 2010, p.35

19. Alistair Darling, *Back from the Brink*, Atlantic Books, 2011, Kindle edition, location 1876

20. https://investors.rbs.com/~/media/Files/R/RBS-IR/Archived/interim2008.pdf

21. Fraser, p.350

22. https://publications.parliament.uk/pa/jt201213/jtselect/jtpcbs/144/14409.htm, para 106

35 'THEY ARE GOING BUST THIS AFTERNOON'

1. http://news.bbc.co.uk/1/hi/8375969.stm

2. http://www.bloomberg.com/data-visualization/federal-reserve-emergency-lending/#/HBOS_PLC/?total=true&mcp=true&mc=true&taf=false&cpff=false&pdcf=false&tslf=false&stomo=false&amlf=false&dw=false/

3. Darling, location 2291

4. *Daily Telegraph*, 16 September 2009

5. Presentation by Tim Tookey to UBS Global Financial Services Conference, New York, 12 May 2009

6. *Financial Times*, 7 October 2008

7. Fraser, p.364

8. *Financial Times*, 24 February 2009

9. Darling, location 2377

10. *ibid.*

11. *ibid.* location 2581

12. *ibid.* location 2477

13. Brown, p.65

14. https://www.bbc.co.uk/news/business-41672212

15. Darling, location 2676

16. https://www.bbc.co.uk/news/business-17944066

36 THE END OF AN 'AULD SANG'

1. https://investors.rbs.com/~/media/Files/R/RBS-IR/annual-reports/rbs-group-accounts-2008.pdf

2. *The failure of the Royal Bank of Scotland*, FSA, p.54

3. The *Guardian*, 23 February 2018

4. https://publications.parliament.uk/pa/jt201213/jtselect/jtpcbs/144/14409.htm, Table 3

5. *Financial Times*, 18 March 2008

6. Lloyds reverted to its original name after spinning off TSB at the behest of the European Commission.

7. https://www.bbc.co.uk/news/uk-scotland-scotland-business-31724967

8. https://www2.gov.scot/Publications/2011/08/09172458/5

9. https://publications.parliament.uk/pa/cm200809/cmselect/cmtreasy/416/416.pdf

10. https://en.wikipedia.org/wiki/Economy_of_Edinburgh

11. https://www.bbc.co.uk/news/business-43729508

12. http://www.parliament.scot/ResearchBriefingsAndFactsheets/S5/SB_16–92_Earnings_in_Scotland_2016.pdf

13. https://www.aberdeenstandard.com/en/who-we-are, https://en.wikipedia.org/wiki/Baillie_Gifford

14. https://positivemoney.org/2018/08/british-public-dont-trust-banks/

15. See: https://www.theguardian.com/business/2016/apr/25/rbs-royal-bank-scotland-legal-claims-damages-small-businesses-bankruptcy, https://www.theguardian.com/business/2018/jun/19/lloyds-hbos-fraud-report-published-reading

16. https://www.globalethicalfinance.org/wp-content/uploads/2018/06/Edinburgh-Finance-Declaration-Overview.pdf

Index

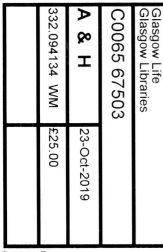

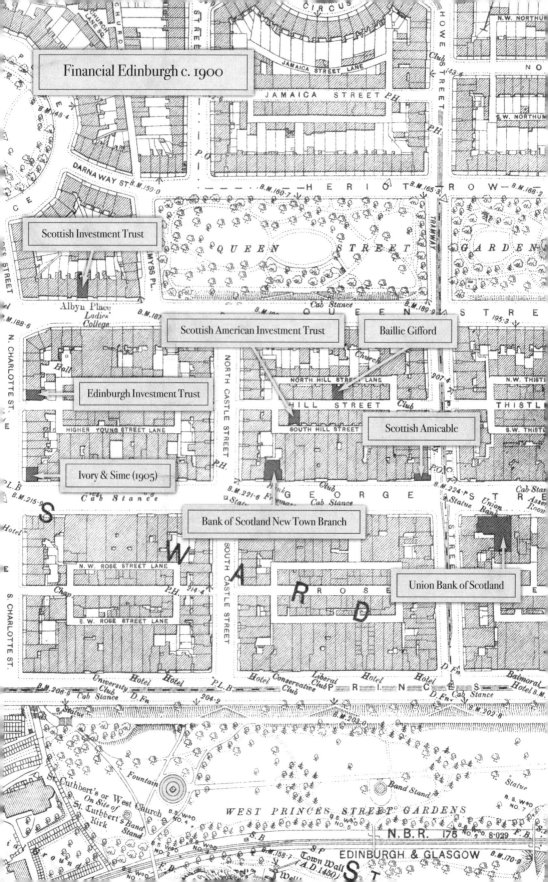

Financial Edinburgh c. 1900

Scottish Investment Trust

Scottish American Investment Trust

Baillie Gifford

Edinburgh Investment Trust

Scottish Amicable

Ivory & Sime (1905)

Bank of Scotland New Town Branch

Union Bank of Scotland